THE TEMPLE IN ĀNDHRADĒŚA

THE TEMPLE IN ĀNDHRADĒŚA

A. SURYAKUMARI

Gian Publishing House
29/6 SHAKTI NAGAR • DELHI-110007 • INDIA

GIAN PUBLISHING HOUSE
29/6, SHAKTI NAGAR
DELHI-110007
Phone : 7213053

ISBN 81-212-0230-2

PRINTED IN INDIA

Published by Mrs. Gayatri Garg for Gian Publishing House and Printed at Suman Printers, Delhi-1100053.

PREFACE

This work entitled "The Temple in Āndhradēśa" is devoted to a study of the temple in its various aspects, namely Construction, Maintenance, Organization, Management, Worship and Festivals. This study is based upon a careful examination of 8,000 inscriptions, on stone and copper plates, found in several districts of Āndhradēśa and a judicious selection of all matter relating to the temple.

The significance and symbolism of the temple, different varieties of temples, and different styles and examples of Āndhra temples have been mentioned briefly in the Introduction. Numerous examples relating to the Construction and Consecration of temples in various parts and the installation and reinstallation of deities are dealt with in Chapter 2. Chapter 3 deals with the varieties of the gifts made to temples and the numerous purposes for which these gifts were made. The management of the temple and the part played in it by workers inside and outside as well as their duties and privileges have been dealt with in Chapter 4. Chapter 5 deals with the organization of the temple and the role of the *Sthānāpati*, *Sthānikulu*, the Village Assembly and the *Śrī Bhaṇḍāram*. Chapter 6 is devoted to a description of various items of worship conducted in the temple as known from the inscriptional sources. Chapter 7, which is the most interesting, describes in detail various temple festivals, annual and periodical, with the help of numerous details available from the inscriptions.

Care has been taken in selecting examples to see that the inscriptions cover the three distinct parts of Āndhradēśa viz., Telangāna, Coastal Āndhra and Rāyalasīma and that they are also representative of various centuries.

This is the first attempt made so far towards determining the working of the temple in Āndhradēśa.

While in my M.A. Final Class I had occasion to survey several Āndhra temples for writing a Dissertation. This roused my curiosity to investigate the working of the temple. Dr. Rama Rao, the Emeritus Professor of History in the Śrī Venkaṭēśwara University, who guided my temple survey, suggested to me the topic which constitutes the title of this work. He guided my work throughout and helped me in studying Sanskrit and Kannaḍa inscriptions. His monographs on several temples of Āndhradēśa have also helped me considerably. I am grateful to him for giving me all the facilities required and his kind encouragement and able guidance.

AUTHOR

LIST OF ILLUSTRATONS

CONTENTS

1

INTRODUCTION

NAMES OF THE TEMPLE

The temple is known as *Dēvālaya* or the place of the god. The other names of the temple are *Dēvagṛha*, meaning the house of god, *Dēvāyatana* and *Dēvakula* meaning the resident of god, *Mandira*, *Bhavana*, *Sthāna* and *Vēsman* meaning waiting or abiding place, dwelling abode, station or abode, entrance or dwelling respectively. The *Samarānganasūtradhāra*[1] gives several other names like *Dēva-dhisuya* or seat, *Surasthāna* or establishment, *Arcā-gṛha*, *Dēvatā-āyatana* or god's residence, *Vibudhāgāra* or a house of god, *Arcāgṛha* or the house of the consecrated image and *Cayita* or a sacred monument piled up like the Vēdic *Agni* or *Citi*. The *Īśānuśivagurudēva-paddhati*[2] calls the temple the *Prāsāda* or the seat and the dwelling of the god. This name is most generally employed to denote the Hindu temple.

THE TEMPLE AS AN INSTITUTION

The Hindu temple is built by devotees as a work of dedication in order to secure merit in this world and the next. To the pilgrim and devotee who goes to the temple it is a *tīrtha*, i.e., holy place. A Hindu temple unlike the Vēdic altar, does not fulfil its purpose by merely being built; it has of necessity to be seen. *Darśana* and worship are the purposes of visiting the temple.

Throughout the centuries, the Hindu temple played an important role in promoting the social, religious and cultural life of the people. It was the centre of religious and cultural education. Schools were attached to the temple for imparting education in the *Vēdas*, *Vēdāngas*, *Itihāsas* and *Purāṇas*. In addition to this, it provided religious education relating to *Śaiva*, *Vaiṣṇava* and *Śākta* and dispensed spiritual

1. *Samarānganasūtradhāra*. XVIII. 25.
2. *Īśānaśivagurudēvapaddhati*. Part III. Ch. XII.

solace and enlightenment through recitation of texts, festivals, processions, music recitals and dances. The sculptures and paintings that adorned the walls of the temples and the icons in the corridors attracted the masses and practically imparted audio-visual education.

The construction of the temple took several years and it provided employment to hundreds of *sthāpatis* or architects and *śilpis* or sculptors and imparted training to those who were still beginners. It also offered employment to the celebrated musicians and dancers of the times.

The villagers used to hold elections and transact public business in the temple premises as though inviting god as witness i.e., *śākṣi.*

The temple was an ideal autonomous institution free from any lay or secular control. It received the best attention of the most powerful rulers of the time and enjoyed the best patronage that they could dispense. It was the recipient of many valuable gifts from all classes of people and provided for the perpetual merit of the donors.

The temple maintained several auxiliary institutions like *maṭhas,* choultries, maternity homes, sanitoria for the convenience and well being of the pilgrims and of its own staff.

SYMBOLISM OF THE TEMPLE

Unlike the mosque and the Church, the Hindu temple is not a mere house of prayer; it has its peculiar symbolism. The Supreme anxiety of the Hindu is *mōkṣa* or release. There are two ways : subjective and objective prescribed for this. The former is realisation of the Supreme through contemplation, the other is realisation through devotion and worship. The latter method requires a concrete symbol. One of these symbols is the temple itself. The Supreme spirit or *Puruṣa* is originally in an unmanifest condition. He is made to manifest himself in a particular shape and form for the convenience of the devotee. The Supreme who is considered to have been manifest in the shape of the temple is known as *Vāstupuruṣa.* The word *'Vāstu'* is derived from the Sanskṛt root *'Vas'* or dwell and *Vāstu* means a dwelling. *Vāstu-puruṣa* thus means the Supreme spirit that dwells. Before the temple structure is raised a magic diagram or *maṇḍala* is drawn on the ground. The *Vāstupuruṣa* or the Supreme spirit accompanied by attendant deities is localized in this square which comes to be known as the *Vāstu-puruṣa-maṇḍala.* The most important part of the temple is the *Garbhagṛha* which actually means the house of the womb. The spirit, thus localised, is developed in the *garbha* or womb and has its birth in the shape of the image enshrined in the *Garbhagṛha.* It goes up step by step and ultimately reaches the pinnacle or *kalaśa* from which it passes into the original unmanifest condition. Thus the temple is the embodiment of the *Puruṣa* or the Supreme spirit. For this reason, it is something to be seen and worshipped. The numerous mythological sculptures found on the walls and pillars are so many aids for concentration. Thus the Hindu temple is god himself to be seen, felt and realised.

VARIETIES OF TEMPLES

Numerous Sanskṛt texts like the *Mānasāra*, the *Suprabhēdāgama*, the *Śilparatna* and the *Īśānaśivagurudēvapaddhati* describe the method of construction of the Hindu temples ana classify these temples on the basis of style and location.

According to these texts, there are three styles—*Nāgara, Drāviḍa* and *Vēsara.* That structure which is round either from the base or the *kanṭha* or *gaḷa* or neck is *Vēsara*; that which is six or eight sided from the base or at the neck is *Drāviḍa* and that which is four sided from the base to the *śikhara* is *Nāgara.* Most of the extant temples are square below the roof. Therefore the expression four sided, is to be taken to refer to the superstructure above the roof. Even here, in most cases, the *prastara* or the lower portion of the *Vimāna* is always four sided. The *Īśānaśivagurudēvapaddhati* makes the position clear when it states that the differences among temples should be decided on the basis of the differences in the *śikhara.*[3] The *Śilparatna* supports this view by stating that the temple whose *śīrṣa* or *śikhara* and *kanṭha* or neck are eight sided is *Drāviḍa*; that which has a round *kanṭha* or neck and *śira* or *śikhara* is *Vēsara* and that which has a *śikhara* of four sides is *Nāgara.* The *Mānasāra* is in agreement with this view.

The *Vāstu* texts also give a geographical classification of temples. They divide India into three regions viz., the country between the Himālayas and the Vindhyas which is designated as *Nāgara*; the area between the Vindhyas and the Kṛṣṇā which is named *Vēsara* and that between the Kṛṣṇā and the Kanyākumārī which is known as *Drāviḍa.* It is clear from what has been stated above that the stylistic classification relates to the structures, while the geographical classification relates to the regions. This same set of three names namely, *Nāgara, Drāviḍa, Vēsara,* appear in both classifications. On this basis, it has been held by recent scholars that both the classifications are identical. But this is untenable. Because in the so called *Nāgara* area we find temples which belong to both the *Nāgara* and *Drāviḍa* styles. Similarly, in the second or *Vēsara* region, we find temples with round or *āmalaka śikhara* as well as those with four sided and six sided *śikharas.* In the third or *Drāviḍa* region again we find temples with round, four faced, six sided and *āyatāsra* or oblong and *gajapṛṣṭa* or apsidal *śikharas.* It is clear, therefore, that the geographical classification is against the stylistic classification. Since the stylistic classification accords with the nature of all extant temples it has to be taken as the most reliable basis for the classification of the temples.

ORISSAN AND NORTH INDIAN TEMPLES

In the Orissan and North Indian temples, we find three varieties of temples, viz., *Rēkhā Dēul, Piḍhā Dēul,* and *Khākharā Dēul.*

Elevation

Rēkhā Dēul

On the elevation, the *Rēkhā Dēul* consists of three main sections, each with

3. *Īśānaśivagurudēvapaddhati.* Vol. III, Ch. 28, Verse 42.

several sub-sections. The first section is the *Bāḍa*, which corresponds to the *Adhiṣṭāna, Kuḍya* and *Kapōta* of the South Indian temple. It consists of many sub-sections like *Pābhāga, Tala, Joangha, Bandhana, Upar Jangha* and *Baraṇda.* The second section which is the *Gaṇḍi* corresponds to the *Prastara* of the South Indian temple. The *Gaṇḍi* consists of several stories or *Bhūmis*, each marked by a *Bhūmi-āmla*, and its sides are curvilinear, divided into three projections named *kōnikāpāgā* and *Rāhā-pāgā* and two recesses or *anurāhā-pāgās*. The corner projections are known as the *Kōnikā-pāgās*, while the central projection is known as the *Rāhā-pāgā*.

Above the *Gaṇḍi* is the *Mastaka* or head, the third section corresponding to the *grīva, śikhara*, and *kalaśa* of the South Indian temple. The *Mastaka* consists of the *Bēki*, a deep recess, the *Āmla* or cogged stone and the *Khapuri* or cupola. Above is the *Kalaśa*. Often the *Āyudha* (sacred weapon) of the deity to whom the temple is dedicated is placed above the *Kalaśa*.

Another distinguishing feature of this type of temple relates to the outer side of three walls included in the *Bāḍa*. Each wall contains, in the earlier examples, three niches projecting from the wall, whose top part goes up on to the *Gaṇḍi*. The two *Kōnikāpāgas* rise above the two side niches while the upper part of the central niche merges into the *Rāhāpāgā*. In later examples, there are five and even seven projections called *Rathas*. Thus are evolved the *triratha, pañcaratha* and *saptaratha* patterns.

Piḍhā Dēul

The *Piḍhā-Dēul* consists of the same parts as the *Rēkhā Dēul* as far as the *Bāḍa* is concerned. The *Gaṇḍi* which is pyramidal in this case, is made up of a number of *piḍhās* or steps diminishing in size. The *Mastaka* of this *dēul* consists of the *bēkī*, above which sometimes there is a *ghaṇṭā* (an enormous bell-shaped member, sometimes ribbed), the *āmla, khapurī, kalaśa* and *āyudha*.

Khākharā Dēul

This third variety of the temple resembles the *Rēkhā Dēul* with regard to the first two sections below the roof. Its distinguishing feature pertains to the third or upper part which is in two sections. These two sections resemble the half of a *khākharā* or pumpkin, placed one above the other. This part is fluted and suggests the *Drāviḍa śikhara* of the South Indian temple.

Axis

On the axis, this temple contains generally four members viz., the *Dēul*, the *Jagmōhan*, the *Nāṭmandir*, and the *Bhōgamṇṭap*. These four members correspond to the *garbhagṛha, antarāḷa, mukhamaṇṭapa* and *mahāmaṇṭapa* of the fully developed South Indian temple. One distinguishing feature, however, is that in the case of the South Indian temple, the four parts mentioned above are integral and form one whole, whereas in the case of the North Indian temple, each member on the exis is an independent structure formally connected with the preceding member and sometimes unconnected.

THE SOUTH INDIAN TEMPLE

Elevation

The elevation of this temple is in two parts separated by the *acchādana* or roof. The portion below the roof generally contains three parts namely, *adhiṣṭāna* or base, *kuḍya* or wall and *kapōta* or cornice. In some cases an additional member, known as the *upapīṭha* or basement, is added below the *adhiṣṭāna*. Above the roof and above the *garbhagṛha* there is one structure known as the *Vimāna*. This *Vimāna* consists of the *prastara* or entablature, the *grīva* or the neck, the *śikhara* or cupola and the *kalaśa* or the finial. Thus there are in all seven or eight parts on the elevation.

Adhiṣṭāna or Base

This is the lowest member on the elevation of the temple. It has a number of component parts. These parts may be decorated or plain, moulded or flat and receding or projecting. The neck of the *adhiṣṭāna* is cut into small compartments, plain or decorated. In some cases, the *adhiṣṭāna* contains a moulded cornice or *kapōta* either plain or decorated with *nāsikas* or gables. In some instances the top of the *adhiṣṭāna* contains a band with a row of elephants, lions or *makaras*.

Kuḍya or Wall

It is the second member on the elevation of the temple and is constructed above the *adhiṣṭāna*. In some cases, walls are built with large blocks of stone without any decoration or ornamentation, but in most cases, they are decorated beautifully. Some walls are decorated with pilasters or *kuḍyastaṁbhas* which are partly built into the wall and partly visible. In some instances the wall is decorated with *kūṭa* or *kuḍu*. This *kūṭa* is constructed on two pilasters and has a cornice and is crowned by a bell shaped *śikhara*. It is located in the corners and also in the interior alternating with other members. Some walls are decorated with *pañjaras* which are of two types namely, *staṁbhapañjara* and *kuṁbhapañjara* which contain a *kūṭa* above a pilaster. In some cases, the wall is decorated with *śālās*, containing a wagon top or vaulted roof decorated with *nāsikas* or gables. The space between the two pilasters may be either decorated with sculpture or may be plain. Another variety of decoration on the walls is the *kōṣṭa* or niche between two pilasters. This *kōṣṭa* is either plain or contains the icon of a deity and its top may be decorated either with a *śālā* or a stepped *vimāna* or a *tōraṇa*. Some *tōraṇas* contain round plumes hanging down on the sides, in some cases the plume stops with the *phalaka* or plank above the pilasters, and in still others the plume distends to the sides. In some cases the *tōraṇa* assumes the form of a dome. The form of this *tōraṇa* helps the identification of the style. In a few instances, the *gavākṣa* or window is placed in the walls in order to admit light and air into the temple interior and many of them contain perforated screens but some have false windows primarily intended for ornamental purposes.

Kapōṭa or Cornice

The third member is the *kapōta* and it is erected above the walls. In some instances it is plain and flat and in most cases it is a curved moulding projecting from the top of the wall. The outer side of the cornice is decorated with gables or *nāsikas* with or without *siṁhalalāṭs* above. In some cases, the *nāsika* contains human or deity heads. The lower side of the cornice is either plain or cut into compartments by vertical and horizontal rafter ends and decorated with rows of lotus buds on the edges.

Prastara or Entablature

The fourth member on the elevation connects the roof of the temple and the *grīvā* or neck. This is of two general varieties, the storeyed variety and the stepped variety, both of which are of the diminishing type. The former is decorated with the series—*kūṭa*, *pañjara*, *śālā*.

Grīvā or *Neck*

The neck is the fifth member and it connects the *prastara* with the crown or *śikhara* of the temple.

Śikhara or *Crown*

The crown is the sixth member on the elevation of the temple. It is the basis for the determination of the order of the *Vimāna*.

Kalaśa or *Finial*

This is the seventh member and it is constructed above the *śikhara*.

Axis

Garbhagṛha or Sanctum

The *garbhagṛha* is the first member and hindmost part on the axis. The walls of the *garbhagṛha* are either plain or decorated with pilasters and niches. The interior is in a semi-dark condition and in its centre will be a linga of Śiva or an image of the deity, set up on a *vēdi*.

Antarāḷa or ante-chamber

This second member, the *antarāḷa* or the ante-chamber is immediately before the *garbhagṛha* and behind the *mukhamaṇṭapa*.

Mukhamaṇṭapa or Hall

The third member is the *mukhamaṇṭapa* which is behind the *mahāmaṇṭapa*. The plan of the *mukhamaṇṭapa* is either square or rectangular. The *mukhamaṇṭapa* is either an open pillared hall or pillared hall with walls on three sides with one or three entrances with or without porches.

Mahāmaṇṭapa or great Hall

This fourth member, found in front of the *mukhamaṇṭapa* is the foremost part of the temple. In most cases it is a latter day addition but in the temples of the Vijayanagara period it formed part of the original monument.

EARLY ĀNDHRA TEMPLES

Temple building activity was in vogue in Āndhradēśa since the first quarter of the third century A.D. With the help of the sculptured slabs that once adorned the *stūpas* of Amarāvati, Gōli, Nāgārjunakoṇḍa, Rāmireḍḍipalli and Jaggayyapēṭa, it is possible to trace the temple construction in Āndhradēśa to very early times. On one of the Amarāvati slabs, the *bahirdvāraśālā* sculptured with a moulded *kapōta* above the *kuḍya* or wall and a *śālā* or wagon top roof above, with six rows of *kalaśas* or finials, is suggestive of a temple or *gōpura* with an *āyatāsra śikhara.*[4] Another sculpture of a building with a square base and four sided roof is suggestive of the *kūṭāgāra* of the *Nāgara* order. The Eastern Cāḷukyan temples of Bikkavōlu are the best examples of this style. A hut sculptured on a slab with a round base and top resembles the *Vēsara* shrine is mentioned in the *Vāstu* texts.[5] A storeyed building containing human heads inside suggestive of the *kapōta* of the cave temples of the Viṣṇukuṇḍins and the Pallavas and the *kūṭas* of the structural temples.[6] The storeyed *Vihāra* with two, three, four and even five gables in each storey, raised round a *Vṛkṣacaitya,* is suggestive of the storeyed *Vimāna* of the latter temples.[7] A building sculptured on a slab with a heavily moulded *kapōta* and ornamentation, resembles the upper part of the facades of the Viṣṇukuṇḍin and Pallava caves,[8] and a single storeyed building with three gables and a row of animals above resembles the cave facades.[9] Two storeyed buildings, containing two gables in the centre of the front of the first floor and a *kūṭāgāra* at either end, are suggestive of an *alpaprāsāda* of the *Nāgara* order found in the second storey of the Anantaśāyī cave of Uṇḍavalli.[10] The slab which contains the *Nalagiridamana* shows the wing of a building with a square base and a *śālā* top adorned with a wide *nāsika* or gable in the front.[11] Long sheds with wagon top shaped roofs appear frequently in these sculptures and are suggestive of the *āyatāsra* shrine.[12] A miniature shrine with a circular *śikhara* and another with an octagonal top suggestive of the *vimānas* of the *Vēsara* and *Drāviḍa* orders. The *Punyaśālā* of Jaggayyapēṭa, with an upper storey and an *āyatāsra* or oblong top with *kalaśas* above, is suggestive of this type of *Vēsara* temples and the *gōpuras.* In most of the Buddhist *tīrthas,* there are apsidal or *gajapṛṣṭa* shaped *caiyta* halls, some with a *pradakṣiṇa* in the interior with either a *caitya* or an image of Buddha in the apse. These are suggestive of the apsidal type of Hindu temple of which there are fine examples at Guḍimallam, Satyavōlu and Cēzerla. At Sālihuṇḍam, there is a rectangular room with a brick platform in the centre containing an image of the Buddha and this suggests the *garbhagṛha* of the Hindu temple with an image in the centre. At Śankaram, there are three structures with Buddha figures or sculptures

4. Sivaramamurthi. *Amarāvati Sculptures,* Pl. XII, Fig. 3.
5. *Ibid.,* Fig. 4.
6. *Ibid.,* Pl. XIV-3.
7. *Ibid* , Pl. XV-1.
8. *Ibid* , Pl. XVII-2.
9. *Ibid.,* Pl., XIX-a.
10. *Ibid.,* Pl. XXIV.
11. *Ibid.,* Pl. XV. 1.
12. *Ibid.,* Pl. XLVII-2.

on the back wall and these resemble the Sōmāskanda panel on the back wall of the *garbhagṛha* in the cave and structural temples of the Pallavas. All these show that buildings of the shapes and forms of the later day Hindu temples existed in Buddhist times and that these must have been adopted by the Hindus as models for their temples. These prototypes of temples are found in the Buddhist or Āndhra-Sātavāhana period.

But the actual structures were found during the course of the excavations in the Nāgārjunakoṇḍa valley and belong to the Ikṣvāku period which followed the Sātavāhana period. A Kumārasvāmi temple existed on site V-7.[13] Another temple, dedicated to the same god, was found on the bank of the Kṛṣṇā built by the Ikṣvāku prince, Cāṁta-Śakti Kumāra.[14] About 200 yards south of the above temple, there was another shrine of Kumāra.[15] At the northern reach of the river Kṛṣṇā, there was a temple of god Śiva known as Puṣpabhadrasvāmi, constructed by the Ikṣvāku King, Ehavula Cāṁtamūla.[16] There was another temple, dedicated to Śiva, with a number of stone lingas found inside it.[17] Another temple dedicated to god Sarvadēva, was built by Elisiri, the chief *talavara*, who was a great devotee of Kumārasvāmin.[18] Another temple or *dēvakula*, dedicated to god Noḍagirisvāmi, also existed here.[19] There was one famous shrine dedicated to Viṣṇu under the name of Aṣṭabhujasvāmi. This temple had three shrines with the *dhvajastaṁbha* opposite them.[20]

With the fall of the Ikṣvākus, the Pallavas came to power and established their sway in the southern and south-western parts of the Ikṣvāku territory. It is known from inscriptions that the temples of god Nārāyaṇa of Dāḷūra and of Viṣṇuhara at Kandukūra existed in Pallava times.[21] An Ānanda gōtra inscription mentions a Śiva temple of god Vaṁkēśvara.[22] The Paraśurāmēśvara temple of Guḍimallam was also raised by the Pallavas in the 8th century.

VARIOUS STYLES

Many styles of art and architecture flourished in Āndhradēśa. Of these, the Early Cāḷukyan, Eastern Cāḷukyan, Kaḷinga, Kākatīya and Vijayanagara are important.

Early Cāḷukyan Style

The Cāḷukyan art and architectural tradition which flourished at Aihole, Paṭṭadakal and Bādāmi between 550-753 A.D. travelled from its epicentre to far distant places like Alaṁpūr, Mahānandi and Satyavōlu in Āndhradeśa. The Cāḷukyas evolved a new idiom to embellish their monuments and thus became pioneers in the field of temple architecture.

13. *Indian Archaeology*, 1955-56, p. 25.
14. *Ibid.*, 1955-56, p. 36.
15. *Ibid.*, Pl. LXIII-c.
16. *E.I.*, XXIV, pp. 19-29.
17. *Indian Archaeology*, 1957-58, p. 8.
18. *E.I.*, XXXIII, pp. 147-149.
19. *Ibid.*, XXXV, pp. 4-7.
20. *Indian Archaeology*, 1958-59, Pl. V, Fig. 5.
21. *E.I.*, VIII, pp. 143-146; *I.A.*, V, pp. 50-53,
22. *I.A.*. IX, pp. 101-103.

Plan

The Early Cāḷukyan temples with curvilinear *Vimānas* and *āmalaka śikharas* exhibit a variety of plan starting with the mere *garbhagṛha* and ending with the complex containing *garbhagṛha, antarāḷa*, porch, *pradakṣiṇa,* walled enclosure and another porch.

Walls

The walls are plain and devoid of decoration. The *garbhagṛha* walls have no angles and recesses, unlike the walls of the *triratha* and *pañcaratha* patterns of North India.

Doorways

The doorways are adorned with carvings and beautiful sculptures at the bases. The architraves are decorated with the *kūṭa, śālā, pañjara* series and the corner beams with lions projecting.

Niches

The *kōṣṭas* or niches are usually plain and in some cases project a little forward. Between the top of the niche and the cornice above the walls there is empty wall space.

Vimānas

The *vimāna* above the *garbhagṛha* has the *kōnikā* and *rāhā pāgās* adorned with vertical rows of gable arches.

Pillars

There are many varieties of pillars in this style of temples. The first variety is the massive square pillar with a big capital. It is decorated with simple brackets, or with sculptured brackets, or with *taranga* alone and sometimes it may be decorated with *ṭaranga* with a *paṭṭa* in the centre, plain or with an animal figure. The second variety is the ornate pillar with a lion on the *pāda, pūrṇakalaśa* at the bottom and the top, fluted shaft and sculptured fillets. In some cases it is decorated with lions projecting from the ends and supporting the roof. The third variety is the square pillar with circular and semi-circular medallions and the last variety is decorated with life size figure brackets belonging to either deities or *mithunas*.

Eastern Cāḷukyan Style

The practice of constructing elaborate temples in Āndhradeśa owes its origin to the time of the Cāḷukyas. The five *ārāmas*, Drākshārāma, Kumārārāma, Amarārāma, Sōmārāma and Kṣīrārāma, that are linked with the anecdote of the victory of Lord Śiva over the Tripuras, are the earliest temple structures that can be ascribed to the Eastern Cāḷukyan rulers in the coastal tract of the Telugu country.

Plan

The plan of these temples shows an interesting variety. There are two general types—single storeyed shrines and double storeyed shrines. All these temples have on the axis the *garbhagṛha*, *antarāḷa* and *mukhamaṇṭapa*. All these parts are found also in the upper floor. Some of the temples are inside *prākāras* while the others do not have the *prākāras*.

Walls

The walls of independent temples like those of Bikkavōlu are decorated with projections with *kōṣṭas* surmounted by *makaratōraṇas* between two pilasters, recesses and projections. Sometimes the *kōṣṭas* have deity icons. The pilasters are crowned by simple bracket capitals.

Kapōṭa or Cornice

It is adorned with *siṁhalalāṭa* gables.

The Roof

The roof contains a row of *yāḷis* in the front and the series *kūṭa, śālā, pañjara* and *kūṭa* behind it.

Vimāna

The base of the *vimāna* contains a row of tall pilasters. The *vimānas* of this period have horizontal rows of diminishing size containing the series—*kūṭa, śālā* and *pañjara*. All these temples are of the *Nāgara* Order.

Kaḷinga Style

The region between the Mahānadi in the north and the Gōdāvari in the south is known as Kaḷinga. The *Mānasāra* and the *Kāmikāgama* mention a separate Kāḷinga style of architecture.

Plan

The temples of Siṁhāchalam and Mukhalingam alone are inside the *prākāras*. All the others stand in the open.

Walls

The walls of the Kaḷinga temple contain narrow projections on either side of a wider projection with a central niche containing sculpture. The pilasters on the walls and the pillar capitals are peculiar. In the recesses of the walls there are *kūṭagāras* with *Nāgara-śikharas*. But the walls of the temple at Mukhalingam are peculiar. They are plain and there is a tapering band in the centre starting in the *adhiṣṭāna* below and ending at the *phalaka* above. All the front walls of the shrines contain a *dvāra* in the centre flanked by a niche on either side.

Cornice

The cornice above the walls is decorated with semi-circular *siṁhalalāṭa* arches and not with gables or *nāsikas* as in the case of the temples of the southern type.

Vimāna

The *vimānas* of the Kaḷinga temples do not have the projecting *kōnikā pāgās, anurāhā pāgās* and *rāhā pāgās* on each face. The faces are flat and the edges are straight and curved only at the top. These temples have *āmalaka śikharas* and belong to the *Vēsara* order like the Early Cāḷukyan temples of Northern Karṇāṭaka and Āndhradēśa. The absence of the *śukanāsa* in this style is peculiar. The *bhūmi āmlas* are present in some cases and absent in others and therefore optional.

Axis

On the axis, only two temples i.e., Madhukēśvara and the Bhīmēśvara of Mukhalingam have the *garbhagṛha, antarāḷa* and a *maṇṭapa* before them. The temple of Simhachalam contains on the three sides of the *garbhagṛha*, a pillared *pradakṣiṇa* and a *bhōga maṇṭapa.* The Dibbēśvara temple at Sārapalli contains only the *garbhagṛha.*

Kākatīya Style

The Kākatīyas of Warangal were great builders and lovers of art and raised numerous temples in their vast empire.

There are two types of temples, one a single shrine, and the other a triple shrine, generally known as *trikūṭa.* Among the single shrines, there are five varieties. The first variety contains the *garbhagṛha, antarāḷa* and *maṇṭapa* with three porches on the three sides. The second variety contains the *garbhagṛha, antarāḷa* and *maṇṭapa* with a single porch. The third variety contains only the *garbhagṛha* and *antarāḷa.* The fourth variety contains the *garbhagṛha* behind an open *maṇṭapa* and finally, the fifth variety contains only the *garbhagṛha.*

The Base

The bases of these temples are of two varieties. A few temples contain a double base with the *upapīṭha* and a broad *pradakṣiṇa* at its top and the *adhiṣṭāna* built above it inside the *pradakṣiṇa.* All other temples have the *adhiṣṭāna* only.

Walls

The artists of this time adopted numerous devices for decorating the outer side of the walls of the temples. The wall surface contains alternating recesses and projections. The central projection contains miniature shrines one and sometimes three one above the other. The other projections contain a pilaster or a *kōṣta* or *śālā* or a miniature shrine of the *Nāgara* Order. The recesses contain a pilaster with a miniature *vimāna* of horizontal bands or a *kūṭa-kōṣṭa,* or *vimāna* under a creeper.

The Roof

On the edges of the roof are to be found a row of miniature *vimānas* built of bricks. This is the peculiar feature of the Kākatīya style. These *vimānas* are similar to the *pañjara* and *śālā* of the Pallava temples and the *cuncu* of the Vijayanagara monuments.

Pillars

The pillars are of two varieties. One variety is made of black granite and lathe turned, polished and decorated with various geometrical and bead designs and human and deity sculptures. The second variety is made of sand stone and is mostly plain, though in a few cases there is figure sculpture of a high order.

Vimānas

These *vimānas* contain diminishing rows of distended *kūṭas* and wide *śālās* or miniature *vimānas.* There is often the *śukanāsa* added at the front base of the *vimāna.*

Miniature Vimānas

These are found in the recesses on the outer side of walls, on the outer side of the low *vēdis* on the *adhiṣṭāna,* on the architrave above the beam and canopies of the entrances of the *antarāḷa* and *garbhagṛha* and *mukhamaṇṭapa.* The miniatute *vimānas* contain five to nine *talas* of horizontal bands of diminishing size and sometimes a conical band in the centre of the front face. They sometime contain an *avatāsra* part above the *gaḷa* and are sometimes crowned by *śikharas* of the *Vēsara* Order.

Miniature Shrines

Miniature shrines are complete temples with a canopy above and a low parapet with an opening in the centre in the front. There is a *kapōta* above the walls and a *vimāna* of horizontal bands of diminishing size crowned by a *Nāgara* or *Vēsara śikhara.* These shrines are found on the side walls of the *antarāḷa,* on the architrave above the entrances and on the outer side of the walls of the *grabhagṛha.*

Carved Entrances

A remarkable feature of this style is the *dvāra* fixed in a large and wide frame consisting of the wall portion, pillars, pilasters and jambs with sculptures. Another feature relating to these *dvāras* is the projecting canopy above the cross beam.

Subsidiary Shrines

The major shrines are surrounded on the four sides by a cluster of minor shrines.

The Vijayanagara Style

The Vijayanagara style of architecture marks a specific improvement on the previous styles. Large *prākāras* or enclosures with entrances surmounted by big *gōpuras* are a special feature. The temples of this time generally contained four members on the axis i.e., *garbhagṛha, antarāḷa, mukhamaṇṭapa* and *mahāmaṇṭapa.* The *Kalyānamaṇṭapa* is another special feature. The same is the case with the Dēvī shrine which is located to the left of the main sanctum.

Wall decoration in this style is also peculiar. Besides the usual pilasters, the niche surmounted by an oblong *vimāna,* and pillars in projections are of new features.

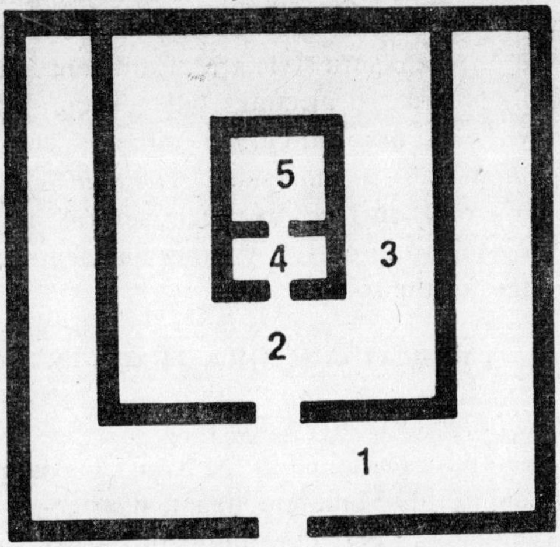

Key to the plan—Bālabrahma temple, Alaṁpūr

1. Inner *Pradakṣiṇa* 2. *Maṇṭapa* 3. Outer *Pradakṣiṇa* 4. *Antaraḷa* 5. *Garbhagṛha*

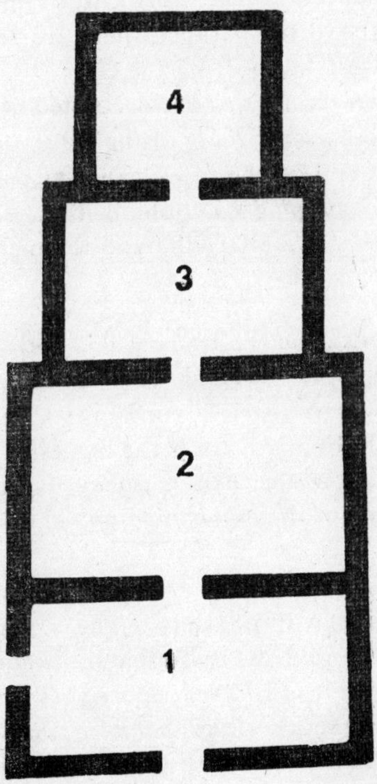

Key to the plan—Gōliṅgēśvara temple, Bikkavōlu

Maṇṭapa 2. *Mukhamaṇṭapa* 3. *Antarāḷa* 4. *Garbhagṛha*

One special feature is the *kumbhapañjara*, a shaft emanating from a vessel below and containing a *kūṭa* above. The cornice is invariably projecting.

The pillars of the Vijayanagara style are of different varieties, e.g., pillar with one, two, three and four pillarets projecting, pillar decorated with *kūṭa, śālā, kūṭa* series all over, pillar with *vāḷi* bracket, curved pillars. The capital of these pillars has a well developed *boḍigai* on the underside. The *mahāmaṇṭapa* is either square or oblong. Sometimes the wall surface between several architectural members is decorated with mythological sculptures. Another new feature is a *cuncu* or a row of arches located on the edges of the roof.

TYPICAL ĀNDHRA TEMPLES

The Bālabrahma Temple, Alaṁpūr (Early Cāḷukyan)

The Bālabrahma temple is situated in the town of Alaṁpūr, the headquarters of a taluk of that name in the Mahaboobnagar district in the Telangana part of Āndhra Pradesh. This temple is a perfect example of Early Cāḷukyan *Vēsara* style.

This temple (pl. I-1) consists of the *garbhagṛha, antarāḷa* and *maṇṭapa* enclosed by a walled inner *pradakṣiṇa*. All these parts are enclosed by another outer *pradakṣiṇa*. The outer *pradakṣiṇa* has on the north, west and south a low parapet cut into narrow compartments. Above the parapet, there are seven short pillars in the north and south and five in the west, supporting the roof.

The walls of the inner *pradakṣiṇa* are decorated with *kōṣṭas*, sculptures, pilasters etc. The *vimāna* above the *garbhagṛha* is of the *catustala* variety of the *Vēsara* Order. The figure of Naṭarāja is found on the face of the *śukanāsa*.

The north wall of the *garbhagṛha* contains a niche with the image of Durga, the niche in the west wall houses Vṛṣabharūḍha and the niche in the south wall contains an icon of Gaṇapati.

The Gōlingēśvara Temple, Bikkavōlu (Eastern Cāḷukyan)

The village of Bikkavōlu situated between the town of Rājahmundry and Kākināḍa, in the East Gōdāvari district, contains six temples of the Eastern Cāḷukyas. Of these, the temple of god Gōlingēśvara is the biggest.

The temple contains on the axis *garbhagṛha, antarāḷa, mukhamaṇṭapa* and another *maṇṭapa*. In between the *mukhamaṇṭapa* and another *maṇṭapa,* there is a narrow passage.

The *garbhagṛha* walls (pl. I-2; II-1) are decorated with *kōṣṭas* containing sculptures, recesses and projections with pilasters The *kōṣṭas* are surmounted by *makaratōraṇas*. The pilasters on the walls have simple bracket capitals. Above the capitals is a row of dwarfs and above it is a *kapōta* adorned with *siṁhalalāṭa* gables. Beyond this row there is a row of the series—*kūṭa, pañjara, śālā, pañjara* and *kūṭa*, each *kūṭa* being adorned with one and each *śālā* with three *siṁhalalāṭa* gables.

The *vimāna* (pl. II-2) above the *garbhgṛha* contains, at its base, a row of eight pilasters and a row of rafter ends. There are twelve beam heads above this and two steps and a narrow *gaḷa*. Above the *gaḷa* is a *Nāgara śikhara* with *siṁhalalāṭa* gable on each side and above it is a *kalaśa* in a double lotus.

The *mukhamaṇṭapa* walls are decorated with pilasters and screens and it contains

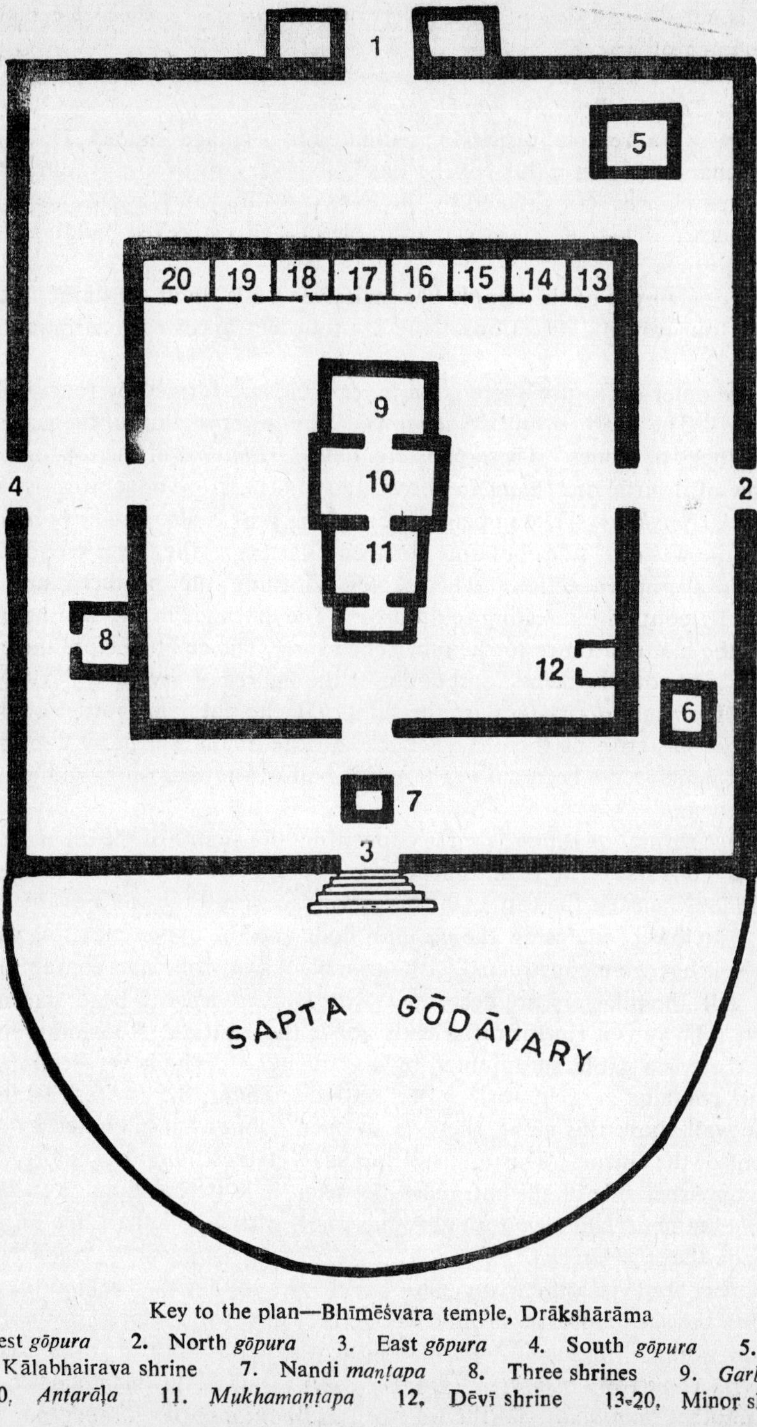

Key to the plan—Bhīmēśvara temple, Drākshārāma

1. West *gōpura* 2. North *gōpura* 3. East *gōpura* 4. South *gōpura* 5. *Maṇṭapa*
6. Kālabhairava shrine 7. Nandi *maṇṭapa* 8. Three shrines 9. *Garbhagṛha*
10. *Antarāḷa* 11. *Mukhamaṇṭapa* 12. Dēvī shrine 13-20. Minor shrines

three small shrines. There is a small shrine on the southern entrance of the *maṇṭapa.* The *antarāḷa* is narrow and devoid of any decoration. In the *garbhagṛha* there is a black granite linga on a *vēdi.*

The Bhīmēśvara Temple, Drākshārāma (Eastern Cāḷukyan)

The Bhīmēśvara Temple (pl. III-1) is situated in a village named Drākshārāma in the Rāmachandrapuram taluk of the East Gōdāvary district in Āndhra Pradēsh. This famous temple was constructed by the Eastern Cāḷukyan King, Cāḷukya Bhīma, in his own name. This is a perfect example of a two storeyed building, standing inside two enclosures.

The outer enclosure of the temple has massive walls built of large blocks of stone. In the four cardinal directions there are four entrances each surmounted by a *gōpura* (pl. III-2).

Inside the outer enclosure there is an inner enclosure formed by four walls also built of stone. The wall is in two sections. The lower section of the wall is plain and built of blocks of stones. These pilasters have *kīrtimukha* at the top. There is a horizontal row of dwarfs or *bhūtamāla* above the pilasters. Above this is a gable adorned with *kīrtimukhas.* The upper section of the wall is also similarly built. But the wall on the western side contains nineteen pilasters in the lower section and the same number in the upper section. The gables adorning the northern and eastern parts of the walls contain interesting sculptures. The entrance in the southern wall is being used as the main entrance to the inner enclosure. The ceiling before the entrance is divided into nine compartments and contains the figures of Śiva and Pārvatī in the centre and of the eight *dikpālakas* on the sides. In the noth-east corner of the inner enclosure, on the eastern side there is a replica of the main shrine. A number of small compartments have been cut in the inner wall of the enclosure and an icon set up in each of them.

The main shrine of Bhīmēśvara is situated in the centre of the inner enclosure. The *adhiṣṭāna* consists of a plain flat band at the bottom, a recess above it and another plain flat band at the top. On this *adhiṣṭāna* stand the walls of the shrine in two sections, the lower enclosing the ground floor and the upper enclosing the upper floor. Both sections were constructed with large blocks of stone and contain pilasters at intervals. All the pilasters are decorated with *kīrtimukha* with bead garlands and capitals above. There is a row of rafter ends above the capitals. Above this row, over each pilaster there is a gable surmounted by a *kīrtimukha.* The lower section of the southern wall contains a niche with a perforated screen in the centre. In the upper section of the wall above this niche, there is an open doorway surmounted by a *gōpura* above the roof of the shrine. This main shrine has a narrow *maṇṭapa* before it in two sections, one on either side of the entrance. Between these two sections is the entrance to the *antarāḷa* and *garbhagṛha* on the ground floor, with a tall shaft like linga set up on a *vēdī* inside the *garbhagṛha.*

The upper floor is similar in plan to the ground floor. Behind the narrow *maṇṭapa* before the shrine on the ground floor, there are two openings in the wall on either side containing a flight of steps leading to the upper floor. To the east on the upper floor is a narrow *maṇṭapa.* On the back wall of this *maṇṭapa,* there is an entrance to another *maṇṭapa.* To the west of this *maṇṭapa,* the *garbhagṛha* and the

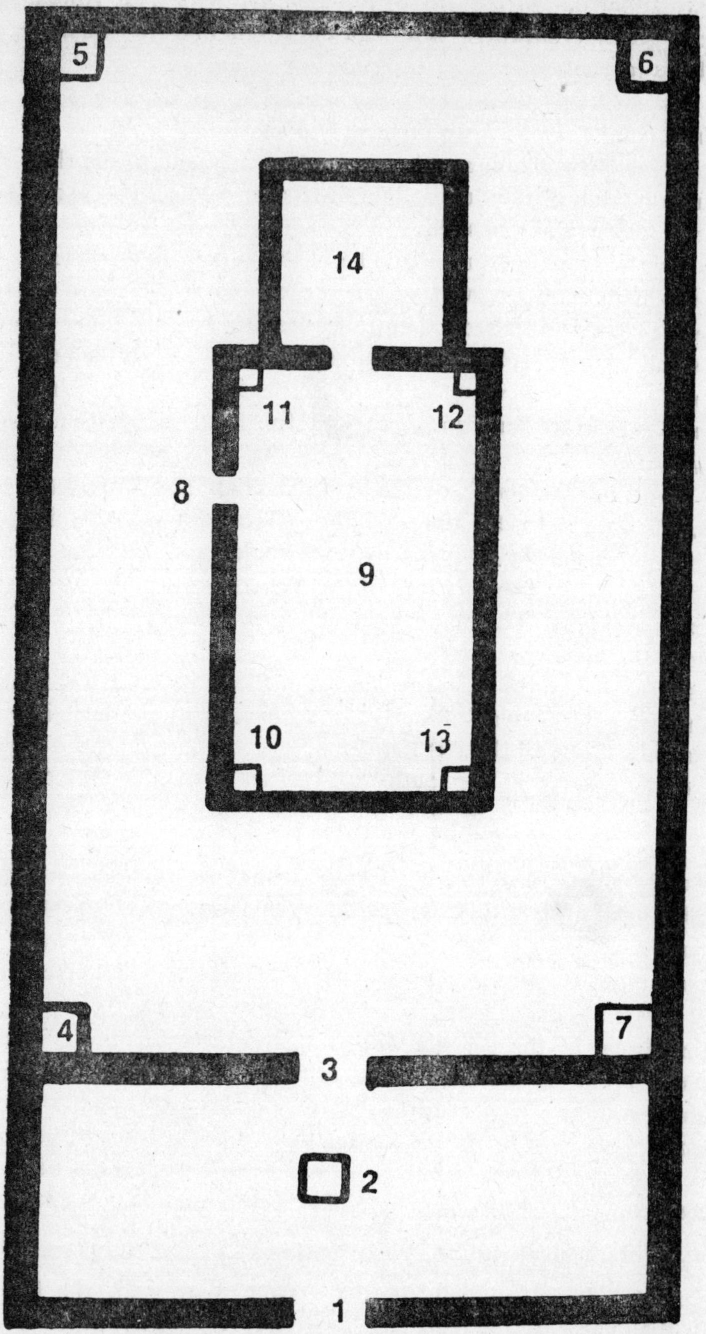

Key to the plan—Madhukēśvara temple, Mukhalingam

1. Main entrance 2. Nandi *Maṇṭapa* 3. Second entrance 4-7. Small shrines
8. Entrance to the *maṇṭapa* 9. *Maṇṭapa* 10-13. Smallshrines 14. *Garbhagṛha*

antarāḷa are situated, surrounded by a *pradakṣiṇa* with two rows of pillars. In the centre of the *garbhagṛha*, there is a linga on a *vēdi* and to the north of the *vēdi*, an image of Umā located.

The Madhukēśvara Temple, Mukhalingam (Kaḷinga)

The village of Mukhalingam is situated on the bank of the river Vaṁśadhāra in the Pātapaṭṇam taluk of the Śrīkākuḷam district in Āndhra Pradēsh. This temple is a good example of the Kaḷinga style.

This temple is situated in the middle of the village on an elevated platform. In the east is the main entrance, with a narrow rectangular courtyard beyond it, a nandi *maṇṭapa* in the centre and a second entrance leading into the inner courtyard. There are four small shrines (pl. IV-1) in this courtyard and in the centre is the Madhukēśvara temple with the *garbhagṛha* and a rectangular *maṇṭapa*. In the four corners of the *maṇṭapa* there are four small shrines (pl. IV-2) each with a curvilinear *vimāna* and *āmalaka śikhara*.

The front or east wall of the *maṇṭapa* contains a wide *dvāra* with a niche on either side. The niche to the right of the *dvāra* contains the figure of a woman standing in *vyatvastapāda* attended by two women and the niche to left contains the figures of two women. The verticals of the *dvāra* are also fully decorated with sculptures and *pūrṇakalaśas*. There are three niches on the walls of the shrine in the south east corner of the *maṇṭapa*.

The south wall of the *maṇṭapa* has six niches with Kumāra, Durgā, Bhūvarāha, Bhikṣāṭana, Śiva, Narasiṁha killing Hiranyakaśipu and another niche with the figure of Naṭarāja. In this wall there is a *dvāra*.

The shrine situated in the south-west corner of the *maṇṭapa* has five niches with sculptures and the shrine in the north-west corner also has five niches with sculptures.

The wall on the north side has several niches containing the sculptures of Śiva, Ekapādamūrti and other standing deities. The shrine in the north east corner of the *maṇṭapa* has six niches with figures. The corner shrines are all alike.

The *maṇṭapa* contains two rows of six pillars each with corresponding pillars in the walls. There are many loose icons inside this *maṇṭapa*.

The *adhiṣṭāna* of the *garbhagṛha* is cut into three sections. The walls are plain and contain a broad projection in the centre. Above the walls there is a low flat *paṭṭa* in three sections. The *vimāna* contains seventeen courses of stone and no *bhūmi āmlas*. On each face of the *vimāna* there is a tapering projection with a gable at the base. There is a double *āmalaka śikhara* with a stone *kalaśa* above it.

There are many interesting icons and sculptures inside this shrine.

Thousand Pillared Temple, Hanumakoṇḍa (Kākatīya)

Hanumakoṇḍa is situated six miles from Warangal, the headquarters of a district of that name in the Telangāna part of Āndhra Pradēsh. At the end of the town, a triple shrine dedicated to Sūryēśvara, Vāsudēvēśvara and Rudrēśvara was constructed in Ś. 1084 or 1162 A.D. by the Kākatīya King, Rudra, in commemoration of his great victories.

This temple (pl. V-1; 2) is the best example of a triple shrine. It is constructed on a double platform and consists of a central *maṇṭapa* or hall with three shrines, Rudrēśvara to the west, the Vāsudēva to the north and Sūrya to the east.

Base

The lowest member on the elevation is the *upapīṭha.* It is mostly buried in the ground. There is a *pradakṣiṇa* at its top, 9′ wide. Inside it is a high *adhiṣṭāna.*

Porch

This is to the south of the central *maṇṭapa,* and has a flight of steps in the middlc leading into the *mukhamaṇṭapa.* It contains four pillars, two in the front and two at the back. The underside of the ceiling is cut into narrow compartments by vertical and horizontal rafters. There is a lotus bud at each angle and a row of buds on the underside of the edges.

There is a low *vēdi* beyond the porch with pillars supporting the roof.

The Rudrēśvara Shrine

This shrine faces the east.

The Walls

The north wall of this shrine is adorned with projection containing pillars and recesses coutaining miniature *vimānas,* niches with deity figures and projections with pilasters. One distinguishing feature is a miniature shrine built in a wide projection in the back wall of the *garbhagṛha* (pl. VI-1). There are three miniature *vimānas* above it each in three projecting sections. The side *vimānas* have seven *talas* and an *āmalaka śikhara.* The central *vimāna* has seven *talas* and an *āmalaka śikhara.* All the *vimānas* have the central conical band with creeper design on it. On the underside of the ceillng of both the front portion and the *garbhagṛha* of the shrine, there is a lotus.

The west or back wall is decorated with projection with pilasters, niches with deity figures, miniature *vimānas* with seven *talas* and *āmalaka śikhara* on a pilaster, projection and projection with a miniature shrine. This wall contains a miniature shrine with three miniature *vimānas* above it. Each of them has five *talas* and a round *śikhara.*

The south wall is decorated with projection with pilasters, recess with a miniature *vimāna* of seven *talas* and round *śikhara* on pilasters, and wide projection with a miniature shrine. There are two lotuses on the underside of the ceiling, one outside and another in the *garbhagṛha.*

Antarāḷa

The entrance of the *anṭarāḷa* has five sections on either side both alike. The architrave above is finely decorated and there is a *makara* at each extremity. Before the *makaras* there are fine figures in dance poses. In the centre is Śiva as Naṭarāja dancing in the *bhujangatrāsa* pose.

In each side wall of the *anṭarāḷa* there is a miniature shrine containing two pillars on either side, jambs, *dvāra,* a plain projecting cornice and a wide *vimāna* in three sections projecting from one another.

Garbhagṛha

The bases of the jambs of the entrance of the *garbhagṛha* are finely sculptured. There is a moon stone before the *paḍi* or base piece. The lintel has been cut into a miniature shrine housing the figure of Gaṇapati. In the *garbhagṛha* there is a carved *vēdi* on which a cylindrical linga was fixed. There are four pilasters in the angles of the walls.

The Vāsudēvēśvara Shrine

This shrine faces the north.

The Walls

The east wall is divided into seventeen sections and decorated like the walls of the Rudrēśvara temple. But some of the sculptures are noteworthy. On this wall there is a niche with the figure of standing Viṣṇu. Another projection, which is in the back wall of the *garbhagṛha,* has a miniature shrine. It has a row of three *vimānas* each with a conical band in the centre and with eight *talas* and a round *śikhara.* The other two walls of this shrine are similar.

Antarāḷa

The *antarāḷa* entrance is in four sections all alike on either side of the *dvāra.* The architrave is finely carved. There is a two storeyed miniature shrine at each extremity. In the centre on a lotus is the figure of Nṛtta-Narasiṁha with a lion's face and dances in the *bhujangatrāsa* pose with the right leg resting on a lotus.

In the *antarāḷa* there are two miniature shrines, one in the north wall and the other in the south wall. There is a full lotus on the underside of the ceiling.

Garbhagṛha

The jamb bases are finely decorated with two *cāmaravāhinis,* Viṣṇu and one woman holding *kalaśa.* The lintel of the upper beam has the figure of Gajalakṣmī. There is a canopy above the *vēdi* in the centre, projecting from the back wall and pilasters in the angles.

The Sūryēśvara Shrine

This shrine is opposite the Rudrēśvara shrine, and faces the west.

The Walls

The walls are decorated as in the other two shrines. There is a broad projection in the back wall of the *garbhagṛha* with a miniature shrine built in it. Above this are three miniature *vimānas.* One side *vimāna* has six *talas* and a round *śikhara* and the other is round from bottom to top. The central *vimāna* has an *āyatāsra śikhara.*

Antarāḷa

The entrance is in three sections with the doorway in the centre and one section on each side. The architrave has a fine representation of Gajāsurasaṁhāramūrti. There are two *makaras,* each with a four handed rider. The space betewen the *makaras* contains three women on each side in dance poses. Between them is Śiva as Gajāsurasaṁhāramūrti dancing in the *lalita* pose.

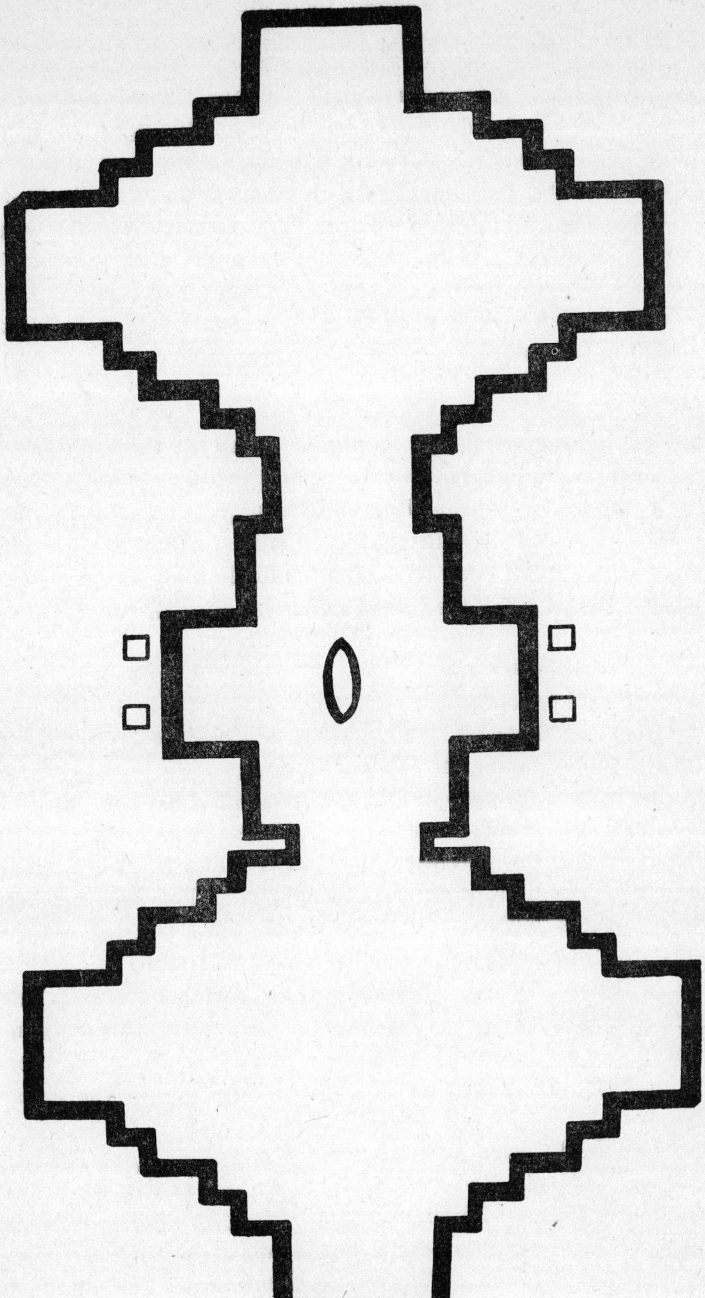

On the two side walls of the *antarāḷa*, there are two miniature shrines.

Garbhagṛha

The entrance of the *garbhagṛha* is in six sections. There are fine sculptures on the bases of the jambs. Each side of the base contains the figure of a man holding up a *cāmara*, a *cāmaravāhini*, Viṣṇu with four hands standing in *dvibhanga*, female deity holding flower in the left hand, standing deity figure with four hands and *cāmaravāhinis*. There is a moon stone before the base, carved in the shape of a lotus creeper with buds shooting out at the ends. In the interior of the *garbhagṛha* there are four pilasters at the four corners. There is a long projecting plank along each of the two side walls and a finely carved canopy projecting from the back wall, above the linga on a *vēdi* in the centre.

Mukhamaṇṭapa

There is a big *mukhamaṇṭapa* common to all the three shrines. It has four richly carved pillars. The underside of the ceiling contains four squares, one inside the other. There are twelve *siṁhalalāṭas* in the angles of the two outer squares and the eight *dikpālakas* round a circle inside the innermost square. This circle contains the figure of Śiva seated in *vīrāsana* with eight hands holding sword, *khēṭa* and *dhanus* among others. There is a full lotus on the underside of each beam.

The Thousand Pillared Maṇṭapa

There is a big *maṇṭapa*, opposite the triple shrine. The platform on which the *maṇṭapa* stands is star shaped in plan. There is a finely carved black granite nandi in the centre of the square facing the triple shrine.

The *maṇṭapa* is raised above an *upapīṭha* and *adhiṣṭāna* and has three porches in the north, east and south. There is a narrow pillared verandah outside the *maṇṭapa* proper connecting the three porches. Each porch consists of a small open pial, containing a pillar and a low *vēdi* on parapet beyond. The walls are decorated with a broad pilaster, recess with a miniature *vimāna* on a pilaster, a projection with a pilaster, recess with a miniature *vimāna* of 14 *talas* and round *śikhara* on a pilaster and projection with a pilaster. The jambs of the entrance on each side have at the base a wide section decorated with a big *pūrṇakalāśa* with a creeper issuing out of it. The lintel contains the figure of Gajalakṣmī. Inside the *maṇṭapa* there is a double square with 12 plain pillars. The roof projects two feet beyond the walls.

The Rudrēśvara Temple, Pālaṁpēṭ (Kākatīya)

The great temple (pl. VI-2) of Pālaṁpēṭ, known as the Rudrēśvara temple, is situated in the small village of Pālaṁpēṭ in the Mulug Taluk of the Warangal district of Āndhra Pradēsh. An inscription set up in the courtyard of this temple states that in Ś. 1135, or 1213 A.D. a famous Kākatīya general, named Rēcerla Rudra, constructed this temple named after himself in the town of Ātukūru and gifted a village to it.

This temple marks the climax of the evolution of architecture in medieval Deccan. It faces the east and is situated inside a compound. It consists of *upapīṭha, adhiṣṭāna, garbhagṛha, antarāḷa, mukhamaṇṭapa* with three porches and a tall *vimāna* above.

The lowest member on the axis is the *upapīṭha*. There is a wide *paradakṣiṇa* on the top of the *upapīṭha*. Inside the *pradakṣiṇa* is the *adhiṣṭāna*. There are three porches in the east, north and south leading into the *mukhamaṇṭapa*. Above the *adhiṣṭāna*, there is a low *vēdi* with openings on the east, south and north. The *vēdi* is decorated with four bands containing a row of elephants, eight petalled lotuses in compartments, a row of fine figure sculptures and four petalled lotuses respectively.

The Walls

In the south wall above the *adhiṣṭāna* there is a broad band decorated with *makara-mukha*, creeper, Gaṇapati seated with two elephants etc. The wall above the band is decorated with pilasters, recess with three miniature *vimānas*, projections with pilasters and *śālās* etc.

In the north wall the band at the base contains four elephants, *makaras*, two elephants, *makaras*, Bhairava between two elephants, Gaṇapati seated between two elephants, etc. The wall above the band is similar in decoration to the south wall.

Garbhagṛha

The south wall has a band at the base decorated with *makara-mukhas*, creepers, elephants, etc The wall above the band is decorated with projection with pilasters with *śālās* above the two central pilasters, recesses with miniature *vimānas* and wide projection with three miniature shrines in a vertical row (pl. VII-1). The base of the lowest shrine contains on the east and west a miniature *vimāna*, a pillar, a miniature shrine and a pillar. The lowest of the three shrines in the vertical row consists of double pillars on each side with a square projection on each containing a small niche. These pillars support a projecting *kapōta* in three sections with a row of lotus buds hanging on the underside. The second and third shrines are similar though smaller.

The west or back wall is similar to the south wall in decoration. The base of these three shrines has on each side two pillars and two miniature *vimānas* on pilasters. The front side contains in a row a pillar, a miniature shrine on a pilaster, nandi, a miniature shrine on a pilaster and a pillar. Above is a miniature shrine on a pilaster and a pillar. Above the miniature shrine is a projecting band with pearl decoration and above it is a recess. There is another band with elephants and *makaras* from whose mouths emanates a creeper forming three arches with the figure of Surya below the central arch. There is another band above which has the figures of four lions in three compartments on the sides and two lions, swans and a woman fighting a lion in the front. There are three *Nāgara vimānas* on the architrave above the entrances of the *garbhagṛha* of the lowest shrine.

The north wall is similar to the other two walls.

On the three sides of the *mukhamaṇṭapa*, on the *vedi* there are thirty eight fine brackets (pl. VII-2) attached to short pillars supporting the heavy roof above.

Vimāna

It is partly fallen and only four *talas* are visible. Each *tala* contains the distended series of *kūṭa, pañjara, kūṭa, pañjara, śālā, pañjara, kūṭa, pañjara* and *kūṭa*. There is a *śukhanāsa* projecting from the base of the *vimāna* and covering the *antarāḷa* below. Its sides are decorated with the series *kūṭa, pañjara, kuṭa, pañjara* and *śālā* in two *talas*.

Interior

All pillars in the *mukhamaṇṭapa* except the four in the centre have finely carved bands in the centre and a rectangular block at the base and top. There is a roll and leaf capital above.

On the *vēdi* on the edges there are seven minor shrines, one to the left of the *antarāḷa* containing the figure of Gaṇapati, another in the north-west corner of the *vēdi* housing the image of Durgā, the third in the north east corner containing the figure of Gaṇapati and the fourth, situated to the left of the entrance containing an icon of Bhairava. The other three are in corresponding positions on the southern half of the *vēdi.*

The central pillars are beautifully carved with fine mythological sculptures.

The *antarāḷa* entrance contains a pilaster and a jamb on either side and contains fine sculptures. The portion above the jambs contains fret work frames with circles containing the figures of dancers and musicians. The verticals and cross beam of the *dvāra* are decorated with diamond cutting and the lintel has the figure of Gajalakṣmī. The architrave contains the figure of Naṭarāja in the centre and Gaṇapati and Dēvī at the extremes. In between are four dancing deities on each side.

Garbhagṛha

The jambs on either side of the entrance of the *garbhagṛha* are in four sections and contain a vertical row of musicians and dancers, vertical row of lions with an elephant at the base and a vertical with creeper design. The lintel is carved into a miniature shrine. The architrave above contains five miniature *vimānas.* The central band of the *vēdi* above the *adhiṣṭāna* is decorated with dance figures in fine poses. In the centre of the *garbhagṛha* there is a *vēdi* with a huge linga.

The Vīrabhadra Temple, Lēpākshi (*Vijayanagara*)

The village of Lēpākshi is situated in the Hindupūr taluk of the Anantapūr district in Āndhra Pradēsh. This temple is a fine specimen of the Vijayanagara style of art and architecture.

This temple is situated on a hillock and the hillock is known as the Kūrmaśaila. Local tradition ascribes the construction of the temple to Virūpanna, a Vijayanagara official, residing at Penugoṇḍa. The local people say that Virupanna built seven *prākāras,* one inside the other, before the temple. Four of them can still be seen. The hillock is reached by a short flight of steps.

This temple (pl. VIII-1) has two enclosures, one inside the other. The outer wall is built of large blocks of stone and plain. There are four entrances in the four cardinal directions. The main entrance is in the north and it is surmounted by a *gōpura.* The outer enclosure contains many structures.

Beyond the northern entrance in the outer wall and slightly to the right is the main entrance to the inner compound. This entrance is also surmounted by a *gōpura,* with many sculptures and a number of *kuḍus* and *śālas* and *kuṁbhapañjaras.* Opposite the entrance there are *balipīṭha* and *dhvajastaṁbha.*

In the inner compound there is a long narrow *maṇṭapa* in the angle formed by the northern and eastern walls. In the south eastern angle there is a hall with a

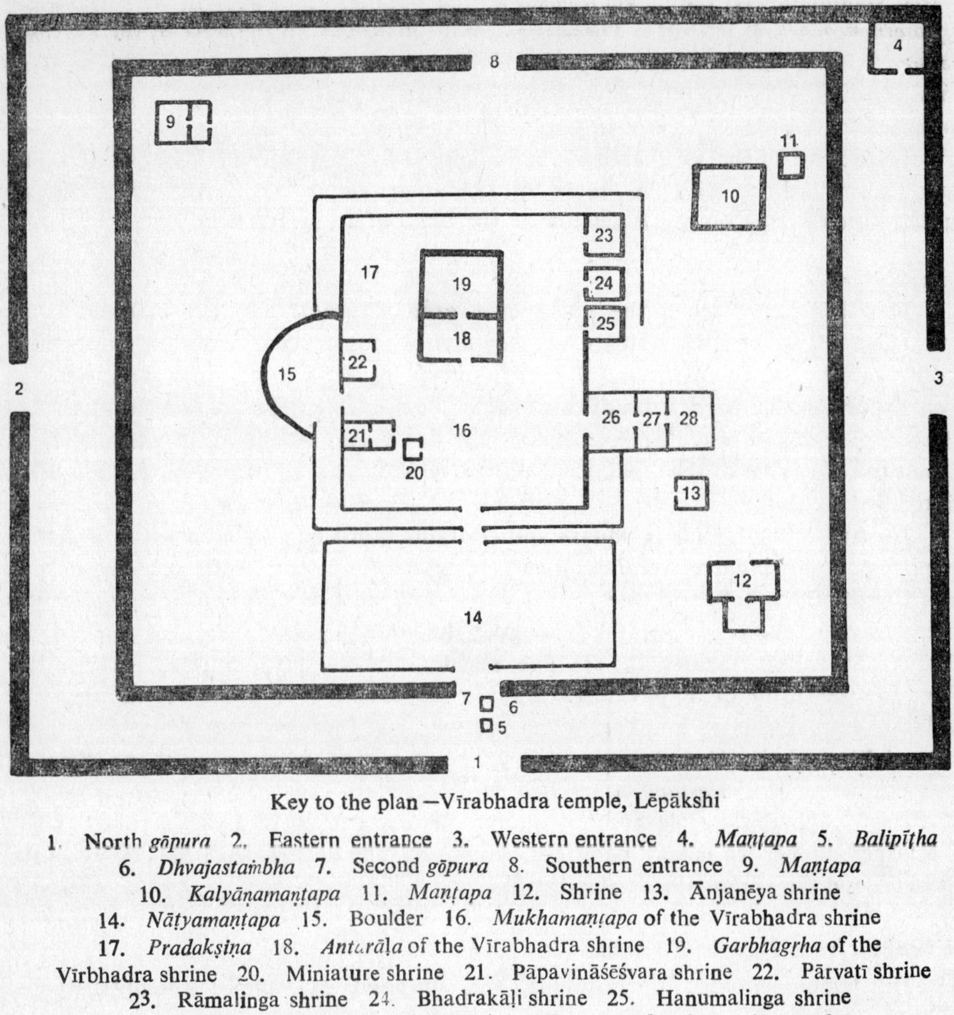

Key to the plan —Vīrabhadra temple, Lēpākshi

1. North *gōpura* 2. Eastern entrance 3. Western entrance 4. *Maṇṭapa* 5. *Balipīṭha* 6. *Dhvajastaṁbha* 7. Second *gōpura* 8. Southern entrance 9. *Maṇṭapa* 10. *Kalyāṇamaṇṭapa* 11. *Maṇṭapa* 12. Shrine 13. Āñjanēya shrine 14. *Nāṭyamaṇṭapa* 15. Boulder 16. *Mukhamaṇṭapa* of the Vīrabhadra shrine 17. *Pradakṣiṇa* 18. *Antarāḷa* of the Vīrabhadra shrine 19. *Garbhagṛha* of the Vīrbhadra shrine 20. Miniature shrine 21. Pāpavināśēśvara shrine 22. Pārvatī shrine 23. Rāmalinga shrine 24. Bhadrakāḷi shrine 25. Hanumalinga shrine 26. *Mukhamaṇṭapa* of the Viṣṇu shrine 27. *Antarāḷa* of the Viṣṇu shrine 28. *Garbhagṛha* of the Viṣṇu shrine

pillared verandah. At the angle formed by the southern and western walls there is a *kalyanamaṇṭapa* (pl. VIII-2). There is a small *maṇṭapa* to the west of the *kalyana-maṇṭapa* with a *vimāna* above it. In the north eastern corner, there is a small *maṇṭapa* with pillars. In continuation of it there is another pillared *maṇṭapa* with sculptures (pl. IX-1).

To the east of the Vīrabhadra temple there is a big boulder. To its western end there is a small shrine with the figure of Gaṇapati and at the eastern end there is a big sculpture of linga on a *vēdi* resting on the hood of a huge serpent.

Main Shrine

This shrine consists on the axis *garbhagṛha, antarāḷa,* a square *maṇṭapa* and a rectangular *nāṭyamaṇṭapa.* This *nāṭyamaṇṭapa* is constructed before the northern entrance to the inner enclosure. There is a square hall to its south and there are seven shrines on the three sides of this hall. The *nāṭyamaṇṭapa* contains a number of pillars of various types. Each of the pillars has a capital ending in *padmaboḍigai.* The entire lower side of the ceiling of this *maṇṭapa* and the beams supporting it are painted.

The hall of the temple is square and contains on its edges pillars with interesting sculptures. It has pillared verandahs on the four sides. The walls on either side of the entrance of the hall and also on the east and west contain bas-relief sculptures representing the story of Siruttoṇḍanāyanār and others. On the three sides of this hall there are seven shrines i.e. (1) The shrine of Gaṇapati, situated between two pillars, (2) the shrine of Pāpavināśēśvara, (3) the shrine of Pārvatī, (4) the shrine of Vīrabhadra consisting of an entrance, a narrow ante-chamber and the cellar, (5) the shrine of Bhadrakāḷī, (6) a shrine with a linga on a *vēdī* inside and (7) the shrine of Viṣṇu consisting of a *maṇṭapa*, ante-chamber and cellar.

The Vīrabhadra temple contains numerous sculptures of great interest. There are a large number of mural paintings decorating the underside of the ceiling of the *maṇṭapas* and the verandahs of this temple.

Śrī Venkaṭēśvara Temple, Tirumala

This temple, situated on Tirumala hill, is a good example of a temple situated inside two *prākāras.*

There is only one entrance in each *prākāra* on the east and *gōpuras* have been constructed over each of them. The space enclosed between each set of *prākāras* is called a *pradakṣiṇa* or circumambulatory passage, the outer one known as the *Saṁpangipradakṣiṇa*, the inner one named *Vimāna-pradakṣiṇa* and the innermost named *Mukkōtipradakṣiṇa*, which is closed for most part of the year.

The first *gōpura* is known as *paḍikāvali-gōpuram.* On the inner side of the first *prākāra* wall is a small *maṇṭapa* with two wings, one on each side and a pathway in the centre. Of these two *maṇṭapas*, the one in the north contains metallic statues of the famous Vijayanagara emperor, Kṛṣṇarāya and his two queens (pl. IX-2). The other contains three statues, one of metal and two of stone, also of Vijayanagara rulers. The metal statue is the statue of king Venkaṭapatirāya and the other two are of Acyutarāya and his queen, Varadāji Aṁma (pl. X-1).

To the south of the Kṛṣṇarāya *maṇṭapa* is the *Ranga-maṇṭapa*, with a small

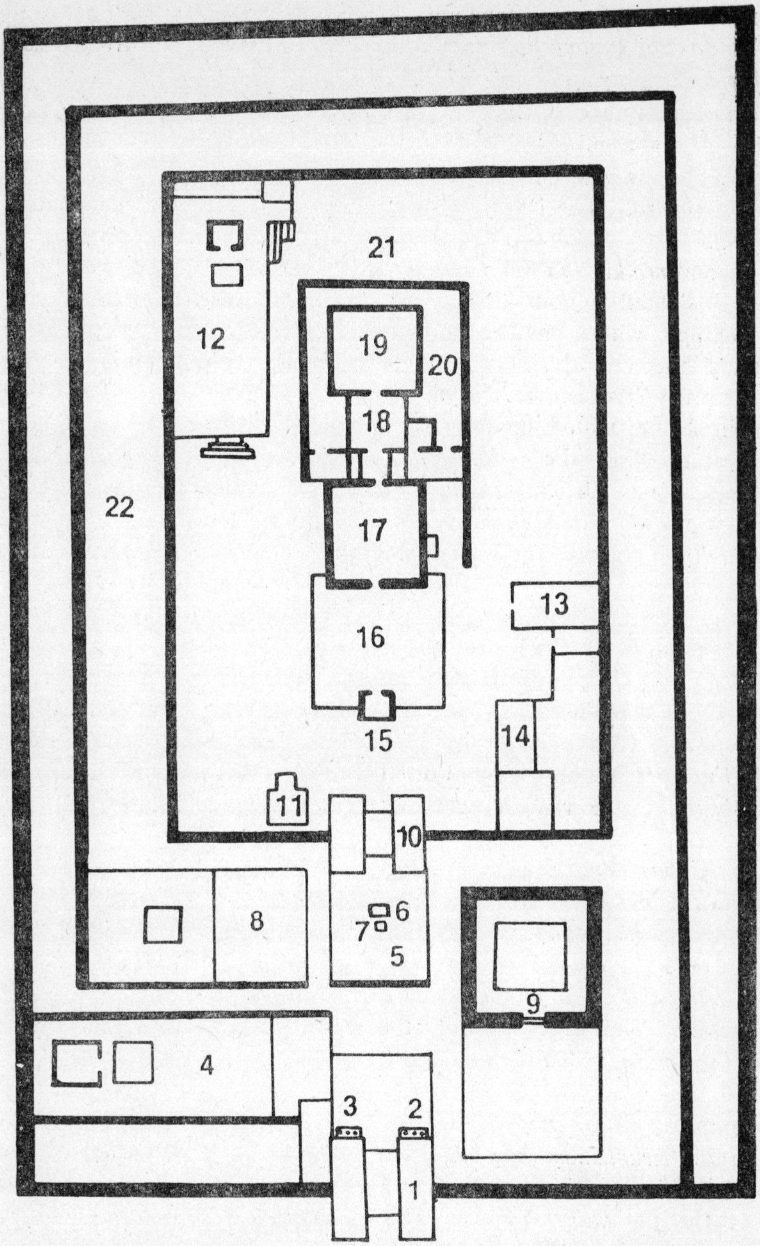

Key to the Plan—Śrī Venkaṭēśvara temple, Tirumala

1. Padikāvali *gōpura* 2. Kṛṣṇarāya and his queens 3. Venkaṭapatirāya Acyutarāya and his queen 4. Ranga-*maṇṭapa* 5. *Maṇṭapa* 6. *Dhvajastambha* 7. *Balipīṭha* 8. *Unjal-maṇṭapa* 9. *Aina*-Mahal 10. Inner *gōpura* 11. Varadarāja shrine 12. *Kalyāṇamaṇṭapa* 13. Rāmānuja shrine 14. Narasiṁha shrine 15. Garuda shrine 16. *Ttrumāmaṇi maṇṭapa* 17. *Snapana-maṇṭapa* 18. *Antarāḷa* 19. *Garbhagṛha* 20. *Mukkōṭi-pradakṣiṇa* 21. *Vimāna-pradakṣiṇa* 22. *Saṁpangi-pradakṣiṇa*

shrine. Next to the *Ranga-maṇṭapa* and extend up to the east wall of the inner *prākāra* is another spacious *maṇṭapa*, named the *Unjal maṇṭapa*, constructed by Sāḷuva Narasiṁha for celebrating the *Annā-ūnjal-tiruṇāḷ*, instituted by him in the year 1473 A.D. In the northern part of the courtyard is another structure now known as the Aina-Mahal, with a shrine behind it.

There is a narrow *maṇṭapa* in the western part of the courtyard touching the second or inner *gōpura*. The *Dhvajastaṁbha* and *Balipīṭha* are placed in the centre of this *maṇṭapa*.

In the second *pradakṣiṇa* immediately to the left of the *gōpura* entrance there is a small shrine dedicated to god Varadarāja. In the southern part of the courtyard is the *Kalyāṇamaṇṭapa*, with a pavilion and a small shrine. In the north-eastern corner of the courtyard there is the shrine of Narasiṁha. Next to it is the shrine of Śrī Rāmānuja, the great Śrīvaiṣṇava Ācārya.

The main shrine, which contains the image of Śrī Venkaṭēśvara, is a complex structure. It starts with the *garbhagṛha* at the western end and ends with the *Tirumāmaṇi-maṇṭapa* at the eastern end. Part of this area ending with the northern and southeru wings of the *Mukkōṭi-pradakṣiṇa* inside is enclosed by a thick stone wall. This *pradakṣiṇa* encloses the *śayana-maṇṭapa*, *antarāḷa* and *garbhagṛha*.

Vimāna

The *vimāna* (pl. X-2) which rises above the *garbhagṛha* is of the *dvitala* type and belongs to the *Vēsara Order*. Each *tala* has the series—*kūṭa, pañjara, śālā, pāñjara* and *kūṭa*. There is a plain narrow step above the two *talas* containing lions in the cardinal directions. Above it is the *gaḷa* or neck and above is a domical *śikhara* adorned with lotus design all over and on the top is the *kalaśa*. There are many Vaiṣṇava sculptures on the *vimāna* which is encased by gilded plates.

Tirumāmaṇi-maṇṭapa

This is a *maṇṭapa* open on three sides and containing sixteen stone pillars. It now serves as the *Āsthāna-maṇṭapa*. To the west of it is the front wall of the *Snapana-maṇṭapa*. There is a finely carved doorway in its centre, known as the *Bangāru-vākili*, flanked by a *dvārapālaka* on either side. The jambs of the doorway are decorated with lotus petals. The lintel contains the figure of Gajalakṣmi and the architrave above has in the centre, a *śālā* surmounted by a *siṁhalalāṭa* gable.

Snapana-maṇṭapa

Next to the *Tirumāmaṇi-maṇṭapa* is the *snapana-maṇṭapa* which contains four central pillars. Beyond this *maṇṭapa* is a narrow compartment with raised pials on each side of the pathway. Farther west is another *maṇṭapa*, now known as the *Śayana-maṇṭapa*. This must have been originally the *antarāḷa*. Next to this *Śayana-maṇṭapa* is the *garbhagṛha*, which contains the image of Śrī Venkatēśvara.

The deity holds *Śaṁkha* and *Cakra* in the two upper hands, keeps the lower right hand in *Varada* and the lower left in *kaṭyavalaṁbita*. The image is fully decorated with various ornaments and clad in fine silk cloths.

GENERAL FEATURES

Temples were built by devotees as tokens of their devotion and piety. The temple was considered as one of the *saptasantānas* and it was raised by all classes of people from Kings down to the ordinary folk. The temples were constructed for both Viṣṇu and Śiva and their attendant deities. Besides temples, devotees were interested in constructing auxiliary buildings like *garbhagṛhas, antarāḷas, vimānas, mukhamaṇṭapas,* special *maṇṭapas, śikharas, kalaśas,* pillars, *prākāras, gōpuras,* steps, choultries and *maṭhas.*

Devotees were not only interested in the construction but also in the reconstruction and renovation of temples, *maṇṭapas* and pillars and in plastering, whitewashing and gilding etc.

The temple was the recipient of various kinds of gifts like villages, lands, gardens, house-sites, tanks, coins, cash, taxes, customs duties, jewels, utensils, animals, oil-mills and requirements of worship like *cāmaras, ālavaṭṭamṣ,* umbrellas, lamps, perfumes, etc.

The temple maintained a number of servants e.g., priests, recitors of sacred texts, decorators, goldsmiths, carpenters, astrologers, lighters, supervisors, proclaimers, potters, etc., and several artistes like flutists, players on *Viṇa*, songsters, players on *mṛdanga*, pipers and drummers and dance troupes for the entertainment of the deity.

The temple had an elaborate and complicated organization. It appointed staff for the proper discharge of various functions and duties. The conduct of its work was entrusted to the *Sthānāpati* who seems to have been the general supervisor. It maintained other agents like the *Sānis*, *Mānis* and *Ayyas* and a treasury i.e., *Śrībhaṇḍāram*. The treasury received many gifts like villages, lands, taxes, cash, animals, lamp-stands etc., from devotees and arranged for the performance of a number of functions like, celebration of festivals, conduct of services and maintenance of lamps, gardens etc.

Worship in the temple was conducted on an elaborate scale starting with the waking up ceremony and ending with the midnight worship and sending the god to sleep. The worship offered in temples is of three main varieties, i.e., *rēpaṭi* or worship offered in the morning, *māpaṭi* or night worship and occasional like the *jāmu* and *ardhajāmu* worship.

One of the attractive features of the temple was the celebration of festivals on a grand scale. The festivals are classified into annual festivals relating to months, months and *tithis,* months and stars, week days, days of particular stars, *Sankrāntis,* special annual festivals, instituted festivals and general festivals.

2

CONSTRUCTION AND CONSECRATION OF TEMPLES

The construction of temples and auxiliary structures and installation of deities was considered an act of great religious merit. The temple was conceived as the manifestation of the Supreme and its construction was, therefore, the best way of worshipping Him. The building of a temple, which is one of the *Saptasantānas*, was expected to confer on the builder several benefits like longevity, health, wealth and prosperity in this world, besides religious merit in the other world. It is for these reasons that many people, from the princes down to the ordinary citizens, vied with one another in building temples.

1. *Purpose of Temple Building*

a. *Expression of Gratitude*

One reason that impelled people to construct temples was the desire to express gratitude to the Almighty for glorious achievements of theirs like conquests. The famous Kākatīya king, Rudradēva (1158-1169), who conquered numerous rival chieftains, annexed their territories and extended his dominions up to the Mālyavanta hill in the north, Kalyāṇi in the west, Śrīśailam in the south and the sea in the east, built a beautiful triple shrine at Hanumakoṇḍa for gods Sūrya, Rudra and Vāsudēva as a token of his gratitude for the conferment of these victories.[1]

b. *Merit of the Dead*

Temples were raised in the name of dead persons and for their religious merit. In Ś. 1172, the Kōṭa queen, Gaṇapāmbā, constructed a temple for god Bētēśvara in the name of her father.[2] Paṇḍāmbikā, the wife of the Koṇḍapaḍamaṭi king, Manmapōta constructed a temple in Ś. 1188, for god Pōtīśvara in her husband's name and another temple for god Paṇḍīśvara,[3] in her own name at Tāḍikoṇḍa. In Ś. 1198,

1. *K.S.* App. Ins, 18 Pālaṁpēṭ.
2. *E.I.* III, Pp, 94-103. Yenamadala.
3. *S.I.I.* X. 408, Tāḍikoṇḍa.

Kuppāṁbikā of the Gōna family built a temple at Būdalūru and installed a linga in it in the name of her dead husband, Malyāla Guṇḍaya, a famous general.[4] The Cōḷa king, Parāntaka, raised a shrine at Toṇḍamānnāḍ, near Kāḷahasti over the corporeal remains of his father, Āditya, for the latter's religious merit.[5] Rēcerla Nāmireḍḍi, a Kākatīya subordinate, raised temples dedicated to gods Kāmēśvara and Kācēśvara and named them after his father and mother.[6] The well known Bētēśvara temple at Pillalamaṟṟi was raised by Erakasāni for the merit of her husband Bēti Reḍḍi.[7] King Rājarāja built in the village of Kaldiṇḍi, two Śiva temples in memory of two Cōḷa generals, who fought and died in the battle with Karṇāṭa forces and named them as Rājarājeśvaram and Uttamasōḍagam.[8] *Mahāmaṇḍalēśvara* Satyāśraya constructed a temple at Eḍeyamaṭha and consecrated therein god Bikkēśvara named after his father, Bikkarasa.[9] In Ś. 1137, *mahāpradhāni sarvādhikāri Sarvadhara* Yiṇḍapa nāyaka built a temple to god Anmēśvaradēva at Gōraṇṭla and named the deity after his father.[10] The Telugu Cōḍa king, Tirukaladēva Cōḍa mahārāja erected at Pabbapalli, a temple for Tirukaḷīśa-mahādēva in the name of his father.[11] Dannaya-sēnāpati's wife constructed the temple of Mallikārjuna at Kaṭṭakūra and the shrines of Annēśvara and Mallēśvara in her husband's name and her own.[12]

c. *Token of Loyalty*

There was also the practice of subordinates constructing temples in the names of their overlords as tokens of loyalty. In Ś. 1054, Paṇḍa, the general of the Velanāḍu king, Gonka, built a temple at Ikṣupalli and installed in it god Gōkēśvara in the name of his overlord.[13] A devotee named Nārabhūpāla, the subordinate of king Pinna, raised a stone shrine in the Kṣīrārāmēśvara temple and installed a linga in it in Ś. 1131 and named it after his overlord, King Allāḍa.[14] A Mādhavanāyaka constructed a temple for god Mallēśvara for the religious merit of his suzerain, *Mahāmaṇḍalēśvara* Gaṇapatidēva Mahārāja.[15] In Ś. 1153, Jāya, the general of the Kākatīya king Gaṇapati built a temple and installed in it Gaṇapēśvara named after the king at Dvīpa.[16] An individual, named Nārāyaṇa, constructed a temple in the name of his king, Cōḍi and named it as the Cōḍīśvara temple in Ś. 1153 at Divi.[17] The temple of Kēśava Perumāḷ was erected in Ś. 1371, by *Daḷavāyi* Malli nāyaniṁgāru for the merit of *Kaṭhāri Sāḷuva* Tippayadēva mahārāja.[18] In Ś. 1402 a temple was

4. *Hyd. Arch. Ser.* No. 13. No. 50.
5. 230 of 1903. Toṇḍamanāḍ.
6. *K.I.A.P.* Ins. No. 13; *Hyd. Arch. Ser.* No. 13. No. 38.
7. *Hyd. Arch. Ser.* No. 13. Part II. No. 42.
8. *E.I.* XXIX. Pp. 57-71. Kalidiṇḍi.
9. 317 of 1937-38. Eṟṟamaṭham.
10. 315 of 1937-38. Gōraṇṭla.
11. 407 of 1915. Babbēpalle.
12. *Hyd Arch. Ser.* No. 19. Km. 4. Kaṭṭakūru.
13. *S.I.I.* VI. 23. Nidubrōlu.
14. *Ibid*, V. 135. Pālakol.
15. *N.D.I.* III. Ongōle 88. Nāguluppalapāḍu.
16. *E.I.* III. Pp, 82-93. Gaṇapavaram.
17. *Ibid.*, III. Pp. 82-93. Gaṇapavaram.
18. 771 of 1922. Daggupāḍu.

constructed for god Rāma by Saṭhakōpadāsar Narasiṁharāya Mudaliār for the merit of King Sāḷuvaya Narasiṁha.[19] Lakṣmīkāntarasu, a servant of Śrī Kṛṣṇarāya, raised a temple for god Prasannakēśava perumāḷ at Koṁmūru, for the merit of the king.[20] In the reign of the Kākatīya king, Gaṇapatidēva, the seṭṭis of the place constructed temples for gods Harēśvara, Sakalēśvara and Gaṇapēśvara in honour of the king at Nagunūr.[21]

d. *Merit of Parents and Gurus*

Temples were constructed by persons for the merit of parents and religious preceptors etc. In Ś. 1059, a Reḍḍi of the Koṇḍapaḍamaṭi country built the temple of Sōmēśvara at Goniyapūṇḍi for the merit of his parents.[22] A person named Mendana constructed a temple for god Sōmeśvara at Lingaṁpāḍu in Ś. 1094 for the merit of his parents.[23] The Paricchēdi king, Bhīmarāju, built a temple and installed in it god Gōpāla in Ś. 1157 for the merit of his parents at Pottūru.[24] Prōla Reḍḍi, who is styled as the ruler of Vērūru, constructed the temple of Bhīmēśvara at Pālaḍuvu in the *Koṇḍapaḍumara* in Ś. 1090, for the merit of his parents.[25] In Ś. 1139, Siddhapa nāyaka raised a temple for god Mallikārjunadēva at Boṁmini in the Śrī *Pāki-nāḍu* for the same purpose.[26] In Ś. 1190, a devotee named Dēvakīputradāsu, constructed a temple for god Cenna Gōpīnātha with his two consorts in the middle of the village of Būrugugaḍḍa in the name of his mother.[27] Sāḷuva Saṁburāyadēva mahārājulu built a temple for god Āndhradēvara at Kūchapūḍi in Ś. 1348, for the religious merit of his father, *Rāyavibhāḷadēva mahārāja*.[28] Bhāva Śiripuram Yatni Manirāju constructed a temple for god Sōmēśvara in Ś. 1534, for the religious merit of his *guru*, Śrī Parvatārādhya, and his parents and forefathers.[29] In Ś. 1689, a temple was erected and the image of goddess Pārvatī was installed in the Mallēśvara temple in the village of Koṇḍapāṭūru by Pāparāja and Mallēśvara for the merit of their ancestors.[30]

e. *Merit of Gōtras*

Some people constructed temples for the religious merit of their *gōtras*. Some Reḍḍis built a temple for god Gōpīnātha in Ś. 1466, for the religious merit of the Śiriyāla *gōtra* to which they belonged.[31]

19. *T.T.D.I.* III. 73; 74 Tirupati.
20. 824 of 1922. Koṁmūru.
21. *Tel. Ins.* I. M. 18. Nāgunūr.
22. *S.I.I.* X. 193 Kāvūru.
23. 286 of 1932-33. Lingaṁguṇṭa.
24. *S.I.I.* X. 282. Pottūru.
25. 325 of 1932-33. Pālaḍugu.
26. *N.D.I.* III. Rapur 36. Koṁpāḍu.
27. *Hyd. Arch. Ser.* No. 13. No. 18. Būrugugaḍḍa.
28. *N.D.I.* III. Podili 26. Kūchapūḍi.
29. *N.D.I.* I. Darsi. 34. Kaṁbhampāḍu.
30. 760 of 1922. Koṇḍapāṭūru.
31. 340 of 1932-33. Toṇḍapi.

f. *One's own Merit*

Individuals built temples in their own name, and for their own merit. In Ś. 1125, Cauṇḍa of the Malyāla family constructed a temple for god Śiva as Cauṇḍēśvara after his name at Koṇḍaparti.[32] Kavalāyi, the wife of *Gaṇḍapeṇḍāra* Ganga sēnāpati of the Kāyasthā family, founded the shrine of Kamalēśvara after her own name in Ś. 1176. In the same year Hacalāṁba, the daughter of king, Allugi, the lord of the town of Moraṭa, founded the shrine of Hacalēśvara after her own name and the Pallava king, Khaṇḍerāya, constructed the shrine and named it as Pallavēśvara[33] at Puṣpagiri and the name *trikūṭa* was given to the group. In Ś. 1183, the famous religious teacher, Viśvēśvara Śivācārya, constituted villages named Mandaram and Velagapūḍi gifted by the Kākatīya king, Gaṇapatidēva and his daughter, Rudrāṁbā respectively, into a new village and constructed a temple for god Viśvēśvara and named it after himself.[34] *Mahāmaṇḍalēśvara* Rājādityarasa erected a temple for Rājādityēś-vara in his own name at Lēṁbalavāḍa during the 8th year of the reign of the later Cāḷukyan king, Tribhuvanamalla.[35] The famous temple at Pālaṁpēṭ was built in Ś. 1135, by Rēcerla Rudra for god Rudrēśvara named after himself.[36] The Eastern Cāḷukyan king, Cāḷukya Bhīma II, built two temples for Bhīmēśvara named after himself, at Drākshārāma and at Cāḷukya-Bhīmavaram.[37] Another Vēngī Cāḷukyan king, Vijayāditya II, built 108 Śiva temples and named them Narēndrēśvara after himself.[38]

2. *Varieties of Temples Built*

Temples constrncted by devotees were of various types and dedicated to the deities of their choice. Some were for Śiva, others for Viṣṇu, some others for Dēvī and still others for the attendant deities.

a. *Temples of Śiva*

Śiva is one of the most popular deities of the Hindu pantheon and evoked the devotion of a large number of people. We find numerous temples dedicated to this god all over the country. Inscriptions which mention the construction of these temples are found in all the three well known parts of Āndhradēśa, viz., the Coastal area, Telangāna and Rāyalasīma and range in dates from the 9th to 19th centuries. People of all classes and sections of society constructed temples for Śiva. In Ś. 1084, the Kākatīya king, Rudra, constructed a temple for gods Rudrēśvara,[39] Vāsudēvēśvara and Sūryēśvara at Hanumakoṇḍa. A minister named Gangādhara, built a temple for god Śiva at Deṁdōḍu.[40] In Ś. 1101, king Tribhuvana Mallidēva Cōḷa and his queen, Lakumādēvī, constructed five temples for god Mallikārjunadēva, Lakṣmaṇēśvaradēva,

32. *Hyd. Arch. Ser.* No. 13. No. 3; Tel. Ins. I. 8. Koṇḍiparti.
33. 304 of 1905. Puṣpagiri.
34. *S.I.I.* X. 395 Mālkāpuram.
35. 159 of 1946-47. Lēmulavāḍa.
36. *Hyd. Arch. Ser.* No. 13. No. 3. I.A. 21. p. 257.
37. Rama Rao, M. *The Eastern Cālukyan Temples*, p. 11.
38. *Hyd. Arch. Ser.* No. 3.
39. *Ibid.*, No. 15. No. 3. I.A. 21. p. 257.
40. *Hyd. Arch. Ser.* No, 13. No. 56. Karīmnagar,

Irungōlēśvaradēva, Mahādēvēśvaradēva and Sūryadēva, at Malyanūr in the *Sire-nāḍu.*[41] The Koṇḍapadamaṭi king, Manma Pōta, erected a temple for god Kāmēśvara at Tāḍikoṇḍa.[42] During the reign of the Eastern Cāḷukyan king, Aṁma II, a temple was constructed for Umāmahēśvara of Vijayavāṭi.[43] *Mahāmaṇḍalēśvara* Paramēśvara Abhidēva Malidēva mahārāja, a Telugu Cōḍa king, built a temple for god Mallikārjuna in Viddarakaṇṭarapuram.[44] The famous Eastern Gāṅga king, Dānārṇava erected in his capital city, a lofty temple for god, Īśa, in the Linga form which he had named Madhukēśa, because it was produced from a *Madhuka* tree.[45] Queen Gaḍiyamadēvī, the wife of the Kōṭa king, Buddharāja, constructed a temple for god Śiva at Nādeṇḍla, in Ś. 1061.[46] Yaṁmarāja *alias* Śrīman *Mahāmaṇḍalēśvara* Nandivarma mahārāja, built two temples for gods Dorēśvara and Irugēśvara at Padaṭūru.[47] A temple for god Śiva was erected at Māvundala by Mandala nāyaka, a subordinate of the Koṇḍapaḍamaṭi king, Maṇḍa Bhūpati.[48] A subordinate of the Velnāḍu king, Rājēndra Cōḷa, constructed a temple for god Vīrēśvara at Guḍimeṭla.[49] *Mahāpraḍhāni Daṇḍanāyaka* Kāmana Perggaḍa, who was a subordinate of Śrī Vatsarāja, constructed a temple for god Iṣṭakāmēśvara, in Ś. 1051.[50] Malyāla Cauṇḍasēnāni, a minister of Kākatīya Rudradēva constructed a temple for god Śiva at Kaṭukuru. He was the grandson of Dannasēnāpati.[51] In Ś. 1175, Iṁmaḍi Viśvanātha *daṇḍanāyaka* constructed temples for gods Bollēśvara, Mallēśvara and Gaṇapēśvara at Jalālpuram.[52] The Viriyāla chief named Malla, built a temple for god Śiva under the name of Mallēśvara at Guṁḍur.[53] In Ś. 1167, Malyāla Guṇḍadaṇḍādhīśa erected a temple for god Nāgēśvara in Vardhamānapura.[54] In Ś. 1091, a temple was constructed for god Nāgēśvaradēva at Madhuvadi by Nāmana, who was the *tantrapāla* of the later Cāḷukyan king, Jagadēkamalla.[55] Mallayasāhaṇi, the *Paṭṭasāhaṇādhipati* of the Yādava king, Singanadēva, constructed a temple for god Jasamēśvaradēva in the capital city of Vellanūru.[56] In Ś. 1670, the members of the Kauta family built a temple for god Oṁkāra Sadāśiva in the village of Kautavari-Agrahārām.[57] Muṁmaḍi Cikkarāya of the Suguṭūru family erected a temple for god Śiva under the name of Candraśēkharasvāmi in Ś. 1722 at Punganūr.[58] A Kallappa Reḍḍi erected a temple

41. *S.I.I.* X. 273. Malayanūr.
42. *Ibid.*, X. 408. Tāḍikoṇḍa.
43. *E.I.* XXIII pp. 161-170. C.P. Tāḍikoṇḍa.
44. *N.D.I.* I. Darsi. 63. Sōmavarapāḍu.
45. *I.A.* XVIII. P. 171. Vizayanagaram.
46. *S.I.I.* IV. 627. Nādiṇḍla.
47. *N.D.I.* III. Udayagiri. 6. Jaḍadēvi.
48. 305 of 1932-33. Mādala.
49. *S.I.I.* X. 542. Gudimeṭia.
50. 21 of App. E. of 1941-42. Amarāvati.
51. *Hyd. Arch. Ser* 19. km. 4. Kaṭukūru.
52. *Tel. Ins.* II. K.I. 7 Jalālpuram.
53. *Hyd. Arch. Ser.* No. 13. No. 24. Gūḍūr.
54. *Tel. Ins.* II. I'I. 6 Vaḍḍamānu.
55. *S.I.I.* X. 230. Madhūḍi.
56. 18 of 1953-54. Mēḍikurti.
57. 286 of 1924. Kautāvāri Agrahāram.
58. C.P, 6 of 1932-33. Punganūr,

for god Nallikadēva at Ūṭukūru, in the *Singattai-nāḍu.*[59] A temple was constructed in Ś. 1660, for god Mātangidēva at Mungamūru by Kēśimareḍḍi Lingā Reḍḍi.[60] Dēmiseṭṭi and Vaidiseṭṭi of the town of Kīrtinārāyaṇapuram and Tuṁbuḷa, built the shrine of Śakalēśvara in Ś. 1150.[61] Malliseṭṭi constructed a temple for god Mallēśvara in Ś. 1678 at Guṇḍlapalle.[62] An individual, named Nāgarāja, erected a temple for god Sāgarēśvara in Ś. 1445 at Mādala.[63] In Ś. 1691, a temple was erected for god Mukṭīśvara by an individual at Mōkṣaguṇḍam.[64] A temple of Śiva, under the name of Sāṁbaśiva, was raised by Karaṇam Rāju Bhaṭu Rāmarāja, a resident of the Bhaṭlapalle-agrahāra.[65] In Ś. 1078, a temple was built for god Mahādēva of Peravali by a woman and her son.[66] A temple was constructed for god Jalapēśa by a Maindaraṁma at Pondugala.[67] In Ś. 1562, Rāvūri Tiṁmappa of the *Viśvakarmakula*, erected the shrine of Nīlakaṇṭhēśvara at Morijaṁpāḍu.[68] Sōmaśivācārya of the Gōḷagi School built the stone temple for god Nāgēśvara of Kaḍalupuri and installed several Nāgakumāras at the place where Janamējaya performed the *Sarpayāga.*[69] In S. 1435, Mahēśvarācārya *alias* Mahēśvarāyati, constructed the temple of Uttarēśvara at Peddakodamguṇḍla.[70] A temple was erected for god Śiva by Mallareḍḍi, a follower of Jainism at Bekkallu.[71] In S. 1358, the son of a servant of the temple of god Mallīśvaradēva of Bezavāḍa, raised a temple for god Pāpavināśana on the bank of the Kṛṣṇa.[72] A Setti, named Gomnaseṭṭi constructed a temple for god Viśvēśvara at Nādiṇḍla in Ś. 1046.[73]

b. *Śaiva-parivāradēvatas*

Separate shrines were constructed for subsidiary deities of the Śaiva pantheon like Gaṇapati, Kumāra and others. An individual constructed a temple for god Gaṇēśvara at Pulipāḍu in Ś. 1160. Another temple was also constructed for god Kuppavināyaka.[74] Śrīgiribhaktuṇḍu erected a temple for god Vighnēśvara to the south of the temple of Mallēśvara of Bezavāḍa in Ś. 1381.[75] A temple for god Kanakagaṇapati was built at Vijayanagaram in Ś. 1440 by *mahāmanḍalēśvara* Singayadēva *mahārāja.*[76] A temple was constructed for god Vināyaka at Morijaṁpāḍu in Ś. 1562, to the east of the Nīlakaṇṭhēśvara shrine by Rāvūri Tiṁmappa of the

59. *N.D.I.* III. Rāpūr. 66. Ūṭukūru.
60. *Ibid.*, II. Kāvali. 44. Munganūru.
61. *K.I.A.P.* Mn. 63. Vardhamānapuram.
62. 276 of 1932-33. Guṇḍlapalle.
63. 289 of 1932-33. Mādala.
64. 256 of 1949-50. Mōkṣaguṇḍam.
65. *N.D.I.* I. Darsi. 5. Bhaṭlapalle.
66. *S.I.I.* X. 138. Peravali.
67. 35 of 1929-30. Pondugala.
68. 92 of 1929-30. Morijaṁpāḍu.
69. *S.I.I.* VI. 81. Pedakaḷḷēpalle.
70. 143 of 1913. Peddakodamaguṇḍla.
71, *Tel. Ins.* II. M. 3. Bekkallu.
72. *S.I.I.* VI. 635. Koṇḍavīḍu.
73. *Ibid.*, X. 82. Nādiṇḍla.
74. *S.I.I.* X. 289. Bējātapuram.
75. *S.I.I.* IV. 776. Bezavāḍa.
76. *Ibid.*, IV. 789. Bezavāḍa.

Viśvakarmakula and the Kāśyapa *gōtra.*[77] Another temple for the same god was constructed at Nallagoṇḍa by Lingāreḍḍi.[78] Lingāreḍḍi erected at Mungamūru a temple for god Vināyaka in Ś. 1660.[79] In Ś. 1073, a minister, named Komma, built the temple of Kumārēśvara at Nārāyaṇapāḍu.[80] An individual, named Prōle nāyaka, the minister of Kōṭa Gaṇapati, constructed a temple for god Kumārasvāmin in Ś. 1160 at Pulipāḍu.[81] Kumārayācama Nāyanimgāru of the Rēcerla *gōtra* clearned the forest and lands in Yāchavaram and Bālyapalle etc., constituted them into a new village, called Subrahmaṇyam and built the temple of Subrahmaṇyēśvara in it in Ś. 1705.[82] The Eastern Cāḷukyan king, Yuddhamalla, the lord of the Salki country, constructed a temple for god Kumāra, his tutelary deity, at Bezavāḍa. God Kumāra is said to have come to Bezavāḍa from Chēbrōlu to see a *jātara* and preferred to stay here and hence this temple was built by the king.[83] Peddanārya, the son of the *tantrapāla* of king Baddega, constructed a temple for god Āditya at Lēmulavāḍa.[84] In Ś. 848, when Pallavadhīra was ruling over the *Mulki* 500, a *mahāsāmanta* raised shrines for eight *Parivāradēvatas* of the Mulkaṁṭhīśvara temple at Kamalāpuram.[85] A temple for the *Parivāradēvatas* was constructed in Ś. 1080 at Guntūr by Pāṇḍyarāja.[86] A devotee, named Annavōtu, the brother of Vēmana, constructed a temple for the *Parivāradēvatas* at Drākshārāma.[87]

c. *Temples of Viṣṇu*

Temples were constructed for Viṣṇu by individuals of different sections and castes. In Ś. 1084, Kākatīya Rudradvēa constructed a temple for god Vāsudēva at Hanumakoṇḍa.[88] The Kōṭa king, Bēta, constructed in Ś. 1173 a temple for god Kṛṣṇa at Mahiṣamardhanagari i.e., Yenamadala, while he was ruling from that place.[89] The Vijayanagara king, Acyutarāya, built a temple for god Acyuta-perumāḷ in Tirupati in Ś. 1460.[90] In S. 1108, a temple was constructed was for god Kuntīmādhava of Śrīpiṭhāpura by Jāyāṁbā, the wife of the Velanāḍu Chief, Manma Gonka, and the mother of Kulōttunga Pṛthvīśvara.[91] In the 33rd year of the reign of the Cāḷukya-Cōḷa king Kulōttunga, Pallavarāja, a subordinate of the king, erected a stone temple for god Viṣṇu at Alaveli.[92] *Mahāmaṇḍalēśvara* Singayyadēva constructed a temple for god Viṣṇu of Guṇḍlamaḍugu in Ś. 1440.[93] Nārāyaṇamantri of the Gautama *gōtra*

77. 92 of 1929-30. Morijaṁpāḍu.
78. *N.D.I.* III. Udayagiri. 11. Nallaguṇḍla.
79. *Ibid.*, II. Kāvali. 44. Munganūru.
80. 314 of 1932-33. Narampāḍu.
81. *S.I.I.* X. 289. Bejāṭapuram.
82. C.P. 2 of 1930-31. Nellore.
83. *E.I.* XV. Pp. 150-159. Bezavāḍa.
84. *K.I.A.P.* Km. 8. Lēmulavāḍa.
85. 235 of 1937-38 Kamalāpuram.
86. *S.I.I.* X. 144. Guntūr.
87. *Ibid.*, IV. 1380. Drākshārāma.
88. *Hyd. Arch. Ser.* No. 13 No. 3. Hanumakoṇḍa.
89. 142 of 1913. Yenamadala.
90. *T.T.D.I.* IV. 123. Tirupati.
91. *E. I.* IV. P. 32. Piṭhāpuram.
92. *Ibid.*, XXII. Pp. 138-145.
93. *S.I.I.* IV. 789. Vijayawāḍa.

constructed a temple for god Nārāyaṇēśa at Telikicheṛuvu in Ś. 1152.[94] Another minister, Dēvaya, erected a temple for god Lakṣmīnārāyaṇa in Ś. 1188 at Tāḷḷapalli.[95] A temple was constructed for god Rāghava at Achalapuri by a minister, named Gōpa, in Ś. 1439.[96] In Ś. 1810, a Venkaṭamantri consecrated the temple of Sītārāmadēva at Yanamadala.[97] A Viṣṇu temple was constructed by Gangādhara, the minister of the Kākatīya king, Rudradēva at Hanumakoṇḍa.[98] In Ś. 1648, a temple was built for god Paṭṭābhirāmasvāmi by Narasiṁhayya of Kundurpi, under the orders of Venkaṭapati nāyaka.[99] Tīrthapādadāsa, who was honoured by king Ananga Bhīma, built the temple of Kūrmanātha at Śrīkūrmam in Ś. 1205.[100] The temple of god Rājanārāyaṇa at Cāḷukya-Bhīmavaram was constructed by Maṇḍaya, a *Vaiśya* of the *Sakaṭamantani-nāḍu.*[101] During the regime of Lakṣmīdēvī Aṁma, the daughter of Rāmakṛṣṇa Muddu-īVrappa nāyaka of Tanjore, and the wife of Kumāra Venkaṭappa nāyaka, the chief of Naragallupālayam built a temple for Paṭṭābhirāmasvāmin in the village of Naragallu.[102] Lakkaya nāyaka, the son of Mupya nāyaka, who was the chief sentry of *mahāpradhāna* Joṁmana Oḍeya, constructed the temple of Varadarājadēva at Hiriya-Velagaṭūru in the *Huli-nāḍu*, in Ś. 1327.[103] An individual, named Bali setti of Tāḷḷūru, who belonged to the Munukula *gōtra,* built a temple for god Vēṇugōpālasvāmi at Dhūlipāḷḷa in the *Bellaṁkoṇḍa-sima* in Ś. 1679, with the permission of Venkaṭanarasiṁha nāyanigaru.[104] In Ś. 1595, a temple was erected for god Madana Gōpālasvāmi in the village of Pulichinta by Gōpāla Pantulu, the son of Raghupati Pantulu, of the Kauṇḍinya *gōtra* and a follower of the Madhva school.[105] The *mahājanas* of the Rēkulagaḍḍa *agrahāra* constructed a temple for god Prasannavallabhadēva in Ś. 1234.[106] A Narasiṁharāya Mudaliyār built a temple in Tirupati in Ś. 1402, for god Raghunātha.[107] In Ś. 1540, a temple was erected for god Raghunāyaka at Lakkarājugārlapāḍu by Raghupati nāyaka, the son of Pinapōtinēḍu, of the Vipparla *gōtra* and a resident of Ōrugaṇṭipura.[108] A woman, named Kottamahālakṣmī, the daughter of Ātukūri Kiccaya, constructed a shrine at Mācavaram for Rāma, Sītā and Lakṣmaṇa.[109] In Ś. 1742, a temple was constructed for god Śrī Venkaṭēśvara at Rājahmundry by Rāja Venkaṭrāya.[110]

d. *Temples of Vaiṣṇava-Parivāradēvatas*

Temples were constructed for the *Parivāradēvatas* of the Vaiṣṇava pantheon like

94. 275 of 1930-31. Telikicherla.
95. 322 of 1930-31. Tāḷḷapalli.
96. *E.I.* VI. No. 2. Mangaḷagiri.
97. 416 of 1915. Yenamadala.
98. *Hyd Arch. Ser.* No. 19. Wg. 2 Hanumakoṇḍa.
99. 102 of 1913. Rāyadurg.
100. *S.I.I.* V. 1179. Śrīkūrmam.
101. *E.I.* VI. pp. 219-223. Cāḷukya-Bhīmavaram.
102. 163 of 1931-32. Nāragallu.
103. 227 of 1931-32. Peddavelagaṭūru.
104. 269 of 1932-33. Dhūḷipāḷḷa.
105. 321 of 1934-35. Pulichinta.
106. 51 of 1929-30. Madinapādu.
107. *T.T.D.I.* II. 73. Tirupati.
108. 284 of 1932-33. Lakkarājugārlapāḍu.
109. 56 of 1929-30. Māchavaram.

Hanumān, Garuḍa etc. A record from Pālakol, dated in Ś. 1562, mentions that a seṭṭi constructed a temple for god Hanumān at Kṣīrārāma.[111] In Ś. 1572, Āryagaṇḍa of the *Kakṣapālamaṇdala* and the Gāṇḍīva *gōtra* raised a temple for god Hanumān at Chintala.[112] A devotee, named Malli seṭṭi, the son of Mallavaram Basavanna of the Vibireseṭla *gōtra*, built a temple for god Hanumantasvāmi in Ś. 1678 near a well.[113] Another Hanumān shrine was erected by Pāppayya, the son of Nārla Gōvinda at Rāmāpuram.[114]

e. *Temples of Dēvi*

Separate shrines were constructed for female deities. In S. 1440, *mahāmaṇḍalēsvara* Singayadēva *mahārāja*, constructed a temple for the goddess Durgādēvī to the west of the Virūpakṣa temple at Vijayanagara.[115] A devotee, named Cittamantri, erected a temple for the goddess Bhadrakāḷi at Kākāṇḍi.[116] A Nārāyaṇa built a temple for the goddess Mahākāḷi at Divi in Ś. 1153.[117] A Rāmamantri raised a temple for the goddess Kāḷi on the bank of the Yōgāgni-tīrtha.[118] In Ś. 1435, a Mahēsvarācārya *alias* Mahēśvarāyati constructed a temple for goddess Kāḷika at Peddakodamguṇḍla.[119] In Ś. 1313, an individual built a temple for goddess Lakṣmīdēvī on the hill at Tangeḍa.[120] Vāsireḍḍi Pōtinēṇḍu, a feudatory of the Reḍḍis, erected a temple for goddess Lakṣmīdēvī at Piṭhāpuram in Ś. 1352.[121]

f. *Village Deities*

The construction of temples for village deities was also in vogue. In Ś. 1160, a temple for the goddess, Brōsinaṁmā, was constructed by an individual at Pulipāḍu.[122] Kākatidēva *alias* Cāmavoḍayālu erected a s one temple for goddess Mānkālaṁmā in Ś. 1328 at Donakoṇḍa.[123] In the reign of the Vijayanagara king, Kṛṣṇarāya, *mahāmaṇḍolēśvara* Singayyadēva *mahārāja* constructed a temple for the goddess, Cengālaṁma, at Changalamaṟri in Ś. 1440.[124] A temple for the goddess Mulangūraṁmā was raised by a king at Mulangūru in the *Kōṭa-bhūmi*.[125] A temple was constructed in Ś. 1509 by Tiṁmanāyaniṁgāru at Tsalivēndra for goddess Gangādēvī.[126]

110. *S.I.I.* V. 117. Rājahmundry.
111. *S.I.I.* V. 120. Pālakol.
112. 281 of 1934-35. Chintala.
113. 276 of 1932-33. Guṇḍlapalle.
114. 37 of 1929-30. Rāmāpuram.
115. *S.I.I.* IV. 789 Bezavāḍa.
116. *Ibid.*, IV. 702. Peddakākāni.
117. *E.I.* III. pp. 82-93. Gaṇapeśvaram.
118. *S.I.I.* IV. 1351. Drākshārāma.
119. 143 of 1913. Peddakodamaguṇḍla.
120. *S.I.I.* X. 565. Tangeḍa.
121. *S.I.I.* VI. 576. Piṭhāpuram.
122. *S.I.I.* X. 289. Bejāṭpuram.
123. *N.D.I.* I. Darsi. 19. Donakoṇḍa.
124. *S.I.I.* IV. 789. Drākshārāma.
125. 259 of 1932-33. Amīnābād.
126. *N.D.I.* I. Darsi 73. Tsalivēndra.

g. *Shrines for Devotees*

Several devotees of Viṣṇu flourished in the early centuries of the Christian era and sang the praises of the god. It was the practice in Vaiṣṇava temples to set up images of these saints known as the Āḷvars and worship them. Besides these Āḷvars, images of the famous Vaiṣṇava religious teacher, Śrī Rāmānuja, were also set up in separate shrines and worshipped The images of the Āḷvars are found at Mangāpuram, the Gōvindarāja and Raghunātha shrines at Tirupati, Tirumala and Śrīkūrmam. In Ś. 1313, an individual constructed a temple for the Āḷvars on the Anantagiri hill at Tangeḍa.[127] The famous religious teacher, Kandāḍai Rāmanujayyangār, built a shrine for Kulaśēkharāḷvār in Ś. 1390.[128] A record from Tangeḍa mentions that a Dēvulenka installed the images of the 12 Āḷvārs in the temple of Vēnugōpalasvāmi at Tangeḍa.[129] Another, from Kāmēpalle, mentions the installation of the Āḷvārs in the temple of Vēṇugōpālasvāmi on the Kaḷyāṇagiri hill to the west of the village of Kāmēpalle by Rājaśēkharuni Śankarayya and his wife, Laccaṁmā.[130] In Ś. 1724, a Calamanna built a temple to Śrī Bhāṣyakāra or Rāmānuja.[131] A beautiful shrine for Naṁmāḷvār was constructed in Ś. 1472 by Āravīḍu Koṇḍarāja at Tirupati.[132]

3. *Auxiliary Structures*

A temple was not always a single building. It had a number of auxiliary structures like *maṇṭapas, prākāras, gōpuras, satras, maṭhas* and *calivēndiris.* The construction of these structures also received the attention of pious devotees.

a. *Construction of Garbhagṛha and Antarāḷa*

While *mahāmaṇḍalēśvara* Siddhirāja Tiṁmayadēva *mahārāja* was ruling over Koṇḍavīdu, the *garbhagṛha* of the Mallikārjuna temple was constructed in Ś. 1470, at the *agrahāra* village of Vipparti *alias* Kṛṣṇarāyapuram situated in the *Koṇḍavīdu-sīma.*[133] In Ś. 1487, a Singarāju built the *garbhagṛha* and *antarāḷa* of the Ādikēśava temple at Kolālapūṇḍi.[134] Rājaśēkharuni Śānkarayya and his wife, Laccaṁmā, erected the *garbhagṛha* and *antarāḷa* of a temple in Ś. 1599, on the Kaḷyāṇagiri hill near Kāmēpalli.[135] A Vīrabhadruḍu raised the *garbhagṛha* and *antarāḷa* of the

127. *S.I.I.* X. 565. Tangeḍa.
128. *T.T.D.I.* II. 36. Tirupati.
129. *S I.I.* X. 557. Tangeḍa.
130. 285 of 1934-35. Kāmēpalle.
131. 357 of 1938-39. Cuddapah.
132. *T.T.D.I.* V. 125. Tirupati.
Similar Examples
S.I.I. X. 141. Edavalli.
Ibid., IV. 927. Iṛlapāḍu.
Ibid., VI. 605. Koṇidena.
Ibid., X. 82. Nādiṇḍla.
321 of 1922. Taṁbaḷḷapalle.
101 of 1921. Mēlpāḍi.
133. 330 of 1934-35. Vipparla.
134. *S.I.I.* X. 746. Kolālapūḍi.
135. 285 of 1934-35. Kāmēpalli.

shrine of god Trikōṭēśvara at Kōṭappakoṇḍa in Ś. 1672.[136] In Ś. 1772, Pullābaṭṭuḍu, the son of Cadalavāḍa Vīranna and his wife Pullaṁmā, built the *garbhagṛha* of the Vīrabhadrasvāmi temple at Uppalūru.[137]

b. *Vimānas*

Inscriptions supply interesting information regarding the construction of the *Vimānas* of temples. In Ś. 1176, a Śaiva teacher, named Śāntaśaṁbhu, constructed the *vimāna* of the temple of god Tripurāntakēśvara at Tripurāntakam.[138] An Akhṣāyi *sēnāpati* built the *vimāna* of the Siṁhāchalam temple with granite stone in Ś. 1190 at the command of king Vīra Narasiṁha.[139]

c. *Mukhamaṇṭapas*

Mukhamaṇṭapas were constructed in temples by various individuals at various times. In Ś. 1057, a Tullila Peṁmaıāju constructed a *mukhamaṇṭapa* for the temple of god Varadarājasvāmi at Kōcherlakōṭa.[140] A record from Eḍavalli refers to the construction of a *mukhamaṇṭapa* for god Svayaṁbhudēva at Eḍavalli in Ś. 1179.[141] In Ś. 1344, the *Śrīmukhamaṇṭapa* with eight pillars was built in the Bhīmēśvara shrine of Cālukya-Bhīmavaram by Mantripregaḍa Annaya and the *niluvu-maṇṭapa* was erected on the occasion of a *makarasankrānti*.[142] The *Teliki-Vēguru*, or the merchant guild of oil-millers, constructed a *mukhamaṇṭapa* in Ś. 1348 in front of god Mallēśvara at Bezavāḍa.[143] In Ś. 1453, Cinaboṁmānāyuḍu, the *śēvaka* of Ayyapparusayya of Koṇḍavīḍu, built a *mukhamaṇṭapa* to the temple of god Vīrēśvara of Enamadala.[144] Veligōṭi Rāyanāyani Lingaṁgāru constructed a *mukhamaṇṭapa* in Ś. 1516 for god Kalimāṇikya Nāyanār of Tūmūru.[145] In Ś. 1742, a *mukhamaṇṭapa* was raised for gods Śrī Venkaṭēśa and Śrī Narasiṁha at Rājahmundry by Basavarāja in the name of Rājā Venkaṭrāya.[146] A record from Chiḍipirāla refers to the construction of a *mukhamaṇṭapa* of the temples of goddesses Pālēṭaṁmā and Māncālāṁmā of Chaḍupurāla by four private individuals of the villages.[147] A certain Kākāṇḍi Maṇḍaya built the *mukhamaṇṭapa* of the temple of god Cenna-Mallikārjuna for the merit of his father, Mallaya.[148]

136. *S.I.I.* IV. 919. Kōṭappakoṇḍa.
137. 287 of 1937-38, Uppalūru.
138 *S.I.I.* X. 345. Tripurāntakam.
139. *Ibid.*, VI. 1142. Simhāchalam.
140. *N.D.I.* I. Darsi. 41. Kocherlakōṭa.
141. *S.I.I.* X. 356. Edavalli.
142. *Ibid.*, V. 36. Bhīmavaram.
143. *Ibid.*, IV. 796. Bezavāda.
144. *Ibid.*, IV. 936. Yenamadala.
145. *N.D.I.* III. Sūḷūrpēṭ. 16. Tuṁmūru
146. *S.I.I.* V. 117. Rājahmundry.
147. 219 of 1937-38. Chidipirāla.
148. 41 of 1929-30.Gāmālapādu.
Similar Examples
S.I.I. VI. 1142. Simhāchalam.
Ibid., V. 39. Bhīmavaram.
N.D.I. III. Rāpur 56. Rāpur.
46 of 1929-30. Naḍikuḍi.

d. *Other Maṇṭapas*

Several devotees evinced keen interest in constructing *maṇṭapas* within the precincts of temples.

While Pallava-Dhīra was ruling over the Mulki 500, a *mahāsāmanta* constructed a *maṇṭapa* in the Mukkeṁṭīśvara temple at Kāmalāpuram in Ś. 848.[149] A Yaṁmarāja *alias* Śrīman *mahāmaṇḍalēśvara* Nandivarma mahārāja, built *maṇṭapas* in Ś. 1024 for gods Dorēśvara and Irugēśvara at Padaṭūru.[150] In Ś. 1057, king Durjaya Maṇḍa nāyaka of the Koṇḍapaḍamaṭi dynasty erected a *mantapa* for god Sōmēśvara at Irṛalūra.[151] In Ś. 1117, a certain Panta nāyaka Pōtaya built a stone *maṇṭapa* for god Śiva at Ēlūr.[152] Nārāyaṇa of the Gautama *gōtra*, who was the minister of king Velanāḍu Manma Gonka, raised a *maṇṭapa* in Ś. 1152 before the temple of god Nārāyaṇēśa at Telikicheṛuvu which he had constructed in the same year.[153] In Ś. 1209, Nallagōpāladēva, who calls himself a dependent of Śrī Modaliṁgāru of the family of Vīra-Nayanadesa, constructed a *maṇṭapa* for god Gōpīnātha at Pulipāḍu for the merit of the king Kākatīya Rudra.[154] A record from Pulivendla, dated in Ś. 12)1, mentions that a *maṇṭapa* was built in the temple of Bhairava of Mōpūru.[155] The big *maṇṭapa* in the temple of Saryanarya perumāḷ at Vikramasingapuram or Nellore was erected in Ś. 1322, by Pulavadalvār *alias* Camayattār.[156] The *maṇṭapa* before the entrance of the Dharmalingēśvara temple at Panchadhārla was constructed by a Cāḷukyan chief named Śrīdhararāja Narēndra *mahāpātra* in Ś. 1350.[157] In Ś. 1434, King Kṛṣṇarāya built the 100 pillared *maṇṭapa* in the temple of Kāḷahastīśvara, when he visited the temple after his eastern campaign.[158] A Tirumala temple inscription, dated in Ś. 1449, states that an individual named Adiyappan, one of the door keepers of king Acyutarāya, erected a *maṇṭapa* in the temple of Śrī Venkaṭēśvara of Tirumala.[159] Another record from the same place, dated in Ś. 1483, mentions the construction of an *Ūnjalmaṇṭapa* by king Āravīṭi Tirumalarāja in the second *prākāra* of the Tirumala temple.[160] Tiṁmāji paṇḍita, the disciple of Satyanidhisvāmin of the *Mādhavācārya-maṭha* and a member of the Sabbinivīsu family constructed *maṇṭapas* in Ś 1587 in the temple of god Rāmēśvara of Kodalūru on the bank of the river Kṛṣṇā.[161] In Ś. 1646, a Rāmireḍḍi, the son of Venkaṭi of Vuppalūru, constructed a *maṇṭapa* for god Agastīśvara at Pālūru.[162] Muṁmaḍi Cikarāyalu, the son of Suguṭūri Iṁmaḍi Cikarāyalu, built a *maṇṭapa* in Ś. 1738 for god Caṇḍēśvara at Cheṛakuvāripalle.[163]

149. 235 of 1937-38. Kamalāpuram.
150. *N.D.I.* III. Udayagiri. Jaḍadēvi.
151. *S.I.I.* IV. 927. Īṛlapāḍu.
152. 269 of 1952-53. Elūr.
153. 275 of 1937-31. Telikicherla.
154. 26 of 1929-30. Pulipāḍu.
155. *S.I.I.* X. 498. Mōpūru.
156. *N.D.I.* III. Nellore 76. Nellore.
157. *S.I.I.* VI. 665. Panchadhārla; *E.I.* XIX. pp. 164-174.
158. *Ibid.*, VIII. 495. Kāḷahasti.
159. *T.T.D.I.* III. 169. Tirumala.
160. *Ibid.*, VI. 168. Tirumala.
161. 302 of 1934-35. Kollūru.
162. 359 of 1940-41. Pālūr.
163. 355 of 1935-37. Cheṛakuvāripalle.

A record from Vallūru, dated in Ś. 1742, states that the stone *mantapa* of the Āñjanēya temple at Kāmalāpūr was built by Bāla Venkaṭareḍḍi as a dedication to god Venkaṭēśvarasvāmin.[164] Moram Vengaya and others of the *Vaiśya* community who claim to belong to the *Ikṣvāku-kula,* constructed a *maṇṭapa* in the temple of Cennakēśava of Vēlpūru in Ś. 1810.[165] An inscription from Vallūru states that Koṇḍayya, the son of Bālaya and grandson of Mēda Rudrapa, raised a stone *maṇṭapa* of 20 *ankaṇas* and dedicated it to god Cennakēśavasvāmi of Vallūru.[166] Another, from Dēvaguḍi, mentions that the *maṇṭapa* in front of the temple of god Talakaṇṭīdēva of the village was erected by Lingāreḍḍi of Chaḍupurēla.[167]

Maṇṭapas were constructed on tank bunds and in gardens. In Ś. 1454, under the orders of the emperor, Acyutarāya, Tāḷḷapākam Tirumalācāryulu, who sung various *Sṛngārasankīrtanas* in praise of Śrī Venkaṭēśa, erected a *maṇṭapa* around the tank at Tirumala.[168] Cōḍa Beharā *mahāpātra* and Śrīhari Narēndra *mahāpātra* constructed a *maṇṭapa* in Ś. 1460 to god Dharmēśvara of Panchadhārla on the banks of the Vaṁśadhārā.[169] In Ś. 1467, Acyutarāya constructed seven *maṇṭapas* for the merit of himself, his queen, his son, his father and his mother at Tirumala.[170] Tāḷḷapākam Tirumala Ayyangār made provision for the construction of the *Nirāḷi-maṇṭapa* in the midst of the *Svāmi-puṣkariṇi* and for the building of a *pradakṣiṇa-maṇṭapa* on the four sides of the banks of the *Puṣkariṇi.*[171] In the reign of Acyutarāya, a *maṇṭapa* was erected in a garden at Tirumala by Āravīḍu Lakṣmīaṁman, one of the ladies in waiting in the royal harem, for god Śrī Venkaṭēśa of Tirumala.[172] In Ś. 1438, Dēyvattan arasu built a *maṇṭapa* in a flower garden for god Śrī Venkaṭēśa of Tirumala.[173] The queen of Śrī *mahāmaṇḍalēśvara* Salakarāju Periya Tirumalayyadēva *mahārāja* constructed in Ś. 1456, a *maṇṭapa* commonly known as Varadanārāyaṇa flower garden *maṇṭapa,* in a garden.[174] In Ś. 1466, Mūrti Nāyakkar constructed a *maṇṭapa* in a flower garden at Tirumala.[175] In Ś. 1467, a flower *maṇṭapa* was constructed by Kuppā Venkaṭattarasu in his flower garden at Tirumala.[176]

Special *maṇṭapas* were constructed by devotees for use on special occasions like the marriage festival, swing festival, hunting festival etc. The Cāḷukyan prince,

164. 436 of 1938-39. Vallūru.
165. 329 of 1934-35. Vēlpūru.
166. 429 of 1938. Vallūru.
167. 326 of 1940-41. Dēvaguḍi.
168. *T.T.D.I.* IV. 52. Tirumala.
169. *S.I.I.* VI. 671. Panchadhārla.
170. *T.T.D.I.* IV. 54. Tirumala.
171. *Ibid.*, IV. 40. Tirumala.
172. *Ibid.*, IV. 125. Tirumala.
173. *Ibid.*, III. 113. Tirumala.
174. *Ibid*, IV. 31. Tirumala.
175. *Ibid.*, V. 19. Tirumala.
176. *Ibid*, V. 64. Tirumala.
Similar Examples :
N.D.I. III. Rāpur 56. Rāpur.
46 of 1929-30. Nādiṇḍla.
S.I.I. X. 109. Dāvulūru.

Contd.

Viśvēśvara, erected a *Kaḷyāṇamaṇṭapa* in Ś.1329 to god Dharmēśa of Panchadhārla.[177] In Ś. 1338 Kirilenka Śirigirinēḍu built a *kalyāṇamaṇṭapa* for god Rāmēśvara of Kṣīrārāma, 16 cubits long, 8 cubits broad and containing 24 pillars on behalf of Naraharinēnimgāru of the village of Manchēḷḷa for the merit of king, Doḍḍaya Allāḍa.[178] A Bhōjanapalle Śrīnivāsayyangāru constructed a *kalyāṇamaṇṭapa* in Ś. 1476, for the purpose of conducting the marriage festival of god Kēśava Perumāḷ at Saṁbaṭūru *alias* Śrībhāṣyapura.[179] The *kalyāṇamaṇṭapa* in the Tirumala temple was built in Ś. 1508, by Avasavaram Connapa for god Śrī Venkaṭēśa of the place.[180] In S.1690, Rāmireḍḍi, the son of Dēvireḍḍi of Muḍiya, erected a *kalyāṇamaṇṭapa* for god Lakṣmī-Cennakēśava of Pālūru.[181] A *kalyāṇamaṇṭapa* was constructed in Ś. 1766, by Tirumalakoṇḍu, the son of Gorre Koṇḍaḍu.[182] A Kṛṣṇamaseṭṭi of the *Vaiśya-kula* built the *kalyāṇamaṇṭapa* in Ś. 1784, for god Lakṣmī-Nṛsiṁha at Tarigoṇḍa.[183]

Sāḷuva Tiṁmarasu constructed a new *bhōga-maṇṭapa* in Ś. 1421, for the religious merit of Śrī Kṛṣṇadēva Mahārāya, in the temple of god Rāmēśvara at

Ibid., X. 144. Gunṭūr.
N.D.I. I. Darśi. 70. Tāḷḷūru.
Ibid., I. Darśi. 19. Donakoṇḍa.
Ibid., II. Kandukūr. 18. Old Chunḍi.
T.T.D I. I. 78. Tirumala.
Ibid., IV. 15, 52. Tirumala
S.I.I. IV. 709. Mangaḷagiri.
T.T.D.I., VI. 7. Tirumala.
280 of 1934-35. Chityāla.
T.T.D.I. VI. 12, 20. Tirumala.
362 of 1940-41. Pālūru.
N.D.I. I. Gūḍūr 44. Kiṣtnaṭnam.
N.D.I. II. Kandukūr. 45. Kōvvūr.
S.I.I. X. 383. Kanchala.
N.D.I. II. Kandukūr 49. Mālakoṇḍa.
T.T.D.I. II. 5. Tirumala.
N.D.I. II. Kandukūr 18, Sōmarājupalle.
S.I.I. VI. 603. Inumeḷḷa.
Ibid., IV. 703. Naṁbūru.
N.D.I. II. Kanigiri. 35. Pōlavaram.
Ibid., III. Rāpūr 57. Saidāpuram.

177. *E.I.* XIX. Pp. 164-174. Panchadhārla.
178. *S.I.I.* V. 133. Pālakol.
179. 279 of 1937-38. Saṁbaṭūru.
180. *T.T.D.I.* VI. 7. Tirumala.
181. 361 of 1940-41. Pālūru.
182. 236 of 1949-50. Bōḍinēnipalle.
183. 448 of 1940-41. Tarigoṇḍa.

Similar Examples
S.I.I. X. 113. Palivela.
Ibid., IV 1379, 1383. Drākshārāma.
Ibid., V. 118. Rājahmundry.
36 of 1940-41. Pālūru.

Madanūru.[184] An inscription from Tāḍipatri, dated in Ś. 1431, refers to the construction of a *bhōgamaṇṭapa* for god Rāmalingēśvara of the place by Sāḷuva Timmayya for the merit of king, Vīranarasiṁha.[185] Another from Mailavaram, records the erection of a *bhōga-maṇṭapa* for god Savita Mallaya of the place by *mahāmaṇḍalēśvara* Rāmayangāru for the merit of Dēvarāya Mahārāya and Hannayaṁmā and Siddhiyaṁmā.[186] In Ś. 1229, Viśvēśvara Jiyana built a *dharma-maṇṭapa* for god Śrī Narasiṁhanātha of Siṁhāchalam.[187] The Hudedars constructed a *dharma-maṇṭapa* in Ś. 1650, for god Kēśavasvāmi at Tartūru.[188]

A *bhadra-maṇṭapa* was constructed by Singana in Ś. 1360 for god Mṛkaṇḍēśvara of Rājahmundry.[189] In the Bhāvanārāyaṇa temple at Sarpavaram, a *ḍōlā-maṇṭapa* was erected in Ś. 1316.[190] In Ś. 1374, a certain Singana built the *ḍōlā-maṇṭapa* for god Śrī Kūrmanātha of Śrīkūrmam.[191] The Reḍḍi king, Anavēma, constructed a *Śanivāramaṇṭapa* in Ś. 1307 for god Bhīmēśvara of Drākshārāma.[192] In Ś. 1179, the *Karavālabhairava-maṇṭapa* was erected in the temple of god Vāsukiravisōmēśvara at Duttiga by Bhaṇḍāru nāyaka and his son, Vīrabhadra nāyaka.[193] In the town of Dirghāsi, a provincial chief, named Vanapati or Banapati, in the service of king Rājarāja of the Gānga dynasty, built a *nāṭyamaṇṭapa* in Ś. 997 in front of the temple of Durgā in that town.[194] In Ś. 1190, an Akhasaya *sēnāpati* raised the *nāṭyamaṇṭapa* in the temple of god Śrī Narasiṁhanātha of Siṁhāchalam at the command of King Vīra Narasiṁha.[195] The Reḍḍi king, Anavēma, constructed a *nāṭyamaṇṭapa* in Ś. 1307, at Drākshārāma in the temple of god Bhīmēśvara.[196] Mallana *alias* Śrī Mādhavadasar built the *Tirumahāmaṇi-maṇṭapa* in Ś. 1339, comprising the *tirumuttinadandal* or flooring, *kaldaram* or stone foundation, the decorative work extending from the *kuradu* or basement up to the *stūpi* or roof and the *meyakkal* hr sloping terrace in the Śrī Venkaṭēśvara temple at Tirumala.[197] A record from the Tirumala temple, mentions the erection of the *nirāḷi maṇṭapa* in the centre of the *Svāmi-puṣkariṇi*.[198] In Ś. 1389, Sāḷuva Narasiṁharāya Uḍaiyar constructed the *Vasanta-maṇṭapa* in the middle of the tank

184. *N.D.I.* III. Ongōle. 71. Māḍanūru.
185. *S.I.I.* IV. 802. Tāḍipatri.
186. 39 of 1937-38. Mailavarm.
Similar Examples
N.D.I. III. Udayagiri 43. Udayagiri.
Ibid., I. Darsi 14. Dēkanakoṇḍa.
T.T.D.I. VI. 25. Tirupati.
187. *S.I.I.* VI. 1002. Simhāchalam.
188. 63 of 1942-43. Ṭarṭūru.
189. *S.I.I.* V. 118. Rājahmundry.
190. *Ibid.*, 27 Sarpavaram.
191. *Ibid.*, V. 1201. Śrīkūrmam.
192. *S.I.I.* IV. 1379. Drākshārāma.
193. *Ibid.*, X 348. Juttiga.
194. *E.I.* IV. P. 314. Dirghāsi.
195. *S.I.I* VI. 1142. Simhāchalam.
196. *Ibid.*, IV. 1379. Drākshārāma.
197. *T.T.D.I.* I. 196. Tirumala.
198. *Ibid.*, IV. 40. Tirumala.

at Tirumala for god Śrī Venkaṭēśa.[199] The *Gāngeyarāya-maṇṭapa* was raised in Ś. 1064 by Kullōttungacōḍa Gonkarāju at Drākshārāma.[200] In Ś. 1196, the *Cōḍa-maṇṭapa* was built to the north of the Bhīmēśvara temple at Drākshārāma by the queen of Vīrabhānudēva of the Eastern Gānga dynasty.[201] A merchant guild, known as the *Akhiladēśāla-Telikivēvuru,* constructed a *nandi-maṇṭapa* in Ś. 1331 before the shrine of god Mallēśvara of Bezavāḍa.[202] The *Hōma* and *Yāga-maṇṭapas* were constructed for god Bhīmēśvara of Drākshārāma by king Anavēma, in Ś. 1307.[203] In Ś. 1768, the *hōmaśālā-maṇṭapa* and kitchen *maṇṭapas* were built for god Narasiṁha at Tarigoṇḍa by Eṟṟappa, the son of Jangama seṭṭi and grandson of Ramagi seṭṭi, a devotee of *guru* Bhāskarācārya and the recipient of boons from the goddess Vāsavāṁbā.[204] In Ś. 1135, Jāya sēnāpati raised a *maṇṭapa* for god Kumārasvāmi of Tāmrapuri for resting after hunting on every *Makarasankrānti.*[205] In Ś. 1135, Jāyasēnāpati got the hunting *maṇṭapa* constructed and painted in it the fight between the gods and demons.[206] A record from Drākshārāma mentions the construction of a *Mṛgayārāma-maṇṭapa,* intended to seatthe deity on the occasion of the hunting festival.[207] Another from Tangeḍa, dated in Ś. 1295, refers to erection of a *Vāhana-maṇṭapa* for keeping various vehicles for god Gōpīnātha of the place.[208] In Ś. 1440, *mahāmaṇḍalēśvara* Singayadēva raised the *Rathōtsava maṇṭapa* for god Rāmacandra of Bezavāḍa.[209] A Kaḍiyam Mācinēniṁgāva built an *āsthāna-maṇṭapa* of stone for god Bhīmēśvara of Drākshārāma for the merit of his overlord, Kāṭamareḍḍi Vēmāreḍḍi and his queen, his son, Komāragiri and his queen.[210]

e. *Śikharas and Kalaśas*

There are several examples of *śikharas* and *kalaśas* being set up by devotees. *Mahāmaṇḍalēśvara Mīsaragaṇḍa* Mangidēva *mahārāja* fixed a golden *śikhara* in Ś. 1281, over the *vimāna* of Tirumaladēva of Tirumala.[211] Sāḷuva Tiṁmarasu erected a pinnacle on the temple of god Rāmēśvaradēva in Ś. 1421 at Madanūru.[212] Nādiṇḍla gōpa set up golden pinnacles in Ś. 1442, on the temple of god Raghunāyaka of

199. *Ibid.*, II. 31. Tirumala.
200. *S.I.I.* IV. 1142. Drākshārāma.
201. *Ibid.*, IV. 1084. Drākshārāma.
202. *Ibid.*, IV. 774. Bezavāḍa.
203. *Ibid.*, IV. 1379. Drākshārāma.
204. 447 of 1940-41. Tarigoṇḍa.
205. *E.I.*, V. pp. 142-151. Chēbrōlu.
206. *Ibid.*, V. Pp. 142-151. Chēbrōlu.
207. *S.I.I.* IV. 1353. Drākshārāma.
208. *Ibid.*, X. 557. Tangēḍa.
209. *Ibid.*, IV. 789. Bezavāḍa.
210. *EI.* IV. Pp. 329-330. Drākshārāma.
Similar Examples
S.I.I. IV. 1142. Drākshārāma.
T.T.D.I. IV. 40. Tirumala.
211. *Ibid.*, I. 179.
212. *N.D.I.* III, Ongole. 71. Mādanūru.

Yajñavāṭika.[213] An inscription from Pinnali, dated in Ś. 1069, mentions the setting up of a *kalaśa* on the local temple of Sītārāmasvāmi.[214] Another from Drākshārāma, dated in Ś. 1326, states that Annadēvamahārāju set up golden *kalaśas* on the temple of god Bhīmēśvara of Drākshārāma.[215] In Ś. 1570, three persons, named Mallinēṇḍu, Gangana and Venkaṭādri, raised a new pinnacle on the temple of god Gōpālarāya at Duvva which was newly constructed by them.[216] Rāmalakṣmaṇadāsa, one of the disciples of Mahant Prayāgadāsa, the then *Vicaraṇakarta* of the *Dēvasthānams* of Tirumala and Tirupati, arranged for the fixing of the *kanaka-kalaśas* or golden vessels over the *vimāna* of Śrī Venkaṭēśvara shrine at Tirumala in Kali Ś. 1010.[217]

f. *Dhvajasthaṁbhas and Balipīṭhas*

Dhvajasthaṁbhas and *balipīṭhas* were set up before temples by pious devotees. In Ś. 1387, Sāḷuva Tirumaladēva *mahārāja*, the son of Gōpayadēva of the *Cōḷamaṇḍalarājya* set up a golden *dhvajasthaṁbha* in front of the temple of Mallikārjuna at Śrīśailam.[218] A certain Jangamarāju installed a *dhvajasthaṁbha* in Ś. 1575, before the temple of god Śrī Cennakēśava of Arivēmula.[219] In Ś. 1760, Lakṣmaṁmā, the wife of Subbarāya, of the Āpstaṁbha *sūtra* and Kāsyapa *gōtra*, erected the *dhvajasthaṁbha* in the temple of Cennakēśavasvāmi at Vallūru.[220] An undated record from Tirupati states that the *dhvajasthaṁbha* in the temple of Śrī Gōvindarājasvāmi of the place was raised by Madarasu Pantulu gāru, as his *ubhaiyam*.[221] A *balipīṭha* was set up before god Ahōbalēśvara at Ahōbalapura by Kannaya, the son of Salam Nāganna,[222] An individual constructed a *balipīṭha* before the temple of god Kēśava at Saṁbaṭūru.[223]

g. *Garuḍasthaṁbha*

Garuḍasthaṁbhas or pillars containing the figure of Garuḍa, were also set up in temples. A Garuḍa pillar was set up before the temple of god Śrī Kēśava at the town of Rāvinūtala in the *Kaṁma-nāḍu* in Ś. 1205, by a brāhmin, named Śrī Padmaya.[224] In Ś. 1321, a similar pillar was installed by the son of Sūru of Ātukūru

213. *E.I.* VI. Pp. 230-239. Koṇḍavīḍu.
214. *S.I.I.* X. 120. Pinnali.
215. *Ibid.*, IV. 1347. Drākshārāma.
216. 15 of 1929-30. Duvva.
217. *T.T.D.I.* VI. 135. Tirumala.
Similar Examples
S.I.I. X. 549. Pinnali.
T.T.D.I. I. 80. Tirumala.
S.I.I. VI. 184. Bāpaṭla.
218. *Meck. Colln.* 15-3-2. p. 215.
219. *N.D.I.* II. Kanigiri. I. Arivēmula.
220. 426 of 1938-39. Vallūru.
221. *T.T.D.I.* VI. 42. Tirupati.
222. 1 of 1946-47. Ahōbalapuram.
233. 274 of 1937-38. Saṁbaṭūru.
224. *N.D.I.* III. Ongōle. 301. Rāvinūtala.

in front of the temple of Lakṣmīnarasiṁhadēva at Puruṣottamapaṭśaṇa.[225] Yallāpragaḍa Dēvarāju set up a Garuḍa pillar in Ś. 1410 in front of the temple of god Kēśavanātha at Peddapalli.[226] An individual consecrated a Garuḍa pillar in the shrines of goddessess Bhūdēvī and Lakṣmīdēvī in the Cennakēśava temple at Kolālapūḍi in Ś. 1487.[227] A quadrangular platform and Garuḍa pillrr were set up in Ś. 1599 in the temple of Rājagōpālasvāmin of the village of Gāmālapāḍu.[228]

h. *Lamp-Posts*

The setting up of *dīpa-sthaṁbhas* or lamp pillars in temples was also considered an act of great piety. Avubalaya and Tirumalayaṁgāru, the sons of Annaṁgaru of Bhōjanapalli-Kaḍamūru, set up a lamp pillar in Ś. 1457 before god Hanumān at Kaḍumūru.[229] In Ś. 1504 an individual, named Yikiya, the son of Doḍḍa-Helegayya, a carpenter, set up an iron lampstand in the temple of Mallikārjuna of Śrīśailam.[230] In Ś. 1710, a lamp pillar was set up by a certain Ayapa Gauḍa at Muttukūru.[231] A lamp pillar was set up in the temple of Rāmēśvaradēva by Lingayya at Gudibaṇḍa.[232]

i. *Nāga-pillars*

Nāga pillars were set up in many temples. This was done by women who longed for children. In Ś. 1028, a *nāga* pillar was set up by Śrīhara-Bhaṭṭa, the *purōhita* of Pottapi Kāmadēvacōḍa, in the temple of god Tripurāntakēśvara at Tripurāntakam.[233] A brāhman, named Dāra, the son of Koṁmana, set up a *nāgasthaṁbha* in Ś. 1051 in front of the temple of Brahmā, Viṣṇu and Śiva, built by him at Mādhavīpaṭṭana or Mācharla.[234] During the reign of the Haihaya king, Vīrakāma, an individual, named Āditya, set up another *nāgasthaṁbha* at Mācharla.[235]

225. *S.I.I.* X. 570. Purushōttamapaṭṭaṇa.
226. 318 of 1936-37. Peddapalli.
227. *S.I.I.* X. 746. Kolālapūṇḍi.
228. 4 of 1929-30. Gāmālapāḍu.
Similar Examples
138 of 1945-46. Peddajūṭūru.
S.I.I. X. 550 Tripurāntakam.
316 of 1934-35. Paṇidem.
370 of 1932-33. Nallaballi.
N.D.I. III. Podili. 28. Maṛripūḍi.
229. 12 of 1942-43. Kaḍumūru.
230. 32 of 1915. *Śrīśailam.*
231. 350 of 1936-37. Muthukūru.
232. 282 of 1934-35. Gudibaṇḍa.
Similar Examples
376 of 1938-39. Eṭūru.
56 of 1942-43. Śrīśailam.
233. *S.I.I.* X. 235. Tripurāntakam.
234. *Ibid.*, X. 27. Gurzāla.
235. *Ibid.*, X. 72. Mācherla.

j. *Other Pillars*

Mere pillars were also set up in temples. In Ś. 1090, a pillar was set up in the temple of god Cōḍīśvaramahādēva at Mōdukūru.[236] An individual set up a stone pillar in the *nandi-maṇṭapa* of the temple of Bhīmēśvara of Māngolanu in Ś. 1237.[237] In Ś. 1326, a pillar was set up in the *mukhamaṇṭapa* of the temple of god Nāgēśvaradēva at Koṇḍavīdu by Rāvipūṇḍi Vīrisetti, the lord of Peaugoṇḍapura, for the merit of his parents.[238] A Gōpasāni constructed a pillar in the eastern side of the *maṇṭapa* in the temple of Śṛngāravallabhasvāmi at Tirupati in Ś. 1345.[239] A Ciṭikoṇḍayya, the son of Singarāja of Piḍugurāṭla, set up a pillar in Ś. 1472 in the local temple of god Gōpīnātha.[240]

Nandi pillars and swinging pillars were also set up in temples. In Ś. 1535, a nandi pillar was set up in the temple of god Sūryanārāyaṇa at Anantapuram by Cavate Sangamayya, the son of Nāgabaṭṭuḍu.[241] Swinging pillars were set up in the temple of Kāmavalli in Ś. 1725 by Kōṭasaciva of Prattipāḍu.[242]

k. *Prākāras and Gōpuras*

The construction of *prākāras* and *gōpuras* to temples was also considered an act of great piety. Many inscriptions supply valuable information in this regard. Yammarāja *alias* Śrīman *mahāmaṇḍalēśvara* Nandivarma *mahārāja*, constructed *prākāras* to the temples of Dorēśvara and Iṛugēśvara of Pādaṭūru in Ś. 1024.[243] The *prākāra* of the temple of Agastyēśvara of Guntūr in the *Oṁgēru-mārga* was constructed in Ś. 1080.[244] Nārāyaṇamantri, the minister of the Velanāḍu king, Manma Gonka, raised the *prākāra* to the temple of Nārāyaṇēśa at Telikicheṛuvu in Ś. 1152.[245] The stone *prākāra* of the temple of god Vēṇugōpālasvāmi of Tangeḍa was erected in Ś. 1295.[246] A devotee, named Lingayya, built the sculptured *prākāra*

236. *Ibid.*, X. 176. Mōdukūru.
237. *Ibid*, X. 511. Mōgallu.
238. 354 of 1936-37. Siddhāntam.
239. 265 of 1930-31. Tirupati.
240. 57 of 1929-30, Piḍugurēḷḷa.
241. 30 of 1943-44. Anantapūr.
242. 266 of 1932-33. Daṁmālapāḍu.

Similar Examples

S.I I. IV. 940. Yenamadala.
Ibid., IV. 660. Guntūr.
Ibid., IV. 694. Koṇḍavīdu.
N.D.I. I. Darsi 13. Darsi.
263 of 1930-31. Tirupati.
226 of 1930-31. Tirupati.
13 of App. E. of 1939-40. Tāḷḷūru.
55 of 1953-54. Niḍugallu.
N.D.I. I. Darsi. 14. Dēkanakoṇḍa.
54 of 1939-40. Tenāli.

243. *N.D.I.* III. Udayagiri. 6. Jaḍadēvi.
244. *S.I.I.* X. 144. Guntūr.
245. 275 of 1930-31. Telikicherla.
246. *S.I.I.* X. 555. Tangeḍa.

round the temple of Mallikārjuna of Srīśailam in Ś. 1334,[247] In Ś. 1354, the *prākāra* of the temple of god Nārāyaṇa at Bhīmavaram was constructed by Mallireḍḍi Pōlasāni.[248] Sāḷuva Timmayya built the *prākāra* in Ś. 1431 to be temple of god Rāmēśvara of Tāḍiparati, for the merit of king Vīranarasimha.[249] In Ś. 1442, Nādiṇḍlagōpa, the nephew of Sāḷuva Timma, raised the *prākāra* of the temple of god Raghunāyaka of Yojñavāṭika or Koṇḍavīḍu.[250] Rājaśēkharuni Śankarayya and his wife, Laccammā, constructed in Ś. 1599, the *prākāras* of the temple on the Kaḷyāṇagiri hill to the west of Kāmēpalle.[251] In Ś. 1742, the compound wall to each of the temples of Śrī Vēṇugōpāla, Śrī Narasimhasvāmi and Śrī Venkaṭēśvarasvāmi at Rājahmundry was built by Basavarāju in the name of Rāja Venkaṭrāya.[252]

A Nandivarma *mahārāja* constructed *gōpuras* to the temples of Dorēśvara of and Iṛugēśvara of Pādaṭūra in Ś. 1024.[253] The *kōṭagōpura* or *gōpura* in the *prākāra* of the temple of god Jōtinātha at Jōti was built by Centa Rāmi nāyaka n Ś. 1169.[254] Nallagōpāladasa constructed the *gōpura* of the temple of Gōpīnātha in Ś. 1209 at Pulipāḍu.[255] King Anavema erected in Ś. 1307, the stone *gōpura* to the temple of god Bhīmēśvara at Drākshārāma.[256] The eastern *gōpura* of the Dharmalingēśvara temple of Panchadhārla was constructed in Ś. 1325 by king Cōḍa.[257] The northern *gōpura* of the same temple was constructed by the same king.[258] After his eastern *digvijaya*, Kṛṣṇarāya visited the Kāḷahastīśvara temple at Kāḷahasti in Ś. 1438 and built the big *gōpura* on the bank of the Suvarṇamukhī stream.[259] The southern *gōpura* of Panchadhāratīra was constructed in Ś. 1452 by Sidhavarājanarēndra

247. *Meck. Collin.* 15-3-2. p. 229. Śrīśailam.
248. *S.I.I.* V. 94. Bhīmavaram.
249. *Ibid.*, IV. 802. Tāḍipatri.
250. *E.I.* VI. pp. 230-239. Koṇḍavīḍu.
251. 285 of 1934-35. Kāmēpalli.
252. *S.I.I.* V. 117. Rājahmundry.
Similar Examples
N.D.I. III. Kāvali. 13. Dūbaguṇṭa.
S.I.I. VI. 1142. Simhāchalam.
26 of 1929-30. Pulipāḍu.
S.I.I. IV. 1379. Drākshārāma.
N.D.I. III Ongōle. 77. Mēḍanūru.
S.I.I. V. 25. Sarpavaram.
S.I.I. VI. 936. Yanamadala.
Ibid., IV. 709. Mangaḷagiri.
N.D.I. II. Nellore 13. Nellore.
T.T.D.I. IV. 40. Tirumala.
N.D.I. III. Udayagiri. 20. Udayagiri.
S.I.I. V. 179. Bāpaṭla.
N.D.I. II. Ongōle 40. Dharmavaram.
S.I.I. IV. 1380. Drākshārāma.
253. *N.D.I.* III. Udayagiri. 6. Jaḍadēvi.
254. *S.I.I.* X. 312. Jōti.
255. 26 of 1929-30. Pulipāḍu.
256. *S.I.I.* IV. 1379. Drākshārāma.
267. *Ibid.*, VI. 657. Panchadārla.
258. *E.I.* XIX. No. 25. Panchadhārla.
259. *S.I.I.* VIII. 495. Kāḷahasti.

mahāpatrungāru.[260] Giriyappa, the *Sthānāpati* of Salakarāja Peda Timmarāju, raised the eastern *gōpura* of the Caṇḍēśvari temple at Nandavaram in Ś. 1458.[261] In Ś. 1550, the Maṭla chief, Anantarāja, erected the *gōpura* at the foot of the first hill called *Gāli gōpuram* on the way to the Tirumala temple and the big *gōpura* at the main entrance of the temple of god Gōvindarāja of Tirupati in Ś. 1632.[262] The big *gōpura* of the temple of god Oāgēśvara of Kaḷḷepalli was built in Ś. 1718 by Rāja Nāgēśvara nāyuḍu.[263] The *Padikāvali gōpura* of the temple of god Śrī Venkaṭēśvara at Tirumala was erected in Ś. 1771, by Dharmadāsuji, the disciple of Mahant Sēvadāsuji in order to please the god at Śēṣādri.[264] Bhīma, the sister's son of Marēḷḷa Annayamantri, constructed the western *gōpura* of the Gōpīnātha temple at Tāḷḷūru.[265]

(l) *Construction of dvāras, jambs etc.*

Another pious act was the construction of doorways, jambs, *tōraṇas*, gateways etc. While Pallava Dhīra was ruling over the *Mulki* 500, a *mahāsāmanta* constructed the doorway of the Mulakanṭīśvara temple in Ś. 848,[266] at Kāmalāpuram. In Ś. 1198 bronze doors were set up to the entrance of the *nāṭyamanṭapa* of the temple of Kṣārāmēśvara of Pālakol for the prosperity of Kōna Gaṇapatidēva by Rājavōli Mallinātha nāyaka[267] An individual built jambs in Ś. 1221 to the entrance or *dvāra* up to the *manṭapa* to the east of the Narendrēśvara temple at Vippaṛṛu.[268] Pōcu Lemka set up a *dvāra* with doors in Ś. 1225 to a *manṭapa* of the temple of god Sōmēśvara of Kārempūḍi, for the merit of Mācaya Nāyaka.[269] In Ś. 1299, Kaḍiyamu Pōtināyuḍu, the servant of Anavēmaya, constructed a bell-tower, door etc., to the central shrine of god Agastyēśvara, of Vāḍapalli formerly built by Pillalamaṛṛi Bēti Reḍḍi.[270] In Ś. 1336 two individuals raised a *tōraṇa*, with a bell

260. *S.I.I.* VI. 669. Panchadhārla.
261. 6 of 1943-44. Nandavaram.
262. *T.T.D.I.* VI. 25. Tirupati.
263. *S.I I.* VI. 79. Peddakaḷḷēpalli.
264. *T.T.D.I.* VI. 134. Tirumala.
265. 10 of App. E of 1939-40. Tāḷḷūru.
Similar Examples
N.D.I. II. Kāvali. 13. Dūbaguṇṭa.
S.I.I. IV. 802. Tāḍipatri.
Ibid., IV. 709. Mangaḷagiri.
355 of 1936-37. Śivaganga.
324 of 1937-38. Prātakōṭa.
60 of 1943-44. Lingāpuram.
S.I.I. VI. 670. Panchadhārla.
T.T.D.I. IV. 40. Tirumala.
N.D.I. III. Udayagiri. 20. Udayagiri.
S.I.I. IV. 1380. Drākshārāma.
266. 235 of 1937-38. Kamalāpuram.
267. *S.I.I.* V. 157. Pālakol.
268. *Ibid.*, X. 487. Vippaṛṛu.
269. *Ibid.*, X. 491. Kārempūḍi.
270. 489 of App. E of 1941-42. Vāḍapalli.

and pillars for god Bhīmēśvara of Bhīmavaram.[271] In the 33rd year of the reign of the Cāḷukya-Cōḷa king, Kulōttunga, Pallavarāja, a subordinate of the king, built a pavilion for god Bhīmēśvara or Drākshārāma.[272] A Mallisetti raised a verandah or *jagati* in Ś. 1347, in the temple of Narasiṁhadēva on the hill in the village of Pillutla for the merit of his master Tiṁma nāyaniṁgāru.[273] Hande Dēmappa nāyaniṁgaru constructed halls in Ś. 1525, in the Mallikārjuna temple at Śrīśailam.[274] In Ś. 1663, the entrance porch or *vākiṭi-mogaśāla* of the temple at Mutukūr was caused to be built by Ceṛakūri Tiṁma Gavunivāru.[275] Subbaṁmā, the wife of Basetti, of Śrīkākulam, erected the main entrance of the Umāmahēśvarasvāmin temple at Bayyanapalle in Ś. 1809.[276]

m. *Construction of Steps*

Construction of steps to temples was also undertaken by devotees at all times. In Ś. 1135, steps to the shrine of god Subbarāya at Dācepalli were constructed by a private individual.[277] The Reḍḍi king, Prōlayavēma, constructed steps to the hills of Śrīgiri and Ahōbalam in Ś. 1259.[278] In S. 1315, the Kadamba princess, Viṭṭhalāṁbā, the wife of Harihara, built steps to the hill on the way to the Pātāḷagangā under instructions given to her by god Mallikārjuna in a dream.[279] Kāṭamareḍḍi Vēmāreḍḍi erected the stone steps leading to Śikharēśvaram at Śrīśailam in Ś. 1327, for the spiritual merit of his master, overlord Kumāragirireḍḍi and his queen.[280] The famous Vijayanagara king, Acyutarāya Mahārāya, constructed steps of granite stone in Ś. 1453 to the *Cakratīrtham* tank as a dedication to god Tiruvēngaḷanātha at Tirupati.[281] In Ś. 1511, Aksatala Tirumala Bhaṭṭa of the Bharadhvāja *gōtra* built a footpath on the Indrakīla hill at Bezavāḍa.[282] The Maṭla chief, Anantarāja, raised in Ś. 1550, the *sōpāna mārga* or the pathway with flight of steps to the Tirumala temple.[283] Upēndraya, the *arcaka* of the Reḍḍi king, Kumāragiri. constructed the

271. *S.I.I* V. 38. Bhīmavaram.
272. *E.I.* XXII. bp. 138-145. Drākshārāma.
273. 95 of 1929-30. Pillutla.
274. 50 of 1942-43. Śrīśailam.
275. 358 of 1936-38. Muthukūru.
276. 332 of 1938-39. Bōyanapalli.
Similar Examples
S.I.I. X. 498. Mōpūru.
9 of 1929-30. Balighaṭam.
S.I.I. X. 28. Dānavulapāḍu.
281 of 1952-53. Tenāli.
404 of 1932-33. Śivaganga.
32 of 1942-43. Sangamēśvaram.
277. 47 of 1929-30. Dāchēpalli.
278. *S.I.I.* X. 559. Śrīśailam.
279. 47 of 1915. Śrīśailam.
280. 43 of 1942-43. Śrīśailam.
281. *T.T.D.I.* IV. 8. Tirupati.
282. 839 of 1917. Bezavāḍa.
283. *T.T.D.I.* VI. 25. Tirupati.

steps leading to the temple of Vasantarāya Narasiṁha of Kottūr.[284] A record from Nādiṇḍla mentions the construction of steps to the local Gōvardhanagiri.[285] Another from ōbalam, states that the steps leading up the hill to the temple of god Mallaṁkoṇḍēśvarasvāmi of the place were built by Vupuvaṭūri Pōtireḍḍi and Yellayya.[286]

n. *Water Reservoirs*

Tanks, wells, canals and channels were excavated by many pious devotees to please the deities. A tank was excavated by Mumranaṁma, the daughter of Koṁmiseṭṭi, in Ś. 996 on the occasion of *Uttarāyaṇa Sankrānti* at Vipparla.[287] Sōmana Peggaḍa, a minister, constructed a tank in Ś. 1057 for god Sōmēśvara of Iṟṟalūra.[288] A Koṁmana built a tank named Drōṇasamudra in Ś. 1073 at Nārāyaṇapāḍu.[289] A Bairapa nāyudu constructed a tank in Ś. 1204, for the enjoyment of the deity of Kākaṭūru.[290] In Ś. 1448, a tank was constructed for god Bhāskarēśvara at Uṇḍavalli on the bank of the river Kṛṣṇā,[291] by four individuals named Pāpiseṭṭi, Tippiseṭṭi, Malliseṭṭi and Kṛṣṇamaseṭṭi of the Murukula *gōtra*. A Tiṁmānāyaniṁgāru excavated a tank in Ś. 1509 for goddess Gangādēvī at Tsalivēndra.[292] Bhōgavōlu Reḍḍi, the son of Yellareḍḍi of the Mantakola *gōtra*, constructed a tank in Ś. 1534 for the temple of god Śiva near Bōgōlu.[293] In Ś. 1722, a tank was constructed near Rāmasamudram by the chief, Suguṭūru Muṁmaḍi Cikkarāya.[294] Three brothers, named Peda-gurappa, Cinna-gurappa and Vōbaṁmā, built a stone tank in Ś. 1758, as a dedication to god Venkaṭēśvara.[295] In Ś. 1390 Nandi Mallareḍḍi constructed the *puṣkariṇi* for god Vijayagōpāladēva at Mannanūr.[296]

In Ś. 1416 Eṟṟamanāyaka, dug a canal, named Eluturti-nadi, from the stream named Elā, brought it up to Gōvāḍa and joined it to Gurugaḍḍa and presented it to god Bhīmēśvara of Drākshārāma.[297] In Ś. 1387 an irrigation channel was excavated at Pērūr for god Śrī Venkaṭēśvara of Tirumala.[298] Guṇḍamadēvī, the queen of Kōṭa Buddharāja, constructed a tank named Guṇḍasamudram at Nādiṇḍla to god

284. 396 of 1926. Kottūr.
285. *S.I.I.* IV. 805. Nādiṇḍla.
286. 46 of 193-940. ōbalam.
Similar Examples
N.D.I. II. Kandukūr. 35. Kandukūr.
Ibid., III. Udayagiri. 43. Udayagiri.
287. *S.I.I.* VI. 586. Vipparla.
288. *Ibid.*, IV. 927. Iṟlapāḍu.
289. 314 of 1932-33. Narnepāḍu.
290. *N.D.I.* II. Kāvali. 33. Kākaṭūru.
291. *S.I.I.* X. 737. Uṇḍavalli.
292. *N.D.I.* I. Darsi. 73. Tsalivēndla.
293. 237 of 1949-50. Bōgōlu.
294. C.P. 6 of 1932-33. Punganūr.
295. 406 of 1938-39. Peddapurla.
296. *Hyd. Arch. Ser.* No. 19. Mn. 18. Mannanūr.
297. *S.I.I.* V. 37. Bhīmavaram.
298. *T.T.D.I.* II. 24. Tirumala.

Mūlasthānamahādēva.[299] In Ś. 1457 a gift was made for the excavation of irrigation of canals in the temple villages of god Śrī Venkaṭeśa of Tirumala.[300]

Wells were also dug by devotees. Cōḍadēva Cōḍamahārāja, Mallidēvarāja and Cikkirāja constructed a well in Ś. 1159 for god Nīlakanṭheśvara at Guḍḷūr for the merit of their parents.[301] In S. 1306, a Nāgana bōyuṇḍu, a palanquin-bearer, constructed a well for providing water for the sacred bath of god Rāmalingēśvara and the attendant deities at Santajūṭūru.[302] Pāpināyaniṁgāru, who was ruling over the *Cheruṅūru-sīma* etc., founded a village called Yellamāṁbapuram, named after his wife, Yellamāṁbā, to the east of Puṣpagiri, in the fields of the village of Mulupala and dug a well in Ś. 1461 for god Viṣṇu.[303] In the village of Guṇḍlapalli, a well was dug in Ś. 1551, for god Vīrabhadra by Payyāvulū Vīrarāghava of the Cuṛukūri *gōtra* for the merit of his chief, Mēdarameṭla Ayyapa nāyaniṁgāru.[304]

o. *Choultries and Maṭhas*

Choultries and *maṭhas* were necessary adjuncts to temples. These were constructed by all classes of people in temples. In Ś. 1449, the stone-car choultry was constructed by Valasam Ellappa nāyakkar as his *dharmam* at Tirupati.[305] Venkataṁmā, the daughter of Rāmanātha and the wife of Eṛakarareḍḍi, built the *dharmaśālā* in Ś. 1792 in order to please god Venkaṭēśvara at Vallūru.[306] *Mahāmaṇḍalēśvara* Satyarasa constructed a *satra* in Ś. 997 for the ascetics, after erecting a temple at *Eḍeyamaṭha* named after his father.[307] In Ś. 1006, in the 15th year of the reign of the Cāḷukya-Cōḷa king, Viṣṇuvardhana, the daughter of a subordinate of the king constructed the *Kulōttunga-cōḍa-satram* before god Yamīśvaradēva at Drākshārāma,[308] in which arrangements were made for feeding 20 brāhmans. In Ś. 1429, Siddapaṇāyani Koppinēniṁgāru granted lands to Goṇḍayya, Kṛṣṇayya and Tiṁmayya for the expenses of maintaining a *satra* at Beḍudūru during the festival occasion at Śrīparvata for the benefit of the pilgrims [309] In Ś. 1169, the *Bhaṇḍāruvumaṭham* was constructed for god Tripurāntakēśvara at Tripurāntakam by Dharma Śivācārya, the disciple of Vimala Śivācārya.[310] In Ś. 1445, Kṛṣṇarāya made a gift to Vyāsatīrtha Śrīpāda Uḍaiyar, for constructing a *maṭham* and he constructed the

299. *S.I.I.* IV. 684. Nādiṇḍla.
300. *T.T.D.I.* IV. 70. Tirumala.
301. *N.D.I.* II. Kandukūr. 22. Guṇḍlūr.
302. 55 of 1953-54. Santajūṭūru.
303. 283 of 1938-39. Chemuḷḷapalle.
304. 277 of 1932-33. Guṇḍapalli.
Similar Examples
92 of 1929-30. Morijaṁpūḍi.
N.D.I. II. Nellore 14. Gaṇḍavaram.
237 of 1949-50. Bōgōlu.
N.D.I. III. Podili. 2. Buḍamarāyalapāḍu.
305. *T.T.D.I.* III. 168. Chandragiri.
306. 437 of 1938-39. Vallūru.
307. 317 of 1937-38. Eṛṛamaṭham.
308. *S.I.I.* IV. 1015. Drākshārāma.
309. 201 of 1950-51. Vanganūru.
310. *S.I.I.* X. 315. Tripurāntakam.

maṭh m at Tirumala and named it after himself.[311] Viśveśvara Śivācārya built a *maṭha* at the town of Mantrakūṭa and another *maṭha* at Elēśvaram to the south of Śrīśailam.[312] A *maṭha* was constructed by the Eastern Cāḷukyan king, Yuddhamalla, in the temple of god Kumārasvāmi at Bezavāḍa.[313] *Mahāpradhāna* Nārāyaṇa Lakṣmīdēva *daṇḍanāyaka*, the general of the Yādava king, Singhanadēva, erected a *maṭha* at Puṣpagiri and named it *Lakṣmīnilaya* after his name.[314] Cadaranga Vīrayya raised a *maṭha* and consecrated Gōkarnalinga therein.[315]

An inscription from Tirupati states that a Rāmānujayyangār, the famous Vaiṣṇava religious teacher, constructed a wooden car for god Śrī Raghunāthan for the merit of *Mahārājādhirāja* Śrī Vīra Acyutarāya Mahārāya at Tirupati.[316] Another car was built by a Yādavarāya queen, the consort of Vīranarasingadēva in the 30th year of his reign, to god Śrī Gōvindaperumāḷ of Tirupati.[317] During the reign of the Vijayanagara king, Sadāśiva a *nīlai-tēr* or stone car was erected with a swing for god Śrī Venkaṭeśa of Tirumula by Basavarasayyar.[318]

'B' *Repair and Renovation*

Pious devotees were not only interested in building temples and auxiliary structures but also in their reconstruction and renovation. The technical word for this renovation is '*jīrnōddhāra*'.

1. *Temples*

Numerous examples are available of temples being renovated by devotees. In Ś. 978, Pergaḍe Bhōgapayya, a subordinate of king Trailōkyamalla, repaired the temple of god Nārāyaṇa built by Cakrēśvara of the Rāṣṭrakūṭa family at Bōdhana.[319] Uḷḷēpalli Bāci Reḍḍi renovated the temple of Kāḷēśvara at Pāluvāya, up to the finial, in Ś. 1177.[320] The temple of god Bhīmanātha of Pingaḷi was reconstructed in Ś. 1214.[321] An individual repaired, up to the *śikhara*, the ruined temple of Sangamēśvaradēva, situated at the holy confluence of the rivers Kṣīrā or Pālēru and Mākēru, about 15 *yōjanas* to the north east of the hill of Śrīśailam in Ś. 1309.[322] A Bommireḍḍi, the son of Singayareḍḍi, of Donakoṇḍa, renovated the temple of Nīlakanṭhadēva on the Udayagiri hill in the *Eṛuva-nāḍu* in Ś. 1324, for the merit of his parents.[323] In Ś. 1424, Kūrmaya *mahāpātra* rebuilt the original shrine of

311. *T.T.D.I.* III. 158. Tirumala.
312. *S.I.I.* X. 395. Mālkāpuram.
313. *E.I.* XV. Pp. 150-59. Bezavāḍa.
314. 410 of 1938-39. Puṣpagiri.
315. 310 of 1936-37. Kūchinapūḍi.
316. *T.T.D.I.* IV. 1. Tirupati.
317. *Ibid.*, I. 86. Tirupati.
318. *Ibid.*, V. 147. Tirumala.
319. *K.I.A.P.* No. 32. Bōdhan.
320. 21 of 1929-30. Puluvāyi.
321. *S.I.I.* X. 472. Pinnali.
322. *N.D.I.* I. Kandukuru. 8. Chennipāḍu.
323. 252 of 1949-50. Mohineenpuram.

Gōpāla at Sarpavaram for the merit of his parents and brother.[324] Śrī Cinna Tirumalayyangār reconstructed in Ś. 1463 the ruined temple of Śrī Venkaṭēśvarasvāmi at Alamēlumangāpuram, situated on the bank of the river Vikalaya.[325] A certain Sōmēśvara rebuilt all the temples which fell into ruins and disuse in the village of Juttiga in the time of the Qutb Shāhi Sultān, Ibrahīm Pādshāh, and got them whitewashed in Ś.1505.[326] In Ś. 1567, Ōbalarāya Kōnēṭināyanimgāru repaired the temple of Pāla-Venkaṭēśvara at Dinnamīdi-Kōḍigipalle *alias* Pālavenkaṭāpura in the *Guyyulūr-nāḍu* in the *Penugonḍadurga*.[327] The temple of Rāmalinga at Mirti-Muppāḷḷa was renovated in Ś. 1604 by Ayyapanēṇḍu, the son of Arikaṭla Kōkanēṇḍu, of the Cedukunūḷḷa *gōtra*.[328] Venkaṭareḍḍi and Annāreḍḍi, the great grandsons of Buṟṟareḍḍi, reconstructed the temples of Nāgēśvara and Vīrabhadrasvāmi in Ś. 1670 at Chintalūru.[329] In Ś. 1704 Yārlagaḍḍa Konḍaraṁmadēśāyi rebuilt the ruined temple of god Nāgēśvara at Peddakaḷḷēpalle.[330] The temple of Lakṣmī-Cennakēśvasvāmin at Chinagārlapāḍu, which was in ruins for several years, was reconstructed in Ś. 1731 by Kaḷḷēpalle Subbārāyuḍu, the *Samuddār* during the administration of the district by Ākumaṇnāṭi Narasayya and Kandāḷam Śrīnivāsācārya under the *Kuṁpiṇīvaru* or the East India Company.[331] The temple of Sītārāmasvāmin at Pedagārlapāḍu, which was originally constructed by Gārlapāṭi Śēṣācalam of Takkeḷḷapāḍu, fell into disuse on account of the famine in the year *Nandana* and his sons, Lakṣmīnārāyaṇa and Subbaya, reconstructed the temple in Ś. 1766.[332] In Ś. 1789, the temple of god Bhāvanārāyaṇasvāmi at Sarpavaram was renovated by Venkaṭamahīpati Gangādhara Rāmarāya.[333] A Muttayya renovated the temple of Lakṣmīnarasiṁhasvāmin in Kali 4959, at Gūḍavalli.[334] Tāḷḷapakkam Cinna Tirumalayyangār reconstructed the ruined temple at Alamēlumangāpuram near the Chandragiri fort.[335]

2. *Manṭapas*

Interesting information is also available from inscriptions regarding the reconstruction and renovation of *manṭapas* and other auxiliary structures besides temples, big and small. In Ś. 1336, repairs were done to the *mukhamanṭapa* of the temple of Cennakēśava of Mahādēvīcherla.[336] The *mukhamanṭapa* of the temple of god Cennakēśava of the same place was rebuilt in Ś. 1351 as its centre gave way.[337] While *mahamanḍalēśara* Siddhirāja Tiṁmayadēva mahārāja was ruling from

324. *S.I.I.* V. 25. Sarpavaram.
325. *T.T.D.I.* II. 144. Mangāpuram.
326. *S.I.I.* X. 749. Juttiga.
327. 80 of 1912. Kōḍigapalli.
328. 313 of 1934-35. Muppāḷḷa.
329. 9 of 1942-43. Chinnalapalli.
330. *S.I.I.* VI. 83. Peddakaḷḷēpalli.
331. 292 of 1930-31. Chinnagārlapāḍu.
332. 27 of 1929-30. Peddagārlapāḍu.
333. 697 of 1926. Sarpavaram.
334. 303 of 1936-37. Guṇḍavalli.
335. *T.T.D.I.* VI. 161. Mangāpuram.
336. *S.I.I.* X. 580. Mācherla.
337. *Ibid.*, X. 583. Mācherla.

Koṇḍavīḍu, the *garbhagṛha* of the Mallikārjuna temple, situated in the *Koṇḍavīḍu-sīma,* was repaired in Ś. 1470, at the *agrahāra* village Vipparti *alias* Kṛṣṇarāya-puram.[338] In Ś. 1587, the eastern *maṇṭapa* which was formerly built by Kōṭa Kētarāja, in the temple of Rāmeśvara at Koḍalūr, a village on the bank of the Kṛṣṇā, was renovated by Timmāji Paṇḍita, a disciple of Satyanidhisvāmin of the *Madhavācārva-maṭha* and a member of the *Sabbinivisu* family.[339]

3. *Pillars*

Piḷlars were also reset and replaced by devotees in temples. The pillar with the image of Garuḍāḷvār in front of the temple of Vēṇugōpālasvāmin at Jūlakallu, in the *Bellaṁkoṇḍa-sīma,* which had been originally set up by Vankāyalapāṭi Rāmalingaya Koṇḍayangāru, was blown down by a storm in the cyclic year, Raktākṣi, and a new pillar was again set up, with an image of Garuḍa in Ś. 1788 by some private individuals.[340] Rājā Mallikārjunaprasādanāyuḍu Bahadūra, renovated the ruined *Dhvajastaṁbha* of the temple.[341]

4. *Tanks*

There are instances of tanks being repaired when they fell into disuse. In Ś. 1454, under the order of the emperor, Śrī Vīra Acyutarāya, Tāḷḷapākam Tirumal-ācāryulu reconstructed the old tank of god Acyutasvāmin.[342] Śrī Mahant Sēvadāsa Satpuruṣa of the *Hathirāṁjī-Maṭham* in Tirupati renovated the *Svāmi Paṣkariṇi alias Śrī Varāhapuṣkariṇi* and Śrīnivāsa *Mahātīrtha* on the Tirumala hill in Ś. 1771.[343] In Ś. 1782, Śrī Mahant Dharmadāsuji of the *Haṭhirāṁji Maṭham* renovated the *Puṣkariṇi* or holy tank known as the *Kapilatīrtham* at Tirupati.[344]

5. *Gilding*

Gilding parts of the temples was also considered an act of great merit. In Ś. 1326, Anadēva mahārāja gilded the temple of Bhīmēśvara at Drākshārāma with gold.[345] The famous Vijayanagara king, Kṛṣṇarāya arranged for the gilding of the *Divya-vimānam* of Śrī Venkaṭēśa of Tirumala and the work was completed in Ś. 1440.[346] In Ś. 1562, the *śikhara* of the temple of Cennakēśava at Nallaballi was renovated and gilded by Tippāreḍḍi.[347] *Mahāmaṇḍaleśvara Mīsaragaṇḍa* Mangidēva mahārāja, a Vijayanagara subordinate, fixed the golden *kalaśa* and gilded the sanctum of she Tirumala temple.[348]

338. 330 of 1934-35. Vipparla.
339. 302 of 1934-35. Kollūru.
340. 293 of f 1930-31. Jūlakallu.
341. 405 of 1932-33. Śivaganga.
342. *T.T.D.I.* IV. 20. Tirumala.
343. *Ibid*., VI. 130. Tirumala.
344. *Ibid.*, VI. 133. Tirumala.
345. *S.I.I.* V. 1347. Drākshārāma.
346. *T T.D.I.* III. 81. Tirumala.
347. 371 of 1932-33. Nallaballi.
348. *T.T,D.I.* I. 180. Tirumala.

6. *Plastering and Whitewashing*

Several devotees arranged for the plastering and whitewashing of temples. An individual got the *maṇṭapa* of the temple of Narēndrēśvara of Vippaṟṟu plastered it in Ś. 1120.[349] In Ś. 1135, Jāyasēnāpati, whitewashed all the temples and placed golden *kalaśas* on the temples of Chēbrōlu.[350] In Ś. 1152, in the reign of the Eastern Gānga king, Aniyanka Bhīma, his general, Jesrāja, got the temple of Bhīmēśvara of Dākshārāma and whitewashed it.[351] A seṭṭi plastered the wall of the temple of god Rāmasvāmi of Addanki for the religious merit of his parents and of himself in Ś. 1326.[352] In Ś. 1352 Vāsireḍḍi Pōtinēṇḍu, the feudatory of the Reḍḍis, got the temple of goddess Lakṣmīdēvaṁmā of Piṭhāpuram plastered.[353] The temples of Narēndrēśvara of Guḍimeṭla and of the attendant deities were got plastered by Kassevuseṭṭi. Kurviseṭṭi and his wife, Sūraṁmā.[354] Nalladiga Rāmacandrayyagāru, the son of Vengaḷa Pāncālayyangāru plastered the *madhvarangam* and other *maṇṭapas* of the temple of god Śrīngāravallabhasvāmi at Tirupati for the merit of his father.[355] In Ś. 1140, an individual whitewashed the temple of god Rāmēśvara at Natta-Rāmēśvaram.[356] A devotee, named Pōcu Lenka, made provision for whitewashing the temple of Sūrēśvara and Kēśava Perumāḷḷu of Kāreṁpūḍi[357] in Ś. 1225 for the merit of Mācaya nāyaka, Nādiṇḍla Gōpa, the nephew of Sāḷuva Tiṁma, arranged for the whitewashing of the *maṇṭapas* and spires of the temple of god Raghunāyaka of Yajñavāṭika or Koṇḍavīḍu.[358] Cokaipātruḍu whitewashed the temple of god Vighnēśvara at Bezavāḍa.[359]

'C' *Consecration*

1. *Purpose of Installation of Deities*

The consecration of images is considered as great as temple construction. Images were installed either in the temple or in the compound of the temple. The consecration was undertaken for the merit of parents, families and of the devotees themselves.

Various deities were installed in temples for the merit of parents. In Ś, 1453, Rangaparāja installed an image at Chinnachāpalle for the merit of his parents.[360] A certain chief installed the images of Viṣṇu and Brahmā at Turimaḷḷa for the merit

349. *S.I.I.* X. 207. Vippaṟṟu.
350. *E.I.* VI. pp. 142-151. Chēbrōlu.
351. *S.I.I.* IV. 1360. Drākshārāma.
352. *N.D.I.* II. Ongōle. 2. Addanki.
353. *S.I.I.* VI. 676. Piṭhāpuram.
354. *S.I.I* X. 544. Koṇakanchi.
355. 274 of 1930-31. Tirupati.
356. *S.I.I.* X. 262. Natha-Rāmēśvaram.
357. *Ibid.*, 491. Kāreṁpūḍi.
358. *E.I.* VI. pp. 223-239. Koṇḍavīḍu.
359. *S.I.I.* IV. 775. Bezavāḍa.
360. 223 of 1937-38. Chinnachāpalle.

of his parents.[361] A Gangiseṭṭi consecrated a deity in the temple of Vīrēśvara at Peddapulivaṟṟu for the merit of his parents.[362]

Deities were installed for the merit of the father alone. In Ś. 1170, the Kākatīya king, Gaṇapatidēva, installed god Mahādēvēśvara in the name of his father at Gajjaram and gifted *angaḍi sunkam* to the god.[363] In the reign of the later Cāḷukyan king, Tribhuvanamalla, the Kākatīya king, Bētarāja, consecrated the image of Varuṇa in the name of his father, Prōlarāja.[364] In Ś. 1135, *mahāsāmanta* Malreḍḍi installed Muppaviśvēśvaradēva, known after his father at Māṭūru.[365] In Ś. 1300, Nēmakūri Annama nāyanimgāru installed god Rāmēśvara at Būrugugaḍḍa in the name of his father.[366] In Ś. 1067, Koṇḍapa nāyaka, who calls himself the lord of Tanarumbaṟu, consecrated the image of Mallikārjunadēva at Vaḍḍavalli for the merit of his father, Madde nāyaka.[367] *Rāyajīvarakṣa-sāmanta Javara* Annaladēva set up the image of Bhengēśvara at Kaṁbhaṁpādu in Ś. 1180, in the name of his father Bheyidēva.[368] In Ś. 1194, Mākanadēvilaṁmangāru set up the image of Gōpīśvaradēva in the name of her father at Taṁmalūr.[369] Nāmadēva Paṇḍita, a subordinate of Gaṇapatidēva Mahārāja, consecrated the image of god Vankēśvaradēva at Durgī and named it after his father.[370]

Some devotees installed images for the merit of their family. A record from Śrīśailam mentions the installation of a linga named Triyaṁbaka, for the prosperity of his family by Anantarasa, the son of Bukkagōparasa, a minister of Harihara.[371]

In some of instances devotees installed images in their own names. The famous Kākatīya king, Gaṇapatīdēva, consecrated at Caitrapura *alias* Mōṭupalli, an image called Kumāra Gaṇapēśvara named after himself.[372] In Ś. 1131, Mēlāṁbikā, the sister of Kākatīya Gaṇapati, and the queen of Ekkaḍimalla Rudra, installed an image of Mailāṁbikēśvara in her own name at Tripurāntakam.[373]

Some devotees set up images for the religious merit of kings and their elders. In Ś. 1212, Cōḍamallidēva mahārāja consecrated the image of Gōpīnātha in Bhīmavaram, for the religious merit of his suzerain, king Pratāpa Rudradēva Mahārāja.[374] In Ś. 1103, Gaṇapamadēvī installed god Rudrēśvara for the merit of *mahāmaṇḍalēśvara* Kōṭa Bētarāja.[375] The Pariccēdi King, Kusumarāja, set up god Gauḍīśvara for the merit of his wife, Sabbama, at Prattipāḍu.[376] In Ś. 1173,

361. 275 of 1949-50. Turimēḷḷa.
362. 325 of 1936-37. Peddapulivaṟṟu.
363. *S.I.I* V. 116. Rājahmundry.
364. *K.S.* App. Ins. No. 2. Kāzipēṭ.
365. *Tel. Ins.* I. M. 9. Rāmannapēṭ.
366. *Ibid.*, I. M. 15. Būrugugaḍḍa.
367. 343 of 1932-33. Vaḍḍavalli.
368. 301 of 1930-31. Kaṁbhaṁpāḍu.
369. *N.D.I.* I. Darsi 72. Taṁmalūru.
370. 306 of 1930-31. Nāgulāvaram.
371. 55 of 1943-44. Śrīśailam.
372. *E.I.* XXVII. pp. 193-197. Mōṭupalli.
373. *S.I.I.* X. 254. Tripurāntakam.
374. *N.D.I.* I. Darsi. 61. Bhīmavaram.
375. *S.I.I.* IV. 930. Yenamadala.
376. *Ibid.*, X. 269. Prattipāḍu.

Damanāmātya installed god Sūrēśvaradēva for the merit of Annaya, the *Kāryābharaṇa* of the Kākatīya king, Gaṇapati, at Kōnātamatkūru.[377] In Ś. 1109, Nāmireḍḍi set up the gods Nāmēśvara. Aitēśvara and Kāṭēśvara at Nāgulapāḍu for the merit of himself and his parents.[378]

Images were also set up for the religious merit of *gurus*. A Vēngaḷappa set up the image of the goddess Lakṣmīdēvī in the Venkaṭēśvara temple at Koyiḷḷakāluva for the religious merit of his *guru*, Tāḷḷapākam Tirumalayyangār.[379]

The installation and reinstallation of deities went along with temple building. Sometimes deities were installed in temples built for this purpose and at others at various places in the precincts of a temple as *parivāradēvatas.*

2. *Installation of Śaivite Deities*

The idols of Śiva under various names were consecrated at various times and various places. Cintāmaṇi Kēśavanāyudu, the ruler of Punungōḍu, consecrated the image of Nīlakaṇṭhēśvara in Ś. 1503.[380] During the reign of the famous Vijayanagara king, Kṛṣṇarāya, Cittamarusuṁgāru installed the image of Angaḍivīrēśvara in Ś. 1440 at Peddakākāni.[381] The Cāgi chief, Pōta, consecrated god Viśvēśvara at Guḍimeṭla on the bank of the Kṛṣṇā.[382] Kandūri Sōmaladēvī, Bhīmarasa and Gangādēvī installed the image of Gangēśvara in the village of Gangāpūr and *Cakravarti* Permāḍirāya, Tribhuvanamalla consecrated the image of Gangēśvara at Sōmaśila.[383] In Ś. 895 *mahāmaṇḍalēśvara* Sōpermāḍi, who was governing from Korapāṭi, installed god Bobbēśvara at Korapōlu.[384] The image of Rājāvīrēśvara was set up in a temple at Drākshārāma by Rāma mantri.[385] In Ś. 1092, a minister named Gangādhara, installed the images of Samartakēśvara and Śiva at Mantrakūṭa and the image of god Acyuta with twenty four *mūrtis.*[386] Rudrasēnāpati consecrated god Rudrēśvara in Ś. 1135 at Ōrugallu.[387] *Mahāmaṇḍalēśvara* Kumāra Mayidēva, the disciple of Nēmicandradēva, consecrated the image of Pārśvadēva.[388] In Ś. 1143 *Paṭṭasāhaṇādhipati* Mallaya Śāhiṇi installed the god Citramēḍi Śrī Jaśamēśvaradēva in the middle of the city of Vellanūru.[389] Śrīmat Śānta Śivagurudēva installed the image of Mahēśvaradēva in Ś. 1176 at Tripurāntakam.[390] In Ś. 1721, Rājāyārlagaḍḍa Ankinēḍu Bahadūr consecrated the image of Vidyāśan-

377. *Ibid.*, X. 337. Konātamatkūru.
378. *K.I.A.P.* 12; *Hyd. Arch. Ser.* No. I. No. 27. Nāgulapāḍu.
379. 396 of 1938-39. Kōyiḷḷakālava.
380. *N.D.I.* I. Ātmakūr. 54. Punungōḍu.
381. *S.I.I.* IV. 702. Peddakākāni.
382. *S,I.I.* X. 542. Guḍimeṭla.
383, *Tel. Ins.* I. Ch. 32. Gangāpūr.
384. *K.I.A.P.* Md. 5. Korapōlu.
385. *S.I.I.* IV. 1351. Drākshārāma.
386. *Hyd. Arch. Ser.* 13. No. 56. Karīmnagar.
387. *K.S.* App. Ins. 18. Pālaṁpēṭ.
388. 154 of 1946-47. Hyderabad.
389. 18 of 1953-54. Mēḍikurti.
390. 14 of 1953-54. Kōḍumurṭi.

karēśvara, the family deity of the Dēvarakōṭa chiefs on the banks of the Śivaganga tank for the private worship of the chiefs of the family.[391] Eṟṟamanāyanimgāru, the co-son-in-law of Guṇḍamanāyanimgāru, installed god Tripurāntakēśvara at Ālugaḍapa in Ś. 1128.[392] In Ś. 1145, the image of Kalyāṇacandraśēkara was set up in the temple of god Bhīmēśvara of Cāḷukya-Bhīmavaram by Dēvaya.[393] A seṭṭi installed the image of Pinnēśvaradēva at Peddaganjām in Ś. 1192.[394] In the 65th year of the reign of the later Cāḷukyan king, Tribhuvanamalla, Vijayāditya Gōvinda installed the image of god Vīravijayēśvara at Donakallu.[395] In Ś. 1088, Mallināyaka consecrated god Mallikārjuna in a temple on the hill at Ikkūru.[396] God Mallināthadēva was installed in Ś. 1159 at Omgūru by Nala Nahīḍu, a servant of *mahāmaṇḍalēśvara* Kāmayadēva mahārāja of the Mukkamṭi-Kāḍuveṭṭi family.[397] In the 17th year of the reign of the Cāḷukyan prince, Viṣṇuvardhana, a Caṭṭapa consecrated god Pārthīśvara on the Indrakīla Hill at Vijayavāḍa.[398] In Ś. 1037, god Sōmēśvara was installed on the occasion of a solar eclipse at Kopparam by Māra, the minister of the Cōḍa chief Kannaradēva.[399]

3. *Vaiṣṇava Deities*

Abundant information is available from numerous records regarding the installation of Vaiṣṇava deities. In Ś. 1077, the Cennakēśava image was installed in the Pamiḍipāḍu-agrahāram.[400] The image of Prasannakēśava was installed in Ś. 1092 by the side of Rudrēśvara at Hanumakoṇḍa by Gadādhara, the minister of Kākatīya Gaṇapati.[401] In the same year, he installed the image of Buddha as an *avatāra* of Viṣṇu at Hiḍimbāśrama. The image of Cennakēśvaraperumāḷ was consecrated at Nāgalāvaram by Immaḍidēvarāya in Ś. 1190.[402] In Ś. 1196 four individuals installed Varada-Gōpīnātha at Amgaḍa.[403] In Ś. 1204, god Śrī Gōpīnātha was consecrated at Vijayanagaram.[404] The images of Rāma and Lakṣmaṇa were installed in Ś. 1256 in the temple of Gōpīnātha at Rājamahēndravaram.[405] In Ś. 1331, the image of Śrī Kaṇṭha Rāmēśvaradēva was set up at Pālēṭikoṇḍa by Vemmanēṇḍu Vennapamgāru.[406] In Ś. 1458, god Gōpālakṛṣṇa was installed in a *tōppu* or garden situated in Tiruchānūr, also known as Vādirājupuram, a suburb of

391. 401 of 1932-33. Śivaganga.
392. *Tel. Ins.* I. M. 7. Ālugaḍapa.
393. *S.I.I.* V. 32. Cāḷukya-Bhīmavaram.
394. *Ibid.*, X. 427. Peddaganjām.
395. *Ibid.*, IX. 236. Dōnakallu.
396. *Ibid.*, X. 159. Ikkūru.
397. 71 of 1939-40. Ogūru.
398. *S.I.I.* X. 16. Bezavāḍa.
399. *Ibid.*, X. 73. Tangēḍumalli.
400. *S.I.I.* X. Pamiḍipāḍu.
401. *Hyd. Arch. Ser.* 13. No. 56. Karīmnagar.
402. *N.D.I.* II. Kanigiri. 24. Nāgalāvaram.
403. *Hyd. Arch. Ser.* No. 19. Ng. 2. Amgaḍa.
404. *S.I.I.* X. 718. Vijayanagaram.
405. *Ibid.*, V. 119. Rājahmundry.
406. *N.D.I.* II. Kanigiri. 34. Perugupalli.

Tirupati.[407] In Ś. 1203, Naraharitīrtha, a *sanyāsin*, and a disciple of Ānandatīrtha, consecrated the image of god Yōgānanda-Narasiṁha in a shrine before the temple of god Kūrmanātha.[408] In Ś. 1635, Tiṁma Reḍḍi of Peddanapāḍu got made the silver and gold images of Madanagōpāla, Kṛṣṇa and installed them in the temple at Peddanapāḍu.[409] A Barugugāru set up an image of Cakra Perumāḷ on the steps in Ś. 1564 at Tirupati.[410] In Kali 4628 an image of Trivikrama was consecrated at Ikṣupuri by king Viṣṇuvardhana of the Cāḷukyan family.[411] The image of Viṣṇu was installed in Ś. 1605 at Gaṇapavaram.[412] An inscription records that the sons of the *Kāṁpu* of the Natavāḍi chief, Pōta, installed god Nārāyaṇa at Koṇakanchi.[413]

4. *Dēvī*

Information is also available about the installation of the images of Dēvī of both the Śaiva and Vaiṣṇava pantheon. A certain *Dānakartta* Subbayya and Venkayya of the Kōmūri *Namaśivayavaṁśa* consecrated the images of goddess Satya-Prasūnāṁbā in Ś. 1334 at Ponnupalli.[414] In Ś. 1348 the image of Gaurī Paramēśvarī, made of *Uttamanīlaśila* or black granite, was installed in the sanctum of the Kumārārāma Bhīmēśvaranagari.[415] The image of goddess Bāla-Tripurasundarī was consecrated in Ś. 1719 at Mācherla.[416] In Ś. 1265, Adidaṁmalaṁgāru, a commander-in-chief, installed a golden image of Gaurī under the name of Trailōkyasundarī in the temple of Tripurāntakam.[417] A minister, named Rudra, set up the image of Durgā at Hanumakoṇḍa.[418] Rājā Yārlagaḍḍa Ankinēḍu Bahadūr installed the image of Nagarapurī-Durgā—Bhavanī, the family deity of the Dēvarakōṭa chiefs, on the bank of the Śivaganga tank for the private worship of the chief.[419] An inscription belonging to the reign of the Eastern Gānga king, Vajrahasta, refers to the installation of the goddess, Bhagavatī at Cintāmaṇi.[420]

The Dēvī images of the Vaiṣṇava pantheon were also installed at various places at various times. In Ś. 1186, the image of Siddha Mahālakṣmī was installed for the prosperity of *Mahāsāmanta* Ceṛaku Immaḍi Viśvanāthadēva at Amrābād.[421] The image of Lakṣmīdēvi and Bhūmidēvī were consecrated in Ś. 1418 in the temple of Cennakēśava of Rāvūru.[422] In Ś. 1569, Bhāṣyam Rāghavācārya, the grandson of Appalācārya, the local *Sthānāpati*, installed the image of Lakṣmī, at Śrīkūrmam as

407. *T.T.D.I.* IV. 94. Tirupati.
408. *E.I.* VI. Pp. 260-266. Śrīkūrmam.
409. 262 of 1937-38. Peddanapāḍu.
410. *N.D.I.* III. Podill, 13. Gārladinne.
411. *S.I.I.* VI. 202. Peddacherukūru.
412. *Ibid.*, IV. 951. Gaṇapavaram.
413. *Ibid.*, X. 544. Kavutāvāri-Agrahāram.
414. 326 of 1936-37. Ponnupalli.
415. *S.I.I.* V. 31. Bhīmavaram.
416. 12 of 1941-42. Mācherla.
417. *S.I.I.* X. 479. Tripurāntakam.
418. *Hyd. Arch. Ser.* No. 19. Wg. 2. Hanumakoṇḍa.
419. 40 of 1932-35. Śivanganga.
420. 359 of 1934-35. Chintāmaṇi.
421. *Corp. Ins. Tel.* Mn. 5. Amrābād.
422. *S.I.I.* X. 730. Santarāvūru.

there was no such image before.[423] The idol of Lakṣmī was set up at Gaṇapavaram in Ś. 1605.[424] A certain Vēngaḷappa installed the image of goddess Lakṣmīdēvī for the merit of his *guru*, Tāḷḷapākam Tirumalayyangār, at Moyiḷḷakālava.[425]

5. *Parivāradēvatas*

Equally interesting information is available about the installation of the *Parivāradēvatas* or attendant deities. In Ś. 1052, the image of Gaṇapati was set up at the western gateway of the temple at Drākshārāma.[426] The minister of the Kākatīya Rudra, named Gangādhara installed the images of Vighnēśvara at Hanumakoṇḍa.[427] A Sevvusāni consecrated the image of Śrī Vighnēśvara in the *Nṛtta-maṇṭapa* of the temple of Śrī Kapilēśvaravāmi at Tirupati in Ś. 1485.[428] In Ś. 1475, the image of god Kumārasvāmi was consecrated at Chēbrōlu.[429] The Kākatīya king, Prōla, installed Jalandhara Bhairava on the hill at Inugurti.[430] The image of Bhairava was set up by a merchant, named Muddanaseṭṭi Gangamalliseṭṭi of Rājamahēndravaram at Śrīśailam.[431] Avagaṇḍiseṭṭi, the son of Cōḍa, consecrated an image of Bhṛngi on the roof of the *maṇṭapa* of the temple of god Jaladhīśa of Ghaṇṭaśālā.[432] The sons of the *kāṁpu* of the Natavāḍi chief, Pōtarāja, installed the image of Brahmā at Koṇakanchi.[433] Koṁmanārya, the son of minister Rāma, set up the image of Yajñēśvara in Ś. 1352 at Chuṇḍi.[434] Mandepūṇḍi Sūrapa nāyaka consecrated the Nandi image in the temple of Sōmanāthadēva at Narnēpāḍu.[435]

Several Vaiṣṇava *parivāradēvatas* were also installed at various places. In Ś. 1429, Mukkapāṭi Singana, the son of Pinna Gōpaya and Baramāṁbikā, and the *mantri* of the village of Bhrigumaṇḍa, set up the image of Hanumān.[436] Narahari-dēva, the *Sthānāpati* of the temple of god Rāmacandrarāya, consecrated the image of Hanumān at Peddanapāḍu.[437] In Ś. 1483, the *Sabhaiyār* belonging to different *gōtras* prepared and installed an image of Hanumān at Tirupati.[438] In Ś. 1479, Vōbularāju of *Sōmavaṁśa* and Ātrēya *gōtra* consecrated the image of Egu Perumāḷ at Veludurti.[439] The image of Garuḍāḷvār was set up by Krānja Pōtarāja in front of the temple of Cennakēśava on the bank of Sagilēru in Paṇḍivīḍu.[440] On the 3rd

423. *Ibid*, V. 929. Śrīkūrmam.
424. *Ibid.*, IV. 951. Gaṇapavaram.
425. 394 of 1938-39. Moyiḷḷakālava.
426. *S.I.I.* IV. 1374. Drākshārāma.
427. *Hyd Arch. Ser.* No. 19. Wg. 2. Hanumakoṇḍa.
428. *T.T.D.I.* V. 172. Kapilatīrtham.
429. *S.I.I.* VI. 105. Chēbrōlu.
430. *Tel. Ins.* I, 3. Inugurti.
431. 23 of 1915. Śrīśailam.
432. 850 of 1917. Ghaṇṭaśālā.
433. *S.I.I.* X. 544, Koṇakanchi.
434. *N.D.I.* II. Kandukūr. 17. Old Chuṇḍi.
435. 328 of 1932-33. Narnēpāḍu.
436. 262 of 1932-33. Bhrigubaṇḍa.
437. 266 of 1937-38. Peddanapāḍu.
438. *T.T.D.I.* III. 20. Tirupati.
439. 296 of 1937-38. Veluḍurti.
440. 44 of 1941-42. Paṇdivīḍu.

day of the dark fortnight of the *Śrāvaṇam* of the year *Kīlaka*, a certain Anumantu caused to be made an image of Sanjīvarāya in Chintalātukūru and consecrated it.[441]

6. *Dvārapālakas*

The images of *Dvārapālakas* were also installed by the devotees. In Ś. 1470, a Nandyāla Nāraparāja installed *Dvārapālaka* images in the inner shrine of Śrī Gōvindarāja of Tirupati.[442] The images of *Dvārapālaka* were made and dedicated to the temple at Kopparti by the stone-cutter, Tippābaṭṭuḍu, the son of Tippābaṭṭuḍu of Tāḍigoṭlu and the *agasāla* or local artisan.[443]

441. *N.D.I.* III. Rāpūr 9. Chintalātukūru.
442. *T.T.D.I.* I. 122. Tirupati.
443. 328 of 1938-39. Kopparti.

3

GIFTS MADE TO TEMPLES

If the construction of temples and the installation of deities were acts of religious merit, any help rendered for the maintenance of temple and the conduct of various items of service therein was considered an act of greater merit. This help was of various forms. Inscriptions found in various parts of the country and ranging in dates from the 9th to the 19th centuries contain numerous instances of varieties of gifts made to temples.

The most important and substantial gift was of villages and land. Kings and high placed individuals made a gift of groups of villages, while others were content with the gift of individual villages, parts of villages, their own shares of villages or plots of land as *vṛttis*. This variety of gift included gardens for growing flowers and vegetables and areca-nut and betel-leaf gardens. Another variety was the gift of house-sites, tanks and canals. Some devotees made gifts of gold, as well as gold dust for several purposes. One very important form of gifts was the gift of coins of several kinds like *māḍa*, *cinnam*, *niṣka*, *ṭanka*, *rūka* etc. Another variety of gifts, mostly made by the well-to-do, was the gift of various ornaments and cloths for adorning the deity. Many kinds of utensils used for cooking, holding of offerings, as well as for the conduct of worship were also endowed to temples. One more popular example of gifts was various taxes collected in villages and from particular communities and tolls and customs duties levied on articles of merchandise. Auxiliaries of worship like flower garlands, *vinjāmaras* and cauries were also given. A popular form of gifts was the gift of lamps to be burnt either daily or on particular occasions. This often included the gift of lamp-stands of different metals and shapes. Animals like cows and buffaloes were given for the supply of ghee for the burning of lamps. A variety of perfumes were required in connection with the ablution and decoration of the deity. Devotees arranged for the supply of all these items.

A. *Purposes of Gift Making*

1. *Religious Merit*

There was an immense variety in the purpose for which these gifts were made. Generally, the donors aspired for merit, for themselves or their dead ancestors or for their masters and overlords in making these gifts. In Ś. 1131, a gift was made by *mahāpradhāni* Talava Pōla Bhīma nāyuḍu to god Tripurāntaka mahādēva for the merit of his father, Dāmanāyaka, his mother, Kāmasāni, and for the welfare of the king.[1] The *lenkas, sahavāsis* and others who had come to Deṁdulūru, made a gift in Ś. 1234, to god Bhīmśēvara for the merit of king, Pratāparūdra Mahārāja.[2] Tiṁmarāja Nandayya made a gift in Ś. 1448, to god Śrī Narasiṁhadēva, for the merit of king Acyutarāya.[3] In Ś. 1447, *mahāmaṇḍalēśvara* Dantalūri Cāgaṇṭidēva mahārājulu made a gift to god Hanumantadēva for the religious merit of his father, Vōjularāju.[4] A Rāpuri Rāghavareḍḍi gāru made a gift to god Sōmēśvara in Ś. 1448 for the merit of his parents.[5] A certain Doṁmarl Pedaraju made a gift to god Cennakēśāva in Ś. 1473 for the merit of the twenty-four families of his community.[6]

2. *Food Offerings*

A large majority of these gifts were made for making food offerings of various kinds to the deities daily. King Karikālacōḷa made arrangements for certain offerings to be made to god Tripurāntaka at Tripurāntakam in Ś. 1028.[7] Kumāra Anantajiyyana made arrangements in Ś. 1192 for an *avasaranaivēdya* daily to the god of Siṁhāchalam.[8] In Ś. 1281, Śrīgiri Nāyaniṁgāru made provision for the supply of midday offerings in the temple of Mallikārjuna at Mandaḍi.[9] Provision was made in Ś. 1390, for offering eight *sandhis* by Vallabhayadēva mahārāja to god Śrī Venkaṭamuḍaiyān of Tirumala.[10] A Singariyaṁgāru made necessary arrangements in Ś. 1453 for *dadhyōdana-avasaram* to god Rāmēśvara of Tāḍiparati.[11] A record from Vāḍapalli, dated in Ś. 1530, mentions that arrangements were made for the supply of daily offerings to god Narasiṁhasvāmin by Talapunūri Kōnappa, who was the head of the administration under Mālik Amil-ul-mulk.[12]

1. 93 of 1929-30. Kottapālem.
2. 268 of 1952-53. Elūru.
3. *N.D.I.* II. Nellore 34-A. Koṁmarapūḍi.
4. *Ibid.*, II. Nellore. 122. Vellāṇṭi.
5. *Ibid.*, II. Kanigiri. 33. Alavalapāḍu.
6. 114 of 1945-46. Alavalapāḍu.
   Similar Examples
   341 of 1938-39. Chintakoṁmudinne.
   N.D.I. II. Kandukur 78. Śingarāyakoṇḍa.
   59 of 1929-30. Guṭṭikoṇḍa.
7. *S.I.I.* X. 62. Tripurāntakam.
8. *Ibid.*, VI. 712 Siṁhāchalam.
9. 65 of 1929-30. Mandaḍi.
10. *T.T.D.I.* II. 35. Tirumala.
11. *S.I.I.* IV. 801. Tāḍpatri.
12. 56 of App. E. of 1941-42. Vāḍapalli.

3. *Offerings on Special Occasions*

Provision was also made for various offerings to be made on special occasions like festivals etc. In Ś. 1215, Vallabha Naṁbyarulu gave 2 *gaṇḍamāḍas* for a food offering to be made on the *Akṣatṛtīya* day to the god of Siṁhāchalam.[13] In Ś. 1367, a cash deposit was made in the temple treasury for certain offerings during *Brahmōtsavam*, celebrated for god Śrī Venkaṭēśa at Tirumala.[14] Provision was made for offerings to god Gōvindarāja of Tirupati during the 20 days of the Summer festival celebrated in Ś. 1392.[15] In Ś. 1405, arrangements were made by Kandāḍai Appacciyār Anna for providing offerings to god Śrī Venkaṭēśa of Tirumala on each occasion of *Punarpūsam* star occurring every month.[16] In Ś. 1408 provision was made for the supply of offerings to god Tiruvēnkaṭamuḍaiyān of Tirumala on each of the thirty days of the festival, *Tiruppuḷḷi-eḷucci*, conducted during the *Mārgaḷi* month.[17] A record from the Gōvindarāja temple, dated in Ś. 1438, states that provision was made for the offering of thirteen *appāpaḍi* to Śrī Gōvindarājan of Tirupati on the thirteen days of the star *Mṛgaśīrṣa*, one *atirasapaḍi* and one *sidaipaḍi* on the day of *Uri-āḍi*.[18] Śrīrāmayyan, made provision in Ś. 1449, at the suggestion of his *ācārya* for offerings to the processional image of Śrī Venkaṭēśa when he visits the *maṇṭapa* constructed by him at Tirumala.[19] In Ś. 1461, Venkaṭatturaivān made arrangements for the supply of offerings to god Śrī Varāhasvāmi enshrined at Tirumala on the 30 days of *Dhanurmāsapūja*.[20] Arrangements were made in Ś. 1466 by Rāmānuja Tiṁmayyar for offerings during *Adhyayanōtsavam*, celebrated in the temple at Tirumala.[21] A Venkamarasa reḍḍi, made provision in Ś. 1506 for making offerings to god Gōvindarāja on the day of Avilāli garden festival newly instituted by him on the prescribed days.[22] In the 64th year of the reign of the Cāḷukya-Cōḷa king, Viṣṇuvardhana, an offering named *aravamudu* was arranged by a subordinate of the king for god Rājanārāyaṇa of Cāḷukya-Bhīmavaram on the occasion of *Tiruśrādhaṇam*.[23]

4. *Feeding the Staff*

The temple received many gifts for feeding its staff, as well as others who were dependant on it. An inscription from Kopparam, dated in Ś. 1037, mentions the gift made to a dance master, named Muppayanāyaka and another gift made to a woman dancer attached to the local temple.[24] Another from Nādiṇḍla dated in

13. *S.I.I.* VI. 1140. Siṁhāchalam.
14. *T.T.D.I.* II. 1. Tirumala.
15. *Ibid.*, II. 45. Tirupati.
16. *Ibid.*, II. 80. Tirumala.
17. *Ibid.*, II. 86. Tirumala.
18. *Ibid.*, III. 208. Tirupati.
19. *Ibid.*, III. 172. Tirupati.
20. *Ibid.*, IV. 138. Tirumala.
21. *Ibid.*, V. 26. Tirumala.
22. *Ibid.*, VI. 6. Tirupati.
23. *S.I.I.* V. 65. Cāḷukya-Bhīmavaram.
24. *Ibid.*, X. 91. Kopparam.

Ś. 1061, states that a gift was made to the musicians, Jakke and Meḍiyam.[25] In Ś. 1053 a gift was made to a *pūjāri* of the temple of Mallēśvara of Bezavāḍa by Nāgadēvuṇḍu.[26] In Ś. 1070 a village was given to god Bhīmēśvara of Koṇidena for the maintenance of its staff.[27] Dēvarāya endowed *vṛttis* for the maintenance of the staff in the temple of god Mallēśvara at Nāguluppalapāḍu in Ś. 1161.[28] A gift of land was made in Ś. 1180 by *Rāyajīvarakṣa sāmanta* Javēśa Annaladēva to *Sthānāpati* Sadāśiva gurudēva, the son of Śāntīśvara Gurudēva.[29] Viśvēśvara Śivācārya, the religious preceptor of Kākatīya Gaṇapati, gave land to 10 dancers, 2 *mukharis,* 8 players of *mardala*, to a Kashmīri singer, 14 women singers, 6 people who beat *karaḍā* and other instruments in the temple of Viśvēśvara of Gōḷagi in Ś. 1183.[30] Provision was made for the maintenance of people, who played on *vīṇā* every day before the god of Śrīkūrmam.[31] In Ś. 1301, 5 *puṭṭis* of land was granted to Umādēvī for serving the god at Siṁhāchalam during the *Gangābhōga*, instituted by king Vīranarasiṁha of the Eastern Gānga family.[32] In Ś. 1324, a Bhaṇḍāru seṭṭi set up a *ghaṭikayantra* and a bell in the temple of Gōpīnātha inside of the fort of Rājamahēndranagara and granted eight *puṭṭis* of land to four *brāhmaṇas* for performing the service of *ghaḍiyārōpacāra* to indicate the hours of worship in the temple.[33] A sum of 25 *gaṇḍamāḍas* was given towards the salary of the person who supplied garlands for the god of Śrīkūrmam in Ś. 1338 by Śāntēśvara, the *Śrīkaraṇam* of the Eastern Gānga king, Vīrabhānudēva.[34] In Ś. 1339, in the reign of the same king, two villages were endowed for the maintenance of staff, who recited the *Purāṇa* by Aṁman *mahāsēnapati.*[35] In Ś. 1356 a field was given to the keeper of the garden of god Rājanārāyaṇa of Bhīmavaram by Jiyyamallasānaṁmā, the wife of Vēmāreḍḍi.[36] A lady devotee of god Raghunāyaka of Bhadrācalam gave a village in Ś. 1546 for the maintenance of temple servants.[37]

5. *Supply of Articles of Worship*

Most of the gifts were intended for providing articles of worship like garlands, requirements of the *tirumanjanam*, lighting lamps, decoration of the deity etc. In Ś. 1269, a gift was made for the supply of a garland 4 cubits long to the god of Siṁhāchalam.[38] A gift was made in Ś. 1324 for the supply of a *tirutōmālā* to the

25. *Ibid.*, X. 107. Nādiṇḍla.
26. *Ibid.*, VI. 762. Bezavāda.
27. *S.I.I.* VI, 610. Koṇidena.
28. *N.D.I.* III. Ongōle. 86. Nāguluppalapāḍu.
29. 301 of 1930-31. Kaṁbhaṁpāḍu.
30. *S.I.I.* X. 395. Mālkāpuram.
31. *Ibid.*, V. 861. Śrīkūrmam.
32. *Ibid.*, VI. 730. Siṁhāchalam.
33. 9 of App. E. of 1939-40. Tāḷḷūru.
34. *S.I.I.* V. 721. Śrīkūrmam.
35. *Ibid.*, VI. 1040. Siṁhāchalam.
36. *Ibid.*, V. 34. Cāḷukya-Bhīmavaram.
37. 305 of 1920. Bhadrāchalam.
38. *S.I.I.* VI. 742. Siṁhāchalam.

same god.[39] In Ś. 1301, gifts were made for the supply of the articles required for the *tirumanjanam* to god Śrī Venkaṭēśa of Tirumala.[40] A gift was made in Ś. 1397 for the purpose of conducting *tirumanjanam* to god Gōvindarāja on the day of *Kṛttikā*, being the day of the *Attai-tirunakṣatram* of Tirumangai Āḷvār.[41] In Ś. 1468, a devotee, named Tāḷḷapākkam Tiruvēnkaṭanāthar, made provision for the *gandhōdaka-tirumanjanam* or *candana-abhiṣēkam* for god Śrī Venkaṭēśa of Tirumala during the five days of the marriage festival.[42] In Ś. 1322, provision was made for lighting a row of lamps in the temple of Mallikārjunadēva at Śrīparvata by seven brothers of the goldsmith caste residing at Guṇḍamangaḷāpura, during the reign of Mallinātha.[43] In Ś. 1218, a gift was made by Udayamāhādēvī the daughter of Mahādēvacakravarti and the queen of Kōna Gaṇapatidēva, for burning 1000 lamps, on the occasion of the *Śivarātri* in the temple of Pālakol.[44] Pinavoḍaya mahādevī, the daughter of Mahādēva Cakravarti of Niḍudaprōlu made provision in Ś. 1228 for a lamp in the same temple.[45]

6. *Maintenance of Auxiliary Institutions*

Some gifts were intended for the maintenance of auxiliary institutions like *maṭhas, satras,* temple gardens etc. In S. 1072, a gift of land was made to the choultry attached to the *Āṇḍāri-maṭham* at Drākshārāma by a certain Cōḍagangabairāgi for feeding visiting ascetics.[46] A village was given in S. 1072 for feeding the visiting ascetics of the choultry to the west of the Bhīmēśvara temple at Drākshārāma on the occasion of the combination of *Siṁhabṛhaspati* by *mahāmaṇḍalēśvara* Kōna Satyarāja.[47] In S. 1075, Bhīmarāju, the son of Satyarāju, gave 33 *kha* of land in Kundūru, for feeding the ascetics living in the *Tiruvīdhi-maṭha* during the marriage festival of Bhīmēśvara of Drākshārāma along with the *ayams.*[48] In S. 1168, a gift was made by certain individuals to gods Kēdāradēva and Gaṇapatidēva of Nandipāḍu for providing rest houses to travellers.[49] In Ś. 1478, Koṇḍayadēva mahārāja granted the village of Gurijipalle in the *Dūpāti-sīma* for maintaining a *Rāmānujakūṭam* in the shrine of Bhāṣyakāra within the temple of Ahōbalēśvara at Diguva-Tirupati.[50] The village of Jakkireḍḍipalle was given by Aṁbadēvarāju for the upkeep of the Jangam choultry and Brāhman choultry at Bezavāḍa.[51] Viśvēśvara Śivācārya granted land to the brāhman choultry, maternity home and sanitorium in the new village, named Gōḷagi constituted by him.[52] Sarvēśvarayyaṁgāru made a gift in Ś.

39. *Ibid.*, VI 742. Siṁhāchalam.
40. *T.T.D.I.* I. 184. Tirumala.
41. *Ibdi.*, II. 62. Tirupati.
42. *Ibid.*, V. 71. Tirumala.
43. 232 of 1930-31. Guṇḍugallu.
44. *S.I I.* V. 125. Pālakol.
45. *Ibid.*, V. 124. Pālakol.
46. *Ibid.*, IV. 1102. Drākshārāma.
47. *Ibid.*, IV. 1104. Drākshārāma.
48. *Ibid.*, IV. 1092. Drākshārāma.
49. *N.D.I.* III. Udayagiri. 14. Nandipāḍu.
50. 61 of 1915. Ahōbalam.
51. *S.I.I.* X. 728. Zakkaṁpūḍi.
52. *Ibid.*, X. 395. Mālkāpuram.

1208 to Mahādēva for maintaining a feeding house at Ālampūr.[53] In Ś. 1440, a gift was made to the *Bhōgasatra* of god Śrī Narasiṁhanātha of Siṁhāchalam.[54] The *Brinjaris* or salt traders made a gift in Ś. 1668 to maintain a *maṭha* at Bandar Rāmayapaṭṭaṇam.[55] In the reign of Rājēndracōḍa of Velanāḍu arrangements were made by a subordinate of the king for feeding 5 ascetics in the *maṇṭapa* in the *tiruvīdhi* of Drākshārāma.[56] Valavan Mārtāṇḍa Muvundavalār granted the *raṭṭaḍikam* of the village of Krunduṟṟu and of *pannasa* land in the village of Vella and Babbaravāḍa in the *Prōla-nāḍu* for feeding 100 people including the teachers in the *Tiruvīdhi-maṭha* at Drākshārāma.[57] In the 33rd year of the reign of the Cāḷukya-Cōḷa king, Kulōttunga, a Pallavarāju, the subordinate of the king, made arrangements for the feeding of the *tapasyins*, and brāhmans in the vicinity of the Brahmēśvara temple of the same place.[58]

7. *Maintenance of Gardens*

Several kinds of gardens were maintained by the temple by receiving gifts from devotees. In Ś. 1092 a gift was made for the maintenance of a flower garden in Chaṭipuram to god Cōḍīśvara mahādēva.[59] An individual made provision in Ś. 1199 for maintaining a fruit and flower garden for god Sūrēśvara at Rāvipāḍu.[60] In Ś. 1299, a gift of land was made for the maintenance of a garden for the god at Palivela by a devotee named Gumḍayamallu.[61] A Dēvarāya Anantarāju made provision for a garden f r god Śṛngārarāya of Mutssumaṟṟi.[62] Arrangements were made in Ś.1385 for the gift of *prasāḍam* each day to the *dāsar* for cultivating the red lotus in a pond at Tirumala.[63] A record from Śrīkūrmam mentions the gift made for the maintenance of a flower garden for god Śrīkūrmanātha of Śrīkūrmam.[64] In Ś. 1313, a gift was made for the setting up of a *bṛndāvanam* to god Rājanārāyaṇa

53. 320 of 1936-37. Malyāla.
54. *S.I.I.* VI. 697. Siṁhāchalam
55. *N.D.I.* I. C.P. 4. Rāmayapaṭṇam.
56. *S.I I.* IV. 1054. Drākshārāma.
57. *Ibid.*, IV. 1281. Drākshārāma.
58. *E.I.* XXII. pp. 138-145. Drākshārāma.
    Similar Examples
    29 of 1929-30. Pedagārlapāḍu.
    S.I.I. X. 404. Santamaguḷūru.
    S.I I. IV. 1296. Drākshārāma.
    Ibid., IV. 1239. Drākshārāma.
    201 of 1950-51. Vangamūru.
    217 of 1937-38. Chiḍipirāla.
    E.I. XXV. pp. 194-198. Santabaṁmāli.
    K.I.A.P. 8. Lēmulavāḍa.
    134 of 1945-46. Nagūru.
59. *S.I.I.* X. 173. Śrīrāmpuram.
60. *Ibid.*, X. 442. Rāvipāḍu.
61. *Ibid.* V, 115. Palivela.
62. 431 of 1940-41. Mutssumṟṟi.
63. *T.T.D.I.* II. Tirumala.
64. *S.I.I.* V. 1240 Śrīkūrmam.

at Bhīmavaram.[65] In Ś. 1319, Gōli Sōmāreḍḍi, set up the *Oḍḍa-Vasanta bṛndāvanam* at a cost of 20 *ṭankas* to god Sarpanātha of Sarpavaram.[66]

8. *Celebration of Festivals*

One important activity in the temple was the celebration of a number of festivals either by the temple or at the instance of the devotees. In Ś. 1096 an individual instituted the *Kottamāvāsyayātra* and the *Māghadarśanōtsava* for god Bhīmēśvara of Drākshārāma.[67] Provision was made for the celebration of the *Śrī Jayanti* festival, in Ś. 1168 in the temple of Siṁhāchalam.[68] A Jihari nāyaka made provision in the temple treasury for the celebration of the *Kumārapunnami* festival every year to the god at Śrīkūrman in Ś.1199.[69]. The *Bāhattaraniyōgālavāru* of the Tripurāntaka temple, made a gift in Ś. 1216, for the celebration of the marriage festival for god Tripurāntakēśvara and his consort, Trailōkyasundarī.[70] In Ś. 1395. Sāḷuva Narasiṁharāya Uḍaiyār instituted the *Ḍōlāmahōtsava* for 5 days for Śrī Venkaṭēśa of Tirumala.[71] In Ś. 1410, provision was made for the celebration of a festival named *tirukkoḍi-tiruṇāḷ* for god Tiruvēnkaṭamuḍaiyān of Tirumala.[72] Provision was made in Ś. 1452 for the celebration of *Brahmōtsavam* for the same god for a period of twelve days from the day of *ankurārpaṇam* to the day of *vidayāṛṛi*.[73] In Ś. 1463 a gift was made for the annual car festival of god Vīrabhadra of Lēpākshi.[74] A gift of money was made in Ś. 1474 by *Vipravinōdins* to gods Hanumantadēva and Remēśvara of the *agrahāra* village of Pinavaḍugūru on the occasion of the *Utthāna-dvādasi*.[75] In Ś. 1 78 a grant of *Vipravinōdi* income realised from the *agrahāra* village of Chinahōtūru *alias* Dēvarāyapuram in the *Vurokoṇḍaventhya* of the *Rāyadurgarājya* by the *Vipravinōdins* for the *Dhanurmāsa* worship of god Cennakēśava of the village[76] A gift of land was made in Ś. 1496 by Krōsipalli Venkaya for celebrating the *Suparṇōtsava-paurṇami* festival for god Tiruvēnkaṭēśvara at *Sangamasthāna*.[77] A certain Kōnēri, a resident of Avilāla village, instituted the Avilāli garden festival in Ś. 1506 for god Gōvindarāja of Tirupati and he made arrangements for the celebration of this festival.[78] In Ś. 1634 an individual, named Tangeḍa Sūrappa, granted permission to celebrate the *Brahmōtsavam* for gods Gōpālasvāmin and Vīrēśvara of Tangeḍa and he made provision for its celebration.[79] In

65. *Ibid.*, V. 86. Bhīmavaram.
66. *Ibid.*, V. 27. Sarpavaram.
67. *Ibid.*, IV. 1162. Drākshārāma.
68. *Ibid.*, VI. 1251 and 1252. Siṁhāchalam.
69. *Ibid*, V. 1236. Śrīkurmam.
70. *Ibid.*, X. 479. Tripurāntakam.
71. *T.T.D.I.* II. 50, Tirumala.
72. *Ibid.*, II. 89. Tirumala.
73. *Ibid.*, V. 6. Tirumala.
74. C.P. 19 of 1937-38. Lēpākshi.
75. 344 of 1920. Chinnavaḍugūru.
76. 403 of 1920. Chinnapōtūru.
77. 162 of 1917. Śēkūru.
78. *T.T.D.I.* VI. 6. Tirupati.
79. 378 of 1926. Tangeḍa.

Ś. 1634, the *Uttara-tiruṇāl*-festival of god Gōpālasvāmi of Tangeḍa, which has been in abeyance since the year Akṣaya, was restored and provision was made for its celebration.[80] In Ś. 1750, arrangements were made for the celebration of the *Vasantanavarātra* festival for god Śrīkūrmanātha of Śrīkūrmam.[81] In the 1st year of the reign of the Rāṣṭrakūṭa king, Dhārāvarṣa Dhruva, a Bālavarman made provision for the celebration of the *maharṇavami* festival for the gods at Alaṁpūr.[82] A gift of land was made for the celebration of *Śrīmahōtsava* for the god of Cāḷukya-Bhīmavaram.[83]

9. *Recitation of the Holy Texts*

Equal attention was paid for arranging for the recitation of the holy scriptures and gifts were made for this purpose. In Ś. 1193 a gift was made by Narahari-tīrtha for the recitation of *Purāṇa* in the temple of Śrīkūrmanātha of Śrīkūrman.[84] In Ś. 1275, a sum of 52 *māḍas* was given for arranging the reading of *Purāṇa* at the time of the offering of the *Gangānarasiṁhabhōga* in the temple of Siṁhāchalam.[85] A certain Sūripeddi instituted in Ś. 1218 the *Puruṣasūkta-nibhandham* to god Śrī Narasiṁhanātha of Siṁhāchalam.[86] Provision was made in Ś. 1272, for the recitation of *Puruṣasūkta* at the time of the *abhiśēka* in the same temple.[87] In Ś. 1461, a person was appointed for the recitation of *Sankīrtanam* in the temple of Siṁhāchalam.[88] A gift was made to two learned persons engaged in singing the *Sankīrtanas* during the sixty-six ablution days yearly in the temple of Śrī Venkaṭēśa of Tirumala.[89] In Ś. 1461, a gift was made for the recitation of the *Gajēndramōkṣa-slōkas* in the same temple.[90] Arrangements were made in Ś. 1287, by Bhīmanapagaḍa for the recitation of *Sahasranāmam* and the *Narasiṁhakāyyam* in the temple of Siṁhāchalam.[91] A sum of 4 *peṇam* per month was paid in Ś. 1467 to a Śrīvaiṣṇava teacher engaged in reading the *Śrī-Bhāṣyam*, of Śrī Rāmānuja in the divine presence of Śrī Venkaṭēśa of Tirumala during the time of ablution.[92] A gift was made to Anantayyangār who recited the *Tiruvenkaṭa Mahātmyam*, which was instituted by Tiṁmarājayyan during *tirumanjanam* or holy bath in Ś. 1467.[93] In Ś. 1465, a brāhman was engaged to read the Śrīnivāsapurāṇam before the presence of Śrī Venkaṭēśa of Tirumala.[94] The recitation of *Kaisika-purāṇam* was arranged in Ś 1457, in the month

80. 379 of 1926. Tangeda.
81. *S.I.I.* V. 1159. Śrīkūrmam.
82. *Tel. Ins.* II. p. 11. Ālaṁpūr.
83. *S.I.I.* V. 80. Cāḷukya-Bhīmavaram.
84. *Ibid.*, V. 1233. Śrīkūrmam.
85. *S.I.I.* VI. 1053. Siṁhāchalam.
86. *Ibid.*, VI. 182. Siṁhāchalam.
87. *Ibid.*, VI. 962. Siṁhāchalam.
88. *Ibid.*, VI. 722. Siṁhāchalam.
89. *T.T.D.I.* V. 46. Tirumala.
90. *Ibid.*, IV. 135. Tirupati.
91. *S.I.I.* VI. 839. Siṁhāchalam.
92. *T.T.D.I.* V. 47. Tirumala.
93. *Ibid.*, V. 53. Tirupati.
94. *Ibid.*, V. 10. Tirumala.

of *Kārttika* by Tiruvēnkaṭa Jiyar in the same temple.[95] A devotee made a gift to the brāhman engaged in reading the *Śrīnivāsa-purāṇam* in the same temple in Ś. 1465.[96]

10. *Repair and Renovation*

Devotees also made gifts specially for renovation and repair of the temples. Provision was made in Ś. 1026, for removing trees on the *vimāna* of the temple, to *kāse* who built the temple of Svayaṁbhudēva of Valivēru.[97] In Ś. 1218, Peddi nāyaka made a gift for removing trees on the *vimāna* of the temple of Siṁhāchalam.[98] In Ś. 1612, the *kāpus* and *Karaṇams* of Chinnaventurla made gifts to Rāmanna who renovated the temple of Cennakēśava Perumāḷ of the village.[99]

B. *Varieties of Gifts Made*

1. *Gifts Relating to Land*

a. *Villages*

Groups of villages were endowed to temples by devotees. The Later Cāḷukyan king, Tribhuvanamalla, gave 44 villages in the 47th year of his reign, to god Tripurāntakēśvara of Tripurāntakam.[100] In Ś. 1028, the villages of Palkūru and Bhōjanicheṛuvu, in the Mārjavāḍa, were given to god Tripurāntaka by king Karikālacōḷa.[101] The villages of Kankaṇamu, Cheṛuvubaṁmukūru, Sōmapalle, Ukkamapalli, Enemadalapāḍu, Rāmasamudram and Nāgasānipalli were given in Ś. 1134 to the same god.[102] In Ś. 1183, the villages of Maṛṛipalli and Alapalapalli were granted to god Mārganārāyana Perumāḷ of Peṇṭrāla by Siddhanadēvulu Vijayadēvuṇḍu of Mukkaṇṭi Kāḍuveṭṭi family.[103] A record from Śrīkākulam, dated in Ś. 1440, mentions the gift of five villages to god Śrīkākulēśvara of the place.[104] Another from Gārladinne, dated in Ś. 1443, refers to the gift of the villages of Gārladinne and Kaṭṭirāḷḷaguṁpu, situated in the *Podali-sīma*, to god Tiruvēngaḍanātha of Veligoṇḍa by Koṇḍamarusayya for the religious merit of Kṛṣṇadēvarāya.[105] In Kali 4928, the Eastern Cāḷukan king, Viṣṇuvardhana mahārāja, gave 3 villages to god Trivikrama of Cherayūru while he was returning from *digvijaya* in which he defeated the king of Kalyāṇi, a traditional enemy.[106]

Single villages were also given by pious devotees to temples. The village of Chākivāḍa in the *Samvā-viṣaya* was granted in Ś. 1003 to god Śiva under the name

95. *Ibid.*, IV. 46. Tirumala.
96. *Ibid.*, V. 10. Tirumala.
97. *S.I.I.* X. 61. Valivēru.
98. *Ibid.*, VI. 868. Siṁhāchalam.
99. 380 of 1940-41. Chinnaventurla.
100. *S.I.I.* IX. 204. Tripurāntakam.
101. *Ibid*, X. 62. Tripurāntakam.
102. *Ibid.*, X. 278. Tripurāntakam.
103. *N.D.I.* II. Kandukūr. 63. Peṇṭrāla
104. *S.I.I.* IV. 981. Śrīkākuḷam.
105. *N.D.I.* III. Podili 14. Gārladinne.
106. *S.I.I.* VI. 202. Peddacheṛukūru.

of Rājarājēśvara, by king Anantavarma Cōḍagangadēva.[107] A village, named Ballikuṛuva, was donated in Ś. 1064, to god Śankaradēva of Koṭṭiyadona as a *dēvabhōga*, by Pottapi Cōḍa of the Telugu Cōḍa family.[108] In Ś. 1174, the village of Bōḍapāḍu, in the *Chilakapāṭikaṁpaṇa*, was given to god Tripurāntakadēva of Tripurāntakam by Rājendracōḍa Cakravarti and his younger brother.[109] The village of Nemilikallu in the *sthala* of Dannalakōṭa was granted in Ś. 1275 to god Tripurāntaka by Māraya Nāyaka.[110] In Ś. 1332 a village was given to god Narasiṁha on the Vēdādri at Rājahmunḍry by Mēlaṁmā, the queen of Kāṭamareḍḍi Vēmareḍḍi.[111] The village of Sirivara along with its hamlets, Manchenahaḷḷi and Māyinakahaḷḷi, was given in S. 1463 to god Vīrabhadra of Lēpākshi at the request of Vīrūpanna *mahīpati* by the famous Vijayanagara king, Acyutarāya.[112] Venkaṭapati Rāyadēva *mahārāyalu* granted a village named Rāva, which was situated in the district of *Arivēlamu* to the local deity Raghunāyaka in S. 1537.[113] In S. 1609 a village was given to god Cennakēśvaradēva of the village of Chēzerla by Śrīmat Dāvu *Surutrāṇu* Maradattamgāru.[114] It is known from an inscription from Bōthpur, dated in the 46th year of the reign of the Later Cāḷukyan King, Tribhuvanamalla Vikramāditya, that a village named Badambuḍu, situated, in the *Kandūr 1000*, was granted to god Rāmēśvara of Nekkoṇḍa by the prince.[115] Another from Kāḷahasti, dated in the 7th year of the reign of the Cōḷa king, Tribhuvanacakravartin Rājarāja, mentions the gift of the village of Kuriyaneri by Saśikulaśalukki Tanininruvenra Vīra Narasingadēvan *alias* Yādavarāya to the god of Nīlagirīśvamuḍaiya Nāyanār at the foot of the hill to the south of the temple of Nāyanār Tirukkāḷatti Uḍaiya Nāyanār at Kāḷahasti.[116]

Parts of villages were also granted to temples. In S. 1439, a Koṇḍiseṭṭi gave half of the village of Cintayapalli which was granted to him by Kṛṣṇarāya, as an *umbaḷika* to God Śrī Venkaṭēśra.[117] Tāḷḷapākkam Tirumalayyangār granted in S. 1452, half of the village of Erraguṇṭayapalli, situated in *Siruvōlu-sīrmai* to god Śrī Venkaṭēśa of Tirumala.[118] In S. 1474, a devotee named Tiruvadiraya, the ruler of *Tiruvadirājyam*, gave half of the village of Kulayapattam, situated on the bank of the river Tāmraparṇi, in the province of *Tiruvaḍi-rājyam* to the same god and another half to goddess Sūḍikkoḍutta-Nācciyār of the consort of Śrī Gōvindarāja of Tirupati.[119]

In some instances villages were renamed by the devotees and endowed to

107. *I.A.* XVIII. pp. 161-165. Viśākhapaṭṇam.
108. *S.I.I.* VI. 624. Koṇidena.
109. *N.D.I.* III. Udayagiri. 48. Yēpilaguṇṭa.
110. *S.I.I.* X. 553. Tripurāntakam.
111. *Ibid.*, X. 577. Uppu Ahōbalam.
112. C.P. 119 of 1937-38.
113. *N.D.I.* III. Udayagiri. 19. Tōṭacheruvupalli.
114. *N.D.I.* I, Ātmakur. 23. Chēzerla.
115. *K.I.A.P.* Mahabūbnagar. 41. Bōṭhpūr.
116. 83 of 1945-46. Kāḷahasti.
117. *T.T.D.I.* III. 119. Tirumala.
118. *Ibid.*, IV. 6. Tirumala.
119. *Ibid.*, V. 158. Tirupati.

temples. In S. 1431. the village of Neladalapāḍu in the *Pennatabāḍi-sthala* in the *Gutti-rājya* was renamed as Vīranarasimhapura and given to god Rāmēśvara of Tāḍiparati by Sāḷuvayyangār, the prime minister of Śrī Vīranarasiṁharāya.[120] An undated record from Yāgaṇṭipalli mentions the gift of the village of Prātapāḍu, renamed Vijaya-Bukkarāyapuram, to god Mallikārjunadēva of the village.[121]

b. *Lands*

The temple was the recipient of various types of lands for various purposes. King Tribhuvanamalla Pottapicōḍa gave land in S. 1064, as *dēvabhōga* to god Śrīsankaramahādēva of Koṇidena.[122] In S. 1157, Nāgadēva, the Telugu-Pallava chieftain, granted 20 *drōṇas* of land to god Bhīmēśvara at Koṇḍanāyanavaram.[123]

120. *S.I.I.* IV. 802. Tāḍipatri.
121. 22 of 1941-42. Yāgaṇṭipalli
122. **Similar Exapmles**
S.I.I. X. 371. Tripurāntakam.
Ibid., VI. 965. Śrīkūrmam.
Ibid., X. 58. Dēgaramūḍi.
449 of 1938-39. Māchelra.
N.D.I. I. Darsi. 48. Mannēpalli.
S.I.I. X. 241. Tripurāntakam.
92 of 1929-30 Kottapālem.
C.P. of 4. 1938-39.
15 of 1953-54. Kōḍumurti.
S.I.I. X. 278. Muṭṭupalli.
Ibid., X. 346. Tripurāntakam.
Ibid., IV. 1048. Drākshārāma.
233 of 1937-38. Gangavaram.
S.I.I. X. 355. Tripurāntakam.
Ibid., IV. 1245. Drākshārāma.
N.D.I. II. Kandukūru. 66. Peṇṭrāla.
S.I.I. VI. 712. Siṁhāchalam.
N.D.I. I. Darsi. 1. Aluvalapāḍu.
Ibid., II. Kāvali. 48. Peddakoṇḍūru.
S.I.I X. 435. Ganikapūḍi.
N.D.I. III. Ongōle. 70. Maddipāḍu.
65 of 1929-30. Mandaḍi.
N.D.I. I. C.P. 2. Turivīḍu.
T.T.D.I. II. 35. Tirumala.
S.I.I. V. 49. Bhīmavaram.
N.D.I. II. Ongōle. 30. Chedaluvāḍa.
T.T.D.I. III. 159. Tirumala.
Ibid., IV. 17. Tirupati.
Ibid., IV. 19. Tirumala.
Ibid., IV. 27. Tirumala.
Ibid., V. 17. Tirupati.
Ibid., V. 77. Tirumala.
Ibid., V. 99. Tirupati.
122. *S.I.I.* VI. 624. Koṇidena.
123. *Ibid.*, X. 284. Koṇḍanāyanavaram.

In S. 1176, a gift of land was made to god Bhīmēśvaradēva of Kroppōlu as *vṛtti*.[124] Śrīmān Baṁma nāyaniṁgāru gifted in S. 1242, 400 *kuṇṭas* of dry land as *vṛtti* to god Iṣṭakāmēśvara mahādēva of Aralur and 100 *kuṇṭas* to another god for the religious merit of king Pratāparudra.[125] Tirumala nāyanimgāru, the son of Pedi nāyuṇḍu of Jakampuṇḍi, granted in S. 1472 several plots of wet and dry land, in Nīṭūru, situated in *Chirabaḍi sīma*, to god Cennakēśava.[126] Yellappanāyaniṁgāru, a *kāryakarta*, gifted land in S. 1478, on the occasion of a solar eclipse, to the temple of Janārdanaperumāḷ of Chintakoṁmudinne for the merit of his overlord Mādirāju Rāmarāju Tirumalarāja Nāgarājayyadēva *mahārāja*.[127] In S. 1509, Maṭli Kumāra Anantarājayya Dēvacōḍa *mahārāja* and others granted land to the god at Āṇimela.[128] Kanugōli Śivarāyanimgāru gave land in S. 1662 to the temple at Takkaḷḷapāḍu.[129] A record from Tuṁmūru, dated in S. 1716, mentions the gift of a *khaṇḍriga* on which ten *tūms* can be sown in the fields of Tuṁbūr to god Nīlakanṭhēśvarasvāmi of the place by *mahārāja Rājā Śrī* Velugōṭi Kumārayācama nāyanivāru.[130] In the reign of the later Cāḷukyan King, Tribhuvanamalla, a gift of two *mattar* of land was made by Mallarasa of Kāḍūru to god Bhujangēśvara.[131] An inscription from Drākshārāma, mentions the gift of 10 *puṭṭis* of *Viṭṭupaṭṭu* to god Mahēśvaradēva of the place by the minister, Anantapāla Daṇḍanāyakulu.[132] Mylāladēvi, the queen of *mahāmaṇḍalēśvara* Vīra Kēśavadēva, donated lands to god Sangamēśvara of Sangamēśvaram.[133]

c. *Gardens*

Several kinds of gardens like flower gardens, fruit gardens, vegetable gardens, areca-nut gardens, betel-leaf gardens, etc., were endowed to temples. In some cases, devotees were interested in presenting lands for laying gardens and in some other cases, in planting trees in the temple gardens.

124. *N.D.I.* III. Ongōle. 67. Koppōlu.
125. *Ibid.*, II. Ongōle. 9. Allūru.
126. 21 of 1953-54. Niṭṭūr.
127. 342 of 1938-39. Chintakoṁmudinne.
128. 234 of 1937-38. Gangireḍḍipalle.
129. 53 of 1939-30. Takkeḷḷapādu.
130. *N.D.I.* III. Sūḷūrpēṭ. 18. Tuṁmūru.
131. 288 of 1952-53. Konganapāḍu.
132. *S.I.I.* IV. 1255. Drākshārāma.
133. *Tel. Ins.* II. Mn. 12. Sangamēśvaram.
Similar Examples
N.D.I. III. Ongōle. 92. Nannūru.
K.I.A.P. Karīmnagar 5. Lēmulavāda.
S.I.I. X. 85. Sattenapalli.
Ibid., IV. 677. Nādeṇḍla.
Ibid., X. 103. Kovvūru.
Ibid., 690., Vizayanagaram.
N.D.I. I. Darsi. 40. Kōcherlakōṭa.
S.I.I. VI. 605. Koṇidena.
Ibid., VI. 640. Koṇidena.
N.D.I. II. Ongōle. 50. Janakavaram.

Contd.

S.I.I. IV. 1133. Drākshārāma.
Ibid., IV. 687. Nādeṇḍla.
Ibid., X. 138. Peravali.
Ibid., X. 157. Gaṇapavaram.
Ibid., VI. 609. Kunkalaguṇṭla.
Ibid., X. 176. Mōdukūru.
Ibid., X. 177. Śiripuram.
Ibid, VI. 124. Appikaṭla.
Ibid, X. 717. Bhīmlipaṭṇam.
Ibid, VI. 120. Ponnūru.
Ibid., VI. 650. Koṇidena.
Ibid., IV. 661. Narasaraōpēṭ.
N.D.I. II. Nellore 62. Nellore.
277 of 1952-53. Kanuparti.
N.D.I. II. Nellore 60. Nellore.
477 of 1940-41. Niḍadavōlu.
268 of 1952-53. Elūru.
N.D.I. II. Kanigiri. 32. Kōḍūr.
S.I.I. V. 138. Pālakol.
44 of 1943-44. Vēlpanūru.
S.I.I. X. 522. Kolakalūru.
Ibid., VI. 592. Kunkalaguṇṭa.
N.D.I. Kandukūr. 40. Kandukūr.
S.I.I. VI. 589. Kunkalaguṇṭa.
N.D.I. I. C.P. 23. Kūchipūḍi.
S.I.I. VI. 730. Siṁhāchalam.
Ibid., V. 29. Sarpavaram.
Ibid., V. Sarpavaram.
Ibid., VI. 731. Śrīkūrmam.
Ibid., V. 46. Bhīmavaram.
Ibid., V. 114. Palivela.
Ibid., VI. 664. Panchaḍhārla.
S.I.I. IV. 687. Nādiṇḍla.
152 of 1945-46. Eṛraballa.
S.I.I. V. 44. Bhīmavaram.
N.D.I. II. Kandukūr. 85. Vīrapalli.
140 of 1945-46. Peddajūṭūru.
N.D.I. II. Udayagiri. 2. Alimēlumangāpuram.
N.D.I. II. Nellore. 122. Vellāṇṭi.
58 of 1942-43. Śrīśailam.
N.D.I. II. Ongōle 41. Boddavaram.
34 of 1939-40. Maḍapūru.
24 of 1943-44. Elamalapalle.
23 of 1939-40. Guṇḍlamaḍa.
314 of 1937-38. Gōraṇṭla.
120 of 1945-46. Cherlōpalli.
N.D.I. II. Kandukūr. 25. Guḍlūr.
336 of 1934-35. Kothapālem.
300 of 1937-38. Veluḍurti.
133 of 1945-46. Nāgūru.
369 of 1938-39. Dēvuni Cuḍḍapah.
36 of 1941-42. Pōrumāmiḷḷa.
215 of 1937-38. Chiḍipirāḷa.

Contd.

A garden consisting of trees like *punnāga*, *sura-punnāga*, *campaka*, *pāṭala*, *vakuḷa*, *aśōka*, and *panasa* was given to god Amarēśvara at Bōni in Ś. 1193 by the general Umāpati, during the reign of the Eastern Gāṅga King, Bhānudēva.[134] In Ś. 1199, a garden consisting of trees like *jāji*, *sēmanti*, *malle*, *virajāji*, *karavīra*, *guri-minda*, *ponna* and *davana* was granted to god Sōmēśvara of Rāvūru by Sāmanta Pōtināyaka.[135] In the reign of the Later Cāḷukyan King, Tribhuvanamalladēva, a flower garden was given to god Harikēśvara of Lēmulavāḍa by Prince Sōmēśvara with the approval of the king.[136] A Gāḍi Dēvarāju gave a flower garden in Ś. 1190 to god Mārganārāyaṇa perumāḷ of Peṇṭrāla.[137] In Ś. 1202 a flower garden was endowed to god Maṇḍukēśavaradēva of Boḍḍēpūṇḍi for the religious merit of Rudrēśvara *Mahārāja* by *mahāmaṇḍalēśvara* Nāgadēva *mahārāja*.[138] The Reḍḍi

19 of 1939-40. Gangapērūru.
364 of 1938-39. Dēvuni Cuḍḍapah.
39 of 1953-54. Chenchu Eṛraguḍi.
162 of 1917. Śēkūru.
N.D I. III. Podili 19. Īgalapāḍu.
Ibid., II. Kanigiri. 15. Kattakiṇḍipalli.
Ibid., I. Gūḍūr. 1. Akkaṁpēṭa.
198 of 1937-38. Animala.
325 of 1937-38. Prātakōṭa.
183 of 1937-38 Kuṇṭrapākkam.
N.D.I II. Ongōle 52. Janakavaram.
Ibid., I. Darsi. 62. Rājanpalli.
251 of 1937-38. Mīrāpuram.
C.P. 36 of 1940-41. Peddapasupula.
49 of 1939-40. Paṭṭapurāyi.
410 of 1938-39. Pushpagiri.
N.D.I. II. Ongōle. 46. Gōnuguṇṭa. Ongōle. 74.
Ibid., III. Udayagiri. 43. Udayagiri.
Ibid., III. Podili. 29. Pāmulapāḍu.
416 of 1938-39. Rudrayagāripalle.
N.D.I. I. Darsi. 22. Donakoṇḍa.
Ibid., II. Nellore. 39-A. Koṁmarapuḍi.
Ibid, II. Kanigiri. 32. Pedda Alavalapāḍu.
Ibid., II. Kanigiri. 5. Dāsalapalli.
S.I.I. IV. 801. Tāḍpatri.
N.D.I. II. Kandukūr. 78. Singarāyakoṇḍa.
347 of 1940-41. Chidipirāḷḷadinne.
259 of 1949-50. Turimeḷḷa.
29 of 1941-42. Śankhavaram.
36 of 1953-54. Penumūḍi.
N.D.I. I. Ātmakūr. 5. Prabhagiripaṭṭaṇam.
S.I.I. V. 1260. Śrīkurmam.

134. *S.I.I.* X. 717. Bōni.
135. *Ibid.*, 442. Rāvipāḍu.
136. *K,I.A.P.* Km. 6. Lēmulavāḍa.
137. *N.D.I.* II. Kandukūr. 65. Penṭrāla.
138. *Ibid.*, Ongōle. 75. Mānikēśvaram.

King, Kāṭayavēmāreḍḍi, gave a flower garden in Ś. 1307 to the god of Kṣīrārāma for the merit of his parents.[139]

Several people presented fruit gardens and arecanut gardens to temples. In Ś. 1246, a fruit garden was granted to the temple of Cenna Mallikārjuna of Kākāni by two individuals, named Krāmja Nāgiseṭṭi and Vallabhiseṭṭi.[140] In Ś. 1336 a fruit garden was presented to god Bhāvanārāyaṇa of Ponnūru by Anavōtanāyanimgāru.[141] In Ś. 1356, a garden consisting of various kinds of fruit plants was presented to god Bhīmēśvara of Bhīmavaram by Vēmāreḍḍi.[142] A garden consisting of mango trees, *nērēḍu, mārēḍu* and *usirika* trees was presented to god Bhāskarēśvara of Uṇḍavilli by three individuals.[143]

In the 13th year of the reign of king Kulōttungacōḍa, a garden consisting of 30,000 areca-nut trees was granted to god Bhīmēśvara of Drākshārāma.[144] An areca-nut garden consisting of 10,001 trees was presented to god Āsaṇṭa-Rāmēśvaramahādēva of Āchaṇṭa, in Ś. 1177.[145] Mango topes and palmyra topes were also granted to temples. In the 39th year of the reign of king Kulōttungacōḷadēva, a mangotope and a jack fruit garden were given to god Viṣṇu of Chāpalapalle by Rājamaladēvan.[146] *Mahāmaṇḍalēśvara* Nāgadēva mahārāja gave a mango tope in Ś. 1202, to god Maṇḍūkēśvaradēva of Boḍḍapāḍu.[147] A record from Durgi, dated in S. 1239, mentions the gift of a palmyra garden to the god at Durgi.[148] A vegetable garden was endowed to god Vankaṭēśvara of Durgi in S. 1173 by Nāmadēva paṇḍita.[149]

In some cases trees were presented to temple gardens. A *sāni* gave 300 trees to god Bhīmēśvara of Drākshārāma.[150] In S. 1084, 1500 areca-nut trees were granted

139. *S.I.I.* V. 155. Pālakol.
 Similar Examples.
 N.D.I. II. Kandukūr. 57. Pākāla.
 S.I.I. X. 438. Duggirāla.
 Ibid., VI. 975, 1151, Siṁhāchalam.
 Ibid., V, 110. Palivela.
 Ibid., V. 1193. Śrīkūrmam.
 Ibid., IV. 950. Gaṇapavaram.
 Ibid., V. 53. Bhīmavaram.
 Ibid., V. 226. Amarāvati.
 Ibid., VI. 676, 677. Piṭhāpuram.
 Ibid., V. 154. Pālakol.
 Ibid., V. 381. Yanamadala.
 Ibid., V. 86. Cāḷukya-Bhīmavaram.
140. *S.I.I.* X. 534. Kākāni.
141. *Ibid.*, VI. 118. Ponnūru.
142. *Ibid.*, V. 34. Bhīmavaram.
143. *Ibid.*, X. 735. Uṇḍavalli.
144. *Ibid.*, IV. 1359. Drākshārāma.
145. *Ibid.*, X. 349. Āchanta.
146. *N.D.I.* III. Venkaṭagiri. 13. Chāpalapalli.
147. *Ibid.*, II. Ongōle. 75. Maṇikēśvaram.
148. *S.I.I.* X. 526. Durgī.
149. *Ibid.*, X. 334. Durgī.
150. *Ibid.*, IV. 1303. Drākshārāma.

to god Ādivināyakadēva of Malya, probably a suburb of Drākshārāma.[151]

In many cases, the temple received lands for the purpose of laying gardens. In Ś. 1092, a gift of land was made for laying a flower garden in Chaṭṭipuram to the local god Cōḍiśvara mahādēva.[152] An individual gave land for fruit and flower gardens to god Sūrēśvara of Rāvūru in Ś. 1199.[153] In Ś. 1220, land was given for the purpose of laying a garden to god Mallināthadēva of Pālūra by Ballirāju Siddhayadēva mahārāja.[154]

A record from Sarpavaram, dated in Ś. 1319, mentions the gift of 3 *kha* of wet land for a *bṛndāvanam*.[155] Another from Śrīkākuḷam, dated in S. 1476, refers to the gift of land for the same purpose.[156] In Ś. 1477, Aubalarāja gave one *puṭṭi* of land at Āmanūru for raising a grove and a flower garden for the benefit of the Ahōbalēśvara temple at Ahōbalam.[157]

d. *House-sites*

Temples received house-sites for lodging their servants. In Ś. 1043, a gift of *pandumu* of land was made to god Bhīmēśvara of Drākshārāma by Satterāju.[158] In S. 1176, a house-site was granted to god Rāmēśvaramahādēva of Velpūru.[159] A house-site was given to god Bhāvanārāyaṇa at Sarpavaram in Ś. 1332.[160] In Ś. 1445, the Vijayanagara king, Kṛṣṇarāya, gave a house-site for building the Vyāsarāya *maṭham* at Tirumala.[161] *Mahāmaṇḍalēśvara* Sēkaradēva endowed a house-site to god Āñjanēya at Kuruvalli during the reign of the Later Cāḷukyan king, Tribhuvanamalla.[162]

e. *Tanks*

Tanks, wells, canals etc., were also granted to temples by devotees. In the 39th year of the reign of Kuḷottungacōḍadēva, a gift of *Paruvalakkal alias Viṣvasamudra,*

151. *Ibid.*, IV. 1099. Drākshārāma.
152. *Ibid.*, X. 173. Śrīramapuram.
153. *S.I.I.* X. Rāvipāḍu.
154. 285 of 1949-50. Pālūru.
155. *S.I.I.* V. 28. Sarpavaram.
156. *Ibid.*, IV. 907. Śrīkākuḷam.
157. 66 of 1915. Ahōbalam.
Similar Examples
S.I.I. V. 155. Pālakol.
Ibid., V. 86. Bhīmavaram.
Ibid., X. 568. Sarpavaram.
327 of 1936-37. Vellaṭūru.
N.D.I. I. Gūḍūr 51. Mādamannūru.
242 of 1937-38. Kōḍūr.
17 of 1937-38. Nandikōṭkūr.
S.I.I. VI. 615. Koṇidena.
158. *S I.I.* IV. 1364. Drākshārāma.
159. *Ibid.*, X. 344. Velpūru.
160. *Ibid.*, V. 14. Sarpavaram.
161. *T.T.D.I.* III. 158. Tirumala.
162. 728 of 1919. Kuruvalli.

a reservoir, was constructed for god Viṣṇu of Chāpalapalle by Rājamalladēva.[163] In S. 1059, tanks were given to god Ballīśvara of Koṭyadona as *dēvabhōga* by Kāmacōḍa Mahārāja.[164] A tank was endowed to god Vaṁkēśvara in the village of Durgi in Ś. 1173.[165] Rācavēma presented a tank in Baddepūṇḍi to god Janārdhana in Ś. 1320, for religious merit of his elder brother.[166] In Ś. 1416, a canal was dug and donaetd to god Bhīmēśvara of Cāḷukya-Bhīmavaram on the occasion of *Uttarāyaṇa Sankrānti* by Eṟṟama nāyanimgāru.[167] In Ś. 1429, Uddaṇḍarāyar Uḷagappan made provision to the temple treasury for excavating the tanks and channels of the temple villages of Śrī Venkaṭēśa of Tirumala.[168] A Śrīnivāsar arranged in S. 1446 to excavate a tank in the temple villages of Śrī Gōvindarāja of Tirupati.[169]

2. *Gifts of Gold and Cash*

a. *Gold*

Gold was also presented to temples. In the 11th year of the reign of the Cōḷa king, Rājarāja, a Muduvaṭṭi, donated one and a half *māḍa* of gold for an evening lamp to the god at Guḍimallam.[170] In the 51st year of the reign of the Pallava King, Kō-Vijayadanti Vikramār, 30 *kalañju* of gold was granted to the image of the Tiruviḷānkōyil-Pērumānaḍigaḷ at Tiruchānūr.[171] A record from Tiruchānūr states that in the reign of the same king, a gift of red gold was made to the same god.[172] Another from the same place, mentions that the Bāṇa king, Vijayāditya, gave gold to gods Tiruviḷānkōyil-Perumānaḍigaḷ Tirumantiraiśālai Perumānaḍigaḷ and Tiruvēnkaṭattu-Perumānaḍigaḷ of Tiruchānūr.[173] In Ś. 820 in the reign of Vijayāditya Mahābali Vānarāya, a gift of 30 *kolañju* of gold was made by Mahādēvī Aḍigaḷ, the mother of this chief, and the wife of Vāṇavidhyādhara, to god Paraśurāmēśvara of Tiruvippiraṁbēḍu.[174] In the 13th year of the reign of the Cōḷa king, Rājarājadēva, 9 *māḍas* of gold were granted for a lamp to Angarayan

163. *N.D.I.* III. Venkaṭagiri. 13 Chāpalapalle.
164. *S.I.I.* VI. 606. Koṇidena.
165. *Ibid.*, X. 334. Durgī.
166. *N.D.I.* II. Kandukūr. 35. Kandukūr.
167. *S.I.I.* V. Chāḷukya-Bhīmavaram.
168. *T.T.D.I.* III. 10. Tirumala.
169. *Ibid.*, III. 161. Tirupati.
    Similar Examples
    S.I.I. IV. 628, 645, 646. Koṇidena.
    N.D.I. III. Udayagiri. 3. Ayyavāripalle.
    Ibid., Udayagiri. 7. Nallagoṇḍa.
    S.I.I. X. 131. Ellamanda.
    N.D.I. II. Nellōre. 106. Sangam.
    K.I.A.P. Mn. 63. Vardhamānapuram.
170. *S.I.I.* VIII. 516. Guḍimallam.
171. *T.T.D.I.* I; 261 of 1904. Tiruchānūr.
172. *Ibid.*, I. 2. Tiruchānūr.
173. *Ibid.*, I. 4. Tiruchānūr
174. *E.I.* XI. pp. 227-228. Guḍimallam.

alias Kāḍuveṭṭi-*sēnāpati* Sevappōttan, one of the generals of Yādavarāya.[175] In Ś. 1473, gold was given to god Madanagōpāḷa of Kāśīpuram by Rācirājadēva *mahārāja*.[176] In Ś. 1165, Periya kandāḍai gave gold for an evening lamp in the temple of Vīrasundaraperumāḷ at Kāḷahasti.[177]

b. *Cash and Coins*

Several gifts of cash and coins were made to temples. In Ś. 1372, gift of money was made to god Bhīmēśvara of Cāḷukya-Bhīmavaram by two individuals on the occasion of a solar eclipse.[178] A gift of money, derived from many lands of the temple, was made to god Kāśīviśvēśvara of the village of Mallaguṇḍla in Ś. 1534 by Paruvata Nāyuḍu.[179] Certain individuals endowed money in Ś. 1676, to goddess Ankālaparamēśvari of Velpunūru.[180]

In S. 1192, a gift of one *māḍa* was made to god Śrī Vallabharāya of Śrīkākuḷam.[181] A gift of 12 *gaṇḍamāḍas* was made in S. 1282 for god Bhīmēśvara of Drākshārāma [182] An inscription from Rajahmundry, dated in S. 1139, refers to the gift of a *permāṇḍi-māḍa* by Nūnkama, the daughter of Kāmasāni, to god Mārkaṇḍēśvara of the place.[183] An inscription from Chēbrōlu, dated in Ś. 1075, states that a gift of thirteen *birudumāḍalu* were made to god of the place.[184] *Cāmaramāḍalu* were given to god Bhāvanārāyaṇa of Bāpaṭla in S. 1057.[185] In Ś. 1041, six *gandhavāraṇamāḍalu* were granted to the same god.[186] An undated record from Bāpaṭla mentions the gift of *gandhahastimāḍas* to the local deity.[187] An inscription from Ellōre mentions the gift of one *bhujabalamāḍa* to god Kēśava of the place.[188] In the 18th year of the reign of the Cōḍa king, Rājarāja, a gift of seven *rūkamāḍas* was made to god Anantīśvara of Kollūru by Būmna, the son of a *sāni* of the temple.[189] In S. 1040, six *uttamagaṇḍamāḍas* were granted to god Agastīśvara mahādēva of Kommūru on the occasion of an *Uttarāyaṇa-sankrānti* by

175. *S.I.I.* VIII. 515. Guḍimallam.
176. *N.D.I.* III. Podili. 24. Kāśīpuram.
177. *S.I.I.* VIII. 530. Kāḷahasti.
Similar Examples.
S.I.I. VIII. 504, 505, 507, 508, 515. Guḍimallam.
298 of 1904 Kāḷahasti.
182 of 1937-38. Kuṇṭrapākkam.
369 of 1934-35.
178. *S.I.I.* V. 48. Bhīmavaram.
179. 17 of 1953-54. Mallaguṇḍla.
180. 41 of 1943-44. Vēlpunūru.
181. *S.I.I.* IV. 957. Vēlpunūru.
182. *Ibid.*, IV. 1261. Drākshārāma.
183. 398 of 1932-33. Rājahmundry.
184. *S.I.I.* VI. 101. Chēbrōlu.
185. *Ibid.*, VI. 170. Bāpaṭla.
186. *Ibid.*, VI. 173. Bāpaṭla.
187. *Ibid.*, VI. 190. Bāpaṭla.
188. *Ibid.*, V. 191. Ellore.
189. *Ibid.*, X. 5. Kollūru.

a Gōkireḍḍi.[190] One *birudamāḍa* was given to the god at Velpūru in S. 1068.[191] A record from Pākāla, mentions the gift of one *gaṇḍagōpālamāḍa* to god Ilangasēnukuliya of the place by four individuals, named Pūsar, Koyimenaka, Rāman and Vallen.[192] Five *gadyānas* were granted to the temple of Rāmēśvaradēva of Ītamukkala in Ś. 1032 by Gosanayya.[193] In Ś. 1080 ten *birudugadyalu* were given to god Sankaradēva of Koṇidena by three *Sthānāpatis*, on the occasion of a *Viṣusankrānti*.[194] Five *kulōttungagadyas* were presented in Ś. 1077 to god Nāgēśvaradēva of Kāza by Dārayaṇāyaka, the *Muduseli* of the Velanāḍu king, Gonkarāja.[195] In Ś. 1058, seven *tyāgigaḍyalu* were donated to the god of Kōṭappakoṇḍa.[196] In Ś. 1127 fifteen *gōkarnagadyānas* were endowed to god Rāmēśvara of Velpunūru by Kēti setti.[197] In Ś. 1062, five *rājanārāyaṇa-gadyānas* were given to god Anantīśvara of Kollūru on the occasion of *Dakṣiṇayana-sankrānti* by Indulasāni.[198] A certain toll officer, named Maṇḍaya, gave a *Kēsari-gadya* to the temple of Bhōgīśvara Mahādēva at Bhaṭṭiprōlu, in Ś. 1160.[199] In Ś. 1382, a sum of 200 *paṇam* was made to the temple treasury of Śrī Venkaṭēśa of Tirumala by Toppu Nāyakkar.[200] Śrīmān Nārāyaṇa Jīyar, the disciple of Śrī Vān-Sathagōpa Jiyar, donated 3,800 *nārpaṇam* in Ś. 1458 to the same treasury.[201] A sum of 250 *rēkhaipon* was made to the same treasury for certain offerings to the deity in Ś. 1456.[202] In Ś. 1456 Kandāḍai Rāmanujayyangār paid a sum of 1200 *pon* or gold coins as the capital to the same treasury of Tirumala.[203] Tāthukkōnaṁman, the queen of Salakarāja Periya Tirumalarāja, gave in Ś. 1457 a sum of 150 *varāhan* to the temple treasury of Śrī Venkaṭēśa of Tirumala.[204] In Ś. 1468, a sum of 300 *gaṭṭivarāhan* a variety of gold coins, were presented to the same treasury by Śrīpati Obalēśvararāju.[205] In Ś. 1473 a gift of twenty *cakram* coins was made to gods Bhōgēśvara and Cennakēśava of Alavalapāḍu by Doṁmari Pedarāju, for the merit of the twenty-four families of his community.[206] An annuity of 25 *varāhas* was made in Ś. 1710 to the local god Rāmalingēśvara and to the goddess Bālātripurasundarī, on the banks of the river, Candrabhāgā, by Nāgulapāṭi Appājīpantulu.[207] A *Karaṇam* granted 500 *ṭankas* to

190. *Ibid.*, X. 78. Koṁmūru.
191. *Ibid.*, X. 117. Vēlpunūru.
192. *N.D.I.* II. Kandukūr. 56. Pākāla.
193. *Ibid.*, II. Ongōle. 79. Mannūru.
194. *S.I I.* X. 57. Koṇidena.
195. *Ibid.*, VI. 996. Śrīkākuḷam.
196. *Ibid.*, IV. 920. Kōṭappakoṇḍa.
197. *Ibid.*, X. 244. Vēlpūru.
198. *Ibid.*, X. 108. Kollūru.
199. 295 of 1936-37. Bhaṭṭiprōlu.
200. *T.T.D.I.* III. 10. Tirumala.
201. *Ibid.*, III. 114. Tirupati.
202. *Ibid.*, IV. 30. Tirumala.
203. *Ibid*, IV. 34. . Tirumala.
204. *Ibid.*, IV. 66. Tirumala.
205. *Ibid.*, V. 75. Tirumala.
206. 115 of 1945-46. Alavalapāḍu.
207. 17 of 1941-42. Mācherla.

the god of Bhīmavaram.[208] In Ś. 1453, a gift of 90 *rūkas* was made to god Kōnēṭi Tiruvēngalappa of Vūṭukūru by Tirumalayyangār, the son of Vīramarājungaru, for the merit of his parents and Sālvaka Narasappa.[209] Ten rupees per annum were gifted in Ś. 1780 by a Peda Narasayya to god Rāmsavāmin of Oṇṭimiṭṭa.[210]

3. *Gifts of Taxes, Tolls and Customs Duties*

Several varieties of taxes collected from certain communities and from villages, tolls and customs duties collected on articles of merchandise etc., were also donated to temples. In Ś. 1035 the *Teliki-vēvuru* remitted the taxes named *ari* on one oil-mill for a lamp to god Śrī Kūrmanātha of Śrīkūrmam.[211] In Ś. 1051, a toll officer, named Māvena, granted a tax named *kōṭi-vīsa,* to god Sakalēśvara at Māvundala.[212] In Ś. 1065 Gongi Reḍḍi, gifted a *vṛtti* including *ālamu,* and *salvisaṁpada* in Manjēru in the *Kaḍalu-nāḍu* to god Bhīmēśvara of Drākshārāma.[213] Taxes like *perusunkamu, vaḍḍarāvalamu, kolucuvīsālu* etc., were given in Ś. 1069 to the god of the village of Peda Kodamaguṇḍla, on the *Viṣusankrānti* by Īṣānageggaḍa the *mudu seli* the of Velanāḍu king, Gonka.[214] In Ś. 1153, the *Ubhayanānādēśis* of the 18 *viṣayas* granted the *ayamu* of the village of Nangepaḍḍa at the rate of one *peddacinnamu* on each *kalañju* to god Gaṇapatīśvara at Gaṇapēśvaram.[215] In Ś. 1170, the taxes *angadi-sunkamu, gōmaṭla, varakavīsamu* and *vedasunkamu* were given to god Mahādēvēśvara at Gajjaram by Upēndradēva Cakravarti in Ś. 1170.[216] This

208. *S.I.I.* V. 45. Bhīmavaram.
209. 341 of 1938-39. Chintakommuāinne.
210. 47 of 1939-40. Oṇṭimiṭṭa.
Similar Examples :
398 of 1932-33. Kōḍūru.
S.I.I. V. 1166. Śrīkūrmam.
Ibid., VI. 957. Śrīkākuḷam.
59 of 1941-42. Māṭumaḍugu.
207 of 1937-38. Nellore.
N.D.I. II. Kāvali 26. Jaladanki.
S.I.I. VI. 625. Koṇidena.
Ibid., X. 101, 244. Kollūru.
392 of 1938-39. Lēbāka.
S.I.I V. 48. Bhīmavaram.
Ibid., IV. 1288. Drākshārāma.
Ibid., V. 706, 1204. Śrīkūrmam.
Ibid., V. 1224, 1248, 1188. Śrīkūrmam.
17 of 1953-54. Malleguṇḍa.
101 of 1943-44. Vēlpunūru.
58 of 1943-44. Tarigoppula.
S.I.I. VI. 844. Siṁhāchalam.
211. *Ibid.*, V. 1316. Śrīkūrmam.
212. 290 of 1932-33. Mādala.
213. *S.I.I.* IV. 1361. Drākshārāma.
214. *Ibid.*, X. 119. Peda-kodamaguṇḍla.
215. *E.I.* III. pp. 82-83. Gaṇapēśvaram,
216. *S.I.I.* V. 116. Rājahmundry.

Upēndradeva Cakravarti donated in Ś. 1175, *pandruvāda-ālamu*, and *raḍrikamu* to god Bhīmēśvara of Drākshārāma [217] In Ś. 1191, a tax named *magama* levied by the *Ubhyanānādēśi* and the *Enamadala-sthalam-pekkanḍru* was granted to god Gannīśvara of Yenamadala.[218] A seṭṭi gave in Ś. 1192, 3 salt pans and the taxes like *ari, appanamu, pullari, mannana, aḍḍavaṭṭa-sunkamu, āyamu* and 3 per cent tax on salt gathered on seven villages to god Pinnēśvaradēva at Peddaganjām.[219] In Ś. 1200, a gift of *buṟṟasunkamu* was made to god Rāmanātha of Penumacca for the merit of king Kākatīya Rudra by Viḍemu Mādaya.[220] In Ś. 1202, the *pradhāni* of the Kākatīya queen, Rudrāṁbā, granted taxes like *panga, kānika* and *mannana* to the gods of the Mōṭupalli village [221] In Ś. 1212, a gift of 1 *duggāni* collected on each horse from the soldiers stationed in the town of Kandukūr was made to god Kanda-Sōmēśvaradēva of Kandukūr which is to the south-east of Śrīparvata.[222] A certain Rudraya-Leṁka gave in Ś. 1241, taxes like *arigoru-pannu, rāca-srōtriyam, kānika* etc., in the village to god Siddhanātha of Chenduvāyi in the *Sakali-Bhūmi* for the merit of the king.[223] In Ś. 1222, the gift of a tax named *māḍabadi*, in the villages of Tāḍuvāyi and Nēlamaṟṟi, at the rate of 2 *vīsas* was made by all the people of each village to god Cenna Mallikārjuna of Tāḍuvāyi.[224] In Ś. 1242, the gift of a tax named *pannasa* to the temple of god Aubaḷanātha by Gunḍaya and Konḍaya nāyaka with the consent of all the *Samayas*. Mention is also made of taxes like *payinḍi* and *singanāthamupannu*.[225] An Inkolani Tirumala donated in Ś. 1370 taxes like *veṭṭi, srōtrīya kaṭnam* and *ayamiralu* to the god at Paruchūru.[226] A tax officer or *suṁka-māniyagāṁḍu*, named Pāparāju Konḍaya, granted taxes realised at Maddūru on several items such as cattle, weights etc., in Ś. 1454 to gods Iṣṭakāmēśvara and Bhairavēśvara of Siddhavaṭam.[227] The tax named *Sthala-sunkamu* was given in Ś. 1458 to god Tiruvēngaḷanātha of Tirumala by Rāyasam Veñgaḷappaṁgāru, who was consecrated by him at Moyillakālava in the *Kalūri-sīma* for the merit of his *guru*, Tāḷḷapākam Tirumalayyangāru.[228] In Ś. 1471, the *vīramuṣṭi* tax was endowed by the *Purāntakas* headed by Komaralingaya, Rācaya etc., at the instance of Siddhabikṣavṛtti-ayya, to the temples of Vīrēśvara and Gāvi Rāmēśvara of Beḍudukūru *alias* Narasiṁhapuram in the *Ganḍikōṭa-sīma* for the merit of Rācavīṭi Vīrēśvara and several *Purāntakas*.[229] Siddhabikṣavṛattaya Nandēla Vīrayya granted in Ś. 1472, the *vīramuṣṭi* income realised in the temple and the village of Chiḍipirāla to god Agastīśvara.[230] The *vipravlnōdins*, Pina-

217. *Ibid.*, IV. 1371. Drākshārāma.
218. *Ibid.*, IV. 935 Yenamadala.
219. *Ibid.*, X. 427. Peddaganjām.
220. *Tel. Ins.* I. 37. Pāmāpuram.
221. *S.I.I.* X. 450. Mōṭupalli.
222. *N.D.I.* II. Kandukūr. 43. Konḍamudurupālem.
223. 5 of 1939-40. Chenduvāyi.
224. *S.I.I.* X. 489. Nandigūḍem.
225. *Hyd. Arch. Ser.* No. 19. Mn. 9.
226. *S.I.I.* X. 586. Paruchūru.
227. 36 of 1939-40. Maddūru.
228. 393 of 1938-39. Moyiḷḷakalava.
229. 306 of 1937-38. Beḍudūru.
230. 205 of 1937-38. Chiḍipirāla.

Gōvindayya, the grandson of Peda-Gōvindayya and others, gave in Ś. 1472, the annual *vartana* of the village of Kopparti to the temple of Siddhēśvara at Koppōlu.[231] In Ś. 1480, Timmarājayyadēva *mahārāja*, granted the taxes like *pannu, siddhāyamu, sunkasūtrālu, kaṭṇam kānika* and *veṭṭivēmu* by the four castes of Mangaḷagiri to the temple of the local deity.[232] In the 49th year of the reign of the Cāḷukya-Cōḷa king. Kulōttunga, the taxes like *valayacuṭṭu, ālamu, pannasa, antarāyamu* and *kiḍera* were made to god Parantakēśvara in the *Uttamacōda-maṇḍalam*, situated in the *Vēngī-nāḍu*, by Jiyyahari Tirumalaya of the *Dimila-nāḍu*.[233] The *mahapradhani* of the Vijayanagara king, Kṛṣṇarāya, named Nādiṇdla Gōparasayyaṁgāru, gifted the *mūlavīsāmu* collected in the *Koṇḍavīḍusīma* on watersheds, saltbeds, market, town and roads used by people like those going to the Tirumala hills as well as taxes collected on articles of merchandise like pulses, vegetables, fruits, spices and cloths to god Raghunāyaka of Yajñavāṭika or Koṇḍavīḍu.[234] An inscription from Drākshārāma registers the gift of *alamu, siddhāya, samastāyamu, antarāyamu, abhinavāyam, salvisampada* and *gaṇṭu* and other taxes to god Bhīmēśvara of the place.[235] A Rāmapaṇḍitulu, granted one *aḍḍa* per every *puṭṭi* of *mānadhānyālu* to god Viśvanātha of Appikaṭla.[236] In the reign of the Vijayanagara king, Sadāśiva, a gift of three *varāhas* of *dombaripannu*, realised from the *agrahāra* village of Bētapalle, to god Tirumaladēva of the village by the *Doṁbaras*.[237]

Tolls collected in various places were also donated to gods. A record from Peda-Gārlapāḍu, records the gift of tolls to the god of the place.[238] In Ś. 1060, the loca and visiting merchants of Prōlavaram granted certain tolls on pack bullocks and cart-loads for providing oblation to god Iṣṭakāmīśvara at Gajjaram.[239] Sāḷuva Gōvindarāja, granted in Ś. 1430, the tolls levied on cattle, and horses and taxes on marriages, festivals etc., to god Agastīśvara at Chadupurēla.[240] In Ś. 1477, *mahāmaṇḍalēśvara* Rāmarāya Cina-Śrīrangarāju Jaggarājayyadēva mahārāja gave tolls collected at the village of Santarāvūru to the temples of Cennarāya and

231. 389 of 1938-39. Kopparti.
232. *S.I.I.* IV. 709. Mangaḷagiri.
233. *Ibid.*, IV. 1226. Drākshārāma.
234. *E.I.* VI. pp. 230-239. Koṇḍavīḍu.
235. *S.I.I.* IV. 1268. Drākshārāma.
236. *Ibid.*, VI. 126. Appikaṭla.
237. 331 of 1920. Bētapalle.
Similar Examples
301 of 1930-31. Tāḷḷapalli.
S.I.I. VI. 219. Amarāvati.
328 of 1915. Kopparam.
430 of 1938-39. Valluru.
20 of App. E of 1941-42. Ulchala.
N.D.I. I. Gūḍur 86. Reḍḍipālem.
319 of 1940-41. Jaṁmalamaḍugu.
S.I.I. X. 135. Pamidipāḍu-Agrahāram.
238. 31 of 1930-31. Pedda-Gārlapāḍu.
239. 294 of 1920. Gajjaram.
240. 214 of 1937-38. Chiḍipirāla.

Rāmayalinga in the village of Santarāvūru.[241] In S. 1401 a gift of toll and other revenues raised in the fair held on every Friday at Lakkhaṇapura by the seṭṭis and *Paṭṭanasvāmis* for the servic. of the goddess Mahālakṣmīdēvī of Haruhe Lakhaṇapura by Vīranāyaka.[242] In Ś. 1482, *mahāmaṇḍalēśvara* Koṇḍarājayadēva mahārāja granted tolls to god Madanagōpālakṛṣṇa of the village of Vēlpucherla.[243]

Customs duties were also donated to gods. In Ś. 1286, the people of all countries came to an agreement in connection with the Friday market established by Kancannaṁgāru, the best of officials in Nellōre and they agreed to devote the fees raised in the market to goddess Iṛukulā Paramēśvari for the religious merit of the above officer.[244] The taxes levied on articles sold in the Chadalavāḍa village, the *sthala* of Raghunāyakulu and on grain, the *aḍagaḍa-sunkamu* and the old *kaṭṇam* collected in *Śri Raghūnāyakulu sthala* were given to god Raghunāyakulu of Chedalavāḍa in Ś. 1481.[245] The taxes on looms etc , and several kinds of *Siddhāyas* accruing in the villages of Chadupurāla and Chapili in the *Gaṇḍikōṭa-sima* were donated in Ś. 1464 to the local deity by three toll-officers.[246]

Other incomes were also presented to temples. A subordinate of Kākatiya Rudradēva, gave in Ś. 1190, money income to the god at Jyōti.[247] In Ś. 1476, the *Vipravinōdins* granted their annual income of six *rūkas* due from the *mahājanas* of the village of Vēmavaram-agrahāram in the *Gandikōāṭa-sīma* to the local god, Lakṣmīkantaperumāḷ.[248] A record from Chandragiri mentions the gift of income from the marriage tax to god Hanumān of the place.[249]

4. *Gifts of Jewels*

The presentation of jewels like *kiritas* of crowns, necklaces, garlands, etc., to gods and goddesses was considered an act of great merit. Various ornaments were presented by people of all positions in life from princes to peasants. Interesting information is available about these gifts.

a. *Kiritas*

The famous Vijayanagara king, Śrī Vīrakṛṣṇarāya Mahārāya, presented a

241. 477 of 1915. Santarāvūru.
242. *S.I.I.* IX. 584. Goṛrepalle.
243. 404 of 1940-41. Vēlpucherla.
244. *N.D.I.* II. Nellore. 78.
245. *Ibid.*, II. Ongōle 31. Chadalavāḍa.
246. 206 of 1937-38. Chiḍipirāla.
    Similar Examples
    34 of 1941-42. Pōrumāmiḷḷa.
    K.I.A.P. Mn. 42. Gangāpuram.
247. 1 of 1939-40. Aṭlūru.
248. 416 of 1940-41. Yāmavaram.
249. 119 of 1945-46. Chandragiri.
    Similar Examples
    S.I.I. X. 422. Durgī.
    Ibid., X. 427. Pedda-Ganjām.
    Ibid., X. 447. Kollūru.

kirīṭam of the following decoration—1,555 weight of gold for *vommeccu* work or basement work for setting the stones, 1,076 weight of solid gold selected for *kundamam* work, 2,822 fine rubies, 160 emeralds weighing 108 *ratulu* or carats, 423 old diamonds weighing 65 *mañjalu,* 3 big rubies including the central one, 10 sapphires, 17 cats eyes and one topaz altogether weighing 663 *ratulu* or carats, 1 string of pearls, gold wire into which the pearls were inserted weighing 15 units, the total weight of the entire crown being 3,308 units, to god Śrī Venkaṭēśa of Tirumala in Ś. 1434.[250] In Ś. 1435, the same king presented three *kirīṭas,* consisting of 405 pearls, 284 old diamonds, 222 rubies 9 cats eyes and 6 sapphires weighing 380 units to the processional images of Śrī Venkaṭēśa of the same place.[251] An Asana nāyaka presented a *kirīṭa* in Ś. 1629 to god Tiruvengaḷanātha of Kaḍapa.[252]

b. *Paṭṭams*

Several donors delighted in presenting *paṭṭams* or diadems to deities. In the 16th year of the reign of the Cōḷa king, Rājēndracōḷa, a *paṭṭam* or ornamental plate for the head worth 52 *kaḷañju* of gold and set with 6 rubies, 4 diamonds and 28 pearls was presented by Parāntakadēvi the chief queen of the king.[253] In Ś. 1267, a gold *paṭṭam* was given to god Amarēśvara of Amarāvati by Vēmayareḍḍi.[254] An individual, named Śrīgirīśvara presented a *paṭṭam,* newly made of gold and gems, to god Śrī Venkaṭēśa of Tirumala.[255] In the 40th year of the reign of Vīranarasingadēva Yādavarāyar, his chief queen granted a *paṭṭam* to god Tiruvenkaṭadēvar of the same place.[256]

c. *Hāras*

Inscriptions supply numerous instances of the presentation of *hāras, kanṭhamālas* and necklaces to gods. In Ś. 1264 Kṛṣṇadēviamma donated one *pahiṇḍipogaḍa-puvula-māla,* one *trisarimuktvālacēru* and two *biḷḷasaramulu* to god Śrī Narasimhanātha of Simhāchalam.[257] One Oḍḍādi Bhīmanapreggaḍa granted a *vaijayantimāla,* set with gems and *sikha-nāga-bhūṣanam* to the same deity in S. 1266.[258] A record from Srīkākuḷam dated in Ś. 1275, refers to the gift of *sannaṁ-*

250. *T.T.D.I.* III. 32. Tirumala.
251. *Ibid.*, III. 60. Tirumala.
252. 366 of 1938-39. Dēvuni-Cuḍḍapah.
Similar Examples
S.I.I. X. 242. Muktiyāla.
Ibid., IV. 765. Bezavāḍa.
253. *T.T.D.I.* I. 14. Tirupati.
254. *S.I.I.* VI. 243. Amarāvati.
255. *T.T.D.I.* I. 193. Tirumala.
256. *Ibid.*, I. 88. Tirumala.
Similar Examples
N.D.I. II. Nellore. 37. Koruṭūru.
S.I.I. IV. 1329. Drākshārāma.
257. *S.I.I.* VI. 983. Siṁhāchalam.
258. *Ibid.*, VI. 836. Siṁhāchalam.

pūsapēru to god Śrīkākolani Vallabharāya by Gangamahādēvulu.[259] Another, from Simhāchalam, dated in Ś. 1343, states that the chief, Oḍḍādi Pratāparudra, gave one pearl necklace and one gold necklace weighing two *vi* and 7 *pa*, to god Śrī Narasimhanātha of Simhāchalam.[260] In Ś. 1425, a *hāra*, named *māmidikāyapēru*, was presented to the same god by Tallu mahāpātrāṇi, the wife of Rāmbhaṭṭu-mahapātrulu.[261] In Ś. 1436 the Vijayanagara king, Kṛṣṇaraya, lead an expedition against Pratāparudra Gajapati and drove him as far as Koṇḍavīḍu, captured the fortress of Udayagiri and on his return journey to his capital, paid a visit to the Tirumala temple and worshipped Śrī Venkaṭēśa, when Cinnādēvi-aṁmā, his queen, presented one *kaṇṭhamāla* with a *padakam* or pendant set with 11 pearls, the central ruby, 2 emeralds and 4 diamonds altogether weighing 200 units.[262] In Ś. 1438, Kṛṣṇarāya, after the conquest of Kōṇḍapalli, Rajahmundry etc., came to the hill, saw the god and presented one *kaṇṭhamālā* and one *śaṁkhu-cakrāla-padakam* to the god and his queens, Cinnādēvī and Tirumaladēvī, gave two pendants.[263] In Ś. 1454, the Vijayanagara emperor, Acyutarāya presented to god Śrī Venkaṭēśa of Tirumala a necklace containing 600 pearls and 10 units of superior gold.[264] Rājāśrī Śivarāja Rāmacandra Yadamatarar Dabirasa presented a gold *kaṇṭhi*, equal to the weight of five *varāhan* and valued at 525 gold coins known as *Śrīrangarājagadyāna* to the same god.[265] In the 8th year of the reign of Aniyanka Bhīma, a gift of *puṣpamālā* or garland of gold flowers was made to the god of Drākshārāma.[266]

d. *Garlands of Gold*

Interesting information is available about the presentation of various kinds of *hāras* or garlands to the deities. In Ś. 1265, seven garlands of pearls were granted to the god of Śrīkūrmam.[267] A garland of 38 lotus flowers was given to god Narasiṁha of Siṁhāchalam.[268] In Ś. 1244, Gangāṁbā, the queen of the Eastern

259. *Ibid.*, IV. 975. Śrīkākuḷam.
260. *Ibid.*, VI. 836. Siṁhāchalam.
261. *Ibid.*, V. 1228. Śrīkūrmam.
262. *T.T.D.I.* III. 70. Tirumala.
263. *S.I.I.* VI. 1170. Siṁhāchalam.
264. *T.T.D.I.* IV. 16. Tirumala.
265. *Ibid.*. VI. 24. Tirumala.
266. *S.I.I.* IV. 1329. Drākshārāma.
Similar Examples
S.I.I. VI. 904. Siṁhāchalam.
Ibid., V. 1169. Śrīkūrmam.
Ibid., V. 1189. Śrīkūrmam.
Ibid., VI. 1065. Siṁhāchalam.
Ibid., IV. 830. Siṁhāchalam.
T.T.D.I. III. Tirumala.
S.I.I. VI. 694. Siṁhāchalam.
T.T.D.I. III. 83. Tirumala.
S.I.I. IV. 1329. Drākshārāma.
267. *S.I.I.* V. 1189. Śrīkūrmam.
268. *Ibid.*, VI. Siṁhāchalam.

Gānga king, Narasiṁha, gave a garland of two lotus buds to god Śrī Kūrmanātha of Śrīkūrmam.[269] In Ś. 1438, Kṛṣṇarāya granted a garland of *śaṁkhas* and *cakras* and his queens Cinnādēvī and Tirumala devī, presented a garland of 500 *varāhas* each to god Śrī Venkaṭēśa of Tirumala.[270]

e. *Valayas*

Equally interesting information is available about the gift of other ornaments like *valayas* and *kaḍiyams* to deities. In Ś. 987, a silver bracelet was given to god Bhīmēśvara of Drākshārāma by Sōmaladēvī.[271] Queen Sabbama, the wife of king Velanāḍu Gonka, granted a *valaya*, weighing 95 *gadyas*, to god Bhīmēśvara of the same place.[272] Koṁmamamahādevī, the queen of Bayyarāju, presented a gold *valaya* weighing 108 *gadyas* to the same god.[273] Śrī Kṛṣṇadēva *Mahārāya* presented one pair of *bhujakīrtis* set with 322 pearls, 360 rubies, 4 sapphires and 247 old diamonds, altogether weighing 573 units for the daily use to the god Śrī Venkaṭēśa of Tirumala in Ś. 1435.[274] In Ś. 1436, the same king gave a *kaḍyam* or *bāhuvalayam* or *vanki*, made of 322 diamonds, 100 rubies, all weighing 275 units to the same god.[275] A gold ring was presented to god Tripurāntaka of Tripurāntakam in Ś. 1278.[276] Kṛṣṇarāya presented one *vajra-mānjkyāla-kaḍiyālajōḍu*, a beautiful ornament to the feet of god Śrī Narasiṁhanātha of Siṁhāchalam in Ś. 1438. The same king presented a pair of *kaḍiyālu*, set with diamonds and *mānikyas* to the same god.[277] Certain jewels like *paṭṭālu* were presented to god Tripurāntaka by *Gaṇḍapeṇḍāra* Tripurāridēva *mahārājulu*.[278] A record from Drākshārāma, dated in Ś. 1065, mentions the gift of *reṇḍu-māṇikyālu-kaṭṭina-pahiṇḍipāṇi* and *samkulu-navaratnamulu-kaṭṭina-pahiṇḍi-pāṇulu-reṇḍu* to god Bhīmēśvara of Drākshārāma.[279] Another from Śrīkūrmam, dated in Ś. 1236 refers to the gift of *śrīhastālu* to the local deity.[280] One record from Siṁhāchalam, dated in S. 1271, mentions the gift of two gold feet to the god by Gangāmahādēvī, wife of Narasiṁhadēva to god Narasiṁha of the place.[281]

f. *Flowers*

Information relating to the gift of gold flowers and leaves to deities is also available from many records. In Ś. 987, a *kalpaka* flower of gold was presented to the god of Drākshārāma by Sōmaladēvī.[282] A big flower of gold was granted to the

269. *Ibid.*, V. 1190. Śrīkūrmam.
270. *Ibid.*, VI. 694. Siṁhāchalam.
271. *S.I.I.* IV. 1007. Drākshārāma.
272. *Ibid.*, IV. 1224. Drākshārāma.
273. *Ibid.*, IV. 1222. Drākshārāma.
274. *T.T.D.I.* III. 60. Tirumala.
275. *Ibid.*, III. 66. Tirumala.
276. *S.I.I.* X. 555. Tripurāntakam.
277. *S.I.I.* VI. 694. Siṁhāchalam.
278. *Ibid.*, VI. X. 431. Tripurantakam.
279. *Ibid.*, IV. 1190. Drākshārāma.
280. *Ibid.*, V. 1216. Śrīkūrmam.
281. *Ibid.*, VI. 933. Siṁhachalam.
282. *Ibid.*, IV. 1007. Drākshārāma.

god of Tripurāntakam in Ś. 1194, by Tripurāridēva *mahārajā.*[283] A certain Mangiraju donated 100 silver flowers to the Nandi of Śrī Bhīmēśvaramahādēva of Drākshārāma in Ś. 1211.[284] King Narasiṁha's wife, Gangāṁbā, gave in Ś. 1244, *mogalirōkulu* to god Śrī Kūrmanātha of Śrīkūrmam.[285] The same queen granted a lotus, two crysunthimum flowers, eight *mogalirēkulu* and four *rasanagamiyālu* in Ś. 1271 to the same god.[286] A record from Śrīkūrmam, dated in Ś. 1425 mentions the gift of *mēḍanūlu-veṇḍicippapūlu* to its god by the wife of Rāmbhaṭṭumahōpādhyāyulu.[287]

g. *Kavaca*

Inscriptions also supply information about the presentation of *kavaca* or encasement to the body of the deities. A Mangiraja presented *mēlukaṭṭu* to god Nandidēvara of the Drākshārāma temple in Ś. 1211.[288] The Eastern Gānga king, Narasiṁha, presented a *pañcavaktra-kōhaḷi* made of gold in Ś. 1344 to god Dharmalingēśvara of Panchadhārla.[289] In Ś. 1417, a *pañcavaktra-kōhaḷi* made of 5 *tolas* of gold to suit the face of the *utsava* image of the god of Śrīkūrman was presented by a seṭṭi.[290] In Ś. 1135, Jaya *sēnāpati*, covered the image of Kumāra of Chēbrōlu with gold.[291]

h. *Miscellaneoas Jewels*

Several kinds of miscellaneous jewels were also donated to deities. Śrī Kṛṣṇadēvarāya presented on big *vududhāra* to Śrī Venkaṭēśvara of Tirumala consisting of five diamonds 4 *aḍḍikas*, 6 middle *aḍḍikas*, these were set with 139 emeralds, 5 gems, 508 old diamonds, 186 rubies including the gold string, weighing altogether 662 units, one *kaṭhāri* or sword with sheath containing 131 old diamonds, 431 rubies and two sapphires, all weighing 198 units the tassel being composed of 3,500 small-pearls and 19 big pearls, 28 rubies fixed at the top of the tassel being 326, in this 43 rubies 15 emeralds, 20 diamonds all weighing 132 units, 24 rubies on the top of this sword consisting of 85 rubies, one emerald and 30 diamonds, weighing 80, one string with 17 *aḍḍigas*, 33 *aḍḍigas* in the shape of the leaves of the peepal tree, thirty pearls, 210 rubies, 58 diamonds and five emeralds altogether weighing 276 units in Ś. 1435,[292] In S. 1454 Acyutarāya presented to the same god a pair of ornaments intended for the daily decoration of his eyes, one string of *taṇikkay* beads made of gold, weighing 10 units of high value, one pair of *valitilaikkay* beads made of pure gold, weighing 10 units, and a big stone ornament containing 900

283. *Ibid.*, X. 431. Tripurāntakam.
284. *Ibid.*, V. 1019. Drāksāhrāma.
285. *Ibid.*, V. 1228. Śrīkūrmam.
286. *Ibid.*, VI. 933. Siṁhāchalam.
287. *Ibid.*, V. 1228. Śiīkūrmam.
288. *Ibid.*, IV. 1019. Drākshārāma.
289. *Ibid.*, IV. 667. Panchadharla.
290. *Ibid.*, V. 1229. Śrīkūrmam.
291. *E.I.* V. pp. 142-151. Chēbrōlu.
292. *T.T.D.I.* III. 60. Tirumala.

pearls.[293] In S. 1194, certain gifts like *mālya* flower, gold leaves and *guṇṭagalu* were granted to god Tripurāntaka of Tripurāntakam.[294] *Mahāmaṇḍalēśvara* Oḍḍādi Pratāpārujunadēva presented in Ś. 1330, one *vāḷi* of 100 *sasukāni* weight, to god Śrī Narasiṁhanātha of Siṁhāchalam.[295] Kopperunjinga, the Later Pallava chief, granted a *tattarikōhaḷa* to god Bhīmēśvara of Drākshārāma.[296] A Gaurīśankara Vinayyangāru gave a *triśūlam, ḍhakkā*, to the Bhīmalinga of Drākshārāma.[297]

i. *Cloths*

One popular item of presentation was cloths. Śrībalidēvaradēvī presented silk cloths in Ś. 1061 to god Mahēśa of Noccaṇḍlapūḍi.[298] A record from Tripurāntakam dated in S. 1212, mentions the gift of cloths like *cīni, mahācīni, ksita-ksauma* and *raktakṣauma* to the local god.[299] In Ś. 1215, the religious, teacher, Naraharitīrtha, made provision for the supply of *manjiṣta-cīralu, vella-cīralu, paṭṭutrāḍu* to god Śrī Rāma at *Śrīkūrmam.*[300] A record from Śrīkākuḷam dated in Ś. 1275, refers to the gift of 12 *venne-ciralu* by Gangamahādēvulu to god Śrīkākolani Śrīvallabharāya.[301] A Pōtinēnimgāru granted *patina-cīralu* to god Bhīmēśvara of Drākshārāma in Ś. 1392 [302] Kṛṣṇarāya after his glorious eastern campaign, visited the Tirumala temple and presented a *kuḷḷāvu* fixed with pearls, rubies, emeralds and sapphires to god Śrī Venkaṭēśa.[303] Mallikārjunarāyaṇḍu gave *pāgālu* to god Bhīmēśvara of Drākshārāma.[304] In Ś. 1442, Kṛṣṇarāya presented to god Tiruvēngaḷanātha, a *pītāṁbaram* or laced silk cloth set with nine kinds of precious stones.[305]

In Ś. 1194, a gift of *gangāvatāram* or a pot with small holes was made to god Tripurāntaka of Tripurāntakam.[306] *Sahasradhāra* of gold was presented to the god of Siṁhāchalam by Oḍḍādi Bhīmana peggaḍa in Ś. 1287.[307] A record from Śrīkūrmam, dated in Ś. 1392, mentions the gift of a silver *Sahasradhārā* weighing 14 *palams* to the local deity.[308]

j. *Mirrors*

Mirrors were also presented to the deities by devotees. In the 34th year of the reign of the Gajapati king, Puruṣōttamadēva, a mirror was given to god Bhīmēśvara

293. *Ibid.*, IV. 16. Tirumala.
294. *S.I.I.* X. 431. Tripurāṇṭakam.
295. *Ibid.*, VI. 946. Siṁhāchalam.
296. *Ibid.*, IV. 1342-B. Drākshārāma.
297. *Ibid.*, IV. 1346. Drākshārāma.
298. *Ibdi.*, IV. 672. Nadiṇḍla.
299. *Ibid.*, X. 465. Tripurāntakam.
300. *Ibid.*, V. 1172. Śrīkūrmam.
301. *Ibid.*, IV. 975. Śrīkākuḷam.
302. *Ibid.*, IV. 1344. Drākshārāma.
303. *T.T.D.I.* III. 80. Tirumala.
304. *S.I.I.* IV. 1374-A. Drākshārāma.
305. *T.T.D.I.* III. 83. Tirumala.
306. *S.I.I.* X. 431. Tripurantakam.
307. *Ibid.*, VI. 882. Siṁhachalam.
308. *Ibid.*, V. 1247. Śrīkūrmam.

of Drākshārāma on the occasion of the *Simhayuktapuṇyakāla*.[309] A metal mirror was granted in Ś. 1064 to the same god by the Velanāḍu king, Kulōttungacōḍa Gonka.[310] Bimmaladēvī, the queen of Vennacōḍayarāju, donated a round mirror to god Bhīmēśvara of the same place in Ś. 1159 on the *paurṇima* day.[311]

5. *Gifts of Utensils etc.*

A variety of utensils used for various purposes were presented to temples by several people. A silver vessel was given in Ś. 987 to the god of Drākshārāma.[312] A general of the Śilāvamśa gave a drinking vessel in Ś. 1051 to god Śrīkūrmanātha of Śrīkūrmam.[313] In Ś. 1135, a gold vessel was granted by Jāyasēnāpati to the deity at Chēbrōlu.[314] Gangāmahādēvī, the queen of Narasimhadēva, gifted vessels for *abhiṣēka* to the god at Simhāchalam in Ś. 1272.[315] In Ś. 1330, two *tambagariyalu* were given for fetching water for the same deity for the *tirumanjanam*.[316] A gold pot and two silver pots were presented to god Bhīmēśvara of Drākshārāma in Ś. 1392 by Pōtanēnimgāru.[317] Kṛṣṇarāya and his queen, Cinnājī-ammangāru, granted in Ś. 1430 a gold vessel weighing 374 *tōlas* for god Tiruvēngaḷanātha of Tirumala for offering milk after night worship.[318]

A number of plates of gold, silver, bronze and brass were presented to the temples. Kṛṣṇarāya and his queen, Tirumaladēvī, granted a gold plate weighing 10 *tolas* for *parimaḷālu-avadharincanu* to the god of Tirumala in Ś. 1434.[319] In Ś. 1438, another plate weighing 44782 *gadyas* to the god at Simhāchalam.[320] In Ś. 1438 the same king gave a gold plate, weighing 4479 *tumkālu* and 2,000 *kānika-māḍalu*, to the god of Simhāchalam, for the merit of his parents.[321] A certain Bayyarāju granted a gold plate weighing 500 *gadyas* to god Bhīmēśvara of Drākshārāma.[322] In Ś. 1057, a silver plate was given to god Śrīkūrmanātha of Śrīkūrmam by a general of the Śilāvamśa.[323] Jayantirāju, the son of Oḍḍādi Arjunadēvarāju, granted a silver plate to the god of Simhāchalam.[324] In Ś. 1350, a brass plate was given to god *Mulasthāna* Siddhēśvaralinga on the occasion of a lunar eclipse at Bhīmavaram.[325]

309. *Ibid.*, IV. 1362. Drākshārāma.
310. *Ibid.*, IV. 1142. Drākshārāma.
311. *S.I I.* IV. 1145. Drākshārāma.
312. *Ibid.*, IV. 1007. Drākshārāma.
313. *Ibid.*, V. 1170. Śrīkūrman.
314. *E.I.* V. pp. 142-151. Chēbrōlu.
315. *S.I.I.* VI. 1052. Simhāchalam.
316. *Ibid.*, VI. 946. Simhāchalam.
317. *Ibid.*, IV. 1344. Drākshārāma.
318. *T.T.D.I.* 39, 41. Tirumala.
319. *Ibid.*, III. 50. Tirumala.
320. *S.I.I.* VI. 696. Simhāchalam.
321. *Ibid.*, VI. 1170. Simhāchalam.
322. *Ibid.*, IV. 1222. Drākshārāma.
323. *Ibid.*, V. 1170. Śrīkūrmam.
324. *Ibid.*, VI. 981. Simhāchalam.
325. *Ibid.*, V. 1350. Bhīmavaram.

Cups were also presented to the deities. In Ś. 1434, Cinnājī-aṁman, the queen of *Mahārājādhirāja Rājaparamēśvara Śrī Vīra* Kṛṣṇarāya presented a gold cup weighing 374 units to Tiruvengaḷanāthadēva of Tirumala for milk offering after the night worship.[326] Tirumaladēvīaṁma, the queen of Kṛṣṇarāya, presented a gold cup of the same weight to the same deity.[327]

Devotees presented *kuḍukalu* or laddles. A record from Bhīmavaram, dated in Ś. 1344, mentions the gift of a *kuḍuka* to the local god.[328] Pōtinēniṁgāru granted copper *kuḍukalu* to god Bhīmēśvara of Drākshārāma in Ś. 1396.[329] In Ś. 1057 an *arghyapātra* was endowed to god Śrī Kūrmanātha of Śrīkūrmam.[330]

6. *Gifts of Requirements of Worship*

Requirements of worship like flower garlands, *vinjāmaras*, cauries etc., were also donated.

a. *Garlands*

A gift was made in Ś. 1276 for the supply of one *doṇḍavanamālā* to the god of Śrīkūrmam every day.[331] In Ś. 1313, provision was made for the supply of one *tulaśimālā* to the same deity.[332] In Ś. 1324 arrangements were made for the supply of a *tirutōmālā* to the same god.[333]

b. *Vinjāmaras*

Vinjāmaras were also presented to the deities. In Ś. 1065, two gold gilded *vinjāmaras* were granted to the god of Drākshārāma.[334] A *sāni* gave a *vinjāmara* with gold handle in Ś. 1150 to god Bhīmēśvara of the same place.[335] Queen Gangāmahādēvulu, presented in Ś. 1275, two *vinjāmaras* with gold handles to god Śrīkākolani Śrī Vallabharāya.[336]

326. *T.T.D.I.* III. 40. Tirumala.
327. *Ibid.*, III. 50-59. Tirumala.
328. *S.I.I.* V. 46. Bhīmavaram.
329. *Ibid.*, IV. Drākshārama.
330. *Ibid.*, V. 1170. Śrīkūrmam.
Similar Examples
S.I.I. IV. 1142, 1343, 1362, Drākshārāma.
Ibid., X. 451. Mallavōlu.
Ibid., V. 131. Pālakol.
Ibid., V. 29. Sarpavaram.
Ibid., V. 46, 47. Bhīmavaram.
T.T.D.I. III. 100. Tirumala.
331. *S.I.I.* VI. 1136. Siṁhāchalam.
332. *Ibid.*, VI. 750. Siṁhāchalam.
333. *Ibid.*, VI. 717. Siṁhāchalam.
Similar Examples
S.I.I. VI. 716, 742. Siṁhāchalam.
Ibid., V. 1223. Śrīkūrmam.
334. *S.I.I.* IV. 1194. Drākshārāma.
335. *Ibid.*, IV. 1372. Drākshārāma.
336. *Ibid.*, IV. 975, Śrīkākuḷam.

c. *Cauris*

Cāmaras or cauries were granted to gods by devotees. Queen Gangāmahādēvī donated in Ś. 1271, two silver *cāmaras* to the deity at Siṁhāchalam.[337] In Ś. 1061, Śrībalidēvaradēvī gave a *cāmāravaḷi* to the god at Nādeṇḍla.[338] Śrī Kṛṣṇarāya presented two *cāmaras* set with nine kinds of gems to god Tiruvēngaḷanātha of Tirumala.[339]

d. *Ālavaṭṭams and Umbrellas*

Ālavaṭṭavms and umbrellas were presented by pious devotees to gods. In Ś. 1275, *ālavaṭṭam* with gold handle was granted to the god at Śrīkakuḷam.[340] Eight umbrellas were given to the god at Śrīkūrmam in Ś. 1236.[341] In Ś. 1275, umbrellas made of silk were presented to the same god by Gangāmahādēvī.[342] A gold umbrella was granted in Ś. 1392 by Pōtanēniṁgāru to the god at Drākshārāma.[343] An undated record from Drākshārāma, mentions the gift of an umbrella made of ivory to the local deity by Mallikārjunarāyaṇḍu.[344]

e. *Lamps*

The most popular item of gift made to temples was lamps. There are hundreds of examples of this gift. A certain Dantigan, the son of Aranili, who was administering the *Pānkara-nāḍu*, situated in the *Kunravattana-kōṭṭam*, donated a lamp in Ś. 876 to god Karaikkandar of the village of Kurichchānūr.[345] King Vīra Rājēndra Cōḷa granted a lamp in Ś. 1089 to god Mallikārjunadēva of Śrīśailam.[346] In Ś. 1193, Uttamaśivagurudēva, the son of Rājagurudēva, presented two lamps to the temple of Bhōgīśvara mahādēva of Bhaṭṭiprōlu.[347] Tōlēṭi Induśēkharadēva Cakravarti gave a lamp to god Śrīkūrmanātha of Śrīkūrmam in Ś. 1222, for the merit of his parents, Viṣṇuvardhana and Bhīmidēvī.[348] In Ś. 1322, provision was made for lighting of a row of lamps in the temple of Mallikārjunadēva at Śrīparvata by seven brothers of the goldsmith community residing at Guṇḍamangaḷāpura during the reign of Mallinātha, the brother of Dēvarāya, who was the agent of Bhikṣāvrtti Siddhaya-Dēvayya.[349]

337. *Ibid.*, VI. 933. Siṁhāchalam.
338. *Ibid.*, IV. 672. Nādiṇḍla.
339. *T.T.D.I.* III. 83. Tirumala.
340. *S.I.I.* IV. 975. Śrīkākuḷam.
341. *Ibid.*, V. 1216. Śrīkūrmam.
342. *Ibid.*, V. 1233. Śrīkūrmam.
343. *Ibid.*, IV. 1344. Drākshārāma.
344. *Ibid.*, VI. 1374 A. Drākshārāma.
345. 26 of 1946-47. Nagari.
346. 59 of 1942-43. Śrīśailam.
347. 307 of 1936-37. Bhaṭṭiprōlu.
348. *S.I.I.* V. 1147. Śrīkūrmam.
349. 232 of 1931-32. Guṇḍugallu.
Similar Examples
S.I.I. X. 59. Juttiga.
17 of App. E of 1939-40. Guḍimūla.
S.I.I. X. 64. Vēlpūru.

f. *Lampstands ana Lamp Pillars*

Devotees presented several kinds of lampstands for keeping lamps in the temples. A lamp-stand weighing 300 *palams* was granted by Cōḍināyaka, the *paḍālu* of the Kalacūri chief, Kāṭamanāyaka, to god Bhīmēśvara of Drākshārāma in Ś. 1021.[350] In Ś. 1029, in the 38th year of the reign of the Cāḷukya-Cōḷa king, Kulōttunga, a silver lampstand was presented to the same god.[351] In S. 1127, a *Puravara* Mancena peggaḍa donated a lampstand to god Śrīkūrmanātha of Śrīkūrmam for the religious merit of his mother, Vasanaṁma.[352] A bronze lampstand was presented in Ś. 1145 to god Bhīmēśvara of Bhīmavaram by Dēvaya.[353] A *tiruvaḷikakōla* was given to god Śrī Narasiṁha of Siṁhāchalam in Ś. 1316.[354] In Ś. 1343 Kūnamanēṇḍu granted a bell metal lampstand with the figures of his mother, himself and his wife sculptured on it to god Bhāvanārāyaṇa perumāḷ at Sarpavaram.[355] In Ś. 1382, Dāhala Cāmurautu gave a lampstand to god Śrīkūrmanātha.[356] In Ś. 1425, a gift of a figure of a lamp bearer was made to the same god.[357] A Kāṭhaka king presented a golden lampstand to the gods of Drāksharama for the merit of the Kākatīya king.[358] A Puṣpāla Pāpana erected the stone lamp post in Ś. 1451, in front of the temple of Cennakēśava of Turimiḷadinne the *agrahāra* of Nācirāju-sōma, which was situated in the *Puṣpagiri-Prāntya* on the north bank of the river Penna, in the *Gaṇḍikōṭasīma.*[359] In Ś. 1721, a *dīpa-sthaṁbha* was set up by Peda Gurvireḍḍi, the son of Vīrā-reḍḍi of Rāyasaṁpalli.[360]

g. *Perfumes*

A number of perfumes were required for worship for ablution etc. In Ś. 1018, a gift of land was made for the supply of sandal to the temple of god Bhīmēśvara of Drākshārāma by the *mahāsthānādhipati* of the temple.[361] In Ś. 1212, provision was made for the supply of *Kuṁkuma,* musk, camphor, *agaru, śrīgandha* etc., to god Tripurāntakēśvara at Tripurāntakam.[362] Provision was made in Ś. 1191 for the supply of *śrīgandha, guggilam* etc., to the god at Durgi.[363] A record from Nellore refers to the provision made for the supply of sandal and basil to god Śrī Talpagiri Ranganāthasvāmi by a dancing girl.[364] Arrangements were made in Ś. 1427 for the supply of *paccaikarpūram* or refined camphor and *kastūri* or musk for performing the *pulugu-kāppu* function to the goddess, Alarmēlmangai Nācciyār, adorning the

350. *S.I.I* IV. 1235. Drākshārāma.
351. *Ibid.*, IV. 1305. Drākshārāma.
352. *Ibid.*, V. 1314. Śrīkūrmam.
353. *Ibid.*, V. 32. Cāḷukya-Bhīmavaram.
354. *Ibid.*, VI. 771. Siṁhāchalam.
355. 694 of 1926. Sarpavaram.
356. *S.I I.* V. 1165. Śrīkūrmam.
357. *Ibid.*, V. 1228 Śrīkūrmam.
358. *Ibid.*, IV. 1342. Drākshārāma.
359. 425 of 1938-39. Tuḍumuladinne.
360. 259 of 1937-38. Rāyasaṁpalli.
361. *S.I.I.* IV. 1229. Drāksāhrāma.
362. *Ibid.*, X. 465. Tripurāntakam.
363. *Ibid.*, X. 422. Durgī.
364. *N.D.I.* II. Nellore 59. Nellore.

bosom of Śrī Venkaṭēśa of Tirumala by a seṭṭi.[365] Provision was made in S. 1466, for the supply of *candanam, damanam,* rose water, musk and refined camphor for god Gōvindarāja of Tirupati by Nārāyaṇa seṭṭi.[366] Udayagiri Dēvarāya Bhaṭṭar arranged for the supply of *candanam* for the *kalabham* decoration, musk, refined camphor, and *gaṁbūra* for the decoration of god Tiruvēnkaṭamuḍaiyān of Tirumala in Ś. 1468.[367] In Ś. 1536 arrangements were made by Venkaṭayyan for the supply of *candanam*, musk, saffron, turmeric camphor, benzoin and *palasam* flowers for the conduct of the *Vasantōtsava* function to god Malaikuniyaninṟa Perumāḷ and Nāccimār of Tirumala.[368] An inscription from Drākshārāma, mentions the provision made by the temple treasury for the supply of sandal paste daily to god Bhīmēśvara of the place at the time of *ardhajāmu*.[369]

7. *Gifts of Animals*

Interesting information is available about the gift of animals like cows, buffaloes, bulls sheep etc., for maintaining lamps in the temples and for the preparation of offerings.

a. *Cows*

In Ś. 1037 and in the 45th year of the region of Velnāḍu Mādhavunḍu *alias* Rājavallabha-Pallavarāyaṇḍu, the lord of Kadambaṁguḍi granted a lamp to god Nārāyanadēva of the Māṇḍayya temple at Cāḷukya-Bhīmavaram in the *Sakaṭamantani-nāḍu* on the occasion of a *Viṣuva-sankrānti*, and gave 20 cows.[370] In Ś. 1055, in the reign of the Velanāḍu chief, Gonka, a gift of 50 cows was made for the *kṣīrābhiṣēka* by the king to god Bhīmēśvara of Drākshārāma.[371] In Ś. 1192, 50 cows were given for two perpetual lamps to god Śrī Narasiṁha on the occasion of the *Dipāvali-mohōtsava*.[372] In Ś. 1205, 100 cows were donated for 2 lamps by Upēndradēva Mallapadēva *mahārāja* to god Śrī Narasiṁhanātha of Siṁhāchalam.[373] In Ś. 1268, 50 cows were endowed for a lamp by the king Lakumarāja of the Cāḷukyas of Vīraghōṭṭam to the same god.[374] A *seṭṭi* presented 50 cows in Ś. 1272 for a lamp to god Śrīkūrmanātha of Śrīkūrmam.[375] In Ś. 1281 one hundred cows were presented for two lamps to the same god.[376] In Ś. 1346, a cow was presented for supplying ghee, milk and curds as part of a food offering to god Nārāyaṇa of

365. *T.T.D.I.* III. 4. Tirumala.
366. *Ibid.*, V. 25. Tirupati.
367. *Ibid.*, V. 91. Tirupati.
368. *Ibid.*, VI. 18. Tirumala.
369. *S.I.I.* IV. 1103. Drākshārāma.
370. *E.I.* VI. pp. 219-223. Bhīmavaram.
371. *S.I.I.* IV. 1138. Drākshārāma.
372. *Ibid.*, VI. 726. Siṁhāchalam.
373. *Ibid.*, VI. 1157. Siṁhāchalam.
374. *Ibid.*, VI. 989. Siṁhāchalam.
375. *Ibid.*, V. 1237. Śrīkūrmam.
376. *Ibid.*, V. 1157. Śrīkurmam.

Cāḷukya-Bhīmavaram.[377] Fifty cows were given in Ś. 1434 for maintaining a lamp in the presence of Śrī Venkaṭēśa of Tirumala.[378]

b. *Buffaloes*

Buffaloes were also donated for the supply of ghee for maintaining lamps in the temple. In Ś 1004, 50 buffaloes were granted by Lakṣmīdēvī, the daughter of Muṁmaḍirāju, for a lamp in the temple at Drākshārāma.[379] Fifty *yinpayeḍlu* were given for a lamp on the condition that one *muṁmaḍibhīma-mānika* of ghee should be supplied daily in Ś. 1143 to the god at Juttiga.[380] In the 2nd year of the reign of Viṣṇuvardhana, fifty buffaloes were granted for the supply of one *sāniyam-bāṭimāneḍu* ghee for one lamp to god Rājanārāyaṇa Viṣṇudēvara at Bhīmavaram on the occasion of *Uttarāyaṇa.*[381] In the 31st year of the reign of the same king, fifty buffaloes were given for the supply of one *rājamāna-mānika* of ghee for a perpetual lamp to god Rājanārāyaṇa at Bhīmavaram.[382] A Mādhava gave 20 buffaloes for a lamp to god Nārāyaṇa of the same place.[383]

377. *Ibid.*, V. 47. Cāḷukya-Bhīmavaram.
378. *T.T.D.I.* III. 25. Tirumala.
Similar Examples
S.I.I. X. 70. Vēlpūru.
Ibid., X. 84. Īmani.
S.I.I. IV. 1158. Drākshārāma.
459 of 1940-41. Tripurāntakam.
S.I.I. V. 208. Taḍikalapūḍi.
340 of 1934-35. Peddakancherla.
S.I I. IV. 780. Bezavāḍa.
305 of 1936-37. Bhaṭṭiprōlu.
289 of 1936-37. Āmulālapalli.
293 of 1936-37. Bhaṭṭiprōlu.
S.I.I. V. 219. Guḍivāḍa.
278 of 1930-31. Telikicherla.
E.I. V. p. 31. Śrīkūrmam.
323 of 1937-38. Malyāla.
S.I.I. V. 33. Bhīmavaram.
T.T.D.I. I. 64, 85. Tirumala.
Ibid., I. 23. Yōgimallavaram.
T.T.D.I. I. 181. Tirumala.
S.I.I. X. 552. Tripurāntakam.
379. *Ibid.*, IV. 1161. Drākshārāma.
380. *Ibid.*, X. 268. Juttiga.
381. *Ibid.*, V. 77. Bhīmavaram.
382. *Ibid.*, V. 71. Bhīmavaram.
383. *E.I.* VI. pp. 219-223. Cāḷukya-Bhīmavaram.
Similar Exapmles
S.I.I. X. 68. Tripurāntakam.
Ibid., X. 110. Koṇidena.
Ibid., VI. 228. Amrāvati.
Ibid., V. 8. Bhīmavaram.
8 of 1941-42. Gōkarṇapuram.
S.I.I. IV. 771. Bezavāḍa.

c. *Sheep and Goats*

Sheep and goats were also presented to temples for maintaining lamps. In Ś. 965, sheep were presented to god Tripuruṣadēva in Valivēru in *Vela-nāṇḍu.*[384] In Ś. 1003, a Vellan presented 100 sheeps for 2 perpetual lamps to Madhukēśvara at Mukhalingam.[385] Fifty sheep were granted in Ś. 1054, to god Amutumūri Amṛtīśvara for maintaining a lamp with one *māna* of ghee per day.[386] In Ś. 1198, 66 ewes were given for lighting day and night, a perpetual lamp, to god Śrī Cennakēśava of Jaladanki.[387] In Ś. 1324, Residasa nāyaḍu, a Kalinga merchant gave 100 sheeps for a lamp to god Śrīkūrmanātha of Śrīkūrmam.[388] In Ś. 1335, 50 sheeps were presented to the Bhīmēśvara linga at Panchadhārla for a *mānadipa* on the occasion of a *Mēṣa sankrānti.*[389] A gift of 96 she-goats and one ram for a lamp was made to god Tirukkālattiuḍaiyar of Kāḷahasti by Ponnavasāni, the wife of Tirukkāḷaiṭṭ uḍaiyār, the *tantrapāla* of Darani-mattu of the *Poyagai-nāḍu.*[390]

d. *Bulls and Cows*

Bulls were also presented to temples. In Ś. 1085 a lady, named Erakama, granted 25 bulls for a lamp to god Bhīmēśvara Mahādēva of Drākshārāma.[391] In Ś. 1132 a gift of 50 bulls were made to god Bhāvanārāyaṇa of Prēmpalli.[392] In the

Ibid., V. 74. Bhīmavaram.
Ibid., V. 67. Bhīmavaram.
384. *S.I.I.* X. 6. Valivēru.
385. *Ibid.*, V. 1125. Mukhalingam.
386. *Ibid.*, X. 90 Amṛitalūru.
387. *N.D.I.* II. Kāvali 23. Jaladanki.
388. *S.I.I.* V. 1180. Śrīkūrmam.
389. *Ibid.*, VI. 656. Panchadhārla.
390. *S.I.I.* VIII. 381. Kāḷahasti.
Similar Examples
S.I.I. X. 7. Nandivelugu.
Ibid., X. 8. Amṛitalūru.
400 of 1932-33. Rājahmundry.
20 of App. E of 1939-40. Guḍimūla.
396 of 1932-33. Elamanchilli.
S.I.I. V. 42. Bhīmavaram.
Ibid., X. 84. Īmani.
348 of 1936-37. Bhaṭṭiprōlu.
S.I.I. X. 94. Sattenapalli.
294 of 1932-33. Mādala.
S.I.I. VI. 247. Amrāvati.
299 of 1936-37. Bhaṭṭiprōlu.
N.D.I. V. Ongōle. 28-A. Chandrapāḍu.
323 of 1934-35. Sanipūḍi.
E.I. VI. p. 159. *S.I.I.* IV. 734. Bezavāḍa
297 of 1936-37. Bhaṭṭiprōlu,
N.D.I. II Kāvali 23. Jaladanki.
147 of 1946-47. Gōpalapaṭṇam.
30 of 1953-54. Elūr.
S.I.I. V. 75. Bhīmavaram.
391. *Ibid.*, IV. 1077. Drāksharama.
392. *Ibid.*, VI. 144. Bāpaṭla.

reign of the Velanāḍu chief, Cōḍa, Prōla Bhīmaya the servant of the chief, granted fifty bulls for a lamp to god Bhīmēśvara of Drākshārāma.[393]

In some cases cows were donated for purposes of offerings. In Ś. 1059, 15 cows were gifted to god Bhīmēśvara of Drākshārāma by Mallirāju.[394] *Mandalīśvara* Prataparudra gave in Ś. 1343, 510 cows to the same god.[395] In Ś. 1407 cows were granted to the local god at Guntūr for purpose of an offering.[396]

8. *Gifts of Oil-Mills*

Numerous records from Āndhradēśa supply information about the gift of oil-mills for maintaining lamps in the temple. An oil-mill was granted to god *Syayaṁbhu* Śrī Mahādēva at Satraśāla in Ś. 1166 for a lamp by a chief.[397] A Buruvumada Malnāyaniṁgāru donated an oil-mills in Ś. 1218 for lamps in the temple of Cenna-Gōpīnātha at Pulipāḍu for the merit of Guṇḍaya nāyaka and Māraya Sāhini, the favourite servants of the Kākatīya king.[398] A record from Rācanapalli refers to the gift of an oil-mill for a perpetual lamp made by the chief, *mahāmaṇḍalēśvara* Rāviyarasa, the son-in-law of Bhuvanaikamalla *mahārāja*, *mahāmaṇḍalēśvara* Kētamallarasa and *mahāmaṇḍalēśvara* Muṁmaḍi Cōḷarasa to Mallikārjuna paṇḍita, the *dēvakarmi* of god Mallikārjuna at Rācayapalli, the head quarters of *Kuḍiyana-40*.[399]

9. *Other Gifts*

Several kinds of miscellaneous gifts like bells, palanquins, images, *nandis*, slaves, *sānis* and *suradāma vṛttis* etc., were donated to temples.

a. *Bells*

In Ś. 1278, the Reḍḍi King, Annapōta, presented 5 elephant bells to god Bhīmēśvara for the merit of his father, King Vēma.[400] A big bell was presented to god Kōpunādhadēva of Palivela on the occasion of a *Makara-sankrānti*, in Ś. 1099.[401] In Ś. 1818, a *dūba-gaṇṭa* was granted to god at Pālakol.[402] A Piriya Rājayyadēva gave a bell to god Mallikārjuna of Śrīśailam in Ś. 1512, for the salvation of his deceased ancestors.[403] Guṁṭipalli Muttarāju who is described as one interested in performing 16 *dānas*, presented golden bells to god Śrīgirinātha of

393. *Ibid.*, IV. 1224. Drākshārāma.
394. *S.I.I.* IV. 1176-A. Drāksharama.
395. *Ibid.*, IV. 966. Drākshārāma.
396. *Ibid.*, IV. 659. Guntūr.
397. 314 of 1930-31. Satraśāla.
398. 24 of 1929-30. Pulipāḍu.
399. 69 of 1941-42. Rāchanapalli.
400. *S.I.I.* IV. 1387. Drākshārāma.
401. *Ibid.*, V. 111. Palivela.
402. *Ibid.*, V. 131. Pālakol.
403. 60 of 1942-43. Śrīsailm.

Śrīśailam.[404] King Vēma granted a bell weighing 12,000 *pālikas* to the temple of Mārkaṇḍēśvara of Rājahmundry.[405]

b. *Tōraṇas*

Tōraṇas were also endowed to temples. In Ś. 1336, a *tōraṇa* with a bell attached to it was presented to the god of Bhīmavaram.[406] The famous Vijayanagara king, Kṛṣṇarāya, presented a *navaratna-prabhāvaḷi* or *makara-tōraṇa* in Ś. 1437, set with nine kinds of precious stones consisting of 25 *kīrtimukha*-leaves, 13,835 *vommeccu* beads, II...weight of gold wire, 7,978 weight of the solid gold, 20 silk fringes hanging on the head of the *makara-tōraṇa* and 5,747 weight of the above said gold fringes. The following 9 kinds of gems were fixed in different parts of the *makara-tōraṇa*, 81 rubies, 10,994 red stones, 754 emeralds, 530 sapphires 40 cats-eyes, 54 agates, 74 topazes 920 old diamonds, 3,933 pearls, 4 prominant sapphires fixed in the place of the eyes, 6 corals and 30 conch-shells.[407]

c. *Prabhas*

In Ś. 1337, a gold *prabha* was presented to god Rāmēśvara of Pālakol by Naraharinēniṁgāru for the merit of the king.[408] The Vijayanagara king, Kṛṣṇarāya, presented a golden *prabhāvaḷi* set with precious stones to god Kāḷahastīśvara of Kāḷahasti in Ś. 1435 for the merit of his parents.[409]

d. *Suradāma-vṛtti*

The *Sānimunnūru* and the *Ayyamunnūru* of Chēbrōlu donated the *suradāmavṛtti* to god Kumārasvāmi of the place in Ś. 1135.[410]

e. *Servants*

A individual gave away his daughter to the temple of Gōpāladēva of Māgallu.[411] Three individuals, named Pōti Reḍḍi, Sēnapareḍḍi and Brahmanaya, granted in Ś. 1140 three slaves to god Sōmēśvara mahādēva of Sangam.[412] In Ś. 1188, the Eastern Gānga king, Vīrabhānudēva, presented 100 women dancers to the Siṁhāchalam temple [413] In Ś. 1339, Nāra donated a woman servant to god Bhīmēśvara of Drākshārāma for the religious merit of the Reḍḍi king, Allāḍa Reḍḍi.[414] King Prōlaya Tiṁma granted a servant for doing all work in Bhīmēśvara temple at Drākshārāma.[415]

404. 46 of 1942-43. Śrīśailm.
405. *E.I.* XIII. pp. 237-259. Vēmavaram.
406. *S.I.I.* V. 38. Bhīmavaram.
407. *T.T.D.I.* III. 76. Tirumala.
408. *S.I.I.* V. 134. Pālakol.
409. *Ibid.*, IX. 489. Kāḷahasti.
410. *Ibid.*, VI. 110. Chēbrōlu.
411. *Ibid.*, X. 588. Māgallu.
412. *N.D.I.* II. Nellore. 103. Sangam.
413. *S.I.I.* VI. 1197. Siṁhāchalam.
414. *Ibid.*, IV. 1378. Drākshārāma.
415. *Ibid.*, IV. 1345. Drākshārāma.

f. *Nandis*

In Ś. 1062, *Paḍālu* Kāṭamanāyaka granted a golden bull and a *nāga* to god Bhīmēśvara of Drākshārāma.[416] A *nandi* image was presented to the temple of Sangamēśvara of Pondugala by Rācapūṇḍi Annamarāja the *karaṇam* of Balemirti for the merit of his elder brother, Śrīgiri Pregaḍa, and his son, Kasuvaya.[417]

g. *Images*

In Ś. 1135 Jāyasēnāpati presented *utsava* or procession images of god Kumārasvāmi and his consorts to the temple of Chēbrōlu.[418] In Ś. 1135, the concubines of the Kōṭa chief, Kēta, gifted an *utsavamūrti* to the temple of Uṇḍavalli.[419] In Ś. 1392 a devotee named Vellenka Pōtinēnimgāru, presented an *utsava* image to the temple of Drākshārāma.[420] In Ś. 1442, Nādiṇḍla Gōparasayyaṁgāru, the nephew of Śāḷuva Tiṁmarasayyangāru, the *mahāpradhāni* of the Vijayanagara king, Kṛṣṇarāya, presented the processional images to the temple of Rāma of Yajñavāṭika or Koṇḍavīḍu.[421] In Ś. 1810, Maddnēni Narasiṁhadāsu, presented the processional images to the temple of Sītārāmadēva of Yanamadala.[422] A certain Peda Śāntalingam and Cina Śāntalingam procured certain processional images and presented them to the temple of Sōmēśvarasvāmin of Kambhampāḍu.[423]

h. *Vehicles*

Giriyappa, the *Sthānāpati* of Salakarāju Peda Timmarāju, donated a palanquin to the goddess at Nandavaram.[424] In Ś. 1337, Mancēḷḷa Naraharinēniṁgāru granted a chariot for the merit of the king Allāḍa to the temple of Kṣīrārāmēśvara of Pālakol.[425] The Maṭla chief, Anantarāja gave in Ś. 1550, a *suvarṇāśva* or golden horse vehicle, a *sindhūra* or elephnat vehicle, a *samarabhūpāla-vāhana* or war chariot, a *padmapītha* or a lotus shaped seat to god Śrī Venkaṭēśa of Tirumala, and to god Gōvindarāja of Tirupati. A *gaja vāhana* or elephant vehicle, *turangama vāhana* or horse vehicle and a *kanaka-mayūra* or golden peacock vehicle, and a *mōhana-vāhana* or syren or demon vehicle were presented to god Śrīkāḷahastīśvara of Kāḷahasti and a *hāṭaka-vṛṣabha-vāhana* or golden bull vehicle to god Siddhavaṭēśvara of Siddhavaṭam.[426] Nandāpurapuri Mallikārjunarāyaḍu presented an ivory palanquin to the god at Drākshārāma.[427] A Rāma mantri gave two seats of gold studded with gems to be used at the time of the god's marriage festival at Drākshārāma.[428]

416. *Ibid.*, IV. 1031. Drākshārāma.
417. 320 of 1934-35. Pondugala.
418. *E.I.* V. pp. 142-151. Chēbrōlu.
419. *S.I.I.* X. 260. Eṛrabālem.
420. *Ibid.*, IV. 1344. Drākshārāma.
421. *E I.* VI. pp. 230-239. Koṇḍavīdu.
422. 416 of 1915 Yanamadala.
423. 375 of 1934-35. Kaṁbahṁpāḍu.
424. 6 of 1943-44. Nandavaram.
425. *S.I.I.* V. 134. Pālakol.
426. *T.T.D.I.* VI. 25. Tirupati.
427. *S.I.I.* IV. 1374-A. Drākshārāma.
428. *Ibid.*, IV. 135. Drākshārāma.

i. *Miscellaneous Gifts*

A record from Cāḷukya-Bhīmavaram mentions the gift of a stone quary in a village in the *Cenganūnṭi-sthalam* to god Bhīmēśvara of the place for the construction of a temple.[429] Another, from Siṁhāchalam, mentions the gift of silver and gold *satha-gōpam* by Gōḍecangalvarāyaniṁgāru in Ś. 1720 to the local god Śrīnarasiṁhanātha.[430] In Ś. 1326, a clock was presented to god Bhāvanārāyaṇa at Sarpavaram by Gōḷi Sōmāreḍḍi.[431] In Ś. 1346 Mantripreggaḍa Sūranaṁgāru presented a *uyyāla-mancam* or swing cot to god Bhīmēśvara of Bhīmavaram.[432]

10. *Process of Gift Making*

Gift of all varieties intended for the temple were made through a separate process. They were first of all registered in the treasury. Then the gift was inscribed in some part of the temple. Sometimes agreements were entered into between the parties or between them and the temple. These are instances of the utilisation of these gifts as settled in meetings. All gifts were made with libation of water. A gift was made with libation of water to god Viśvanātha of Gudimetta.[433] A native of Perumulaiyar, named Vāgīsapperumāḷ, the temple accountant of Yōgimallavaram, attested the transaction of a gift to the god of Yōgimallavaram.[434] In some cases, the transaction of the gift was witnessed both by the temple accountant and the *Mahāsabha.*[435] In some cases, the transaction was witnessed and signed by the Periya Nāṭṭar.[436] In some instances, the gifts made by devotees were registered in the *Avanakkalari* or the registration office and witnessed by the *Ācārya puruṣas.*[437] Sometimes agreement was arrived at among merchants to contribute for the requirements of the Vīrabhadra temple at Maṭṭipenṭra.[438] In Ś. 1457 the gift was accepted in an agreement by the superintendants of the treasury of god Tirukkāḷahasti.[439] In some cases the gifts were settled at a conference of the disciples of the deity in the temple premises.[440] In the 19th year of the reign of the Yādavarāya king, Tirukkālattidēva, the gifts made by him were made in an assembly of the Avilāli village. But in the reign of the Cōḷa king, Maduraikoṇḍa Kopparakēsari, an endowment was registered by the members of the *Sabhā* and members of the town.[441] The gifts

429. *Ibid.*, V. 43. Cāḷukya-Bhīmavaram.
430. *Ibid.*, VI. 1192. Siṁhachlam.
431. *Ibid.*, V. 10. Sarpavaram.
432. *Ibid.*, V. 39. Bhīmavaram.
433. *Ibid.*, X. 468. Guḍimeṭla.
434. *T.T.D.I.* I. 35. Yōgimallavaram.
435. *Ibid.*, I. 38. Yōgimallavaram.
436. *Ibid.*, I. 40. Tirupati.
437. *T.T.D.I.* I. 205. Tirumala.
438. 3 of 1908. Cuṁbum.
439. 152 of 1924, Kāḷahasti.
440. *S.I.I.* X. 503. Śrīśailam.
441. *T.T.D.I.* I. 81. Tirumala.

made to the temple of Gōkarnēśvara of Penumūli was registered on a stone and installed in front of the temple in Ś. 1236 by Dodelavōte Pōtingāru for the merit of Kākatīya king, Pratāparudra.[442]

442. *S.I.I.* X. 509. Penumūli.
Similar Examples
S.I.I. X. 777. Konakoṇḍa.
Ibid., 774. Bollavaram.
T.T.D.I. I. 81. Ṭirumala,

4

MANAGEMENT OF THE TEMPLES

The temple was a multipurpose institution which played a dominant role in moulding the religious, social and cultural life of the people throughout the centuries. It is a complex institution, and employed a large number of persons belonging to different professions. It had to attend to various kinds of work like the conduct of worship, preparation of offerings, preparation of sandal, perfumes etc., decoration, lighting, entertainment, recitation of sacred texts, running choultries and *maṭhas*, maintaining schools and hostels, providing accommodation and comforts to the staff and the visiting pilgrims, repair and renovation, safe keeping of jewels, distribution of *prasādams*, management of properties, keeping accounts, arranging for processions, keeping watch and ward etc., besides celebration of various festivals, obligatory, optional and instituted.

1. *Nature of Staff*

The temple staff was of several types. Some servants of temple were individually employed while some were hereditary employees. The Mālakoṇḍa grant of Kandukur, states that *Mahārāja* Śrī Mallaya Reḍḍi granted the hereditary right of conducting worship to Viṣṇu at the villages of Cherukūru, Kamayapalli, Ādūru and Paṇṭarāla and their hamlets to Mālakoṇḍa Kēśava Dīkṣita, the priest of the temple of god Viṣṇu of Malyādri.[1] Another inscription from Ānimala, records the provision made in favour of Timmappa and stipulates that he and his descendants should make use of the gift and discharge their assigned duties properly.[2] Another epigraph from Yōgimallavaram, mentions that a Vāgīspperumāl, a native of Perumulaiyār was the holder of the hereditary right of the temple accountant's post in the local temple of Parāśarēśvara.[3]

1. *N.D.I.* I. C.P. 5. Mālakoṇḍa.
2. 203 of 1937-38. Animala.
3. *T.T.D.I.* I. 35. Yōgimallavaram.

2. *Maintenance of Staff*

The temple staff were maintained in various ways, viz., by the temple treasury, by payment of salaries, by cash gifts, through *vṛttis* and by means of gifts of *prasādam.*

a. *By the Treasury*

Some of the staff were paid and maintained by the *Śrī-Bhaṇḍāram* or the temple treasury. Nārāyaṇasēnāpati made arrangements in Ś. 1213 for a gift to the *Bhaṇḍāram* of the temple of Siṁhāchalam for maintaining the staff of the temple.[4] In Ś. 1227, Vāsudēvajiyyanaṁgāru made provision in the temple treasury for the maintenance of two gardeners.[5] The Oḍḍādi chief, Arjunadēva, made provision in the *Bhaṇḍāram* for the maintenance of the staff of god Śrī Narasiṁhanātha of Siṁhāchalam.[6] In Ś. 1318 *bhōgaparīkṣa* Ānjanīyuṁgāru made a gift to the treasury for the maintenance of the staff of the same temple.[7] In Ś. 1311, Queen Nīlādēvī, the consort of the Eastern Gānga king, Vīranarasiṁha, made provision in the *Śrī-Bhaṇḍāram* for the maintenance of the staff of the same temple.[8] In Ś. 1336, Gōvindadēvamahāpātra made provision in the treasury for maintaining servants to hold *cāmaras* at the time of *dhūpa.*[9] In S. 1356, 20 *ṭankas* were made to the temple treasury of god Bhīmēśvara of Bhīmavaram for the maintenance of a gardener.[10] The treasury of the Tirumala temple made provision in Ś. 1454, for the maintenance of staff like cooks, *tiruppaṇiyal* or temple servants, *vāgai* or officers, fuel suppliers etc.[11] A record from Tirupati, dated in Ś. 1457, mentions that the *Śrībhaṇḍāram* made provision for the maintenance of the temple staff.[12] Another record from the Tirumala temple, dated in Ś. 1466, also states that the temple treasury made arrangements for the maintenance of the temple staff.[13] A certain Puruṣōttamajiyyaṁgāru made provision in the treasury for the maintenance of a servant who was incharge of the *Khaṇḍadharā-koluyu* for god Śrīkūrmanātha of Śrīkūrmam.[14]

b. *By Gifts of Devotees*

The staff was mostly maintained by the grants and gifts made by the devotees. In Ś. 1006, Jayana endowed land for the maintenance of staff in the temple of Bhīmēśvara of Drākshārāma.[15] Śiriyamudāsiri donated in Ś. 1035 three *malla-māḍas* for the maintenance of servants who were incharge of the *cāmara-koluyu* in the

4. *S.I.I.* VI. 904. Siṁhāchalam.
5. *Ibid.*, V. 1151. Śrīkūrmam.
6. *Ibid.*, VI. 876. Siṁhāchalam.
7. *Ibid.*, VI. 1033. Siṁhāchalam.
8. *Ibid.*, VI. 1008. Siṁhāchalam.
9. *Ibid.*, V. 1167. Śrīkūrmam.
10. *Ibid.*, V. 34. Bhīmavaram.
11. *T.T.D.I.* III. 18. Tirupati.
12. *Ibid.*, III. 39. Tirupati.
13. *Ibid.*, IV. 19. Tirumala.
14. *S.I.I.* V. 1219. Śrīkūrmam.
15. *Ibid.*, IV. 1016. Drākshārāma.

temple of Siṁhāchalam.[16] In Ś. 1054, Kāpaya nāyaka made gifts for the maintenance of the staff in the temple of Bhīmēśvara of Duṁbaṟuta.[17] In Ś. 1075, Arusugoṇḍalarāvuta, the brother-in-law of the king, Kāmarṇavadēva, granted the taxes like *yalayacuṭṭu, samastāyam, kōru, antarāyamu* and *abhinavāyamu* to the temple of Cōḍaganga Mādhavadēva and its musicians, dancers and priests.[18] In Ś. 1172, arrangements were made by Dēhusāhasamalla, a subordinate of the king Vīranarasiṁha, of the Eastern Gānga family for maintaining a group of 20 women dancers and accompanying artistes.[19] In Ś. 1190, arrangements were made for the maintenance of the staff in the temple at Durgī, by *Karaṇam* Nēmaya.[20] In Ś. 1349. 20 silver *ṭankas* were presented by Ellamadēvī, the wife of king Vīrabhānudēva, for holding two umbrellas and two *ālayaṭṭams* in the temple of Siṁhāchalam.[21] In Ś. 1499, land was given to the artisans attached to the temple of Cennakēśvaradēva at Molagavalli.[22] The Velnāḍu chief, Kulōttungacōḍa Gonka, made provision for the maintenance of several workers in the temple of Rāmalingasvāmi at Sātulūru.[23]

The temple staff were maintained by many kinds of gifts made by the pious devotees like villages, lands, *vṛttis*, salaries paid from interest accruing from on cash deposits, provision of shares of *prasādam*, grant of house-sites etc.

c. *Gifts of Villages*

Villages were donated for the maintenance of the staff. In Ś. 1005, the Eastern Gānga King, Anantavarma Cōḍa Ganga, endowed the village of Murupāka in the *Eṛaḍa-viṣaya* to god Narēndrēśvaradēva of Murupāka for the conduct of *nṛtta, gīta* and *vādya*.[24] In Ś. 1067, a village named Dēvarapalli was granted to the priest of the temple of Mānyapalle.[25] Mangayadēva *mahārāja*, the son of *mahāmaṇḍalēśvara* Śankidēva *mahārāja*, gave a village to the *naṁbi* or the priest in Ś. 1292 for the merit of his parents Śankidēva and Muṁmala dēvī.[26] In Ś. 1431, Hoṁnapa nāyuḍu presented the village of Būḍedapāḍu in the *Pāṇem-sīma* to the priests of god Paṇikēśvara of Pānaya for conducting services in the temple.[27]

d. *Gift of Land*

The staff also received land gifts from devotees. According to an inscription from Bezavāḍa, dated in Ś. 1053, a gift of 4 *kha* of land was made to the *pūjāris* of the temple of Mallēśvara of the place by Nāgadēvuṇḍu.[28] Another from Durgī,

16. *Ibid.*, V. 756. Siṁhāchalam.
17. *Ibid.*, X. 89. Tubāḍu.
18. *S.I.I.* X. 707. Rellivalasa.
19. *Ibid*, VI. 1188. Śrīkūrmam.
20. *Ibid.*, X. 422. Durgī.
21. *Ibid.*, VI. 1082. Siṁhāchalam.
22. 729 of 1919. Molagavalli.
23. *S.I.I.* X. 97. Sātulūru.
24. *JAHRS.* XXII. pp. 9-17.
25. *N.D.I.* I. Darsi. 48. Mannēpalle.
26. 338 of 1938-39. Chinnadēsaripalle.
27. 165 of 1913. Ilapaṟṟu.
28. *S.I.I.* VI. 762. Bezavāḍa.

dated in Ś. 1191, mentions the gift of 20 *na* of land to the conch-blowers in the local temple.[29] In Ś. 1210, a gift of 2 *na* of wet land and 2 *kha* of *yelipolamu* were made to a *pujāri* of the temple of Amarēśvara of Amarāvati.[30] In Ś. 1343, a Rangukaṭṭyuṇḍu granted 1 *puṭṭi* of land to Gangamarāṇi for doing the *cāmara-koluvu* at the time of the *dhūpas* in the temple of Siṁhāchalam.[31] In Ś. 1490, a gift of land was made by Daḷavāyi nāyaniṁgāru to pipers and drummers for rendering services in the temple of Cennakēśava Perumāḷ at Gollala-Uppalapāḍu.[32] A certain Venkaṭapati Rājuṁgāru granted land as a *sarvamānya* to drummers and pipers of the temple of Cennarāya of Vanjavāka. In Ś. 1536.[33] In Ś. 1681, a gift of a field named *maṭa* and *pallimuntham* was made in Rājaṁpalli village to three artisans who carved the temple of Gōpālasvāmi of Rājyaṁpalli.[34] Elamanci Cōḍa Gangadēvarāju of the Cāḷukyan family donated 2½ *puṭṭis* of wet land to two women for waving *cāmaras* at the time of the *alaṁkāra* in the temple of Siṁhāchalam.[35] A gift of 800 *kuḷi* of land was made by Vīmarasan of Tyāgasamudrappaṭṭi for the maintenance of two men employed in the Alalasundaran flower garden of god Kāḷahastīśvara.[36] The *Sabhaiyār* and the *Mahēśvaras* of Guḍimallam made a grant of land to the goldsmith attached to the temple of Paraśurāmēśvara of Guḍi-mallam.[37] The *Reḍḍis* and *Karaṇams* of the village of Sarparājapuram granted land to Vāṁbhaṭlu, the *arcaka* of the temple of Rāmēśvarasvāmin of the village of Sarparājapuram.[38]

29. *Ibid*, X. 422. Durgī.
30. *S.I.I.* VI. 225. Amarāvati.
31. *Ibid.*, VI. 777. Siṁhachalam.
32. 377 of 1940-41. Gollalauppalapāḍu.
33. *N.D.I.* I. Gūḍūr. 10. Vanjavāka.
34. *Ibid.*, I. Darśi. 61. Rājaṁpalli.
35. *S I I.* VI. 705. Siṁhāchalam.
36. 92 of 1922. Kāḷahasti.
37. *S.I.I.* VIII. 526. Guḍimallam.
38. 146 of 1946-47. Sarphrājapuram.

Similar Examples

S.I I X. 74. Kopparam.
Ibid., IV 677. Nādiṇḍla.
Ibid., X 91. Dāvulūru.
Ibid., VI. 624. Koṇidena.
Ibid., X. 159. Ikkūru.
Ibid., X. 164. Maṇḍapāḍu.
Ibid., X. 138. Peravali.
Ibid., X. 151. Tiṁmāpuram.
N.D.I. I. Darśi. 49. Mannēpalli.
S.I.I X. 188. Jonnalagaḍḍa.
N.D.I. II. Kavali. 10. Chinnakrāka.
S.I.I. VI. 207. Peddacheṛukūru.
Ibid., X. 289. Bējaṭpuram.
N.D.I. III. Ongōle. 88. Nāguluppalapāḍu.
S.I.I. X. 422. Durgī.
Ibid., VI. 751. Siṁhāchalam.

Contd.

e. *Gifts of Vṛttis*

Vṛttis were also allotted to several employees of the temple by devotees. In Ś. 1072, Nūṁkisetṭi granted *vṛttis* for the staff of the temple of god Ballīśvara at Koṭyadona.[39] Singadēva *mahārājulu*, a subordinate of Kākatīya Gaṇapatidēva, donated a *vṛttis* in Ś. 1175 for a *pujāri* of the Rāmalinga temple at Chandalūru.[40] In Ś. 1526, Sarvappa Aśvārāyaniṁgāru presented *vṛttis* to the servants of the temple of Śrīkūrmanātha of Śrīkūrmam.[41] An inscription from Cāḷukya-Bhīmavaram mentions the *Vṛttinibandha* or gifts of *vṛttis* to the servants of the temple of god Rājanārāyaṇa in the western part of Cāḷukya-Bhīmavaram.[42] The *Vidvan-mahājanas* of a village and *mahāmaṇḍalēśvara* Jiḷḷēḷḷa Rangapati rājayyadēva *mahārāja* gave *vṛttis* to an artisan named Tirumalayya of the Viṣṇu temple at Nemaḷḷadinne in Ś. 1533.[43]

f. *Gift of Cash*

Coins like *māḍas, niṣkas, cinnams* etc., current in those days, were also given for the upkeep of the temple servants. Queen Gangādēvī gave 8 *cinnas* to the recitors of the *nāmasankīrttanas* in the temple of god Śrīkūrmanātha of Śrīkūrmam in Ś. 1263.[44] In Ś. 1301, 20 *gaṇḍamāḍas* were granted to the temple treasury for the maintenance of a *sāni* for rendering service in the same temple.[45] Elamanci Cōḍagangadēvarāja of the Cāḷukyan family donated 21 *padmanidhi-gaṇḍamāḍas* for maintaining two women to wave cauries in the temple of Siṁhāchalam.[46] A record from the Gōvindaraja temple of Tirupati, dated in Ś. 1461, mentions the gift of 2 *paṇam* to the reader of the *Gajēndramōkṣa-ślōkas*.[47] Another from the same place, dated in Ś. 1468, states that 2 *rēkhai-pon* and 4 *paṇam* were given to the persons engaged in the water shed established at the *Paḍikāvali gōpuram* of the temple of Śrī Venkaṭēśvara of Tirumala.[48]

Ibid., VI. 707. Siṁhāchalam.
Ibid., X. 774. Bollavaram.
N.D.I. II. Kandukūr. 11. Chennipāḍu.
Ibid., II. Kandukūr. 79. Sāmarājupalli.
Ibid., II. Kandukūr. 19. Gaṇḍavaram.
S.I.I. IV. 633. Nādeṇḍla.
Ibid., X. 238. Pedapalakalūru.
Ibid., VI. 633. Bhīmavaram.
205 of 1940-41. Vēlpucherla.

39. *S.I.I.* IV. 605. Koṇidena.
40. *N.D.I.* I. Ongōle. 28. Chandalūru.
41. *S.I.I.* V. 1260. Śrīkūrmam.
42. *Ibid.*, V. 82. Cāḷukya-Bhīmavaram.
43. 353 of 1940-41. Nemaḷḷadinne.
44. *S.I.I.* V. 1227. Śrīkūrmam.
45. *Ibid.*, V. 1207. Śrīkūrmam.
46. *Ibid.*, VI. 705. Siṁhāchalam.
47. *T.T.D.I.* IV. 135. Tirupati.
48. *Ibid.*, V. 89. Tirupati.

g. *Salaries*

Salaries were paid to some workers in the temple out of the interest on cash deposits made by devotees. In Ś. 1201 a Babbimahāsēnāpati granted land to the temple treasury for the salaries to *dāsaris*, who were in charge of the flower garden of Śrīkūrmanātha.[49] In Ś. 1207, Gaurāju of Jantarnāḍu, donated *māḍas* to the treasury of the Siṁhāchalam temple for the maintenance of a gardener.[50] A sum of 14 *gaṇḍamāḍas* were made to the temple treasury for the salaries of two *dāsaris* who were in charge of a flower garden of the Śrīkūrmam temple in Ś. 1267 by an individual.[51] Vatsarāyuṇḍu gave in S. 1294, 5 *gaṇḍamāḍas* to a servant who supplied a *tirumāla*, 4 cubits long to god Śrī Narasiṁhanātha of Siṁhāchalam at the time of *tiruvajāmu*.[52] In Ś. 1415 land was given by *mahāmaṇḍalēśvara* Anantarāju Kōnamarājaydēva *mahārāja* and the *Sthānikas* of the temple of Śrī Cennarāya of Miruṭūru to the musicians of the temple in lieu of their salaries.[53] In Ś. 1457, a sum of 1750 *nārpaṇam* was paid to the temple treasury of Tirumala, by two women for the maintenance of the staff.[54] Vangāpuram Nārayaṇa Seṭṭi, presented 48,900 *nārpaṇam* to the temple treasury as capital. The staff of the temple were maintained with the interest accruing from it.[55] In Ś. 1035, 3 *padmanidhimāḍas* were paid to the *Śrī-Bhaṇḍāram* of the Siṁhāchalam temple for the salary of the people, who were in charge of the *vinjāmara* service.[56]

h. *Allotment of Prasādam*

The temple staff were allotted share in the *prasādam* or food offered to the deity. In S. 1035, three *padmanidhi-mallamāḍalu* were presented for the supply of 1 *kuncamu* of *prasādam* to a person who was to wave the *cāmara* at the time of the two *dhūpas* in the temple of Siṁhāchalam.[57] A Narasiṁhabhārati, made arrangements in Ś. 1281, for the supply of 5 *kuncams* of *prasādam* to some of the temple staff like flutists and songsters of the same temple.[58] In Ś. 1302, the Eastern Gānga king, Vīranarasiṁha made arrangements for the distribution of *prasāda* to the temple servants who were in charge of the *Khaṇḍadhāra-koluvu* for god Śrīnarasiṁha of Siṁhāchalam.[59] In S. 1303 Śankarajiyana made provision for the gift of *prasādam* for a woman servant who decorated the floor with coloured powder before the god of Siṁhāchalam.[60] In Ś. 1312, provision was made for the supply of *prasādam* to Rāghava Bhārati Śrīpāda, the disciple of Vāsudēva Bhārati Śrīpāda, with the stipulation that he would serve the god at the time of the *dhūpas*.[61] In Ś.

49. *S.I.I.* V. 1238. Śrīkūrmam.
50. *Ibid.*, VI. 713. Siṁhāchalam.
51. *Ibid.*, V. 1240. Śrīkūrmam.
52. *Ibid.*, VI. 742. Siṁhāchalam.
53. 410 of 1926. Miḍuṭūru.
54. *T.T.D.I.* IV. 40. Tirupati.
55. *Ibid.*, V. 25. Tirupati.
56. *S.I.I.* VI. 756. Siṁhāchalam.
57. *Ibid.*, VI. 756. Siṁhāchalam
58. *Ibid.*, VI. 890. Siṁhāchalam.
59. *Ibid.*, VI. 741. Siṁhāchalam.
60. *Ibid.*, VI. 738. Siṁhāchalam.
61. *Ibid.*, VI. 859. Siṁhāchalam.

1331 Kauśalyādēvī, the wife of Kaḷingapātra Mangalarāju made provision for the gift of *prasādam* for a servant, in order to hold the *ālavaṭṭam* at the time of the *dhūpa* in the temple of Siṁhāchalam.[62] A record from Śrīkūrmam, dated in Ś. 1339, mentions the gift of *prasādam* to a woman servant of the local temple.[63] A certain Sāhasamallu made provision for the gift of *prasāḍam* for the man who was intended for doing *sankīrtana* and *meyigāpu-arcana* at the time of two *dhūpas* in the same temple in Ś. 1348.[64] In S. 1469, a Śrīnivāsayyangār, authorised the distribution of *prasādam* and *paṇyāram* among the temple officials of Tirupati.[65] The *Sthānattār* of the temple of Tirumala made arrangemnets in Ś. 1557 for the distribution of *prasādam* among the temple officials.[66]

3. *Varieties of Temple Servants*

A large number of servants were maintained by the temple for various purposes. Some of the staff like priests, reciters of sacred texts, decoraters, players on the *vīṇā*, cleaners, cauri-bearers, *ālayaṭṭam* bearers, bearers of mirrors etc., were in charge of the work in the interior and others were in charge of the external work of the temple. They were torch bearers, watchmen, bearers of vehicles, gardeners, garland makers, gold-smiths etc.

A. *Workers in the Interior*

1. *Priests*

The priest or *pūjāri*, who generally conducted worship, was an important functionary. He was maintained either by the temple or by the devotees through gifts of villages, lands, assignments of dues etc. *Mahāmaṇḍalēśvara* Balli Cōḍa *mahārājulu* made a gift in Ś. 1088, for the maintenance of the *pūjāri* of the temple of Śrī Cōḍēśvara Mahādēva of Mānyapalli.[67] In Ś. 1093, Sēnapa nāyaka, a subordinate of king Rājēndra Cōḍadēva, granted land to the *pūjāri* of the temple of Cōḍiśvara of Mōdukūru.[68] In Ś. 1175 a gift was made to priests of Rāmēśvara of Pulipāṭi for their maintenance.[69] King Kāṭaya Vēma Reḍḍi made provision in Ś. 1312 for maintaining the priests, Singaya and Vengaḷa, of the temple of god Gōpīnātha of Rājamahēndranagara.[70] A record from Sarparājapuram, dated in Ś. 1598, states that the *Reḍḍis* and *Karaṇams* of the village made provision for the maintenance of Vābaṁbhaṭlu, the *arcaka* of the local god, Rāmēśvarasvāmi.[71] The Nandāpura chief, Vīra-Viśvaṁbara, granted 10 *garśe* of land to a *pūjāri* of the two

62. *Ibid.*, VI. 710. Siṁhāchalam.
63. *Ibid* , V. 1167. Śrīkūrmam.
64. *Ibid.*, VI. 708. Siṁhāchalam.
65. *T T.D.I.* V. 92. Tirupati.
66. *Ibid.*, VI. 1. Tirupati.
67. *N.D.I.* I. Darśi 49. Mannēpalli .
68. *S.I.I.* X. 176. Mōdukūru.
69. *Ibid.*, X. 289. Bējāṭpuram.
70. *JAHRS.* XI. pp. 191-205. Kōrukoṇḍa.
71. 146 of 1946-47. Sarpharājapuram.

temples of Mallikārjuna of Śrīśailam for providing daily offerings during the three courses of worship in the day.[72]

2. *Reciters of Sacred Texts etc.*

One important and interesting activity in the temple is associated with the recitation of religious and sacred texts like the *Vēdas, Purāṇas, Viṣṇustōtras, Puruṣasūkta, Gajēndra-mōkṣam slōkas, Venkaṭācalamahatmyam, Śrīnivāsakalyāṇam,* etc.

Many people were appointed for doing *Vēdapārāyaṇam*. In Ś. 1355, provision was made for employing 24 *mahājanas* of Śrīnivāsapuram to do *Vēdapārāyaṇam* before god Tiruvenkaṭamuḍaiyān at Tirumala.[73] Two people were appointed for the recitation of *Vēdas*, each day, in the presence of Śrī Venkaṭēśa of the same place.[74] In Ś. 1718, 5 *gaṇḍamāḍas* were presented by an individual to recite the *Viṣṇustōtram* at the time of *rēpaṭidhūpa* in the temple of Śrīkūrmam by Kācu *sandhivigrahi*.[75] In Ś. 1305 Caṁpumahāsēnāpati made provision in the temple treasury for the maintenance of a brāhman named Odyapeddibhaṭṭu for the recitation of *Vēdas* in the temple,[76]

Arrangements were also made for the recitation of the *Purāṇas* before the god. A record from Śrīkūrmam, dated in Ś. 1193, states that Narasiṁhatīrtha made provision for the recitation of the *Purāṇas* in the local temple.[77] A record from Malkāpuram, dated in Ś. 1183, refers to the recitation of the *Sāmavēda* in the temple.[78] Another from Nādeṇḍla mentions the maintenance of 4 *Pauraṇikas* in the local temple.[79]

Equal importance was attached to the recitation of the Tamil *prabhandhams* composed by the Vaiṣṇava Āḷvārs and gifts were made for the maintenance of persons who recited them. In the 4th year of the reign of the Telugu Pallava king, Vijayagaṇḍagōpāla, a gift was made for the maintenance of the reciters of the *Tirumoḷi* songs composed by Tirumangai Āḷvār before god Gōvindarāja of Tirupati.[80] According to a record from Bhīmavaram, a gift was made to Sundara-brahmamārāya, the reciter of *Tiruvamudi*.[81] In Ś. 1481 a gift was made to two persons who recited the *prabhandham* in the Tirumala temple.[82] Provision was made by Rāmabhaṭṭar for the maintenance of the people who were in charge of the *anusandhānam* of the *prabhandham* of the Āḷvārs in the temple of Gōvindarāja of Tirupati.[83]

72. C.P. 20 of 1925-26. Śrīśailam.
73. *T.T.D.I.* I. 201. Tirumala.
74. *Ibid.*, I. 200. Tirumala.
75. *S.I.I.* VI. 1022. Siṁhāchalam.
76. *S.I.I.* V. 1096. Siṁhāchalam.
77. *S.I.I.* V. 1233. Śrīkūrmam.
78. *Ibid.*, X. Mālkāpuram.
79. *Ibid.*, IV. 663. Nādeṇḍla.
80. *T.T.D.I.* I. 61. Tirupati.
81. *S.I.I.* V. 82. Bhīmavaram.
82. *T.T.D.I.* II. 62. Tirupatti.
83. *Ibid.*, IV. 18. Tirupati.

Various *stōtras* were also chanted in temples. In Ś. 1272, provision was made for the recitation of the *Puruṣasūkta* at the *abhiṣēka-avasaram* in the temple of Siṁhāchalam.[84] A gift was made to an individual in Ś. 1318, for reading the *Viṣṇu-stōtramu* in the same temple.[85]

The performance of *Sankīrtanas* or singing the god's names was another important customs in temples. A Narasiṁhabhārati made provision in Ś. 1281, for keeping two flutists and 8 women singers to form two batches which did the *sankīrtanam* at the time of the *dhūpa* in the Siṁhāchalam temple.[86] A Gōvindajiyya appointed a Garuḍadāsu in Ś 1312, to recite the *sankīrtanam* in the same temple.[87] A record from Mangaḷagiri refers to the provision made for the maintenance of the *Bhāgavatas* who recited the *sankīrtana* in the local temple.[88]

An interesting item was the *Vinnapam* service or soliciting the permission of the deity to commence the rite. Provision was made in Ś. 1271 for the maintenance of the people who did the *vinnapam* in the temple of Śrī Kūrmanatha of Śrīkūrmam.[89] A record of Ś. 1418, mentions the gift made to the *vinnapaṁsēyuvār* of the temple.[90] In Ś. 1461, a gift was made to the reader of the *Gajēndramōkṣa-slōkas* in the temple of God Gōvindarāja of Tirupati.[91]

Provision was also made for the maintenance of the reciters of *Tiruvēnkaṭa-mahātmyam* in the Tirumala temple. An inscription from Tirumala dated in Ś. 1413, refers to the reading of *Tiruvēnkaṭamahātmayam* which was composed and presented by Pasinḍi Venkaṭatturaivar *alias* Jiyar Rāmanujayyangār before the god.[92] In Ś. 1469, provision was made for the recital of the *Tiruvēnkaṭamahatmyam* in the same temple.[93]

3. *Decoraters*

The practice of decorating the floor with various designs with coloured powders was a custom of holy antiquity in the temples Inscriptions supply many instances. Provision was made by the wife of Śūrēśvarajiyana in Ś. 1303, for the maintenance of a woman who decorated the floor with designs before the god of the temple at Siṁhāchalam.[94] A gift was made to Jannama in Ś. 1309 for decorating the floor before the same god.[95] A person was appointed in Ś. 1298 to decorate the floor before the same god with *kōlamu* or coloured designs once in a week.[96]

84. *S.I.I.* VI. 962. Siṁhachalam.
85. *Ibid.*, VI. 1022. Siṁhāchalam.
86. *Ibid.*, VI. 890. Siṁhāchalam.
87. *Ibid.*, VI. 722. Siṁhāchalam.
88. *Ibid.*, IV. 710. Mangaḷagiri.
89. *S.I.I.* V. 1191. Śrīkūrmam.
90. *T.T.D.I* II. 135. Tirumala.
91. *Ibid.*, IV. 135. Tirupati.
92. *Ibid.*, II. 95. Tirumala.
93. *Ibid.*, V. 92. Tirupati.
94. *S.I.I.* VI. 738. Simhāchalam.
95. *Ibid.*, VI. 1127. Simhāchalam.
96. *Ibid.*, VI. 1128. Simhāchalam.

4. *Players of the Viṇā*

Many varieties of artistes were appointed for playing on musical instruments at the time of worship. Of these, the players on the *viṇā* occupied a prominent place. In Ś. 1212, a *Brāhmaṇapaṇḍita* made a gift for the *brahma-viṇāsvastyayana* to god Kūrmanātha at Śrīkūrmam.[97] Provision was made in Ś. 1278, for the maintenance of two women who played on the *viṇā* before the god at Siṁhāchalam.[98] A gift was made in Ś. 1296, for *viṇā-koluvu* to be performed daily before the god at Siṁhāchalam.[99] According to a Ānimala inscription, a gift was made in the village of Pālem to a certain Tiṁmappa on the condition that he and his descendants should play the *viṇā* and *kinnara* instruments in the local temple of god Sangamēśvara.[100]

5. *Cauri-bearers*

Many servants were appointed for waving *cāmaras* at the time of the conduct of various services in the temple. Provision was made in the Siṁhāchalam temple treasury in Ś. 1035, for holding *vinjāmara* at the time of the *ubhayadhūpas* to god Śrī Narasiṁhanātha.[101] In Ś. 1298, a gift was made to a woman for waving the *cāmara* at the time of *candanalagi* in the same temple.[102] Arrangements were made by Gōvindayya for waving the *vinjāmaras* in Ś. 1312 in the same temple.[103] A record from Śrīkūrmam, dated in Ś. 1339 a gift of a *cāmara* with a gold handle was made and a woman was appointed for holding it.[104]

6. *Ālavaṭṭam-bearers*

In Ś. 1302 provision was made for holding *ālavaṭṭam* at the time of *rēpaṭi-dhūpālu* before god Narasiṁhanātha of Siṁhāchalam.[105] Kauśalyādēvī, the wife of Kaḷingaparīkṣa mahāpātra Mangaḷarāju, made provision in Ś. 1331, for the *ālavaṭṭamu-koluvu* daily at the time of *rēpaṭṭi-dhupālu* in the Siṁhāchalam temple.[106]

7. *Bearers of Mirrors*

Servants were also appointed to hold mirrors before the god. In Ś. 1298, a person was appointed for holding a mirror once a week before the god of the Siṁhāchalam temple.[107] Another person was appointed for holding a mirror before the same god daily at the time of *rēpaṭi-candanalagi.*[108]

97. *Ibid.*, V. 1150. Śrīkūrmam.
98. *Ibid.*. VI. 955. Siṁhāchalam.
99. *Ibid.*, VI. 1134. Siṁhāchalam.
100. 203 of 1937-38. Ānimala.
101. *S.I I.* VI. 756. Siṁhāchalam.
102. *Ibid.*, VI. 751. Siṁhāchalam.
103. *Ibid*, VI. 722. Siṁhāchalam.
104. *Ibid.*, V. 1167. Śrīkūrmam.
105. *Ibid.*, VI. 707. Siṁhāchalam.
106. *Ibid.*, VI. 710. Siṁhāchalam.
107. *Ibid.*, VI. 1228. Siṁhāchalam.
108. *Ibid.*, VI. 1099. Siṁhāchalam.

B. *External Workers*

The functions discharged by the temple were of a varied nature. For this reason, many people were appointed for rendering services outside the sanctum. These external workers were torch-bearers, watchmen, bearers of vehicles, gardeners, garland makers, goldsmiths, astrologers, lighters, supervisors, *paccaḍikkārar*, proclaimers, street sweepers, *tirumanjana-śālaiyan*, *Īyunni Appayān*, etc.

1. *Nivandakkārar or Bearers of Vehicles*

People were appointed for carrying the *vāhanams* or vehicles like palanquins, flags etc., of the god and provision was made for their maintenance. In Ś. 1418, provision was made for the bearers of the *vāhanam* for god Śrī Venkaṭēśa at Tirumala by Kandāḍai Rāmānujayyangār.[109] Arrangements were made by Vangāpuram Nārāyaṇa seṭṭi for the maintenance of bearers of flower palanquins during the procession through the eight streets at Tirupati during *Damanārōhaṇa-Vasantōtsava-tirunāḷ*.[110] In Ś. 1460, arrangements were made for carrying the *Vaikuṇṭha-vimānam* through the streets after the decoration of god Gōvindarāja at Tirupati.[111] Provision was made for servants who carried the *Garuḍa-vāhanam* through the eight streets and to the bearer of Tiruvaḷi Āḷvan at Tirupati.[112]

2. *Bearers of Flags, Torches and Umbrellas*

Umbrellas and flags were carried by servants during processions and provision was made for their maintenance. Arrangements were made in Ś. 1457 by Rāmabhaṭṭārayyan for the maintenance of the bearers of umbrellas in the Tirumala temple.[113] In Ś. 1469, provision was made for the bearers of flags during the procession of god Śrī Venkaṭēśa of Tirumala.[114] Torch-bearers were also maintained by the temple. In Ś. 1457, a gift was made for the bearers of torches during the procession arranged for the same god at Tirumala.[115] Another gift of cash was made to the bearers of lights in Ś. 1469 for the same god during the procession at Tirumala.[116]

3. *Watchmen*

Several people were appointed in the temples for keeping watch at the gates. According to a record from Śrīkūrmam dated in Ś. 1263, Nārāyaṇadaḷapati appointed a man, named Kattula Kūnapanāyuḍu, to serve at the *Cittaradvāram* of Śrīkūrmanātha temple of the place, at the time of *ubhayadhūpālu*.[117] In Ś. 1296, arrangements were made for a woman to keep watch at the *Dharmadvāra* of the

109. *T.T.D.I.* II. 135. Tirumala.
110. *Ibid.*, V. 25. Tirumala.
111. *Ibid.*, IV. 127. Tirupati.
112. *Ibid*, IV. 135. Tirupati.
113. *Ibid.*, VI. 61. Tirumala.
114. *Ibid.*, V. 92. Tirupati.
115. *Ibid.*, IV. 61. Tirumala.
116. *Ibid.*, V. 92. Tirupati.
117. *S.I.I.* V. 1181. Tirupati.

Siṁhāchalam temple which was built by Dharmadāsujiyana.[118] An inscription from the Tirumala temple, dated in Ś. 1428, contains provision made for the location of watchmen at the corners.[119] Another from Tirupati, dated in Ś. 1468, mentions that provision was made for *talaiyāris* or night-watchmen [120] An undated record from Tripurāntakam, mentions the appointment of servants who kept watch, day and night at the *maṭha* of the local temple.[121]

4. *Time-keepers*

In Ś. 1418, provision was made for the maintenance of *Muttukkārar* or the time keeper at the Tirumala temple.[122] Arrangements were made in Ś. 1428, for the maintenance of a time-keeper in the same temple.[123]

5. *Suppliers of Flowers and Garlands*

Many people were appointed for the supply of flowers and garlands to deities. In Ś. 1313, Viśvanādhamahāsēnāpati made arrangements for a woman to supply one *doṇḍavanamālā* to the god of Siṁhāchalam.[124] Bhāvasāhasumallu made provision in Ś. 1350 into the temple treasury for the supply of one *doṇḍavanamālā* with *jarajhaṁpā* to the god of the same place.[125] In Ś. 1352, arrangements were made for a man who supplied the *tulaśī* garland to god Śrī Narasiṁhanātha of Siṁhāchalam by Paramapuruṣa Śrīpāda.[126] In Ś. 1468, provision was made for the maintenance of flower suppliers to god Gōvindarāja at Tirupati.[127] Arrangements were also made for the suppliers of garlands for god Śrīkūrmanātha of Śrīkūrmam.[128]

6. *Astrologers*

Astrologers were also maintained by the temple for fixing auspicious times for the performance of items of worship. A record from Timmāpuram, dated in Ś. 1083, mentions that provision was made for an astrologer in the local temple.[129] Another from the Tirumala temple, dated in Ś. 1505, states that arrangements were made for the maintenance of the Vengaṇṇan or the temple astrologer.[130] In Ś. 1053, a gift was made to Sūriyabhaṭlu for fixing the *muhūrtham* for the installation of god Gōkśēvara in Javaramu.[131] Provision was made in Ś. 1469 by Īyunni Appayyan for fixing *muhūrthams* at the Tirumala temple.[132]

118. *Ibid.*. VI. 1136. Siṁhāchalam.
119. *T.T.D.I.* III. 7. Tirumala.
120, *Ibid.*, V. 89. Tirupati.
121. *S.I.I.* X. 388. Tripurāntakam.
122. *T.T.D.I.* III. 135. Tirumala.
123. *Ibid.*, III. 7. Tirumala.
124 *S I.I.* VI. 801. Siṁhāchalam.
125. *Ibid.*, VI. 1085. Siṁhāchalam.
126. *Ibid.*, VI. 796. Siṁhāchalam.
127. *T.T.D.I.* V. 88. Tirupati.
128. *S.I.I.* V. 1384. Śrīkūrmam.
129. *Ibid.*, X. 151. Timmāpuram.
130. *T.T.D.I.* VI. 5. Tirumala.
131. *S.I.I.* X. 151. Timmāpuram.
132. *T.T.D.I.* V. 92. Tirupati.

7. *Lighters*

Several people were appointed for burning lamps in the premises of the temple. Four persons were appointed in Ś. 1384, for the service of lighting lamps in the Tirumala temple.[133] In Ś. 1418, provision was made for the maintenance of a *Tiruvēnkaṭapiccan* or a lamp-lighter in the temple of Śrī Venkaṭēśa of Tirumala.[134]

8. *Supervisors*

Several records mention that supervisors or *Kangāṇippan* were appointed in temples and arrangements made for their maintenance. A record from Tirumala temple, dated in Ś. 1418, mentions that a gift was made to *Kangāṇippan*.[135] In Ś. 1430, arrangements were made for the maintenance of a supervisor in the temple at Tirumala.[136]

9. *Kaikkōlar*

Kaikkōlars or people who were in charge of the decoration of the *maṇṭapas* were also maintained by the temple. In Ś. 1418, a gift was made to a *kaikkōlar* for his maintenance.[137]

10. *Paccaḍikkārar or Distributors of Prasādam*

Some people were appointed for the distribution of *prasādams* in the temples. In Ś. 1418, provision was made for the maintenance of a *paccaḍikkārar* at the Tirumala temple.[138] A gift was made in Ś. 1463, for *paccaḍikkārar* in the same. temple.[139]

11. *Street Sweepers*

The temple maintained a number of sweepers. A record from the Tirumala temple, dated in Ś. 1418, states that a gift was made to the *tiruvīdhimunaiyār* or street sweeper.[140]

133. *Ibid.*, II. 12. Tirumala.
134. *Ibid.*, II. 135. Tirumala.
135. *Ibid.*, II. 135. Tirumala.
136. *Ibid.*, III. 16. irumala.
Similar Examples
T.T.D.I. III. 11.
Ibid., IV. 54, 59, 61.
Ibid., V. 2, 25, 83, 84, 88, 90.
Ibid., VI. 6, 20, 80.
137. *T.T.D.I.* III. 7. Tirumala.
Similar Examples
T.T.D.I. III. 29, 105.
Ibid., IV. 26, 29, 54, 59, 61, 67, 92, 129, 135.
Ibid., V. 2, 8, 25, 38, 88, 89, 90, 92, 171.
Ibid., VI. 3, 12, 21, 22, 24.
138. *T.T.D.I.* II. 135. Tirumala.
139. *Ibid*, V. 2. Tirumala.
Similar Examples
T.T.D.I. V. 84, 89, 90.
Ibid., VI. 3.
140. *T.T.D.I.* II. 135. Tirumala.

12. *Proclaimer*

Proclaimers were also included in the temple staff. Provision was made in Ś. 1418, for *tiruvettuvāgai* or proclaimer in the Tirumala temple.[141]

13. *Goldsmiths*

The preparation and repair of numerous ornaments and utensils used in the temple required the services of goldsmiths. A record from Śrīkūrmam, dated in Ś. 1271, mentions that provision was made for the maintenance of 3 goldsmiths in the temple.[142]

14. *Paḍuvayakkārar*

Paḍuvayakkārar or the keeper of the articles of stores was also maintained by the temple. A record from Tirupati, dated in Ś. 1468, mentions that a *paḍuvayakkārar* was maintained by the Tirumala and Tirupati temples.[143]

15. *Cooks etc.*

Cooks were appointed in temple kitchens for the preparation of the *naivēdyas* or sacred food etc., offered to the deities. In Ś. 1127, four cooks were appointed in the temple of Amarēśvara of Amarāvati and provision was made for their maintenance.[144] A record from the Tirumala Temple, dated in Ś. 1418, mentions that arrangements were made for the appointment of *Tēvaiyāḷ* or temple cooks.[145] Another from the Gōvindarāja temple, Tirupati, dated in Ś. 1430, states that provision was made for the cooks in the temple.[146] An undated record from Bhīmavaram, refers to the provision made for the maintenance of cooks who prepared *amudu*.[147] Another from Tripurāntakam, mentions that *vṛttis* were allotted to cooks in the *maṭha* and the choultry of the Tripurāntakēśvara temple.[148]

16. *Water Suppliers*

The supply of water received considerable attention. Water was required for the bath of the god, for the kitchen, for the *maṭha* and for the *calivēndiris*. Arrangements were made for the supply of water for all these purposes. In Ś. 1006, two women were donated by Jayamā for supplying water for the temple of Drāk-

141. *Ibid.*, II. 135. Tirumala.
142. *S.I.I.* V. 1191. Śrīkūrmam.
143. *T.T.D.I.* V. 89. Tirupati.
144. *S.I.I.* VI. 558. Amarāvati.
145. *T.T.D.I.* II. 135. Tirumala.
146. *Ibid.*, III. 13. Tirupati.
147. *S.I.I.* V. 66. Bhīmavaram.
148. *S.I.I.* X. 388. Tripurāntakam.
Similar Examples
S.I.I. X. 395. Mālkāpuram.
T.T.D.I. III. 135. Tirumala.
Ibid., IV. 54, 61, 67, 167.
Ibid., V. 25, 34, 84, 90, 94.
Ibid., VI. 1, 3, 6, 12, 20, 21, 22.
411 of 1938-30. Puṭlaṁpalli.

shārāma.[149] An inscription from the Gōvindarāja temple, Tirupati, dated in Ś. 1467, mentions that provision was made for maintaining the persons who supplied water to the pilgrims and for the maintenance of a watershed established in the *maṇṭapa* constructed on the western side of the Vyāsa-Uḍaiyar's *maṇṭapa,* situated in the northmāda street of Śrī Gōvindarāja temple in Tirupati. It also states that, arrangements were made for the additional charge to the water suppliers who supplied extra water during the *Puraṭṭāsi-brahmōtsavam* celebrated for god Śrī Venkaṭēśa of Tirumala and for the maintenance of *Śālai-vāsal* or the manager of the watershed.[150] In Ś. 1191, a gift was made to a brāhmin who supplied water for the *tirumanjanam* of the god at Durgī.[151] In Ś. 1213, a man was appointed for supplying one *kāvaḍi* of bathing water to the god of Siṁhāchalam.[152] *Mahāmaṇḍalēśvara* Kōna Bhīmarāja's son, Rāmanātha, instituted a *calivēndiri* or watershed in Ś. 1240, at Kṣīrārāma and gifted a house-site, and land to the Brāhmin who supplied water to it.[153]

17. *Fuel Suppliers*

Fuel suppliers were also maintained in the temples. In Ś. 1034, provision was made in the Drākshārāma temple for maintaining a fuel supplier.[154] Similar arrangements were made for the maintenance of the *singa-muṛai* or the fuel suppliers in Ś. 1437 in the Tirupati temple.[155] A gift was made in Ś 1460, to the fuel suppliers of the same temple.[156]

18. *Potters*

Pots of various sizes and kinds were required for use in a temple. Suitable provision was made for their supply. A record from Drākshārāma, dated in Ś. 1034, refers to the gift made to a potter.[157] Another from Malkāpuram, dated in Ś. 1183, mentions that provision was made for the maintenance of potters.[158] In Ś. 1467, arrangements were made for the maintenance of a potter who supplied pots every month in the Tirupati temple.[159] An undated record from the Gōvindarāja

149. *S.I.I.* IV. 1015. Drākshārāma.
150. *T.T.D.I.* V. 61. Tirupati.
151. *S.I.I.* X. 422. Durgī.
152. *Ibid.*, VI. 904. Siṁhāchalam.
153. *Ibid.*, V. 128. Pālakol.
154. *Ibid.*, IV. 1248. Drākshārāma.
155. *T.T.D.I.* III. 105. Tirupati.
156. *Ibid.*, III. 13. Tirupati.
Similar Examples
T.T.D.I. IV. 18, 39, Tirupati.
Ibid., IV. 67, 134, 135, 154.
Ibid., V. 10, 25, 84, 88, 89, 90, 92.
Ibid., VI, 3, 6, 12, 20, 21, 22, 24.
157. *S.I.I.* IV. 1248. Drākshārāma.
158. *Ibid.*, X. 395. Mālkāpuram.
159. *T.T.D.I.* V. 61. Tirupati.

temple, Tirupati, mentions that arrangements were made to *kuṁmara-svarūpam* or potters.[160]

19. *Pāṇi-muṛai or Basket Suppliers*

Many people were appointed for the supply of baskets. In Ś. 1430, provision was made for the maintenance of basket suppliers in the Tirupati temple.[161] Arrangements were made in Ś. 1430 for maintaining the *pāṇi-muṛai*, for supplying baskets to the temple of Tirumala.[162]

20. *Mēkarai-Svarūpam or Suppliers of Brass-vessels*

The temple maintained suppliers of brass vessels. Provision was made in Ś. 1457, for *mēkarai-svarūpam* in the temple at Tirumala.[163] In Ś. 1504, a gift was made to *mēkarai-svarupam* in the same temple.[164]

21. *Repair and Renovation*

Several artisans and skilled workers were employed in temples and provision was made for their maintenance. A record from Valivēru, dated in Ś. 1026, refers to the gift made to a *kāse* or mason who built the temple of Svayaṁbhudēva of Valivēru and undertook to do repairs to the temple from time to time.[165] In Ś. 1319, *mahāmaṇḍalēśvara* Apratimalla Gangayadēva Cōḍa *mahārāja* made a gift to a stone-cutter or *kāse* Camayabaṭṭuḍu, who constructed the temple of god Bhairava-dēva of Gōṭūru.[166] A gift was made in Ś. 1418, to the *śippiyār* or *śilpi*-engravers in the Tirumala temple.[167] An inscription from Isakala, dated in Ś. 1484, mentions the gift of a *mānya* by Rāmidēvuni Virupayyaṁgāru of Nāgalūṭi to the artisans, Çinavīrōju Tarigoppula and Pōcamōju, for their having brought the images meant for processions for the temple of Kēśava at the village.[168] In Ś. 1533, a gift was

160. *Ibid*, VI. 80. Tirupati.
Similar Examples
S.I.I. VI. 677. Nādiṇḍla.
Ibid, VI. 1384. Drākshārāma.
T.T.D.I. II. 135. Tirumala.
Ibid, VI. 5, 80, Tirumala.
161. *T.T.D.I.* III. 13. Tirupati.
162. *Ibid*, III. 29. Tirumala.
Similar Examples
T.T.D.I. III. 105,
Ibid, IV. 39, 54, 67.
Ibid., V. 10, 25, 89, 90, 92, 171.
Ibid, VI. 3, 6, 12, 22, 74, 80.
163. *T.T.D.I.* IV. 67. Tirumala.
164. *Ibid.*, VI. 3. Tirumala.
Similar Examples
T.T.D.I. V. 88, 90.
165. *S.I.I.* X. 61. Valivēru.
166. 384 of 1938-39. Gōṭūru.
167. *T.T.D.I.* III. 7. Tirumala.
168. 64 of 1943-44. Isakala.

made by *Vidvanmahājanas* of the village of Nemaḷḷadinne and *mahāmaṇḍalēśvara* Jiḷḷēla Rangapatirājayyadēva *mahārāja* to the artisan, Tirumalayya, for his having prepared a fresh image of god Nāgavula Cennakēśava at Nemaḷḷadinne[169] On the occasion of the consecration of the temple of Kāśīviśvanātha at Bollavaram in Ś. 1619, a gift was made to an architect for his services[170] Fields were gifted in Ś. 1651 to three artisans who built the temple of god Gōpālasvāmi of Rājaṁpalli.[171] The *kāpus* and the *karaṇams* of Chinnaventurla granted lands to Rāmanna, the son of Ghaṭṭu Kēśavaya, who renovated the temple of Cennakēśava Perumāḷ, originally consecrated by Paraśurāma and to the sculptors Tippaya and Ayyana.[172] Another from Peddamuḍiyam refers to the grant of land as *mānya* made by the 108 *mahājanas* of Brāhmalamudiyam-agrahāram to artisans who built the *śikhara* to the temple of Narasiṁha of the place and for its upkeep and repairs.[173] A record from Pālakol states that the *Pañcāhanaṁvāru* of the place remitted a tax in favour of a mason named Sūrāsari, who attended to the repairs of the temple of god Rāmalinga of the place.[174]

22. *Carpenters*

Many carpenters were maintained by temples. A gift was made in Ś. 1006 to a man who was in charge of the wood work of the temple at Drākshārāma.[175] In Ś. 1452, money was granted to a carpenter for his services in the Tirumala temple.[176] An inscription from the Gōvindarāja temple, Tirupati, dated in Ś. 1466, states that provision was made for carpenters for making and painting the *mahāmēru* images.[177]

169. 353 of 1940 41. Nemaḷḷadinne.
170. *S.I.I.* X. 774. Bollavaram.
171. *N.D.I.* I. Darsi 61. Rājaṁpalli.
172. 380 of 1940-41. Chinnavenuturla.
173. 358 of 1940-41. Peddamuḍiyam.
174. *S I.I.* V. 159. Pālakol.
Similar Examples
S.I I X. 144. Guntūr.
30 of 1941-42. Śankhavaram.
372 of 1940-41. Bhīmaguṇḍam.
405 of 1940-41. Vēlpucherla.
23 of 1941-42. Yāgaṇṭipalli.
T.T.D.I. II. 135.
Ibid., III. 7, 105.
Ibid., , IV. 18. 39, 54.
T.T.D.I. V. 8, 10, 25, 84, 88, 89.
Ibid., IV. 3, 6.
Ibid., III. 105.
Ibid., IV. 26, 39, 54, 59, 67, 129, 134, 135.
Ibid., V. 8, 25, 38, 88, 90.
175. *S.I.I.* IV. 1015. Drākshārāma.
176. *T.T.D.I.* IV. 53. Tirumala.
177. *Ibid.*, V. 25. Tirupati.
Similar Example
T.T.D.I. IV. 129. Tirumala.

23. *Custody of Jewels and Utensils*

Repairs to jewels and utensils were also undertaken by the temple authorities and people were appointed for attending to this work. A record from the Tirumala temple, dated in Ś. 1417 mentions that an agreement was entered into between Kandāḍai Rāmānujayyangār and the *Sthānattār* of the Tirumala temple relating to the repairs, renewal and making of jewels, gold vessels and silver vessels of Śrī Venkaṭēśa and Śrī Gōvindarāja which were in a damaged, broken and tattered condition. It also states that under the orders of Sāḷuva Narasiṁha, the hereditary right was conferred upon Kandāḍai Rāmanujayyaṁgār as the custodian of the key of the treasury of the temples and he accepted the advice of the *Sthānattār* with regard to the above repairs etc., and also agreed to effect the repairs in the presence of the *Sthānattār*.[178]

24. *Accountants*

Accountants were maintained in temples. A record from Yōgimallavaram, dated in the 7th year of the reign of the Cōḷa king, Tribhuvanacakravartin Śrī Rājarājadēva, mentions the hereditary nature of the temple accountant's post in the temple and his right to attest the gifts.[179] Another from the Gōvindarāja temple, Tirupati, dated in Ś. 1557, states that a certain Peṛiya Piḷḷai was appointed as the chief accountant of the temples at Tirumala and Tirupati.[180]

25. *Councillor*

A record from the Tirumala temple mentions the provision made for the maintenance of a chief councillor of the temple.[181]

C. *Entertainers*

Many kinds of artistcs were appointed for the entertainment of the god. These included *mukharī*, the conch blower, the flutist, songsters, players of *mṛdanga*, *nāgasvara*, *āvaja* etc.

1. *Mukharīs*

Several records mention the appointment of *mukharīs* in temples. In Ś. 1054, a gift was made to a *mukharī* in the temple of Gōkarnēśvara of Dāvulūr.[182] According to an inscription from Mālkāpuram, dated in S. 1183, a provision was made for two *mukharīs* in the temple of Viśvēśvara of Gōḷagi.[183] A record from Siṁhāchalam, dated in Ś. 1221, mentions that Varadarāja Śrīpāda made arrangements for two batches of *mukharīs* to provide entertainment to god Viśvēśvara of the place.[184] Another, from Pedamalakūru, states that a *mukharī* was maintained in

178. *T.T.D.I.* II. 133. Tirumala.
179. *Ibid.*, I. 35. Yōgimallavaram.
180. *Ibid.*, VI. 22. Tirupati.
181. *Ibid.*, IV. 129. Tirumala.
182. *S.I I.* X. 91. Dāvulūru.
183. *Ibid.*, X. 395. Mālkāpuram.
184. *Ibid.*, VI. 941. Siṁhāçhalam.

the local temple of Vēṇugōpālasvāmi,[185] One *mukharī* was maintained in the temple of Śrīkūrmanātha of Śrīkūrmam in Ś. 1172.[186]

2. *Conch-blowers*

Conch-blowers and conch-bearers were also appointed in the temples. Provision was made in Ś. 1037, for keeping a conch-bearer in the temple of Sōmēśvara of Kopparam.[187] A *śankhuvari* or a conch blower in the temple of Gōkēśvara of Dāvulūru was maintained by the temple in Ś. 1054.[188] In Ś. 1080, a gift was made to the conch-blowers or *śankulavāru* of the temple of Agastyēśvara of Gunṭūr.[189] A conch-blower, named Brahmama, in the temple of Komara Bhīmēśvara of Cheṛakūru, received a gift in Ś. 1131,[190] In Ś. 1191, provision was made for the maintenance of *ēkaśaṁkulavāru* and *dhavaḷaśaṁkulavāru* in the temple of god Gōpīnātha at Durgī.[191] A record from Sōmarājupalle mentions the gift made to a *śaṁkugārlu* of the local temple.[192]

3. *Bhēri-carrier*

Provision was made for the maintenance of a man who carried the *bhēri* in the temple of god Kūmārabhīmēśvara of Cheṛukūru by Kōṭa Kēta.[193] A gift was made to individual named Janakasundara for playing on the *Bhērī* in the Siṁhāchalam temple.[194]

4. *Flutists*

Flutists or *vaṁsekaras* also received gifts for serving in the temple. In Ś. 1053, the flutist Malla in the temple of Nādiṇḍla received a gift for his service.[195] Provision was made in Ś. 1191 for a flutist in the temple of god Gōpīnātha at Dugya.[196] Two

185. *Ibid.*, X. 238. Padamalakūru.
186. *Ibid.*, V. 1188. Śrīkūrmam.
187. *Ibid*, X. 74. Kopparam.
188. *Ibid.*, X. 91. Dāvulūru.
189. *Ibid.*, X. 144. Gunṭūr.
190. *Ibid.*, VI. 207. Peddacherukūru.
191. *Ibid.*, X. 422. Durgī.
192. *N.D.I.* II. Kandukur 79. Sōma.ājupalle.
Similar Examples
S.I I. X. 151, Tiṁmāpuram.
Ibid., X. 177. Siripuram.
Ibid., IV. 677. Nādeṇḍla.
Ibid., VI. 624. Koṇidena.
S.I.I. X. 159. Ikkūru.
Ibid., X. 164. Mandapāḍu.
N.D.I. III. 47. Rāpūr. Pulicherlapāḍu.
S.I.I. V. 66, 80, Bhīmavaram.
Ibid., IV. 663. Nādiṇḍla.
Ibid., X. 88. Pāmulapāḍu.
193. *S.I.I.* VI. 127. Paddacherukūru.
194. *Ibid.*, VI. 1052. Siṁhāchalam.
195. *Ibid*, IV. 677. Nādiṇḍla.
196. *Ibid.*. X. 422. Durgī.

flutists were maintained by the temple of Siṁhāchalam in S. 1212.[197]

5. *Players of the Mṛdanga*

Maddelakārulu or people who were skilled in playing on the *mṛdanga* were also maintained by the temple for the entertainment of god. A *maddalika,* named Bōta, in the temple of god Sōmīśvara of Kopparam, received a gift in Ś. 1037, for his maintenance.[198] In Ś. 1093, provision was made for the maintenance of *maddaliya* named Varṇa and *maddaliya* Dēvana in the temple of god Rāmīśvara of Siripuram.[199] A gift was made in Ś. 1133, to a *maddlelṇḍu.*[200] Three people who played on the *mṛdanga* were maintained by the temple of god Vankēśvara at Dugyapaṭṭaṇa in the *Palli-nāḍu* in Ś. 1173.[201] In S. 1183, eight people were appointed to play on *maddela* in the temple of god Viśvēśvara at Gōḷagi.[202] Six people were appointed to play on the *maddela* in the temple of god Śrīkūrmanātha of Śrīkūrmam in S, 1172 by Baddakuravadēvu Sāhasamalluḍu.[203]

6. *Ḍōlānāgasvara or Pipe and Drum Service*

Several artistes who played on pipe and drum were also maintained by the devotees. In S. 1418 a gift was made to the *nāgasvarakārar* and drummers of the temple of Tirumala.[204] A record from Veludurti, dated in S. 1472, mentions that a gift was made by Kūnapuli Iṁmaḍi Basivināyanigāru to the barber, Cinnōju, for performing daily the *ḍōlānāgasvara* service in the temple of god Cennarāya in the

197. *Ibid.*, VI. 1137. Siṁhāchalam.
 Similar Examples
 S.I.I. X. 74. Kopparam.
 Ibid., X. 177. Siripuram.
 Ibid., X. 144. Guntūr.
 Ibid., IV. 663. Nādiṇḍla.
198. *S.I.I.* X. 74. Kopparam.
199. *Ibid.*, X. 177. Siripuram.
200. *N.D.I.* III. Rāpūr. 47. Pulicherlapāḍu.
201. *S.I.I.* X. 334. Durgī.
202. *Ibid.*, X. 395. Mālkāpuram.
203. *Ibid.*, V. 1188. Śrīkūrmam.
 Similar Examples
 S.I.I. IV. 677. Nādiṇḍla.
 Ibid., X. 89. Tubāḍu.
 Ibid., X. 91, Dāvulūru.
 Ibid., X. 97. Sātulūru.
 Ibid., X., 107. Nādeṇḍla.
 Ibid., VI. 624. Koṇidena.
 Ibid., X. 144. Guntūr,
 S.I.I. X. 159. Ikkūru.
 Ibid., VI. 207. Peddacheṛukūru.
 Ibid., X. 422. Durgī.
 Ibid., VI. 663. Nādeṇḍla.
 Ibid., V. 66, 80. Bhīmavaram.
 Ibid., X. 238. Pedamalakūru.
204. *T.T.D.I.* II. 135. Tirumala.
205. 294 of 1937-38. Veludurti.

village.[205] Another from Bōyarēvula, dated in Ś. 1482, states that provision was made for Mangala Ankōju for performing the drum service to god Tiruvēngaḷanātha of Guṁḍūru by *mahāmaṇḍalēśvara* Tiṁmarājayyadēva mahārāja.[206] *Daḷavāyi* Nārappanāyaniṁgāru made a gift in Ś. 1499, to the pipers and drummers for serving in the temple of Cennakēśava Perumāḷ at Gollala-Uppalapāḍu.[207] In Ś. 1536, provision was made by Venkaṭapatirājuṁgāru for drummers and pipers in the temple of god Cennarāya of Vanjivanka.[208]

7. *Players of Āvajam*

Āvaja is a kind of musical instrument played in temples and people were appointed for playing on it. An individual who played the *āvajam* in the temple of Gōkēśvara of Dāvulūru received a gift in Ś. 1054.[209] In Ś. 1131, provision was made for the *āvajam* Dāse of the temple of Komara Bhīmēśvara of Cheṛukūru.[210] Arrangements were made in Ś. 1173, for the maintenance of one *āvajakāṇḍu* in the temple of god Vankēśvara at *Dugya-Paṭṭaṇa.*[211] In the temple of Śrī Narasiṁhanātha of Siṁhāchalam also a woman was appointed for this purpose.[212]

8. *Songsters*

Several songsters were maintained by the temple and they received many gifts from the temple treasury as well as from the pious devotees. A songstress named, Gaurī, and another individual named Āditya, both of the temple of Sōmīśvara of Kopparam, received a gift of land in Ś. 1037.[213] Fourteen women singers and one Kaṣmīrī singer were appointed in Ś. 1183, in the temple of Viśveśvara of Gōḷagi by Viśveśvara Śivācārya.[214] A gift was made in Ś. 1191 to ten songsters of the Durgī temple.[215] In Ś. 1418 a gift was made to the *pāḍuvār* or songsters at Tirumala temple.[216]

9. *Players of other Musical Instruments*

Several other musical instruments were played by many artistes in the temple. In Ś. 1191, a gift was made to a *kāhaḷakāḍu* who played on the *Kāhaḷamu*. Another

206. 40 of 1943-44. Bōyarēvula.
207. 377 of 1940-41. Gollala-uppalapāḍu.
208. *N.D.I.* I. Gūḍūr 110. Vanjavanka.
Similar Examples
349 of 1940-41. Garisaḷūru.
T.T.D.I. V. 89. Tirupati.
Ibid., VI. 5. Tirumala.
209. *S.I.I.* X. 91, Dāvulūru.
210. *Ibid.*, VI. 207. Peddacherukūru.
211. *Ibid.*, X. 334. Durgī.
212. *Ibid.*, VI. 1052.Siṁhāchalam.
Similar Examples
S.I.I. X. 422. Durgī.
N.D.I. III. Ongōle 88. Nāguluppalapāḍu.
213. *S I I.* X. 74. Kopparam.
214. *Ibid.*, X. 395. Mālkāpuram.
215. *Ibid.*, X. 422. Durgī.
216. *T.T.D.I.* II. 135. Tirumala.

gift was made to *Vīranatiṇḍlavāru* and to *Sannagāḷavāḍu* and *Peddagavurravāru* in the temple of god Gōpīnātha at Durgya.[217] *Khāhaḍlavāṇḍu* and *Jagaḍavāṇḍu* were also maintained by the temple. The *jagaḍa* is a kind of cymbal consisting of rows of bells attached to it. People who played on a small pipe which is intended for *śṛti* were also maintained in the temple of Bhīmavaram.[218] In the temple of Śrīkūrmam a *khāhadlakāḍu* was also maintained in S. 1172.[219] An instrument named *bōyuvid-dhavallabhi*, a kind of bamboo instrument with holes, was also played in temples and people were maintained in the temple of Nādiṇḍla for this purpose.[220] Six people, who played on *karaḍa* were appointed in S. 1183 in the temple of god Viśvēśvara of Gōḷagi.[221] One *karaḍakāṇḍu* was maintained in the temple of Siṁhāchalam in Ś. 1172.[222]

10. *Dance Troupes*

Several dancers and dance troupes were appointed in temples for the entertainment of the god. In Ś. 1059, provision was made for a dancer and to a woman dancer by name Āya, in the temple of Śaktīśvara of Nūteki.[223] A gift was made in Ś. 1061, for maintaining a dancer named Dādapōjumalle.[224] In Ś 1075, a gift was made in the village of Taṭārāma for the dancing girls in the temple of god Cōḷaganga Mādhavadēva.[225] Tripurāntakamahārāja made provision in Ś. 1151, for the dancing girls of the temple of god Tripurāntakēśvara of Tripurāntakam.[226] In Ś. 1212, a gift was made to the temple treasury for keeping a dance group of eight women in the temple of Siṁhāchalam.[227] Provision was made in Ś 1213, for the maintenance of four women dancers in the same temple.[228] A Venkaṭapati Rājuṁgāru made a gift in Ś. 1536, for the dancing girls in the temple of Vanjevanka.[229] In Ś. 1418, a gift was made to the *naṭṭuvar* or dancers of the Tirumala temple.[230] An undated record from Palivela refers to the provision made for the *nṛttānganas,* in the local temple.[231] Another, from Bhīmavaram, mentions the gift to a dancer

217. **Similar Examples**
S.I.I. IV. 677. Nādeṇḍla.
Ibid., X. 89. Tubāḍu.
Ibid., X. 192. Nūtakki.
Ibid., X. 107. Nādeṇḍla.
N.D.I. III. Rāpūr. 47. Pulicherlapāḍu.
S.I.I. IV. 663. Nādeṇḍla.

217. *S.I.I.* X. 422. Durgī.
218. *Ibid.*, V. 80. Bhīmavaram.
219. *Ibid.*, V. 1188. Śrīkūrmam.
220. *Ibid.*, IV. 663. Nādiṇḍla.
221. *Ibid.*, X. 395. Mālkāpuram.
223. *Ibid.*, X. 102. Nūtakki.
224. *Ibid.*, X. 107. Nādiṇḍla.
225. *Ibid.*, X. 707. Rellivalasa.
226. *N.D.I.* I. Darsi 57. Pōṭlapāḍu.
227. *S.I.I.* VI. 1137. Siṁhāchalam.
228. *Ibid.*, VI. 902. Siṁhāchalam.
229. *N.D.I.* I. Gūḍūr 110. Vanavalla.
230. *T.T.D.I.* II. 135. Tirumala.
231. *S.I.I.* V. 105. Palivela.

named Sōmayya of the local temple.[232] In S. 1183, 10 dancers were maintained in the temple of god Viśveśvara at Gōḷagi by Viśveśvara-Śiva the preceptor of the Kākatīya king Gaṇapatidēva and Rudrāṁbā.[233]

D. *Intermediaries*

Sometimes certain services were instituted to the temple like lighting of lamps, celebration of festivals, etc. Animals like cows, goats, sheep, buffaloes were placed in the charge of individuals subject to the condition that they were to supply the required quantity of ghee to the temple. Such people were intermediaries between the temple and the donor. In the 14th year of Rājarājadēva, the residents of Mannaipūṇḍi accepted the gift and undertook to conduct a festival for god Tippalādīśvaramuḍaiya Nāyanār in Tiruccukanūr in the *Kudavūr-nāḍu* and they paid the cost of the accessories required for the celebration of the festival in the *Śrī-Bhaṇḍāram*.[234] A gift of 6 cows was made for the purpose of a lamp to god Rāmalingēśvara of Vēlpūru and the gift was entrusted to *dēvavaḍugulu* for the proper utilization of the gift in Ś. 1034.[235] A record from Koṁmūru, dated in Ś. 1040, mentions the gift of 6 *gaṇḍa-māḍas* for keeping a perpetual lamp before god Agastīśvara of the place and the gift was entrusted to Muppabōyuṇḍu for the supply of one *nandimānika* of ghee every day.[236] In Ś. 1041, a gift was made to the *Koṁmūrisānimunnūru* and they had to supply one *nandimānika* of ghee per day to the temple of the same place for keeping a lamp.[237] In Ś. 1063, the protection of the

232. *Ibid.*, V. 80. Bhīmavaram.
233. *Ibid.*, X. 395. Mālkāpuram.
Similar Examples
N.D.I. III. Udayagiri 6. Jaḍadēvī.
S.I.I. X. 74. Kopparam.
Ibid., X. 89. Tubāḍu.
Ibid., X. 91. Dāvulūru.
Ibid., VI. 624. Koṇidena.
Ibid, X. 144. Gunṭūr.
Ibid., X. 177. Siripuram.
Ibid., VI. 207. Peddacheṛukūru.
N.D.I. III. Rapur 47. Pulicherlapāḍu.
Ibid., III. Ongōle 88. Nāguluppalapāḍu.
S.I.I. X. 334. Durgī.
N.D.I. I. Darsi 22. Toṁmalūru.
Ibid., II. Kāvali 48. Koṇḍūru.
Ibid., I. Ātmakūr 25. Chirmāna.
S.I.I. V. 1204. Śrīkūrmam.
Ibid., VI. 1052, 1078. Siṁhāchalam.
T.T.D.I. III. 7. Tirumala.
N.D.I. II. Kandukūr 79. Somarājupalli.
234. *T.T.D.I.* I. 38. Yōgimallavaram.
235. *S.I.I.* X. 71. Vēlpūra.
236. *Ibid.*, X. 78. Koṁmūru.
237. *Ibid.*, X. 80. Ponnūru.

gift was entrusted to the *Sthānāpatis*, *Sānimunnūru* and *Nibhandhakāru*.[238] In S. 1066, a gift was made to the temple of Jaladhīśvara of Ghaṇṭaśāla *alias* Cōḍa-Pāṇḍyapuram and it was entrusted to the *Sānimunnuru* for the supply of ghee at the rate of *sāniyamāna* per day.[239]

238. *Ibid.*, X. 110. Juttiga.
239. *Ibid.*, X. 115. Ghaṇṭaśāla.

5

ORGANIZATION OF THE TEMPLE

The temple was a highly organized institution. It received immense variety of gifts and had to arrange for the performance of a number of services and functions. The management of the temple had to be very efficient. The conduct of its work seems to have been entrusted to the *Sthānāpati* who seems to have been the general supervisor. There were other agents like the *Sānis, Mānis* and *Ayyas*. The Śrī *Bhaṇḍāram* or the temple treasury also played a vital role. Inscriptions supply interesting information about all these agents of temple organization.

1. *The Sthānāpati*

a. *Appointment of Sthānāpati*

Inscriptions mention the appointment of the *Sthānapati.* In Ś. 1037, a scholar of *Śaivāgamas,* named Mallikārjuna, was appointed as the *Sthānāpati* of the temple of god Sōmēśvara of Kopparam by a *sēnāpati.*[1] A record from Rellivalasa, dated in S. 1081, mentions the conferment of the office of the *Sthānāpati* of the temple of god Cōḷaganga Mādhavadēva on Kaḍapāka Puruṣōttama-Bhaṭṭa and his son, Brahmarāya by Eṛapōta nāyaka.[2]

b. *Receiving Gifts*

Many records register a variety of gifts made to the *Sthānāpati* obviously as an agent of the deity. In Ś. 1077, a gift of 10 *puṭṭis* of land was made to Mādajiyya, the *Sthānāpati* of the temple of Śiva, by the elders of the village of Dayyālarēyūru.[3] A record from Ikkūru, dated in Ś. 1088, mentions the gift of 1 *kha* and 10 *na* of land made to the *Sthānāpati* of the Rāmasvāmi temple of the village.[4] The *Sthānāpati*

1. *S.I.I.* X. 73. Tangēḍumalli.
2. *Ibid.*, X. 709. Rallivalasa.
3. *N.D.I.* II. Ongōle 18. Bollavarapāḍu.
4. *S.I.I.* X. 159 Ikkūru.

of the temple of Mārkaṇḍēyasvāmi of Rājahmundry received a gift of 3 *mattars* of the land in Ś. 1098.[5] A gift of land was made in Ś. 1140, on the occasion of a lunar eclipse, to the *Sthānādhipati* of the temple of god Cōḍēśvaramahādēva, located in the *Samavidyāsthāna*.[6] An inscription from Kaṁbhampāḍu, dated in Ś. 1180, states that some land was granted to *Sthānāpati*, Cōḍaśiva-Gurudēva of the local temple.[7] In Ś. 1330, the Telugu Cōḍa chief, Annadēva, gave land to Niśsanka Kāmaya the *Sthānāpati* of the temple of Mahānandigirilinga near Pōlavaram.[8] Another from Amarāvati, dated in the 2nd year of the reign of Kulōttungacōḷadēva, states that a Sikkar-Uḍaiya Seṭṭiyār donated a garden land with a spring to the *Sthānāpati* of the local temple of Mangēśvaradēva.[9] In Ś. 1055, twenty-five cows were given to Puṣpātmajiya, the *Sthānādhipati* of the temple of god Mahādēva of Tripurāntakam.[10] A palmyra garden was granted in Ś. 1093 to a *Sthānāpati* of the temple of Rāmēśvara of Śiripuram on the occasion of an *Uttarāyaṇa-sankrānti*.[11] A record from Ālaṁpūr, dated in the 4th year of the reign of the Kalacūri king, Āhavamalla, mentions the gift of income derived from tolls on various transactions to Kēśavarāśi, the *Sthānāpati* of the temple of god Gaurēśvara.[12] Another from Siddhēśvaram, dated in S. 983, refers to the gift of toll-income collected on the river at Siddhēśvara to the disciple of the ascetic, Kalyāṇaśakti, the *Sthānāpati* of the temple of god Siddhēśvara.[13] In C.V.E. 39, and in the reign of the Later Cāḷukyan King, Tribhuvanamalla, a gift was made to Vitaraṇēndrarāśi paṇḍita, the *Sthānāpati* of god Brahmēśvara of Ālaṁpūr, by *mahāmaṇḍalēśvara* Mallarasa.[14] In the 72nd year of the same reign, a gift was made to Dharaṇīndrarāśipaṇḍita, the *Sthānāpati* of the same temple by Abhinavasarasvatī, the queen of the king.[15]

Making Gifts

Besides receiving gifts, the *Sthānāpatis* were also making gifts themselves. Śrīmadvisiṣṭulapaṇḍitulu, the *mahāsthānādhipati* of the temple of Drākshārāma, made a gift of land for the purpose of laying a garden for god Bhīmēśvara of Drākshārāma.[16] Ten *birudugadyalu* were endowed by three *Sthānāpatis* in Ś. 1080, to god Śankaradēva of Koṇidena on the occasion of a *Viṣu-sankrānti*.[17] In Ś. 1099, Vyāsatīrtha paṇḍita, the *Sthānāpati* of the temple at Tripurāntakam made a gift of land to the local god Tripurāntakēśvara.[18] A gold plate weighing 2,000 *ṭankas* was

5. *Ibid.*, X. 194. Rajāhmundry.
6. C.P. 4. of 1938-39.
7. 301 of 1930-31. Kaṁbhaṁpāḍu.
8. 293 of 1920. Pōlavaram.
9. *E.I.* XXXI. pp. 269-276. Hēmavati.
10. 459 of 1940-41. Tripurāntakam.
11. *S.I.I.* X. 177. Śiripuram.
12. *K.I.A.P.* Appendix 32. Ālaṁpūr.
13. 38 of 1942-43. Siddhēśvaram.
14. *K.I.A.P.* 108; *Tel. Ins.* pp. 41-42. Ālaṁpūr.
15. *Tel. Ins.* I. Ch. 30 Ālaṁpūr.
16. *S.I.I.* IV. 1256. Drākshārāma.
17. *Ibid.*, VI. 625. Koṇidena.
18. *Ibid.*, X. 196. Tripurāntakam.

granted in Ś. 1569, to gods Surabhēśvara, Pāpavināśadēva, and Rāmayadēva of Sattevōlu by *Sthānāpati* Peda Gangajiyya.[19] In the 49th year of the reign of the Later Cāḷukyan King, Tribhuvanamalla, a gift of lamp was made by the *Sthānāpati* Rāmēśvararāśi paṇḍitulu to god Bhīmēśvara of Drākshārāma.[20]

There is evidence to show that the *Sthānāpati* received several benefactions from devotees for specific purposes. In Ś. 1055, a gift was made by Rājēndra to a *Sthānāpati* for the maintenance of a lamp in the temple of god Mahādēva of Tripurāntakam.[21] The Velanāḍu king, Cōḍa, gave a lamp in Ś. 1058 and the *Sthānāpatis* of the temple were commissioned to maintain this charity.[22] In Ś. 1057, the *Sthānāpatis* accepted a gift on the occasion of a solar eclipse, in order to keep a lamp burning in the temple of god Rāmēśvara of Chāmcalūru.[23]

Sthānāpati as Manager

The *Sthānāpatis* were appointed as managers of the donated lands, villages etc., and they were requested to protect the gifts made by the devotees to temples. A gift was made by the feudatory named Māmala Mallaya to god Viśvanātha at Siddhēśvara and the management of the gift was handed over to the *Sthānāpati* of Sangamēśvara and Bhāskarakṣētra.[24] In S. 1161, a gift was made by Mādhava nāyaka to god Mallēśvara of Nāguluppalupāḍu and the gift was made into the hands of the *Sthānāpatis* for further security.[25]

c. *Collection of Taxes*

The *Sthānāpatis* used to levy taxes and collect them for various purposes. A record from Turimeḷḷa, dated in Ś. 1569, registers a gift made to gods Surabhēśvara, Pāpavināśanadēva and Rāmayadēva of Sattevōlu and refers to the levy of a fee on marriages and *upanayanams* performed in these temples by *Sthānāpati* Peda Ganga-Jiyya.[26]

d. *Installation of Images etc.*

It is also known from inscriptions that images were installed by the *Sthānāpatis*. A record dated in Ś. 1569. mentions that originally there was no Lakṣmī image at Śrīkūrmam, and that Bhāṣyam Rāghavācārya, the grandson of Appalācārya, the local *Sthānāpati*, installed this goddess.[27] Another from Peddanapāḍu, states that

19. 258 of 1949-50. Turimeḷḷa.
20. *S.I I.* IV. 1229. Drākshārāma.
21. 459 of 1940-41. Tripurāntakam.
22. *S.I.I.* V. 160. Pālakol.
23. *Ibid.*, X. 97. Sātulūru.
    Similar Examples
    S.I.I. VI. 161. Pālakol.
    Ibid., X. 12. Juttiga.
    N.D.I. III. Ongōle 79. Mannūru.
24. 40 of 1942. 43. Siddhēśvaram.
25. *N.D.I.* III. Ongōle 86, 88. Nāguluppalapāḍu.
26. 258 of 1949-50. Turimeḷḷa.
27. *S.I.I.* V. 1164. Śrīkūrmam.

Naraharidēva, the *Sthānāpati* of Rāmacandrarāya, consecrated the image of Hanumān at Peddanapāḍu.[28]

In Ś. 1077, Setajiyya the *Mūlasthānāpati* of the temple of Janakavaram, was ordered to build the temple *maṇṭapa* and perform daily worship with lights and offerings.[29] A certain Vinayāditya Satyāśraya made a gift to Kāśmīra Paṇḍitadēva, the *Sthānāpati* at Panchalinga, for annual repairs and upkeep of temples.[30]

e. *Acting as Witness*

In some cases the *Sthānāpatis* were requested to act as witnesses to the benefactions made to the temples by the devotees. An inscription from Dēvaguḍi, dated in Ś. 1316, mentions the sale of the worshipping rights and the attached land by Bāca-Jiya, Pōlama and others of the Talakaṇṭidēva temple to five other Jiyas. As witnesses to this transaction were cited the *Sthānāpatis* of the temple of god Rāmēśvara and Eṛamadala-Jiya the *Sthānāpati* of the temple of god Talakaṇṭidēvī and others.[31]

2. *Sthānikulu*

The *Sthānikulu* or *Sthānaṁvāru* or *Sthānattār* were also closely associated with temple organization. The office of the *Sthānika* came to be regarded in certain cases, as hereditary in certain families. If the trustee, who had originally secured the office, had a number of sons, his office, after his death was regarded as common property, and was divided equally among his sons. Thus, the place of a single trustee would be taken by a board of trustees within a generation or two. It is said in an inscription at Dēvaguḍi, that the *Sthānikas* were the six sons of one Cinnajiyya, who probably had held the trusteeship of the temple.[32] Although the trust boards of some of the temples had sprung up in this fashion, it is extremely unlikely that all of them have had a similar origin. Most of them probably were created by the government, one of whose principal duties was to look after the well being of the temples.

The *Sthānikas* received gifts made to temples and the gifts made to themselves. In Ś. 1425, a village of Pāṇem was gifted to four *Sthānikas* of the Paṇikēśvara temple for the merit of Iṁmadi Narasingarāja *mahārāja*.[33] In Ś. 1488, Śrī Ajātavīra-śaivasiddhā Bhikṣāvṛtti Ayyavāru of Śrī Kailāsamu on the Śrī Parvata gifted the income named *viramuṣṭi pannu* to the *Sthānikas* of the temple of Sangamēśvaram.[34]

The *Sthānikas* administered lands and other properties belonging to the temple.

28. 266 of 1937-38. Peddanapāḍu.
29. *N.D.I.* II. Ongōle 51. Janakavaram.
30. 50 of 1953-54. Panchalingāla.
31. 332 of 1940-41. Dēvaguḍi.
32. L.R. 15. p. 82.
33. 166 of 1913. Pāṇem.
34. 431 of 1923. Samgamēśvaram.

They received gifts of money and lands on behalf of the god.[35] A record from Kāḷahasti, dated in Ś. 1438 registers the gift of money to the *Sthānikas* of the local temple by Mādenāyaka.[36]

Acquisition and Disposal of Properties

The *Sthānikas* extended the temple estate by the acquisition of fresh lands by purchase.[37] They disposed of the temple property when the ceremonies of the temple demanded ready money.[38] They made *dāśabandha* grants either for repairing or for rebuilding the temple.[39] They also cancelled the debts by purchasing the mortgaged property.[40] They invested the money deposited in the temple treasury by donors and others in a manner profitable to the temple.[41] The *Sthānikas* had some judicial functions also, they investigated the cases involving the theft of the temple properties and punished the culprits.[42]

Assenting Gifts

The *Sthānikas* received gifts made to temples and their consent was necessary for the making of these gifts. In Ś. 945, a gift was made to god Bhāvanārāyaṇa for *angarangabhōga* and *dhūpadīpanaivēdya* and this was entrusted to the hands of *Sthānaṁvāru* for protection.[43] In the 17th year of the reign of king Viṣṇuvardhana, a gift was made to god Vāsukiravisōmēśvara at Juttiga and it was entrusted to the care of the *Sthānaṁvāru* of the place.[44] A cash gift was made to the temple of god Agastyēśvara of Guntūr in Ś. 1464, by Pōli Reḍḍi and the amount was entrusted to the *Sthānikas* with certain stipulations.[45] A record from Bhīmavaram, dated in Ś. 1350, states that, Viśvēśvaragurudēva made a gift of *Suvarṇadhēnu, Kāṁśyapātrō-pakaraṇādulainapanulu* to god Bhīmēśvaradēva on the occasion of a lunar eclipse with the consent of the *Sthānaṁvāru.*[46] Another from Sarpavaram, dated in Ś. 1316, mentions the consent of the *Sthānaṁvāru* for making a gift.[47] In Ś. 1438, the *Sthānikas* of the Kāḷahastīśvara temple granted money to the temple for the king's merit.[48]

It is not clear, however, who these *Sthānaṁvāru* were. Etymologically the word

35. *M.E.R.*, 1925. Kāḷahasti.
36. *S.I.I.* IX. 505. Kāḷahasti.
37. 7 of 1922; LR 36. Vāṇipeṇṭa, pp. 485-486.
38. 446 of 1921; 321 of 1○21, Tiruvennainallūr.
39. L.R. 15. Dēvaguḍi. p. 80.
40. 179 of 1924. Kāḷahasti.
41. *M.E.R.*, 1925. Kāḷahasti.
42. 185 of 1894; *S.I.I.* V. 479; Tirukkalkunram, 446 and 321 of 1921 above, and *S.I.I.* V. 479 fall technically outside Āndhradēśa, but are included for their unique value, as such instance are, so far, not found in inscriptions from Āndhradēśa.
43. *S.I.I.* VI. 139. Bāpatla.
44. *Ibid.*, X. 13. Juttiga.
45. 207 of 1937-38. Chiḍipirāla.
46. *S.I I.* V. 52. Bhīmavaram.
47. *Ibid.*, V. 27. Sarpavaram.
48. *Ibid.*, IX. 575. Kāḷahasti.

means "those belonging to or in charge of the *sthānam* or place or institution". Since the word is in the plural, it means, obviously a group of people. It does not seem unreasonable to conclude that these *Sthānaṁvāru* were a kind of Managing Committee or the board of trustees of the concerned temple. Each board of *Sthānikas* had a president known as *Sthānāpati* or *Sthānācārya.* It is not possible, at the present stage of our knowledge, to state the exact number of *Sthānikas* comprising a board. The Dēvaguḍi epigraph states that there were six *Stnānikas* managing the affairs of the local temple, but as they were sons of the same father, Cinnajiyya, its evidence cannot be relied upon in fixing the normal strength of the board of the *Sthānikas* of the time. It also implies that the *Sthānaṁvāru* had the power to accept or reject a gift made that gifts could not be made without their consent.

Mēlunāyakulu

Mēlunāyakulu or the supervisors also played a great role in the temple organization. Provision was made by Kulōttunga Cōḍa Gonka in Ś. 1057, to Mēlunāyakamalle, Mēlunāyakasūre of the temple of god Rāmēśvara of Chaṁcalūru.[49] In Ś. 1172, ten *mēlināyakulu* were maintained in the temple of Śrī Kūrmanātha Śrīkūrmam by Baḍḍakuruva Sāhasamallunḍu.[50] A *mēlunāyaka* was maintained in Ś. 1433, by the treasury of Śrī Vēnkaṭēśa of Tirumala.[51] The same treasury maintained the *mēlnāyakam* of the temple in S. 1468.[52]

3. *Sānis, Mānis and Ayyanulu*

a. *Their Number*

Inscriptions belonging to the 11th and 12th centuries of the Christian era invariably mention the *Sāni* three hundred as associated with the *Sthānāpati* in the management of the temple charities. In other instances the *Sānis* are mentioned along with *Mānis* in connection with temple affairs. It is interesting to note that at this early period 300 women of the place had a voice in the temple management.[53] This suffix *Sāni* was applied to the names of married women as a mark of respect. Certain names like Namundari Bēti-reḍḍi's wife, Kūnasāni and her mother-in-law, Sūrasāni and her father-in-law, Anasūrapa-reḍḍis are mentioned in an inscription dated in Ś. 1237. Another from Juttiga dated in Ś. 1237, mentions the names of Attilireḍḍī's mother, Mēḍamareḍḍisāni and his father, Nāgireḍḍi.[54] What the nature and status of these *Sānis* were, it is difficult to state. It seems hazardous to put down all of them as prostitutes which the word now indicates in its degraded sense. Evidence there is in some inscriptions of Juttiga, of *Sānis* leading married lives.[55]

49. *Ibid.*, X. 97. Sātulūru.
50. *Ibid.*, V. Śrīkūrmam.
51. *T.T.D.I.* III. 20. Tirupati.
52. *Ibid.*, V. 71. Tirumala.
53. 735 of 1902; *S.I.I.* X. 268. Juttiga.
54. *S.I.I.* X. 511, 512. Juttiga.
55. *Ibid.*, X. 13. Juttiga.

A record dated in the 18th year of the reign of Rājarāja, mentions *Sānulu* and *Mānulu.*[56] Another from Juttiga, dated in the 15th year of the reign of Viṣṇuvardhana refers to 300 *Sānis* and *nibandhakārulu.*[57] One other from Vēlpūru, dated in Ś. 1034, mentions *Sānimunnuru.*[58] A record from Chēbrōlu dated in Ś. 1075, mentions 300 *Sānis*, 300 *Avyanulu* and 300 *Māṇis.*[59] Another from Śrīkākuḷam, dated in Ś. 1077, mentions *Sānikāṁpulu.*[60] Another from Chēbrōlu, mentions 300 *Sānis*, 300 *Ayyanulu* and *nibandhakāru.*[61]

b. *Receiving Gifts*

Gifts made to temples were entrusted to these *Sānis*, *Mānis* and *Ayyanulu.* In Ś. 1064, a gift of land was made to the *Sānis* and *Mānis* by Tribhuvanamalladēva Pottapicōḍa.[62] Part of the village of Jonnaprōlūru was granted in Ś. 1070 to the *Sānis* and *Mānis* by the king Tribhuvanamalladēva Cōḍa.[63] In Ś. 1072, a gift of land was made on the occasion of a *Viṣu-sankrānti* to the *Sānis* and *Mānis.*[64] A record from Yēnikapāḍu, dated in Ś. 1096, mentions the gift of land made to the *Sānis* and *Mānis* on the occasion of an *Uttarāyaṇa-sankrānti.*[65] Another from Panchadhārla, dated in Ś. 1359, refers to the gift of 4 *kha* of land made to the *Sānis* for their services to the temple.[66] Another refers to the gift of *kulōttunga-māḍas* to *Sānimunnuru.*[67]

c. *Trustees of Gifts*

Several records register gifts made to temples and entrusted to the *Sānis*, *Mānis* and *Ayyanulu* and *Dēvakarmulu.* In Ś. 945, a gift was made to a god and it was entrusted to the *dēvakarmulu.*[68] A record from Bāpaṭla, dated in Ś. 1038, mentions a gift made to a god and states that it was entrusted to the *dēvakarmulu.*[69] Another from Pālakol, dated in Ś. 1058, states that the *Sānis* were commissioned to maintain a charity.[70] In Ś. 1075, a gift was made to a god and it was entrusted to the 300 *Sānis* and 300 *Ayyanulu.*[71] Mention is also made of a gift made in Ś. 1085, and of its being attested to *Valayacuṭṭina-bindyasānimunnuru.*[72] In Ś. 1143, a lamp was given and the 300 *Sānis* and *nibhandhakāru* were asked to maintain it.[73]

56. *Ibid.*, X. 5. Kollūru.
57. *Ibid.*, X. 12. Juttiga.
58. *Ibid*, X. 80. Koṁmūru.
59. *Ibid*, VI. 10. Chēbrōlu.
63. *Ibid.*, IV. 996. Śrīkakūḷam.
61. *Ibid.*, VI. 113. Chēbrōlu.
62. *Ibid*, VI. 624 Koṇidena.
63. *Ibid.*, VI. 610. Koṇidena.
64. *Ibid*, VI 605. Koṇidena.
65. *Ibid.*, X. 193. Yenikapāḍu.
66. *Ibid.*, VI. 668. Panchadhārla.
67. *Ibid.*, X. 229. Masulipaṭṇam.
68. *Ibid.*, VI. 139. Bāpaṭla.
69. *Ibid.*, VI. 135. Bāpaṭla.
70. *Ibid.*, V. 160. Pālakol.
71. *Ibid.*, VI. 101. Chēbrōlu.
72. *Ibid.*, IV. 989. Śrīkakūḷam.
73. *Ibid.*, X. 268. Juttiga.

d. *Making Gifts*

Gifts were made by the *Sānis* themselves to temples. A record from Chēbrōlu, dated in Ś. 1135, mentions the gift of *suradāmavṛtti* to god Kumārasvāmi of the place by the *Sāni* 300 and *Ayyanulu* 300 of the place.[74]

e. *Their Status*

The available examples do not help us to determine exactly the status of these temple agents. The numberals 300, often added after the *Sānulu, Mānulu* and *Ayyanulu*, cannot be explained. Probably, they indicate their strength. *Dēvakarmulu* means workers of the god, meaning the temple employees. Their association with the *Sānulu, Mānulu* and *Ayyanulu* may be taken to imply that these too were temple employees. A certain Amarināyaka made a gift in Ś. 1163, to god Agastīśvara at Kolakalūru and it was entrusted to *Sāni-māni-nibandhakāṇḍru.*[75] Another record from Śēkūru mentions that a gift was entrusted to *Sāni-māni-nibandhakāṇḍru.*[76] *Sāni-māni-nibandhālu* means the department of the *Sānis* and *Mānis*, if *nibandhālu* is taken to be the equivalent of *niyōgālu* which are mentioned in connection with the organization of the state (cf. *Bāhattari-niyōgas* and 72 *niyōgalavāru*). In some instances the *Sānis* were hereditarily serving the god. A record from Juttiga mentions that the three hundred *Sānis* in the temple were hereditarily serving the god Vāsukiravisōmēśvara of the place.[77]

4. *Sabhaiyār*

The *Sabhaiyār* were another agency associated with the temple. In Ś. 1466, a gift of ½ *paṇam* was made to the *Sabhaiyār* for arranging to carry Naṁmāḷvār from the sanctum to the car on the day of the star *Vaiśākham*, occurring on the 10th day of *Adhyayanōtsavam* celebrated for the Āḷvār.[78] One *paṇam* was granted to the *Sabhaiyār* for carrying the image of Śrī Viṭṭhalēśvara in a procession.[79] A record from Tirupati, dated in Ś. 1466, states that 2 *paṇam* was paid to the *Sabhaiyār* as *tirumun kānikkai* for conducting the festival in a garden-*maṇṭapa* at Tirumala on the eleven days of the *Brahmōtsavam.*[80] Another, from Tirumala, dated in Ś. 1457, refers to the gift of one *paṇam* to the *Sabhaiyār* for the erection of a pandal.[81] One record from the same place states that the *Sabhaiyār* were entrusted with the duty of guarding against the taxation of tax free land granted to the temple for the purpose of conducting a service.[82] An inscription from Tiruchānūr, dated in the 29th year of the reign of the Cōḷa King, Kō-Parākēsarivarman, registers the gift of 40 *kalañju* of gold to the *Sabhaiyār* of Tiruccōgunūr for burning a lamp.[83] In the 23rd

74. *Ibid.*, VI. 110. Chēbrōlu.
75. *Ibid.*, X. 292. Kolakalūru.
76. *Ibid.*, X. 405. Śēkūru.
77. 744 of 1920. Juttiga.
78. *T.T.D.I.* V. 34. Tirupati.
79. *Ibid.*, V. 90. Tirupati.
80. *Ibid.*, V. 88. Tirupati.
81. *Ibid.*, IV. 67. Tirumala.
82. *Ibid.* I. 8. Tirumala.
83. *Ibid*, I. 12. Tiruchānūr.

year of the reign of the Cōḷa king, Rājarāja, an individual, named Brahmamarāyan deposited with the Sabhaiyār of the village of Yōgimallavaram, 26 *kalañju* of gold accurately weighed with the *dharmakattalai* stone.[84] A sum of 4 *kalañju* of gold was granted to the *Sabhaiyār* of Tiruccūkanūr for making an offering to god Tiruvēnkaṭamuḍaiyān in the sanctum.[85]

It is evident from these examples that the *Sabhaiyār* or the committee of the village in which the temple was situated was also closely associated with the temple and played an important part in receiving gifts and fulfilling the wishes of the donors.

5. *Niyōgas*

Several inscriptions mention the *niyōgālavāru* in connection with the management of the temple. One record from Tripurāntakam mentions the *Bāhattariniyōgālavāru.*[86] Another from the same place mentions the *Bāhattari-niyōgālavāru* as making a gift for the celebration of the marriage festival of god Tripurāntakēśvara.[87] The word *Bāhattari* means 72 and *niyōga* means department.[88] Other records mention *Bāhattariniyōgas* and a head of these *niyōgas* named *Bāhattari-niyōgādhipati.*[89] Inscriptions of the ancient period mention the *niyōga* as government official. It may be inferred from this that *niyōga* meant a department. It is obvious that as in the state, there were 72 departments in the temple also. Probably different types of temple servants were grouped together into one department or another.

6. *Overseers*

Officers called the overseers of the temple are mentioned in a Kambadur grant dated in Ś. 1478.[90] The nature of the work which they performed is nowhere stated It is not unlikely that they were government officials, probably belonging to the religious endowment department, supervising the work of the *Sthānikas* in administering temple properties.

7. *The Temple Cāvaḍi*

Every temple had its own *Cāvaḍi* or office, where one or more *Karaṇams* kept the accounts of its properties. The office of the *Karaṇam* was hereditary, although the appointment was made at first by the emperor or his provincial representative. For instance, Rāmarāja-kōnēṭi-Timma, who was the governor of Udayagiri, about Ś. 1474, appointed one Vīragangayya, as the hereditary *Karaṇam* of the temple of Raghunāyaka at Udayagiri. According to the grant recording his appointment he was to maintain the accounts of the villages belonging to the temple and of the dues

84. *T.T.D.I.* I. 18. Yōgimallavaram.
85. *Ibid.*, I. 129. Tiruchānūr.
86. *S.I.I.* X. 173, 465. Śrīrāmāpuram, Tripurāntakam.
87. *Ibid.*, X. 479. Tripurāntakam.
88. *Ibid.*, X. 502. Tripurāntakam.
89. *Ibid.*, X. 369, 400. Tripurāntakam.
90. 94 of 1913. Kaṁbadūru.

on articles that were sold therein. In addition to these, he had probably to draft leases which the temple authorities granted to its tenants and to keep a register describing the various kinds of taxes due to the temple treasury. His salary was fixed at 1 *varāha* a month or 12 *varāhas* in a year. Besides, he was entitled to get from the temple four *paḍis* of *prasādam* every day.[91] A record from Ellanūru states that the members of the Cittiramēḷi guild appointed Vyāpakadēva, a pupil of Yajina Jiyyar of Puṣpagiri as the *Śrī Kāryam* of the temple of god Cittiramēḷi-Desamīśvaramuḍaiyār of Vellatūrpaṭṭaṇam.[92]

8. *The Śrībhaṇḍaram*

The *Śrī-Bhaṇḍāram* or the temple treasury played a vital role in the organization and functioning of the temple.

The *Śrī-Bhaṇḍāram* received various gifts like villages, lands, coins, taxes, animals, vessels, lampstands, camaras. channels, canals etc. The *Pōn-Bhaṇḍāram* or gold treasury and jewellery store of the temple was also maintained by it. Gifts were also made to this *bhaṇḍāram* and the famous religious teacher, Kandāḍai Rāmānujayyangār, was the manager of this department at Tirumala.[93] The *Tiruppaṇi-Bhaṇḍāram* or the treasury of the public works pertaining to temples was also maintained by the temple. Gifts were also made to this *Bhaṇḍāram.* The study of inscriptions shows that the *Śrībhaṇḍāram* was the main treasury and the others were of auxiliaries attached to it. The *Poṇ-Bhaṇḍāram* and the *Tiruppaṇi-Bhaṇḍāram* received grants from the *Śrī-Bhaṇḍāram* as well as gifts from devotees for specific purposes. The treasury of god Vīra Narasingapperumāḷ in Śrīnivāsapuram was called *Appan-Śrī-Bhaṇḍaram* and gifts were also made to this treasury.[94]

a. *Gifts of villages*

Villages were granted to the *Śrī Bhaṇḍāram.* In Ś. 1470, six villages were given to the temple treasury of Tirumala.[95] Four villages were given to the *Śrī Bhaṇḍāram* as *tiruviḍaiyāṭṭam* to god Tiruvēnkaṭamuḍaiyān in Ś. 1389.[96] A record dated in S. 1438, mentions the gift of three villages to the temple treasury of god Śrī Venkaṭēśa of Tirumala, for the merit of king, Kṛṣṇarāya.[97] Two villages were granted to the *Śrībhaṇḍaram* in Ś. 1470, by Nandyāla Nārapparāju.[98] A record in Ś. 1390 states that a village was donated to the *Tiruppaṇi-bhaṇḍārattār* or officers of the public works treasury as a *maṭhappura.* It also states that the *Bhaṇḍāram* should collect the income from the above said village.[99]

b. *Gifts of Land*

Several kinds of land were also granted to the *Śrībhaṇḍāram.* A certain

91. LR 42. Udayagiri. No. 19.
92. 6 of 1953-54. Ellanūru.
93. *T.T.D.I.* II. 135. Tirumala.
94. *Ibid.*, I. 224. Tirupati.
95. *Ibid.*, IV. 29. Tirumala.
96. *Ibid.*, II. 34. Tirumala,

Viśvanādhājiyana gifted some land in Ś. 1229 to the treasury of the Siṁhāchalam temple.[100] Two individuals gifted five *puṭṭis* of land to the treasury of Śrīkūrmanātha temple of Śrīkūrmam in Ş. 1373.[101] In Ś. 1364, land was given to the temple treasury by Kaḷingadaṇḍapāṭiparīkṣa Śrīrenmallu Komaragirimahāpātruḍu.[102]

c. *Gift of Taxes*

The *Srībhaṇḍāram* or the Temple Treasury was the recipient of gifts of various kinds of taxes. A record from the Tirumala temple, dated in Ś. 1378, mentions that in lieu of the *svarnādāyam* or income derived in gold coins and *dhanyavargam* or taxes collected in the shape of grain and all other dues collected from the *sarvamānya* village of Alipuram were gifted to the *Śrībhaṇḍāram.*[103] Another, from the same place, dated in Ś. 1395, states that, the *Kar-koḍai, kaḍamai, ponvari* and other incomes realised from the 215 *kuḷi* of wet land in the village of Alipuram were gifted to the Śrībhaṇḍāram.[104]

d. *Gifts of Cash*

Very interesting information is available about the gift of a variety of coins to the temple treasury. In Ś. 1380, a sum of 1000 *nārpaṇam* was received by the *Śrībhaṇḍāram* of the Śrī Venkaṭēśvara temple of Tirumala.[105] Seven *rekhai-pon* was paid in the temple treasury by *Dēsantari* Perulalayyan, the manager of Tiruvēnkaṭanāthan flower garden at Tirumala.[106] In Ś. 1198, seven *parke-gaṇḍamādas* were made over to the temple treasury of the Śrīkūrmam temple.[107] A certain Puṇḍikōma Jiyyaṁgār granted 22 *telikaṭṭu-gaṇḍamādas* to the *bhaṇḍāram* of the Siṁhāchalam temple.[108] A sum of 25 *sasukāni-ṭankas* collected from a village were given in Ś. 1364 to the Kaḷinga *Bhaṇḍāram* of the same temple.[109] In Ś. 1313, five gold-*ṭankas* were deposited in treasury of the Śrī Narasiṁhanātha temple at Siṁhāchalam.[110] In Ś. 1317, gold coins were granted to the *Śrībhaṇḍāram* of Śrī Venkaṭēśa of Tirumala in Ś. 1456.[111] A certain Māmiḍiaṁmā donated 7 *malla-māḍas* to god Śrīkūrmanātha in Ś. 1168.[112] In Ś. 1125, seven *surabhi-gadyas* were presented to the *Śrībhaṇḍaram* of the Siṁhāchalam temple by Rēkamanāyaka.[113] Śrīrāmabhaṭṭōpādhyāyula gave 10

97. *Ibid.*, III. 109. Tirupatti.
98. *Ibid.*, V. 122. Tirupati.
99. *Ibid,*, II. 35. Tirumala.
100. *S.I.I.* VI. 805. Siṁhāchalam.
101. *Ibid.*, V. 1199. Śrīkūrmam.
102. *Ibid.*, VI. 839. Siṁhāchalam.
103. *T.T.D.I.* II. 4. Tirumala.
104. *Ibid.*, II. 53, 54, 55. Tirumala.
105. *Ibid.*, II. 8, 9, 10, 16, 17. Tirumala.
106. *Ibid.*, V. 96. Tirumala.
107. *Ibid.*, V. 1168. Śrīkūrmam.
108. *Ibid.*, VI. 833. Siṁhāchalam.
109. *Ibid.*, VI. 868. Siṁhāchalam.
110. *Ibid.*, VI. 844. Siṁhāchalam.
111. *Ibid.*, VI. 806. Siṁhachalam.
112. *T.T.D.I.* IV. 34. Tirumala.
113. *S.I.I* V. 1304. Śrīkūrmam.

biragōṭṭapu-gadyas in Ś. 1129 to the same treasury.[114] The Eastern Gānga king, Nissankabhānudēva, granted 4 silver *ṭankas* in Ś. 1349, to the *Śrībhaṇḍāram* of the Śrī Narasiṁhanātha temple.[115] The same treasury received a gift of 5 *padmanidhi-gaṇḍamādas* in Ś. 1289.[116] A sum of 30 *paidi-malla-māḍas* was given to the same temple treasury in Ś. 1271.[117] In S. 1316, the *Śrībhaṇdāram* of the same temple received a gift of 4 *punu-gaṇḍamādas.*[118] A record from Siṁhāchalam dated in Ś. 1330, mentions the gift of 4 *sanubhuja-gaṇḍamādas* to the temple treasury.[119] Another from the same place, dated in Ś. 1123, states that a sum of ten *tyāgi-māḍas* was given to the temple treasury.[120] In Ś. 1267, fourteen *gaṇḍa-parka-māḍas* were received by the treasury of the Śrīkūrmam temple.[121]

e. *Gifts of Animals*

The *Śrībhaṇḍāram* received gifts of animals for the supply of ghee required for maintaining lamps and for the preparation of various food offerings to the deities. In Ś. 1066, twenty seven cows were granted by Sōmāṇḍiyaṁmā, the consort of Kulōttungacōḍa Gonka, to the *Śrībhaṇḍāram* of the Kumārasvāmi temple.[122] A certain Varadanapeggaḍa, made a present of 40 cows in Ś. 1297 to the temple treasury.[123] The Eastern Gānga king, Nissanka Bhānudēva, gave 50 cows in S. 1349 to the temple treasury of Siṁhāchalam.[124] In Ś. 1303, 300 cows were granted to the same *Śrībhaṇḍāram* by Oḍḍādi Arjunadēva.[126] In Ś. 1344, Paṇditavarajiy-yanaṁgāru donated 50 cows to the treasury of Śrīkūrmanātha of Śrīkūrmam for a lamp.[127] A record from the Tirumala temple, dated in Ś. 1435, mentions the gift of 200 cows to the temple treasury.[128] An undated record from the same place, men-

114. *S.I.I.* VI. 1178. Siṁhāchalam.
115. *Ibid.*, VI. 1182. Siṁhāchalam.
116. *Ibid.*, VI. 808. Siṁhāchalam.
117. *Ibid.*, VI. 815, 816. Siṁhāchalam.
118. *Ibid.*, VI. 11225. Siṁhāchalam.
119. *Ibid.*, VI. 771. Siṁhāchalam.
120. *Ibid.*, VI. 884. Siṁhāchalam.
121. *Ibid.*, VI. 1177. Siṁhāchalam.
122. *Ibid.*, V. 1240. Śrīkūrmam.
Similar Examples
T.T.D.I. II. 233. Tirupati.
Ibid., II. 31, 37, 41, 43, 57. 58, 63, 69.
Ibid., III. 178.
Ibid., V. 96.
Ibid., V. 96.
S.I.I. V. 1287. Śrīkūrmam.
Ibid., VI. 896. Siṁhāchalam.
Ibid., VI. 835, 919, 1122. Siṁhāchalam .
Ibid., V. 1248. Śrīkūrmam.
123. *S.I.I.* VI. 135. Bāpaṭla.
124. *Ibid.*, VI. 794. Siṁhāchalam.
125. *Ibid.*, VI. 808. Siṁhāchalam
126. *Ibid.*, VI. 789. Siṁhāchalam.
127. *Ibid.*, V. 1174. Śrīkūrmam.
128. *T.T.D.I.* III. 88. Tirumala.

tions the gift of 32 cows and one young bull.[129] All these gifts were intended for the supply of stipulated quantities of ghee for burning lamps and for preparing various o erings to the deities in temples.

f. *Gilts of Articles*

Gifts of articles used for worship like *cāmaras*, *vinjāmaras*, *tiruvaḷikakōlas* etc., were also received by the *Śrībhaṇḍāram*. A record from Śrīkūrmam, dated in Ś. 1336, mentions the gift of two gold *pahiṇdi-rasana-kamaśvēta-cāmaras* or cauris with gold handles by *mahāpatra* Gōvindadēva.[130] Another, from Siṁhāchalam, dated in Ś. 1363, mentions the gift of 4 *vinjāmaras* and 4 *cāmaras* to the temple treasury.[131] Two *tiruvaḷika-kōlalu* or torches were given in Ś. 1330 to the treasury of the same temple.[132]

g. *Gifts of Lamps*

Numerous inscriptions mention gift of lamps to the temples and some of them were given to the *Śrībhaṇḍāram*. In Ś. 1066, provision was made for keeping up a lamp to the temple treasury of Siṁhāchalam.[133] A certain Varadanapeggada, granted a lamp to the same treasury in Ś. 1291.[134] One *nandāviḷakku* was given to god Tiruvēnkaṭamuḍaiyān or Śrī Vēnkaṭēśa and it was left in the care of the *Tiruppaṇi-Bhaṇḍārattār* or repairing committee.[135]

h. *Gifts of Lampstands*

Lampstands were also presented to the temple treasury. In Ś. 1271, Queen Cingamadēvī, the consort of Oḍḍādi Jayantika dēvarāja, gave a *dīpa-pratima* or lampstand with an image to the temple treasury of Siṁhāchalam.[136] In Ś. 1325, a brass lampstand which had a swan at its head was presented by Kūnaparāju and a bronze image holding lamps was also donated to the treasury of the same place.[137] In Ś. 1346, Śrī Karaṇalingusēnāpati granted a lampstand with an image to the same treasury.[138] A certain Śītādēvī, the wife of Svapnēśvara Jiyyana, gave a lampstand with an image to the treasury of Śrīkūrmam temple.[139]

i. *Gifts for the Supply of Garlands*

Many gifts were made to the treasury for the supply of flower garlands. In S. 1271, provision was made for the supply of a *tirumala* to the god of Siṁhāchalam.[140]

129. *Ibid*, I. 113. Tirumala.
130. *S.I.I.* V. 679. Śrīkūrmam.
131. *Ibid.*, 1248. Siṁhāchalam.
132. *Ibid.*, VI. 884. Siṁhāchalam.
133. *Ibid.*, VI. 811. Siṁhāchalam.
134. *Ibid.*, VI. 794. Siṁhāchalam.
135. *T.T.D.I.* I. 113. Tirumala.
136. *S.I.I.* VI. 968. Siṁhāchalam.
137. *Ibid.*, VI. 865. Siṁhāchalam.
138. *Ibid.* VI. 970. Siṁhāchalam.
139. *Ibid.*, V. 1211. Śrīkūrmam.
140. *Ibid.*, VI. 898. Siṁhāchalam.

Provision was made in Ś. 1219, for the supply of a *cengalyamālā.* in the treasury of the temple of Siṁhāchalam.[141] A certain individual named Vāraṇāsi kaṭakāna Garuḍadāsamahāsēnāpati, made a gift to the *Śrībhaṇḍāram* of the same temple for the supply of a *doṇdavanamāla.*[142] Paramapuruṣa Śrīpādālu, the disciple of Jñānatīrtha Śrīpādālu, the *maṭhādhipati* of Bēlūr, arranged with the *Śrībhaṇḍāram* of the same temple for the supply of a garland of *tulaśi* leaves to the god in Ś. 1352.[143] A record from Śrīkūrmam dated in Ś. 1251, mentions the provision made for the supply of flowers to the temple treasury to decorate Rāma, Lakṣmaṇa and Sītādēvī.[144]

j. *Gifts of Offerings*

The temple treasury received various kinds of gifts for providing food offerings to the deities. Provision was made by Mantyana Permāḍi Gōpāluṇḍu to the treasury for the supply of one *kunceḍu* of milk and *viḍyam* to god Śrīkūrmanātha of Śrīkūrmam.[145] In Ś. 1226, Bhōdenabbināyaka, made provision in the temple treasury for the supply of an offering named *uppannamu* to god at the time of *tirunāḷa-pānkanyadivyamahōtsavas.*[146] A certain Arjunalenka made provision in the treasury for the supply of an offering named *sēmantikhiri* to god Śrī Narasiṁhanātha of Siṁhāchalam in Ś. 1296.[147] Varadana peggaḍa made a gift to the treasury for the supply of an offering named *jīnu* to the same god at the time of the night *dhūpa* in Ś. 1299.[148] In Ś. 1300, Kaḷingabeharāmadhi *mahāsēnāpati* gave 10 *gaṇḍamāḍas* to the treasury for the supply of four *manōharalaḍḍu* to be offered to the god at the time of *māpaṭidhūpa.*[149] An offering, named *trigunipālakalaśalu* was prepared and made to the god daily by the *Śrībhaṇḍāram* in Ś. 1321, on the basis of a gift made by Siriyaṁmā, the sister of Oḍḍāi Dēvarāja.[150] The *Śrībhaṇḍāram* made provision in Ś 1372, for making an offering named *tirupponakam* each night to god Vīranara-siṁhaperumāḷ at Śrīnivāsapuram.[151] In Ś. 1390, the treasury of the Tirumala temple received a gift for the offering of eight *sandhis* or food offerings to god Tiruvēnkaṭa-muḍaiyān daily.[152] In Ś. 1397, the *Bhāṇḍaram* agreed to arrange for the offering of *ara amudusirappu* to a god.[153] Offerings like the *nāyakataligai* and iddali-nādi were made to the god by the temple treasury in return for gifts received by it, in

141. *Ibid.*, VI. 896. Siṁhāchalam.
142. *Ibid.*, VI. 852. Siṁhāchalam.
143. *Ibid.*, VI. 796. Siṁhāchalam.
144. *Ibid.*, V. 1172. Śrīkūrmam.
145. *Ibid.*, V. 1166. Śrīkūrmam.
146. *Ibid.*, VI. 969. Siṁhāchalam.
147. *Ibid.*, VI. 1122. Siṁhāchalam.
148. *Ibid.*, VI. 874. Siṁhāchalam.
149. *Ibid.* VI. 923. Siṁhāchalam.
150. *Ibid.*, VI. 872. Siṁhāchalam.
151. *T.T.D.I.* 112. 112. Tirupati.
152. *Ibid.*, II. 35. Tirumala.
153. *Ibid.*, II. 57. Tirupati.

Ś. 1426.[154] Provision was made in Ś. 1435, for offering daily 1 *naḷi* of *pāḷedu-kuḷaṁbu* or thick boiled milk with the cream formed over it, to god Śrī Venkaṭēśa of Tirumala during the *tiruvardhajāmam* or the worship in the early part of the night by the *Śrībhaṇḍāram*.[155]

2. *Functions*

The *Śrībhaṇḍaram* discharged several other functions besides receiving gifts.

a. *Celebration of Festivals*

Several festivals were celebrated by the temple treasury in return for a number of gifts received from devotees for that purpose. In Ś. 1430, provision was made for the celebration of the *Anna-Ūnjal-tirunāḷ* for god Śrī Gōvindarāja of Tirupati.[156] In Ś. 1168, arrangements were made for the celebration of the *Amāvāsya* festival by the treasury of the Śrīkūrmam temple.[157] A Narasiṁhamahāmuni arranged for the conduct of the *Grāmapradakṣiṇa* festival every month in Ś. 1178, on the day of his birth star, *Uttarāṣādha*, by the *Śrībhaṇḍaram* in lieu of a gift made by him in the Śrīkūrmam temple.[158]

b. *Maintaining Lamps*

Śrībhaṇḍaram maintained lamps in the temple, by receiving gifts. In Ś. 1364, a gift was made to the treasury of the Siṁhāchalam temple for the maintenance of a lamp by a *mahāpatra*.[159] A certain Rēkamanāyaka made a gift to the same temple treasury, on the occasion of a *Karkāṭāka-sankrānti*, for the maintenance of a lamp in his name in the temple, in Ś. 1125.[160] In Ś. 1129, on the occasion of *Mēṣa-sankrānti*, arrangement for maintaining a lamp in the same temple was made by Śrī Rāmabhaṭṭōpādhyāya.[161] The Eastern Gānga king, Niśśanka Bhānudēva, made a gift to the *Śrībhaṇḍāram* of the Siṁhāchalam temple in Ś. 1349, for the maintenance of a

154. *Ibid.*, III. 1. Tirumala.
155. *Ibid.*, III. 88. Tirumala.
 Similar Examples
 T.T.D.I. II. 24, 18, 23, 34, 35, 53, 58, 94.
 Ibid., III 109, 178.
 Ibid., V. 29.
 S.I.I. V. 1204, 1287. Śrīkūrmam.
 Ibid., VI. 135, 844. 875, 1122. Siṁhāchalam.
156. *T.T.D.I.* III. 13. Tirupati.
157. *S.I.I.* V. 1304. Śārīkūrmam.
158. *Ibid.*, V. 1291. Śrīkūrmam.
 Similar Examples
 T.T.D.I. III. 181. Tirumula.
 Ibid., IV. 188. Tirumala.
 S.I.I. V. 1249. Śrīkūrmam.
 Ibid., VI. 969. Siṁhāchalam.
159. *S.I.I.* VI. 805. Siṁhāchalam.
160. *Ibid.*, VI. 1178. Siṁhāchalam.
160. *Ibid.*, VI. 1182. Siṁhāchalam.

lamp.[162] A record from the Tirumala temple, mentions the provision made by its *Bhaṇḍāram* for the maintenance of a *andāviḷakku* in the temple.[163]

c. *Arranging Services*

The temple treasury also undertook to arrange for the performance of various kinds of services. An inscription from Siṁhachalam, dated in Ś. 1288, mentions the provision made by its treasury for waving a *cāmara* at the time of the *ubhayadhūpālu* before god Narasiṁhanātha of Siṁhāchalam in lieu of a gift made by Kaḷinga-parīkṣa Gangādharajiyana.[164] Another record from the same place, dated in Ś. 1289, mentions the gift made to the treasury of the Śrīnarasiṁhanātha temple for the performance of the daily *cāmara* service at the time of the *ubhayadhūpālu* to the same god.[165] In Ś. 1336, arrangements were made by the *Śrībhaṇḍāram*, for the *cāmara* service with gold handle to god Śrī Kūrmanātha of Śrīkūrmam.[166] A Komara-guru mahāpātra made arrangements through the *Śrībhandaram* for the service of *ālavaṭṭamu* at the time of the *dhūpa* in the Siṁhāchalam temple in Ś. 1300.[167] The service of holding a *tiruvaḷika-kōla* or torch was also arranged by the same temple treasury. Gabirumahāsēnāpati made a gift in Ś. 1316, for the service of *tiruvaḷika-kōla* at the time of *candanalagi* to god Śrī Narasiṁha of Siṁhāchalam.[168] In Ś. 1305, provision was made by the *Śrībhaṇḍāram* for *divyakōla nibhandhālu* daily, at the time of *ubhayadhūpāḷu* to the same god.[169]

The *Śrībhaṇḍāram* made arrangements for *koluvu* or durbar. In the 7th year of the reign of the Eastern Gāṅga king, Vīranarasiṁha, provision was made by the *Śrībhaṇḍāram* of the Śrīkūrmam temple for the performance of the *Khaṇḍadhāra-koluvu* by Kumāra Puruṣottamadēvajiyya.[170] The temple treasury received a donation in Ś. 1142, for the purpose of arranging for the *Āsthanam-koluvu* on the day of the *Uttaraphalguṇi-nakṣatra.*[171]

d. *Supply of Garlands*

Several gifts were made to the temple treasury for the supply of garlands for worship. In Ś. 1271, a cash gift was received by the treasury for the supply of one

162. *Ibid.*, VI. 803. Siṁhāchalam.
163. *T.T.D.I.* I. 113. Tirumala.
 Similar Examples
 S.I.I. IV. 794, 811. Simhāchalam.
 T.T.D.I. V. 135. Tirupati.
164. *S.I.I.* VI. 813. Siṁhāchalam.
165. *Ibid.*, VI. 815. Siṁhāchalam.
166. *Ibid.*, V. 1248. Śrīkūrmam.
167. *Ibid.*, VI. 851. Siṁhāchalam.
168. *Ibid.*, VI. 771. Siṁhāchalam.
169. *Ibid.*, VI. 807. Siṁhāchalam.
 Similar Exapmles
 S.I.I. V. 1225, Śrīkūrmam.
 Ibid., VI. 884. Siṁhāchalam.
170. *S.I.I.* V. 1219. Śrīkūrmam.
171. *Ibid.*, VI. 1167. Siṁhāchalam.

tirumāla daily.[172] Muktadēvī, the wife of Vāranāsikaṭakāna Jalēśvaramahāpātra, made arrangements with the treasury of the Siṁhāchalam temple for the supply of one *tirutōmāla* daily to the god.[173] In Ś. 1291, the same *Śrībhaṇḍāram*, accepted a gift for the supply of a *cengalvamālā* or a garland of *cengalva* flowers to the same god. For the supply of one *doṇḍamālā* for the *bhōga* a gift was made by the wife of Taṁmajiyya to the same *Śrībhaṇḍāram* in Ś. 1316.[175] In Ś. 1352, a Paramapuruṣa Śrīpādālu made provision with the same treasury for the supply of a *tulasidaṇḍa* or a garland of *Tulasi*-leaves to the god.[176] An inscription from Tirumala, dated in Ś. 1413, states that a gift was made to the temple treasury for 4 round flower garlands of the shape of the full moon on the days of *Yugādi* and *Dīpāvaḷi* to adorn Tiruvēnkaṭamuḍaiyān and Śrī Gōvindarāja by *mahāmaṇḍalēśvara* Baicirāju Tiṁmayadēva *mahārāja*.[177] Provision was made by the treasury of the Siṁhāchalam temple in Ś. 1215, for the supply of flowers to the deities Rāma, Lakṣmaṇa and Sītādēvī in the temple of Śrī Kūrmanātha of Śrīkūrmam.[178]

e. *Tirumanjanam*

The temple treasury made arrangements for the performance of *tirumanjanam* or holy bath to deities by receiving gifts from devotees. A record from the temple of Kapilatīrtham mentions that provision was made by the *Śrībhaṇḍāram* of Tirumangaiāḷvār for performing *tirumanjanam* to god Gōvindarāja in the month of *Kārtika*, on the day of the *attai-tiru-nakṣatram* of Tirumangaiāḷvār.[179] In Ś. 1298, arrangements were made in the treasury of the Śrīkūrmam temple for performing the *pancāmrta-abhiṣēka* to the *mūlabēra* of Śrīkūrmanātha by Śrī Naraharitīrtha Śrīpāda.[180] Provision was made in Ś. 1283, by the treasury of the Siṁhāchalam temple for the supply of water for the purpose of *abhiṣeka* to the god of the place by Maddala Malli seṭṭi.[181] Mādēvimahādēvī, the queen of the Eastern Gānga king, Śrīniśśanka Bhānudēva, arranged with the same temple treasury for conducting *tirumanjanam* to the god.[182] A record from the Tirumala temple, dated in Ś. 1406, states that a gift was made to a *Rāmanujakūṭam*, and the *Sāttaḍa-ekāki-Śrivaisṇavas* who lived in it were required to supply the articles for the *Alagappiranār* and *Tirumagaluḍan-Varuvar-tirumanjanam* in the temple of god Gōvindarāja of Tirupati.[183]

172. *Ibid*, VI. 898. Siṁhāchalam.
173. *Ibid*, VI. 856. Siṁhāchalam.
174. *Ibidi.* VI. 896. Siṁhāchalam.
175. *Ibid.*, VI. 767. Siṁhāchalam.
176. *Ibid.*, VI, 796. Siṁhāchalam.
177. *T.T.D.I.* II. 94. Tirumala.
178. *S.I.I.* V. 1172. Śrīkūrmam.
Similar Examples
S.I.I. VI. 773, 810, 844, 852, 865. Siṁhāchalam.
179. *T.T.D.I.* II. 62. Tirupati.
180. *S.I.I.* V. 1249. Śrīkūrmam.
181. *Ibid.*, VI. 864. Siṁhāchalam.
182. *Ibid.*, VI. 1069. Siṁhāchalam.
183. *T.T.D.I.* II. 81. Tirumala.

f. *Management of Lands*

The *Śrībhaṇḍāram* also looked after temple lands and arranged for the provision and improvement of means of irrigation like channels, canals and tanks. In Ś. 1123, a channel was excavated by the treasury of the Siṁhāchalam temple on receiving a donation.[184] The *Śrībhaṇḍāram* of the Tirumala temple received a gift in Ś. 1399, for the improvement of irrigation channels from the taxes due from the *tiru-viḍaiyāṭṭam* or temple villages.[185] In Ś. 1471, the same temple treasury excavated the *Rāmanujakālvay* in the *Tiruviḍaiyāṭṭam* village of Vikramādityamangaḷam.[186] A record dated in Ś. 1439, mentions the excavation of an irrigation tank by the same *Śrībhaṇḍāram* on receiving a gift.[187] Another, from Tirupati, dated in Ś. 1459, refers to the renovation of the Tirumala Nāyakkar channel by the *Bhaṇḍāram*.[188]

g. *Watersheds*

Watersheds or *cali-vendiris* were also maintained by the temple treasury. In Ś. 1455, the *Śrībhaṇḍāram* of the Tirupati temple agreed to maintain watersheds, including one on the southern side of *Anaiṟṟu-maṇṭapa*, situated in front of the temple of Śrī Gōvindarājan and another situated in a *maṇṭapa*.[189]

h. *Gardens*

Inscriptions also show that *Śrībhaṇḍāram* received gifts for the maintenance of gardens. In Ś. 1200, the *Bhaṇḍāram* of the Siṁhāchalam temple made arrangements for the planting and improvement of a flower garden.[190] Arrangements were made in Ś. 1267, through the treasury of the Śrīkūrmam temple, for laying a garden by Cīkaṭi Dharmarājusiṣṭu Acyutapradhānulu.[191] The *Śrībhaṇḍāram* of the Siṁhāchalam temple made arrangements in Ś. 1335, for laying out a *Ippavanam*.[192] The treasury of the Tirumala temple cutivated the *nandanavanam* at the bund of the *triukkōnēri* and the other *tirukkōnēri* laying at the bund of the *Narasingarāya-kōneri* and appointed the *Sāttāḍa Śrīvaiṣṇavas* to be in charge of the cultivation.[193]

i. *Repairs*

Repairs to vessels, jewels etc., were undertaken by the *Śrībhaṇḍāram* as well as by the *Ponbhaṇḍāram*. A record from the Tirumala temple, dated in Ś. 1417, mentions that the *Śrībhaṇḍāram* made arrangements for effecting the necessary repairs

184. *S.I.I.* VI. 1177. Siṁhāchalam.
185. *T.T.D.I.* II. 69. Tirumala.
186. *Ibid.*, III. 118. Tirumala.
187. *Ibid.*, III. 156. Tirupati.
188. *Ibid.*, IV. 19. Tirupati.
Similar Examples
T.T.D.I. II. 2. Tirupati.
Ibid., I. 223. Tirupati.
189. *T.T.D.I.* III. 161. Tirupati.
190. *S.I.I.* VI. 912. Siṁhāchalam.
191. *Ibid.*, V. 1240. Śrīkūrmam.
192. *Ibid.*, VI. 848. Siṁhāchalam.
193. *T.T.D.I.* II. 51. Tirumala.

to the jewels and ornaments and gold and silver vessels belonging to Tiruvēnkaṭa-muḍaiyān and Gōvindarāja from time to time.[194] The famous religious teacher, Kandāḍai Rāmanujayyangār, was the head of the *Ponbhaṇḍāram* of the Tirumala temple. The *Tiruppaṇibhaṇḍāram* was in charge of the construction and repairs of the buildings of the temples. A certain Viśvanādhajiyyana made a gift to the *Śrībhaṇḍāram* of the Siṁhāchalam temple for the construction of *Dharma-maṇṭapa* in Ś. 1229.[195]

j. *Purchases*

The *Śrībhaṇḍāram* received gifts for the purchase of vessels and other articles used in the temple. In Ś. 1287, the *Śrībhaṇḍāram* of the Siṁhāchalam temple purchased silver *kaḍavalu* and silver *rēkulu* for *aṣṭamangaḷāla* at the time of the *dhūpa* and one silver vessel for offering milk on receiving a gift from Oḍḍādi Bhīmana Peggaḍa.[196] The same treasury purchased two *taṁbagariyalu*, one *vāli* and two *śribhujālu* from out of a gift from Pratāpārjuna, the son of Vīrārjuna.[197]

k. *Recitation of Texts*

The temple treasury also arranged for the recitation of *Purāṇas*, *Vēdas* etc., in the temple. In Ś. 1275, a Gānga queen, named Gangādēvī, made a gift to the treasury of the Siṁhāchalam temple for arranging for the recitation of *Purāṇa* at the time of the *Gangānarasiṁha-bhōga*.[198] A record from the Tirumala temple, dated in Ś. 1355, mentions that since *Vēdapārāyaṇam* ceased, Tirukkalikandhidāsar Alagappiranār, represented to Uḍaiyan Dēvana Uḍaiyar, that *Vēdapārāyaṇam* be restored as the charity of Dēvarāya Mahārāya and obtained as a *srōiriyam* the half share of the *Rājabhaṇḍāram* and made it over to 24 persons who recited the *Vēdas* and since it proved insufficient for the support of these 24 persons and they requested the *Sthānattār* that the other half share be also granted to them. Tirukkalikanridāsar Alagappiranār arranged the payment of money as the half share of *Bhaṇḍāram* as assessed revenue.[199]

Āvaṇakkaḷari

A department named *Āvaṇakkaḷari* was maintained by the temples. The duty of this department was to register and preserve the documents of the temple.[200]

The inscriptional evidence cited above indicates clearly that several agencies were associated with and responsible for the management of the temple including receiving of gifts from donors and fulfilling their wishes. The *Sthānādhipati* seems to have been a kind of general manager or supervisor of the temple. The *Sthānaṁvāru*

194. *Ibid* , II. 133. Tirumala.
195. *S.I.I.* VI. 1002. Siṁhāchalam.
196. *Ibid.*, VI. 839. Siṁhāchalam.
197. *Ibid.*, VI. 946. Siṁhāchalam.
198. *Ibid.*, VI. 1053. Siṁhāchalam.
199. *T.T.D.I.* I. 199. Tirumala.
200. *Ibid* , I. 231. Tirupati.

or groups of employees of the temple also performed similar duties. The *Sabhaiyār* or the village committee also was associated with the temple management. The more important than all these agencies was the *Śrībhaṇḍāram* which received, arranged for and regulated gifts and services.

6

WORSHIP IN THE TEMPLE

Hinduism prescribes four principal objectives or *Puruṣārthas* for an individual viz., *Dharma* or righteousness, *Artha* or accumulation of material goods, *Kāma* or satisfaction of physical desires and *Mōkṣa* or salvation. According to this theory of *Puruṣārthas,* the pursuit of the two central objectives of *Artha* and *Kāma,* which relate to this mundane world, should be regulated by *Dharma* and so fashioned as to lead to *Mōkṣa* or salvation. The supreme objective is *Mōkṣa.* This *Mōkṣa* is variously defined as the realisation of one's self, or merger in the Supreme Spirit or escape from the cycle of births and deaths. Two principal means of obtaining *Mōkṣa* are mentioned viz , *Jñāna* or right knowledge attained through contemplation and *Bhakti* or devotion. The contemplation and realisation of the unmanifest Brahman requires prolonged *sādhana* or practice spread over several lives and is beyond the reach of the ordinary individuals. Therefore Brahman is conceived of as manifest in some shape or form and worshipped. The devotee creates a personal god, loves him, worships him and surrenders himself unto him. The form of this manifest personal god is called *Arca-avatāra* or worshipable form. This worship may be either private, as in the case of householder worshipping their family gods in their own houses or public. Public worship is localised in temples. This *arcā* type of worship requires an image. The Supreme is conceived in many forms as Śiva, Viṣṇu or Dēvī each in different varieties. An image representing one of these deities is installed in a temple and forms the object of worship.

A number of Sanskrit texts, known as the *Āgamas,* lay down detailed instructions about the making of these images and the process of their worship. These are of three types, Śaiva, Vaiṣṇava and Śākta. The worship conducted in a temple from dawn to midnight and various festivals celebrated are elaborately described in these *Āgamas.* Inscriptions found in temples mention, in relation to gifts conveyed through them, many interesting details.

The main idea behind *arcā* or worship is to treat the deity as immediately present in the image in the sanctum and render all varieties of personal service to the deity. This workship ordinarily consists of *Ṣōḍasōpacāra*[1] or sixteen items—*Dhyāna* or contemplation, *Āvāhana* or localisation, *Āsana* or offering a seat, *Pādya* or washing the feet, *Arghya* or washing the hands, *Ācamaniya* or taking in a small quantity of water, *Snāna* or bath, *Vastra* or clothing, *Yojñōpavīta* or placing the sacred thread, *Gandha* or smearing sandal paste, *Mālyā* or decoration with garlands and flowers, *Dhūpa* or waving incense, *Dīpa* or showing a lamp, *Naivēdya* or offering food, *Nirājana* or waving a lamp and *Mantrapuṣpa* or offering of a tribute. Of these, *Snāna* or *Snapana*, *gandha*, decoration with garlands flowers and jewels, *Dhūpa* and *Naivēdya* are done on an elaborate scale in temples.

The technical word used in the inscription to denote worship in a temple is *anga-ranga-bhōga*. *Anga* means the body and *bhōga* means enjoyment. *Angabhōga* therefore means, every service rendered to the body of the deity like bath, perfuming and decoration. *Ranga* means outside or external and therefore *rangabhōga* means every other service like *dhūpa*, *dīpa*, *naivēdya* and *arcanā*.

Worship offered in temples is of three main varieties. According to the time—*rēpaṭi* or worship offered in the morning, *māpaṭi* or night worship and occasional like the *jāmu* and *ardhajāmu* worship.

1. *Morning Worship*

This is the main worship conducted in the temple. The other items are more or less repetitions on a minor scale with many constituent items omitted. The morning service is very elaborate and consists of several items, as mentioned below.

a. *Waking Ceremony*

Worship in the temple starts early in the morning and the first item is to wake the deity from his sleep. Several inscriptions mention this service. During the 27th year of the reign of the Cōḷa king, Kulōttungacōḷadēva, provision was made for offering to be made to god Kāḷahastīśvara of Kāḷahasti during the early morning raising ceremony.[2] Provision was made in S. 1441, in the reign of Kṛṣṇarāya, for making offerings to the same god in the months of *Māsi*, *Vaigāsi* and *Purāṭṭasi* at the time of the early waking service.[3] Another record also mentions offering made to the god during this service.[4] This practice is continued to this day in many temples. The *Suprabhātam* or the waking up service which is gone through at 4 a.m. every day is one of the impressive and popular items of worship in the Śrī Venkaṭēśvara temple at Tirumala. Provision was made in S. 1298, by Sanajiyyana

1. *S.I.I.* V. 1212. Śrīkūrmam.
   Similar Examples
   Ibid., VI. 219. Amarāvati.
   Ibid., X. 737. Uṇḍavilli.
   E.I. XIV. pp. 34-353. Kanuma.
2. 94 of 1922. Kāḷahasti.
3. 172 of 1924. Kāḷahasti.
4. 185 of 1924. Kāḷahasti.

for singing *mangaḷagitālu* on the flute and on *mukhari* at the time of *prabhātasamaya* in the temple of Śrī Narasiṁhanātha of Siṁhāchalam.[5] The elaborate worship starts with this service.

b. *Early Morning Service*

The regular morning worship started after this waking service. During this service, various kinds of offerings were made and lamps were lighted before the god. In the 13th year of the reign of the Cāḷukya Cōḷa king, Kulōttunga, a gift was made for the worship of the god of Drākshārāma in the early hours of the morning.[6] In Ś. 1439, in the reign of the famous Vijayanagara king, Kṛṣṇadēvarāya, arrangements were made for lighting four lamps and offering a flower garland to the god on this occasion in lieu of the gift of a village.[7] A food offering, named *tirumandirappōnagam*, was made to god Kāḷahastīśvara of Kāḷahasti, in the months of *Puraṭṭāsi*, *Panguṇi* and *Vaikāsi* in the time of the Cōḷā king, Kulōttungacōḷadēva.[8] A devotee deposited 10,00 *paṇam* for making a food offering to god Kāḷahastīśvara in Ś. 1436.[9] In Ś. 1454, another individual gave 1000 *paṇam* for a silver plate for making a food offering on this occasion.[10] In Ś. 1462, a gift of 200 *pōn* was made for food offerings to be made to the same god in the *Mārgaḷi* on this occasion.[11] In Ś. 1455, Tiṁmarāja Salakarāja, the agent of *mahāmaṇḍalēśvara* Salakarāja Tirumalayadēva mahārāja, made arrangements for the same purpose.[12] Gangaiyasāhariyār endowed lands in Ś. 1178, for the early morning service in the temple of god Uḍaiyar Nāyanār at Siddhavaṭam.[13] A record from Tripurāntakam, dated in Ś. 1212, also mentions the early morning worship of god Tripurāntakamahādēva of the place.[14]

c. *Tirumanjanam, Ordinary*

Abhiṣēka or giving of a holy bath to the deity every day was a prominent item in temple worship. In Ś. 1285 and 1298 provision was made for the daily *tirumanjanam* to Śrī Narasiṁhanātha of Siṁhāchalam by Lakumana seṭṭi.[15] Tallamadēvī

5. *S.I.I.* VI. 1116. Siṁhāchalam.
6. *Ibid.*, IV. 1359. Drākshārāma.
7. 139 of 1922. Kāḷahasti.
8. 94 of 1922. Kāḷahassi.
9. 176 of 1922. Kāḷahasti.
10. 183 of 1922. Kāḷahasti.
11. 162 of 1922. Kāḷahasti.
12. 170 of 1924. Kāḷahasti.
13. 33 of 1939-40. Māchupalle.
14. *S.I.I.* X. 464. Tripurāntakam.
    Similar Examples
    147 of 1922. Kāḷahasti.
    168 of 1924. Kāḷahasti.
    164 of 1922. Kāḷahasti.
    176 of 1922. Kāḷahasti.
    113 of 1922. Kāḷahasti.
    155 of 1924. Kāḷahasti.
15. *S.I.I.* VI. 791, 1123. Siṁhāchalam.

Mahādēvī, the queen of the Eastern Gānga king, Vīra Śrī Nissanka Bhānudēva, made provision in Ś. 1344, for *tirumanjanam* to god Śrī Narasiṁha of Siṁhāchalam.[16] An inscription from Tirumala, dated in Ś. 1395, among other things, mentions that provision was made for *tirumanjanam* for Malaikiniyaninṛa perumāḷ and Nāccimār.[17] Another, from Tirupati, dated in Ś. 1397, describes among other things, that provision was made for *tirumanjanam* for god Gōvindarāja of the place.[18]

d. *Tirumanjanam, Special*

Elaborate *tirumanjanam* was conducted on special occasions like festivals etc. A record of the 9th century refers to the provision made for the conduct of *tirumanjanam* on the two *Ayana-sankrānti* days and the two *Viṣu-sankrānti* days to a silver image of god Śrī Venkaṭēśvara of Tirumala.[19] In the 9th year of the reign of the Cōḷa king, Rājarāja, a gift was made for the conduct of *tirumanjanam* on the *Sankrāmaṇam* day to god Parāśarēśvara of Jōgimallāvaram.[20] An inscription from Tirupati, dated in Ś. 1230, states that arrangements were made for the performance of *tirumanjanam* and *snapanam* to god Gōvindarāja of Tirupati, on the days of the *Kaiśikadvādaśi, Mārgaḷi-dvādaśi, Makara-sankrāmaṇam* and *Citra-viṣu.*[21] *Tirumanjanam* was performed in a *maṇṭapa* at Tirupati is Ś. 1457, on the day of *Citra-viṣu* to god Gōvindarāja and his consorts and Senai-Mudaliyār at Tirupati,[22] In Ś. 1467, the Tirumala temple treasury accepted a gift for conducting *tirumanjanam* on the 5 days of the *Pallavōtsavam* to god Śrī Venkaṭēśvara of Tirumala.[23] Instructions were issued by Kandāḍu Rāmānujayyangār to his disciples in Ś 1386 regarding the conduct of a special *tirumanjanam* named the *Alagappiranār-tirumanjanam* at Tirumala.[24] God Gōvindarāja of Tirupati and his two consorts, Śrī and Bhū, used to visit a tank for receiving *tirumanjanam* on the occasion of the *Yajurvēda-upākarma* day. The famous Vaiṣṇava teacher, Śrī Rāmānuja made arrangements for the above *abhiṣeka.*[25]

At the time of the *tirumanjanam* the deity was decorated with flowers and garlands and holy texts like the *Puruṣaśūktam, Sankīrtanas, Śrī Bhāṣyam* etc., were recited. Offering like *viḍyam* was also part of this worship. Arrangements were

16. *Ibid.*, II. 1069 Siṁhāchalam.
17. *T.T.D.I.* II. 50. Tirumala
18. *Ibid.*, II. 62. Tirupati.
19. *Ibid.*, I. 7. Tiruchānūr.
20. *Ibid.*, I. 36. Jōgimallavaram.
21. *Ibid.*, I. 98. Tirupati.
22. *T.T.D.I.* IV. 39. Tirupati.
23. *Ibid*, V. 51. Tirumala.
24. *Ibid.*, II. 22. Tirumala.
25. *Ibid.*, II. 29. Tirupati.
    Similar Examples
    S.I I. VI. 904. Siṁhāchalam.
    T.T.D.I. II. 62. Tirupati.
    Ibid., IV. 215. Tirumala,

made in Ś. 1296, for presenting a *tirumālā* to god Narasiṁhanātha of Siṁhāchalam, after the *tirumanjanam.*[26] Provision was made in Ś. 1313, for the offering of a garland of *tulaśī* leaves to the same god on the same occasion.[27] In Ś. 1312, Gōvindajiyya provided for the offering of a *viḍyam* to the same god at the time of the *tirumanjanam.*[28] Arrangements were made in Ś. 1272, for the recitation of *Puruṣaśūkta* at the time of the *abhiṣēka* of the same god.[29] The performance of *Sankīrtana* was arranged by a Gōvindadāsu in Ś. 1213, before the same god at the time of *tirumanjanam.*[30] In Ś. 1543, provision was made for the recitation of the *Śrībhāṣyam* of Śrī Rāmānuja before god Śrī Venkaṭēśvara of Tirumala during the sixty *tirumanjanam* days.[31] Provision was made in Ś. 1435, by certain individuals for the supply of flower garlands made of *pannīr* and *caṁpak* flowers, offered to god Kāḷahastīśvara of Kāḷahasti during the sacrificial bath.[32]

f. *Other Abhiṣēkas or Ablutions*

Other kinds of *abhiṣēka* like *Kṣīrābhiṣēka* or bathing with milk and *Pañcāṁṛtābhiṣēka* or bathing with five liquids were also performed to the deity. In Ś. 1215, an ascetic named Naraharitīrtha made provision for the conduct of *pañcāṁṛtābhiṣēka* to the *mūlabēram* and to the *utsava* image of the god of the Śrīkūrmam temple on the day of the star, *Jyēṣṭa* and *Śukla-Paurṇimā* in the month of *Vṛṣabha* every year.[33] Pārvatī mahādēvī, the queen of the Eastern Gānga king, Vīra Narasiṁha, arranged a *bhōga* in Ś. 1328 to be offered before the *pañcāṁṛtābhiṣēka* to god Narasiṁhanātha of Siṁhāchalam.[34] In Ś. 1489, provision was made for the *pañcāṁṛta* to god Rāmēśvara of Yeṛaguḍi by *mahānāyakācārya* Mali nāyanigāru of Kaṁbhālapāḍu for the merit of his father.[35]

Several individuals made provision for obtaining water for the *tirumanjanam.* A gift was made in Ś. 1285 for the supply of one pot of water for the god's *tirumanjanam* at Siṁhāchalam.[36] A certain Nārāyaṇa *sēnāpati*, made provision in Ś. 1313, for the supply of one *kāvaḍi* of water for the performance of *abhiṣēka* of the same god.[37] *Mahāmaṇḍalēśvara* Pratāpārjunadēva, made arrangements for the supply of water with two *taṁbagariyas* to the same god in Ś. 1330.[38]

Several kinds of perfumes etc., were used during the course of the *tirumanjanam.* A devotee made provision in Ś. 1301, for the supply of one *palam* of *candanam*, I

26. *Ibid.*, VI. 750. Siṁhāchalam.
27. *Ibid.*, VI. 722. Siṁhāchalam.
28. *Ibid.*, VI. 962. Siṁhāchalam.
29. *Ibid.*, VI. 722. Siṁhāchalam.
30. *Ibid.*, VI. 731. Siṁhāchalam.
31. *T.T.D.I.* V. 47. Tirumala.
32. *N.D.I.* III. Suḷūrpēṭ. II. Tummūru.
33. *S.I.I.* V. 1249. Śrīkūrmam.
34. *Ibid.*, VI. 731. Siṁhāchalam.
35. 37 of 1953-54. Chenchu-Eṛṛaguḍi.
36. *S.I.I.* VI. 946. Siṁhāchalam.
37. *Ibid.*, VI. 791. Siṁhāchalam.
38. *Ibid.*, VI. 1334. Siṁhāchalam.

uḷākku of gingelly oil, musk and saffron.[39] An inscription from the Tirumala temple dated in Ś. 1367, states that provision was made for the supply of ½ *palam* of sandal paste and 1 *uḷākku* of gingelly oil for the *tirumanjanam* and ½ *palam* of *candanam* for *tiruvārādhanam* or worship.[40] Arrangements were made in Ś. 1390, for the supply of gingelly oil and ½ *palam* of thick paste of sandal for the *kalabham* decoration or fixing on the chest, 2 *palam* of *mēḍitta candanam* or soft sandal for smearing the body of the image.[41] Provisions was made for *tirumanjanam* in Ś. 1395, which required the supply of 1 *uḷākku* of gingelly oil for use while conducting the *snapana tirumanjanam* 1½ *palam* of sandal paste, 1 *palam* of sandal from which water was not squeezed and tender cocoanuts for paste for fixing on the deity's chest 614 *palam* of sandal paste, rose-water and crude camphor.[42] The ablution required the supply of 1 *aḷākku* of gingelly oil, 4 *palam* of *candanam*, and 1½ *palam* of sandal paste, *kastūrikāpu* or musk, *karpūrakkāppu* or refined camphor 1 *kalañju* of crude camphor for the *hārati* offering, napkins, ½ *palam* of sandal paste, musk and turmeric. These articles were to be supplied from the income of the village of Gunḍipūnḍi granted by Sāḷuva Narasiṁharāya.[43] In Ś. 1454, arrangements were made for the supply of 1½ *palam* of perfumed *candanam*, 3 sacred threads, ½ *palam* of perfumed *candanam* was presented during the time of ablution, one rose-water pot was supplied during the time of civet oil ablution on every Friday, 2 *palam* of perfumed *candanam*, 365 pair of sacred threads and 52 rose water pots for 52 civet oil ablution days. These articles were to be supplied from the income of a village granted to the temple.[44]

g. *Application of Perfumes*

(i) *Punugukāppu* : The application of perfumes including *punugukāppu* to the deity's body after the *abhiṣēka* was an important item in temple worship. *Punugu* means civet oil, *kāppu* means smearing the body. Therefore the word *punugukāppu* means the application of civet oil to the body of the deity. In Ś. 1356 provision was made for *punugukāppu* to god Śrī Venkaṭēśvara of Tirumala by Alagappiranār, one of the Śrī Vaiṣṇavas of Tirupati.[45] A record from Tirumala, dated in Ś. 1427, mentions the arrangements made for the *pulugu-kāppu muṛai* or civet oil ablution to god Tiruvēnkaṭamuḍaiyān of Tirumala along with the *Paccai-karpūri* and musk on alternate Friday.[46] The Vijayanagara king, Kṛṣnarāya, visited the Tirumala temple in Ś. 1438 and made a gift for the expenses of *pulikāpu* on every Thursday.[47]

39. *T.T.D.I.* I. 220. Tirumala.
40. *Ibid.*, II. 38. Tirumala.
41. *Ibid.*, II. 50. Tirumala.
42. *Ibid.*, II. 81. Tirumala.
43. *Ibid.*, IV. 14. Tirumala.
44. *Ibid.*, I. 207. Tirumala.
 Similar Examples
 T.T.D.I. II. 62, 88, 94, 97, 105, 110.
 Ibid., III. 7, 8.
45. *T.T.D.I.* III. 4. Tirumala.
46. *Ibid.*, III. 80. Tirumala.
47. *Ibid.*, IV. 36. Tirumala.

Provision was made by the temple treasury in lieu of a gift made, for *pulugukkāppu-muṟai* to be conducted for god Śrī Vēnkaṭēśa of Tirumala on the 13 days of the star *Mṛgasīrṣam* in every year.[48] In Ś. 1483, a gift was made for the *pulugukkāppu* to god Tiruvēnkaṭamuḍaiyān during 52 *pulugukkāpu* conducted on 52 Fridays occurring in every year.[49] A record from Eṟṟaguḍi records the gift of a plot of land for the *pulugukāppu* service to god Rāmēśvara of the place by Mali nāyanimgāru.[50] Certain individuals made gift to the *Śrībhaṇḍāram* of Tirumala for the purpose of celebrating the civet oil ablution for god Śrī Vēnkaṭēśa of Tirumala on all the 52 Fridays occurring in every year.[51]

Punugukkāppu required a variety of articles and elaborate arrangements were made for their supply. It required powdered or pressed *pulugu* or civet squeezed of oil, and refined camphor for the holy face of the god, and I *kalañju* of camphor and sandal made into a soft paste, 2 *mārakkal* of rice measured with the *Malaikiniyaninṟ-akāl*, 1 *nāli* of ghee, 200 *palam* of jaggery and 1 *uḷākku* of pepper and 1 *palam* of *candanam*.[52]

Certain offerings were made to the deities at the time of the *punugukkāppu*. An inscription from Tirumala, dated in Ś. 1456, mentions that, provision was made by the temple treasury, in lieu of a gift, for the propitiation of god Śrī Vēnkaṭēśa of Tirumala with 53 *vaḍa* on 53 Fridays, occurring in every year when the god was having the *pulugukkāppu muṟai*.[53] Another from the same place, dated in Ś. 1427, states that arrangements were made for one *Nārāyaṇa-taḷigai* and one *appāpaḍi* to be offered to Tiruvēnkaṭamuḍaiyān during the *pulugukkāppu-muṟai*.[54]

(ii) *Candanalagi*: Arrangements were also made for the supply of sandal etc., for application to the deity's body after the *abhiṣēka*. The word *Candana* means sandal and *lagi* means application. Various services were also gone through during the conduct of *candanalagi*. In Ś. 1298, a gift was made to a woman for waving *cāmara* at the time of *candanalagi* to the god of Simhāchalam.[55] The *ālavaṭṭam* service was arranged at the time of *candanalāgi* to the same deity by the Reddi king, Anavema Reddi in Ś. 1297.[56] Provision was made for holding a mirror before god Narasimhanātha at the time of *candanalāgi* and to decorate the floor with coloured powder at the same time by the sister of Kaḷingaparīṣka Śankarajiya nāyaka.[57]

Large quantities of sandal was required for the service of *candanalāgi* and arrangements were made for its supply. In Ś. 1045, provision was made for the supply of sandal for god Bhīmēśvaradēva of Drākshārāma in the 47th year of the

48. *Ibid.*, V. 167. Tirumala.
49. *Ibid.*, V. 167. Tirumala.
50. 37 of 1953-54. Chenchu Eṟṟaguḍi.
51. *T.T.D.I.* I. 207. Tirumala.
52. *Ibid.*, V. 167. Tirumala.
53. *Ibid.*, IV. Tirumala.
54. *Ibid.*, III. 4. Tirumala.
55 *S.I.I.* VI. 751. Simhāchalam.
56. *Ibid.*, VI. 785. Simhāchalam.
57. *Ibid.*, VI. 882. Simhāchalam.

reign of the Cōḷa king, Kulōttunga.[58] A gift was made to the temple treasury of Śrīkūrmam in Ś. 1137, for the supply of sandal to the local god.[59] A record from Tripurāntakam, dated in Ś. 1272, mentions the provision made for the supply of musk, camphor, *agaru* and *śrīgandha* for the application to god Tripurāntakēśvara.[60] Another from Siṁhāchalam, dated in Ś. 1298, states that arrangements were made for the *candanalāgi* to god Śrī Narasiṁhanātha of Siṁhāchalam.[61] In Ś. 1435, certain individuals, named Narasanāyaka, Iṁmūru Matakkal and Narasiṁha, made provision for the supply of scents including camphor, saffron and *tastakaṭṭai* or sandal wood paste to god Kāḷahastīśvara of Kāḷahasti.[62] A dancing girl made arrangements for supplying sandal and basil to god Śrī Talpagiri Ranganāthasvāmi of Nellore.[63] In the reign of the Cōḷa king, Rājarāja, provision was made for the supply of sandal paste to god Tirukkālatti Uḍaiya Nāyanār of Kāḷahasti by Śaśikula Cāḷukya.[64] In Ś. 1231, provision was made for one sandal ball by the Cāḷukyan king, Viśvanātha to god Śrīkūrmanātha of Śrīkūrmam.[65] A record from Siṁhāchalam, dated in Ś. 1301, states that arrangements were made for the *candanalāgi*.[66]

h. *Decoration*

Cloths : After smearing the body with perfumes, the deity was decorated with *turāvi, kuḷḷāvu, kaṁcuka, pītāṁbara, kaṭivastra* and *ciralu* and other kinds of cloths. A Mallikārjuna presented *pāgālu* or turban to god Bhīmēśvara of Drākshārāma.[67] After his glorious eastern campaign, Kṛṣṇarāya visited the Tirumala temple and gave in Ś. 1438, a *kuḷḷāvu* with pearls, rubies, emeralds and sapphires fixed in it.[68] In Ś. 1442, the same king presented to god Tiruvēngaḷanātha, a *pītāṁbaram* or laced silk cloth set with nine kinds of precious stones.[69] Śrībalidēvara dēvī presented silk cloths in Ś. 1061, to god Mahēśa of Nocceḍlapūḍi.[70] A record from Tripurāntakam, dated in Ś. 1212, mentions the gift of cloths like *cīni, mahācīni, kṣitakṣauma* and *raktaṣksauma* to the local god by Aṁbadēva mahārāja.[71] Another, from Śrīkākulam, dated in Ś. 1275, refers to the gift of 12 *venne-ciralu* or a kind of cloths by Gangāmahādēvulu to god Śrīkākolani Śrī Vallabharāya.[72] Potinēnimgāru granted *patina-ciralu* to god Bhīmēśvara of Drākshārāma in Ś. 1392.[73]

58. *Ibid.*, IV. 1374-A. Drākshārāma.
59. *Ibid.*, V. 1287. Śrīkūrmam.
60. *Ibid.*, X. 465. Tripurāntakam.
61. *Ibid.*, VI. 751. Siṁhāchalam.
62. *N.D.I.* III. Sūḷurpēṭ. 11. Tuṁmūru.
63. *Ibid.*. II. Nellore. 59. Nellore.
64. 168 of 1922. Kāḷahasti.
65. *S.I.I.* V. 1214. Śrīkūrmam.
66. *Ibid.*, VI. 733, 785, 958, 1087, 1116. Siṁhāchalam.
67. *Ibid.*, IV. 1374-A. Drākshārāma.
68. *T.T.D.I.* III. 80. Tirumala.
69. *S.I.I.* VI. 882. Simnāchalam.
70. *Ibid.*, IV. 672. Nādiṇḍla.
71. *Ibid.*, X. 465. Tripurāntakam.
72. *Ibid.*, IV. 975. Śrīkākuḷam.
73. *Ibid.*, IV. 1344. Drākshārāma.

Jewels : Various kinds of jewels and weapons etc., adorned the body of the deity and it was a practice in temples to decorate the deity with weapons like *śaṁkha*, *cakra*, *gaḍa*, *triśūla*, *khaḍga* etc. and jewels like *kirīṭa*, *pathakam*, *graivēyaka*, or *kaṇṭhamālā*, *hāra* or necklace *bhujakīrti* or *kēvūra*, *valayas* or bangles, *kaṭisūtra* or buckle, *manjīras* etc., and this was done after the decoration with cloths. In Ś. 1434, Kṛṣṇarāya granted a *kirīṭam* to the processional image of Śrī Vēnkaṭēśa of Tirumala.[74] Asana nāyaka presented a *kirīṭa* or crown in Ś. 1629, to god Tiruvēngaḷanātha of Dēvunicuḍḍapah.[75] A record from the Tirumala temple, dated in Ś. 1352, states that Śrīgirīśvara presented a *paṭṭam*, newly made, of gold and gems, to god Śrī Vēnkaṭēśa of Tirumala.[76] In Ś. 1264, Kṛṣṇadēviammā gifted one gold *pagaḍapūvula-mālā*, one *trisarimuktyāla-cēru* and two *biḷḷa-saramulu* to god Śrī Narasiṁha of Siṁhāchalam.[77] Cinnādēvī, the queen of Kṛṣṇarāya, presented one *kaṇṭhamālā* with a *padakam*, set with 11 pearls, the central ruby, 2 emeralds and 4 diamonds altogether weighing 200 units to god Śrī Vēnkaṭēśa of Tirumala in Ś. 1436.[78] A gold garland consisting of 38 lotus flowers was presented to god Śrī Narasiṁha of Siṁhāchalam.[79] In Ś. 1244, Gangāṁbā, the queen of the Eastern Gānga king, Narasiṁha, donated a garland of two lotus buds to the same god.[80] Queen Sabbamā the wife of king Velnāḍu Gonka, presented a *valaya* to god Bhīmēśvara of Drākshārāma.[81] The famous Vijayanagara king, Kṛṣṇarāya presented a *kaḍiyam* or *bāhuvalayam* or *vanki* to god Śrī Vēnkaṭēśa of Tirumala in Ś. 1436.[82] A gold ring was presented to god Tripurāntaka in Ś. 12/8.[83] A record from Drākshārāma, dated in Ś. 1065, mentions the gift of *reṇḍu-māṇikyamulu-kaṭṭina-pahiṇḍi-pānulureṇḍu* to god Bhīmēśvara of the place.[84] Kṛṣṇarāya gifted one *vajra-māṇikvāla-kaḍivāla-jōḍu*, a beautiful ornament to the feet of god Śrī Narasiṁhanātha of Siṁhāchalam.[85] A record from Śrīkūrmam dated in Ś. 1425, mentions the gift of *meḍanūlu-venḍicippapūlu* to the local god.[86] Mangirāja gave *mēlukaṭṭu* in Ś. 1211 to god Nandidēvara of Drākshārāma.[87] In Ś. 1417, a *pancāvaktra-kōhaḷi* made of 5 *tōlas* of gold to the face of the *utsava* image of god Śrīkūrmanātha of Śrīkūrmam.[88]

Yajñōpavīta : Sacred threads or *vajñōpavitas* made of thin twisted gold wires or cotton was placed on the body of the deity after the *tirumanjanam*. A record from the Tirumala temple, dated in Ś. 1454, states that, provision was made for the supply

74. *T.T.D.I.* III. 32. Tirumala.
75. 366 of 1938-39. Dēvuni-Cuḍḍapah.
76. *T.T.D.I.* I. 193. Tirumala.
77. *S.I.I.* VI. 983. Siṁhāchalam.
78. *T.T.D.I.* III. 30. Tirumala.
79. *S.I.I.* VI. 933. Siṁhāchalam.
80. *Ibid.*, VI. 694. Siṁhāchalam.
81. *Ibid.*, IV. 1224. Drākshārama.
82. *T.T.D.I.* III. 66. Tirumala.
83. *S.I I.* X. 555. Tripurāntakam.
84. *Ibid.*, IV. 1190. Drākshārāma.
85. *Ibid.*, VI. 696. Siṁhāchalam.
86. *Ibid.*, V. 1228. Śrīkūrmam.
87. *Ibid*, IV. 1019. Drākshāama.
88. *Ibid.*, V. 1229. Śrīkūrmam.

of 3 *vajñōpavītams* to god Tiruvēnkaṭamuḍaiyān during his ablution.[89] Another, from Siṁhāchalam, dated in Ś. 1281, mentions the arrangements made for the supply of two *vajñōpavītams* to god Śrī Narasiṁha of the place.[90] Another record, from the same place, dated in 1272, states that Gangādēvī, the queen of the Eastern Gānga king, Vīranarasiṁha, made provision for the supply of one *vajñōpavita* to the same god.[91] Arrangements were made for the supply of *vajñōpavita*, made of thin twisted gold wire to the same deity in Ś. 1259, by Jayantarāju, the son of Oḍḍādi Arjunadēva.[92]

Flowers : After the decoration with cloths and jewels, the deity was decorated with various kinds of flowers and garlands. Arrangements were made in Ś. 1469, for the supply of flowers for the worship of god Parāśarēśvara at Jōgimallāvaram.[93] In Ś. 1278, a devotee, named Jōgisēnāpati, made a deposit for the supply of a garland, 4 cubits long and consisting of all flowers, daily to god Śrī Narasiṁhanātha of Siṁhāchalam.[94] Provision was made for the supply of flower garlands to god Śrīkūrmanātha of Śrīkūrmam by an individual, named Pōtarāja, in Ś. 1064.[95] A record from the Tirumala temple, dated in Ś. 1413, states that the *Śribhanḍāram* of the temple made provision, in lieu of a gift received from Baicarāja Tiṁmayadēva mahārāja, for the supply of full round flower garlands of the shape of the full-moon to gods Śrī Gōvindarāja and Śrī Vēnkaṭēśa.[96] Another, from Siṁhāchalam, dated in Ś. 1296, regīsters a gift made for the supply of a *donḍavanamālā*, or garland which reached up to the knees, to god Śrī Narasiṁha every day.[97] Paramapuruṣa Śrīpāda, the disciple of Jñānatīrtha Śrīpāda, made a gift in Ś. 1352, for the purpose of offering a *tulaśi-donḍavanamālā* to the same deity.[98] The Gajapati king, Pratāpa Śrī Puruṣōttamadēva, made provision in Ś. 1364, for the supply of five *tulaśi* garlands to god Śrī Narasiṁha and minor deities.[99] *Tōmālā* or a garland, hanging from the shoulders up to the foot, was presented by the devotees. A Cingu *sēnāpati*, in Ś. 1269, made arrangements for the supply of a *tōmālā* daily to the same god.[100] *Tōmala-sēva* was arranged in Ś. 1455, by Nārāyaṇa Seṭṭiyār to god Śrī Vēnkaṭēśa of Tirumala and provision was made for the supply of offerings during this service.[101]

i. *Arcanā*

Arcanā was an important item of worship, which was gone through after the decoration of the deity. An individual instituted the *Sahasranāmārcanā* in Ś. 1132

89. *T.T.D.I.* IV. 14. Tirumala.
90. *S.I.I.* VI. 889. Siṁhāchalam.
91. *Ibid.*, VI. 932. Siṁhāchalam.
92. *Ibid.*, VI. 981. Siṁhāchalam.
93. *T.T.D.I.* V. 136. Tirupati.
94. *S.I.I.* VI. 1131. Siṁhāchalam.
95. *Ibid.*, V. 1223. Śrīkūrmam.
96. *T.T.D.I.* II. 94. Tirumala.
97. *S.I.I.* VI. 1136. Siṁhāchalam.
98. *Ibid.*, VI. 796. Siṁhāchalam.
99. *Ibid.*, VI. 844. Siṁhāchalam.
100. *Ibid.*, VI. 716. Siṁhāchalam.
101. *T.T.D.I.* VI. 27. Tirumala.

to god Śrīkūrmanātha of Śrīkūrmam.[102] The emperor, Acyutarāya, visited Śrī Vēnkaṭēśa of Tirumala in Ś. 1454 and himself performed the *arcanā* to god Śrī Vēnkaṭēśa, while the *arcakas* recited the *Śrīnivāsa-Sahasr.. nāmam* or 1008 appellations of the god, in the presence of his queen, Varadājī aṁman and son, Kumāra Venkaṭādri, on his first visit to Tirumala temple.[103]

j. *Dhūpa*

The *Dhūpa* or waving of incense was conducted, after the *arcanā* was performed. In Ś. 1302, arrangements were made to hold the *ālavaṭṭamu* at the time of the morning *dhūpa* before god Śrī Narasiṁha of Siṁhāchalam.[104] Provision was made in Ś. 1318, for reciting *Viṣṇustōtramu* at the time of *rēpaṭidhūpa* before the same god.[105] Haradāsa Sāhasamalla, the Simādrihbōgaparīkṣa, made provision in Ś. 1338, for the supply of a vessel full of curds to be offered as *madhuparkam* at the time of the morning *dhūpa* to the same god.[106] A *tōmālā* was presented to the deity in Ś. 131.5, at the time of *dhupa* conducted in the temple of Siṁhāchalam.[107] Food offerings like *tirumaḍapali* etc., were also offered to god Śrīkūrmanātha of Śrīkūrmam, during the time of *dhūpa.*[108]

Several kinds of services were arranged, during the time of *ubhayadhupālu.* Provision was made for holding *cāmaras,* umbrellas etc.[109] Recitation of *Sankīrtana* was also arranged[110] in the temple of Siṁhāchalam. In Ś. 1221, provision was made for singing *mangaḷagītālu* before the deity, during the time of *ubhayadhūpālu* by Varadagiri Śrīpāda in the same temple.[111]

Arrangements were made in Ś. 1316, for the offering of one plateful of food on the two *sandhyas* to god Bhāvanārāyaṇa of Sarpavaram.[112] Provision was made in Ś. 1271, for two women to play on *Vīnā* and 2 women to follow at *ubhayasandhyalu,* before god Śrī Narasiṁhanātha of Siṁhāchalam.[113]

k. *Dīpa*

Immediately after the waving of the incense the *dīārādhana* or showing a light of ghee or oil to the deity was done. In Ś. 1477, Mantramūrti Pinna Basuvaya, made provision for the offering of lights or *dipārādhana* to god Hanumanta of Uluchala in *Kandanavōli-sīma.*[114] In Ś. 1236, a gift was made to god Mallikārjuna of

102. *S.I.I.* V. 1212. Śrīkūrmam.
103. *T.T.D.I.* IV. 16. Tirumala.
104. *S.I.I.* VI. 755. Siṁhāchalam.
105. *Ibid.*, VI. 1022. Siṁhāchalam.
106. *Ibid*, VI. 709. Siṁhāchalam.
107. *S.I.I.* VI. 745. Siṁhāchalam.
108. *Ibid.*, V. 1242, 1153. Śrīkūrmam.
109. *Ibid.*, V. 1207, 1225, Śrīkūrmam. VI. 739. Siṁhāchalam.
110. *Ibid.*, VI 890, 933, 708. Simhāchalam.
111. *Ibid.*, VI. 941. Siṁhāchalam.
112. *Ibid.*, V. 4. Sarpavaram.
113. *Ibid.*, VI. 955. Siṁhāchalam.
114. 52 of 1953-54. Ulchala.

Gonuvīḍu and to the god Bhīmēśvara of the same place for a light by Gangireḍḍi, the servant of Oḍayālu.[115]

1. *Naivēdya*

A large number of *naivēdyas* or food offerings were made to deities on an elaborate scale. Several people made a variety of gifts for this purpose. A gift was made in Ś. 1378, by Sāḷuva Narasingadēva for instituting *Udayakāla-sandhi* each in his name to god Tiruvēnkaṭamuḍaiyān of Tirumala.[116] In Ś. 1385, provision was made for the supply of four *tiruppōnakam* daily to be offered to the same god along with the *siru-kālai-sandhi* or morning offering.[117] A record from Sarpavaram, dated in Ś 1326, mentions the gift made for instituting a food offering named *Sṛngāra-bhoga* in the morning consisting of *appamulu* and *tirubōnamu* containing green gram, pudding, ghee, milk, betal nut and pepper to god Bhāvanārāyaṇa of the place.[118] Another from the Gōvindarāja temple, Tirupati, states that Kandāḍaī Rāmānujayyaṁgār arranged a *dadhyōdana-sandhi* for the propitiation of Gōvindapperumāḷ daily in the morning.[119] In Ś. 1467, arrangements were made for the offering of one *alaṁkāra-taḷigai* containing *rājānatiruppōnakam* to god Tiruvēnkaṭamuḍaiyān of Tirumala.[120] In the 36th year of the reign of the Cōḷa king, Kulōttungacōḷadēva, provision was made for the offering of *mantrabonamu* and *biṭṭamudu* to god Bhīmēśvara of Drākshārāma.[121]

Special kinds of offerings were also instituted by devotees in their names. A gift was made in Ś. 1231, for the conduct of *Viśvanātha-bhōga* to god Śrīkūrmanātha of Śrīkūrmam.[122] Gangāmahādēvī, the queen of Narasiṁhadēva, instituted two *bhōgas*, *Gangānarasiṁha-bhoga* and *Pārvatī-bhōga*, to god Śrī Narasiṁhadēva of Siṁhāchalam in Ś. 1272.[123] The Eastern Gānga, king, Pratāpavīra-Narasiṁha, instituted the *Gangā-bhōga* in Ś. 1310, to goddess Umādēvī.[124] Aṁbudēva *mahāsēnāpati* instituted *Nissanka-bhānu-bhōga* for the merit of king Bhānudēva to the god of the temple of Siṁhāchalam.[125] *Uttamadēvimahādēvi-bhōga* was also instituted in the same temple daily in Ś. 1316.[126] A *bhōga* was instituted for god Dharmalingēśvara of Panchadhārla in Ś. 1416.[127] In Ś. 1441, the emperor Kṛṣṇarāya, instituted a *bhōga* to god Śrī Narasiṁha of Siṁhāchalam, which required 1 *palam* of sandal, 2 *ma* of *agaru*, 1 *ci* of *kastūri*, 4 *ci* of musk, 4 *ci* of rose water, 1 *ci* of saffron, 4 flower garlands, rice, *pāyasa*, vegetables, *sārasētulu*, *ariselu*, *manōharams*, *appālu*,

115. *N.D.I.* II. Kanigiri. 7. Gozalaviḍū *alias*. Vāgupalle.
116. *T.T.D.I.* II. 4. Tirumala.
117. *Ibid.*, II. 17. Tirumala.
118. *S.I.I.* V. 5. Sarpavaram.
119. *T.T.D.I.* II. 141. Tirupati.
120. *Ibid.*, V. 55. Tirumala.
121. *S.I.I.* IV. 1288. Drākshārāma.
122. *Ibid.*, V. 1214. Śrīkūrmam.
123. *Ibid*, VI. 1275, 1057. Siṁhāchalam.
124. *Ibid.*, VI. 730. Siṁhāchalam.
125. *Ibid.*, VI. 1040. Siṁhāchalam.
126. *Ibid.*, VI. 1037, 1323. Simhāchalam.
127. *Ibid.*, VI. 661. Panchadhārla.

karpūrakāntulu, vaḍalu, kākarulu, pānakālu, curds, arecanuts, betel leaves, black pepper and *kāraṁbhu* etc.[128] The Eastern Gānga king, Anantavarman, appointed Guṇḍyana and Pōtaya as the officers in charge of the *nartakadēva* Gaṇika, *Vādyakara* and *gāyaka* of *Trikaḷingadēva-bhōga* service in the temple of Śrīkūrmam.[129] In Ś. 1456, provision was made for the supply of an *avasaram* or offering in the name of *Varadājidēvī aṁma-avasaram* and Kṛṣṇarāya's *avasaram* at Tirumala to god Śrī Venkaṭēṣa.[130] An offering named *ven-pongal-taḷigai* was offered to the same god daily in Ś. 1470, during the Rāmarājayyan's *avasaram.*[131] Provision was made by Koyilkelvi Vannaṁmalai Rāmanuja Jiyar in Ś. 1468, for the offering of one *vellai-tiruppōnaka-taḷigai* daily during the Rāja's *avasaram* to god Śrī Tiruvēnkaṭa-muḍaiyan installed by him in the shrine near the *sannidhi* street in Tirupati.[132] Five *pancadārapongal* or modern *sarkkarapongal-taḷigai* was offered to god Śrī Venkaṭēśa of Tirumala in Ś. 1528, daily during the *dadhyōdana-avasaram.*[133]

In Ś. 1381, a certain offerings were made along with the *Bukkarāya-sandhi* to god Śrī Venkaṭēśa of Tirumala [134] The *Acyutarāya-sandhi* was also instituted in the name of the emperor Acyutarāya in Ś. 1468 to the same god.[135] For the propitiation of Tiruvēnkaṭamuḍaiyān, one to eight *sandhis* were made by the devotees.[135a]

A large variety of general food offerings were also made to the deity besides those made on particular occasions. Śiriyaṁmā, the sister of Oḍḍādi Dēvarāja, made provision in Ś 1321, for the supply of a food offering named *triguṇipālakala-śalu* daily to the god of Siṁhāchalam.[136] Arrangements were made for the offering of *upāhāra* to god Dharmalingēśvara of Panchadhārla.[137] In Ś. 1453, a gift was made for the offering of *dadhyānnam* by Śingārayyaṁgāru to god Rāmēśvara of Tāḍipatri.[138] A record from Śrīkūrmam, dated in Ś. 1137, states that, provision was made for the offering of *maḍapali* to god Śrīkūrmanātha of the place.[139] Another, from Peṭṇrāla. dated in Ś. 1180, states that arrangements were made for the offering named *amṛtapaḍi* to a god.[140] After his conquest of Jantarnāḍu in Ś. 13,3, the Oḍḍādi king, Pratāpārjuna, made provision for the food offering *amṛtamaṇihi* to god Śrī Narasiṁha of Siṁhāchalam.[141] The queen of Rājēndra arranged for the supply of an offering of *pālamudu* and *tairamudu* to god Śrī Venkaṭēśa of Tirumala.[142] An

128. *Ibid.*, VI. 695. Siṁhāchalam.
129. *Ibid.*, V. 1010. Mukhalingam.
130. *T.T.D.I.* IV. 29. Tirumala.
131. *Ibid.*, V. 120. Tirumala.
132. *Ibid.*, V. 80. Tirupati.
133. *Ibid.*, VI. 14. Tirumala.
134. *Ibid.*, II. 7, 9. Tirumala.
135. *Ibid.*, V. 81. Tirupati.
135a. *Ibid.*, I. 197, 219. Tirumala.
136. *S.I I.* VI. 872. Siṁhāchalam.
137. *Ibid.*, VI. 664. Panchadhārla.
138. *Ibid.*, IV. 801. Tāḍpatri.
139. *Ibid.*, V. 1287. Śrīkūrmam.
140. *N.D.I.* II. Kandukūr. 52. Penṭrāla,
141. *S.I I.* VI. 966. Siṁhāchalam.
142. *T.T.D.I.* I. 27. Tirumala.

offering named *ōgiram* was made to a god in Ś. 1164.[143] A record from the Tirumala temple, dated in Ś. 1436, mentions the provision made for the purpose of three *pāyasa-harivāṇa* plates to be offered daily to god Śrī Venkaṭēśa of Tirumala.[144] A certain individual made provision in the *Śrībhaṇḍāram* foı an offering named *dōsai-paḍi* to be offered to god Gōvindarāja of Tirupati in Ś. 1453.[145] Offerings like *junnu-paḍi* and *vellai-tiruppōnaka-taḷigai* were offered to the god of Tirumala.[146] In Ś. 1296 and 1313 arrangements were made for an offering *sēmanthakhiri*, and *pappucīdi* to god Narasiṁhanātha of Siṁhāchalam.[147] Offerings like *rājāna-tiruppōnakam* and two *paruvamudu-paḍi-tiruppōnakam* were made to god Tiruvēnkaṭa-muḍaiyān of Tirumala in Ś. 1386.[148] A record from the Gōvindarāja temple, Tirupati, dated in Ś. 1441, mentions the provision made for the offering of *appā-pāḍi, atirasa-paḍi, gōdhi-paḍi, vaḍai-paḍi iḍḍali-paḍi, dōsai-paḍi, sukhīyan-paḍi* and *kunukku-paḍi* to god Śrī Gōvindaperumāḷ of Tirupati.[149] Another from the Tirumala temple, dated in Ś. 1450, mentions the arrangements made for the offering of *paruppuvial* to Śrī Venkaṭēśa as *aravamudu-siruppu* by Uḷagapperumānār of Paramēśvaramangaḷam.[150] Two inscriptions, from the same place, dated in Ś. 1443 and 1460 mention the provision made for the supply of offerings like *bhētanikai* or a kind of sweet cake and *gōdhumai-tiruppaṇyāram* or wheat cake to god Śrī Venkaṭēśa of Tirumala daily.[151] Offerings like *nāyakataḷigai* and *alankāra-taḷigai* were aslo made to the same god in Ś. 1460 and 1467.[152]

143. *S.I.I.* X. 295. Aḍavirāvulapāḍu.
144. *T.T.D.I.* III. 91. Tirumala.
145. *Ibid.*, III. 179. Tirupati.
146. *T.T.D.I.* V. 75. Tirumala.
147. *S.I.I.* VI. 835, 1122. Siṁhāchalam.
148. *T.T.D I.* II. 21. Tirumala.
149. *Ibid.*, III. 134. Tirupati.
150. *Ibid.*, III. 178. Tirumala.
151. *Ibid.*, III. 148, IV. 132. Tirumala.
152. *Ibid.*, IV. 113, V. 55. Tirumala.

Similar Examples

S I.I. VI. 814. Siṁhāchalam.
Ibid., VI, 589, Kunkaḷaguṇṭa.
Ibid., V. 44. Bhīmavaram.
Ibid., VI. 232. Amarāvati.
Ibid., VI. 659. Panchadhārla.
Ibid.. VI. 602. Inumeḷḷa.
Ibid., V. 1178. Śrīkūrmam.
N.D.I. II. Kandukūr. 52. Pākāla.
S.I.I. II. 806. Simhāchalam.
Ibid., X. 228. Nādeṇḍla.
Ibid., X. 334. Durgī.
Ibid., X. 490. Unnava.
S.I.I. VI. 867. Siṁhāchalam.
T.T.D.I. III. 105, 117, 145. Tirumala, Tirupati.
Ibid., II. 12, 57. Tirumala, Tirupati.
Ibid., I. 82, 194. Tirumala.

Contd.

m. *Nīrājana*

After the *naivēdya*, another service, named *nīrājana*, was performed. This was of two kinds, namely waving a lighted lamp or waving lighted camphor before the god. In Ś. 1087, Eṟrama nāyaka the subordinate of Velanāṇṭi Rājēndra Cōḍa made provision for a perpetual camphor lamp with a metal lampstand to god Bhīmēśvara of Drākshārāma.[153] In Ś. 1434, king, Kṛṣṇarāya gifted 25 silver plates for *ārati* to god Kāḷahastīśvara.[154] During the reign of the Telugu-Pallava king, Vijayagaṇḍa-gōpāla, a deposit was made for a camphor light to god Śrī Vēnkaṭēśa of Tirumala.[155] A record from Drākshārāma registers a gift of perpetual camphor lamp with a metal stand to god Bhīmēśvara Mahādēva of the place by Dēkana Mādhava, the minister of Velanānṭi Gonka.[156]

n. *Tāṁbūla*

After the *nīrājana* or *hārati*, the deity was served with a *viḍyam* or *tāṁbūla* or arecanut plus betel leaves. In Ś. 1094, arrangements were made for the supply of betel leaves and arecanuts to god Kēśvadēva of Gōvardhana by Muttana.[157] A record from Durgī, dated in Ś. 1191, mentions the supply of *viḍyam*, betel leaves and arecanuts to god Gōpīnātha of Dugya by *karaṇam* Nāmaya.[158] Another, from Śrīkūrmam, dated in Ś. 1198, mentions the supply of one *viḍyam* to be offered to the god of the place.[159] Another, from Palivela, records the provision made for *tāṁbūla* to god Gaṇapati of the place.[160] Some seṭṭis made a gift of 500 leaves per cart load of betel leaves for the service of god Jakkēśvara of Ūbacherla.[161]

c. *Mantrapuṣpa*

After the *tāṁbūla*, *puṣpānjali* and *mantrapuṣpa* were offered. In Ś. 1194, in the reign of the Kākatīya queen, Rudrāṁbā, *Gaṇḍapeṇḍara* Aṁbadēva mahārāja donated a village to several priests who recited the *mantrapuṣpa* in the Tripurāntakēśvara temple at Tripurāntakam.[162] Provision was also made for *Bhāgayataseva* and chanting of *mantrapuṣpam* to god Cennakēśava of Niṭṭūru by Rāmalinga nāyanimgāru.[163]

S.I.I. IV. 1114. Drākshārāma.
Ibid., V. 1166. Śrīkūrmam.
Ibid., V. 1224. Śrīkūrmam.

153. *S.I.I.* IV. 1195. Drākshārāma.
154. *Ibid.*, IX. 487, 488. Kāḷahasti.
155. *T.T.D.I.* I. 67. Tirumala.
156. *S.I.I.* IV. 1169. Drākshārāma.
157. *Ibid.*, IV. 808. Nādeṇḍla.
158. *Ibid.*, X. 422. Durgī.
159. *Ibid.*, V. 1166. Śrīkūrmam.
160. *Ibid.*, V. 105. Palivela.
161. *Ibid.*, IX. 232. Ubhacherla.
162. *Ibid.*, X. 432. Tripurāntakam.
163. 23 of 1953-54. Niṭṭūru.

2. *Madhyāhnapūja or Midday Service*

The *madhyāhnapūja* or midday worship was a repetition, on a minor scale, of the morning *pūja.* There were many *naivēdyas* made to the deity. In Ś. 1077, a gift was made for the supply of rice required for an offering, at the midday to god Bhīmēśvara of Drākshārāma.[164] An offering named *kuḍumulu* was offered to god Vināyaka during the same time in S. 1088 in lieu of a gift received for this purpose.[165] In Ś. 1281, Śrīgiri Nāyanimgāru, made a gift for the *naivēdya* at the *madhyāhnavēḷa* to god Mallikārjunadēva of Mandaḍi.[166] A gift was made in Ś. 1360, for a *naivēdya* as *madhyāhna-avasaram* or midday offering to god Mṛkaṇḍēśvara of Rājahmundry.[167] In Ś. 1167, the Eastern Gānga King, Vīranarasiṁha Rāvutadēva and his two consorts gifted 25 cows for milk offering to be made to the god at Śrīkūrmam at the time of *madhyāhna-sejja avasaram.*[168] Provision was made in Ś. 1231, by Viṣvanāthadēvajiyyana, for the *madhyāhna-sejjabhōga* to the same god.[169]

3. *Evening Service*

The evening part of the worship started with a brief *tirumanjanam.* Mallirāju made provision in Ś. 1059, for the supply of milk for the *kṣirābhiṣēka* to god Bhīmēśvara of Drākshārāma.[170] Twilight lamps were lighted during the first evening service of god Tirukkāḷatti during the 27th year of the reign of the Cōḷa king, Kulōttungacōḷadēva.[171] Adavallan Gangaikoṇḍan *alias* Iṛugōlan, made provision for burning 20 lamps in 20 lampstands, from the evening till the close of the midnight service, in the temple of Kāḷahastīśvara.[172] Provision was made for the garland, offered at the time of *māpaṭidhūpa* to the god of Siṁhāchalam in Ś. 1337.[173]

4. *Night Service*

The night worship started with the *abhiṣēka* and ended with the *ēkantasēva* or sending the god to sleep. A record from Siṁhāchalam, dated in Ś. 1324, mentions the arrangements made for the *tirumanjanam,* conducted during the night to god Śrī Narasiṁha of the place.[174] After this *abhiṣēka* the deity was decorated with

164. *S I I.* IV. 1153. Drākshārāma.
165. *Ibid.*, IV. 1099. Drākshārāma.
166. 65 of 1929-30. Mandaḍi.
167. *S.I.I.* V. 118. Rājahmundry.
168. *Ibid.*, V. 1294. Śrīkūrmam.
169. *Ibid.*, V. 1214. Śrīkūrmam.
170. *Ibid* , IV. 1176-A. Drākshārāma.
171. 84 of 1922. Kāḷahasti.
172. 151 of 1922. Kāḷahasti.
173. *S.I.I.* VI. 838. Siṁhāchalam.
    Similar Examples
    S.I.I. VIII. 530. Kāḷahasti.
    90 of 1922. Kāḷasasti.
174. *S.I.I.* VI. 1031. Siṁhāchalam.

various kinds of flower garlands like *doṇḍavanamālā, tōmālā* etc.[175] In Ś. 1303, five *gaṇḍamāḍas* were made for holding the *ālavaṭṭam* at the time of the *tiruvajāmu-avasaram* in the temple of Siṁhāchalam.[176] *Dhūpa* was also offered during the night worship after decoration. Various kinds of offerings like *triguṇipālakalaśalu, mantrobōnamu, sēmantikhīri, jīnu* etc., were offered to the deity during the *rātridhūpa* or night *dhūpa* and provision was made for this purpose.[177] A certain Nārāyaṇadēva, a subordinate of king Narasiṁha, instituted a *bhōga*, named *Nārāyaṇa-bhōga* in his name in Ś. 1219, to god Śrī Narasiṁha of Siṁhāchalam, to be offered after the *rātridhūpa*.[178] Various kinds of offerings were made during the night worship. In Ś. 1299, Oḍḍādi king, Arjunadēva, made provision for the *appala-bhōga* to be offered to the god of Śrīkūrmam during night.[179] *Tirukkanāmaḍai* was offered daily at the time of the *rāpaḍi* or night offering to Śrī Gōvindapperumāḷ of Tirupati in Ś. 1378.[180] One *appāpaḍi* was offered daily during the *rāppaḍi* each day to the same deity in Ś. 1385.[181] Provision was made in Ś. 1435, for the supply of 1 *nāli* of *pāleḍu-kuḷaṁbu* or thick boiled milk with cream formed over it to god Tiruvēnkaṭa-muḍaiyān of Tirumala during *tiruvardhajāmam*.[182]

5. *Midnight Service*

Arrangements were made in Ś. 1072, for a *naivēdya* offered at the time of *niśārdha.yāmasamaya* to god Bhīmēśvara of Drākshārāma.[183] A Prōliya peggaḍa, made a gift for the *naivēdya*, offered during midnight, to god Gōvardhanasvāmi of Nādiṇḍla.[184] Two kinds of food offerings like *tiruveḷuccipaḍi* and *ardhāyāmupaḍi* were arranged to the god of Tirumala, during the 7th year of the reign of a Cōḷa king.[185] A record from Drākshārāma, registers the gift of five *dāyajagadala-māḍas* to the local temple treasury for offering sandal paste daily at the time of the *ardhajāmu* worship to god.[186] In Ś. 1473, a devotee named Rāyasam Venkaṭādri made arrangements for a swing every night after the *ardhajāmam* worship to god Aḷagappiranār or Śrīkoluvu Śrīnivāsamūrti of Tirumala.[187]

At stated intervals the god comes out in procession and perhaps sees to the comfort of his attendant deities. In Ś. 1469, land was gifted by *mahāmaṇḍalēśvara*

175. *Ibid.*, VI. 717, 721, 742, 1115. Siṁhāchalam.
176. *Ibid.*, VI. 918. Siṁhāchalam.
177. *Ibid.*, IV. 1021. Drākshārāma.
178. *Ibid.*, VI. 876. Simhāchalam.
179. *Ibid.*, V. 1204. Śrīkūrmam.
180. *T.T.D.I.* I. 223. Tirupati.
181. *Ibid.*, 20, 47. Tirupati.
182. *Ibid.*, III. 88. Tirumala.
183. *S.I.I.* IV. 1182. Drākshārāma.
184. *Ibid.*, IV. 687. Nādiṇḍla.
185. *T.T.D.I.* I. 35. Yōgimallavaram.
186. *S.I.I.* IV. 1093. Drākshārāma.
187. *T.T.D.I.* V. 129. Tirumala.

Kōnayyadēvamahārāja to god Cennarāya of Mirutūru for the daily procession in a palanquin.[188]

The night worship came to an end with sending the god to sleep. In Ś. 1303, Oḍḍādi Arjunadēva, made provision for the supply of ten *kuṁcams* of milk, honey and sugar to god Śrī Narasiṁha of Siṁhāchalam, offered at the time of *Sejja-avasaram* daily as *Arjuna-bhōga*.[189] This *sejja-avasaram* is corresponds to the *Ekantasēva* of Tirumala.

188. 409 of 1926. Miḍuṭūru.
189. *S.I.I.* VI. 789. Siṁhāchalam.

7

FESTIVALS IN THE TEMPLE

The celebration of festivals has been an important and attractive feature of the functioning of the temples. It enhanced the popularity and sanctity of temples. Most of the donations made to temples relate to this aspect and indicate its importance.

Festivals conducted in temples are generally known by the name *utsava* or *tiruṇāḷ*. The compound word *utsava* consists of two words, *ut* and *sava*. Of these, *ut* means high or great and *sava* means *savana*, *yajña* or sacrifice. Among the several sacrifices, that an individual is asked to perform (*pitṛ-yajña*, *ṛṣi-yajña*) *dēva-yajña* or the worship of a deity is considered the greatest. Thus the celebration of a festival constituted the greatest sacrifice or worship offered to the god.

These utsavas may be broadly divided into two categories—those prescribed by the *Āgamas* and those instituted by devotees.

Utsavas prescribed by the *Āgamas* are of several varieties. One is *Śāntika* or those celebrated for warding of evils like draughts and pestilences. The second is *Aicchika* or those performed by individuals for the increase of their welfare and the third is the *Kālika* or those celebrated in a particular month in every year. The *Kālika* festivals may be of varying duration, celebrated for one to nine days. This nine day festival is the best festival according to the *Āgamas*. Special worship is offered during the first two days on a grandscale. On other days, it is shortened. Special items however like the car-festival, *vasantōtsavam* and *puṣpayāgam* are to be conducted on particular days. The *Brahmōtsavam* is the best example of a *Kālika* festival of nine days duration.

These festivals have been classified into annual festivals relating to months ; months and *tithis* ; months and stars ; week days ; days of particular stars ; *sankrāntis* and special annual festivals.

1. *Annual Festivals Celebrated in Particular Months*

a. *Tiruppaḷḷi-eḷucci*

This festival is also known as psalm singing festival, *tirupaḷḷi-eḷucci* and *Mārgaḷi* festival which was of 30 days duration. This festival was celebrated for 30 days in the month of *Mārgaḷi* in both the Viṣṇu and Śiva temples In Ś 1312, one *tiruvōḷakkam* was offered on each of the middle ten days during the *tiruppavvai* or psalm-singing celebrated in the month of *Mārgaḷi* within the hearing of Śrī Venkaṭēśa and Nāccimār of Tirumala.[1] Offerings were made in Ś. 1436, to Periya Perumāḷ or the original image on each of the 30 days of the *tiruppaḷḷi-eḷucci*, as *Dhanurmāsa-pūja*.[2]

This festival was celebrated for god Gōvindarāja of Tirupati in Ś. 1367. Offerings were made to him on the 30 days of *Mārgaḷi*.[3] In Ś. 1415, thirty *paruppu-viyal-tiruppōnakam* was offered with one *tirukkaṇamāḍai* on the day of *tuvvakkam* during this festival.[4]

In Ś. 1469, this festival was celebrated also for god Śrī Janārdana Perumāḷ of Tirupati. Special lights were maintained during this day.[5]

In the temple of god Narasiṁha, abiding in the temple of Tiruvēnkaṭamuḍaiyān or Śrī Venkaṭēśa, this festival was celebrated in Ś. 1415.[6]

An undated record from Sulurpet mentions the gift of land made for the purpose of the celebration of the *tirumārgaḷi* festival for god Nāgēśvara of the place by the consort of Taiṁmadidēvan.[7] Another from same place dated in the second year of the reign of the Telugu-Pallava king, Vijayagaṇḍagōpāla, mentions the gift of land for the performance of this festival during the sacred month of *tirumārgaḷi* for the god of the place by Rājēndra Cōḷa Muṁmaḍi Vaiduṁba *mahārāja*.[8]

b. *Mārgaḷi-Nirāṭṭōtsavam*

This festival, which was also celebrated in the month of *Mārgaḷi* for Sūḍikodutta-Nācciyār or Āṇḍāḷ, the consort of Śrī Gōvindaperumāḷ of Tirupati. It was celebrated for seven days in Ś. 1451, but its duration was increased to nine days in Ś. 1452. In Ś. 1451, this festival was celebrated, commencing on the 24th day of the month and ending on the day of *Makara-Sankraṇam. Adhivāsa tirumanjanam* was conducted on the night previous to the day of *ankurārpanam* being the 23rd day. This festival was started with the *pañcāmṛta-tirumanjanam* which was followed by procession through the streets. After the procession the goddess was seated in her bed-chamber and offerings were made to her.[9] In Ś. 1455, the deity was taken in

1. *T.T.D.I.* I. 187. Tirumala.
2. *Ibid.*, III. 98. Tirumala.
3. *Ibid.*, I. 212. Tirupati.
4. *T.T.D.I.* II. 100. Tirupati.
5. *Ibid.*, V. 101. Tirupati.
6. *Ibid.*, II. 101. Tirumala.
7. *N.D.I.* III. Sūḷurpēṭ. 4. Sūḷurpēṭa.
8. *Ibid.*, III. Sūḷurpēṭ. 8. Sūḷurpēṭa.
9. *T.T.D.I.* III. 181. Tirupati.

procession to a tank and offerings were made after her return to the temple.[10] In Ś. 1463, a car procession was arranged on the 7th festival day. After the procession she was seated in the *Yāga-śālā* in the shrine of Teyvanaka-Perumāḷ.[11] In Ś. 1453, on the 5th festival day various kinds of offerings were made to her.[12] In Ś. 1557, she was seated in the front *maṇṭapa* of Śrī Lakṣmīnārāyaṇa perumāḷ on the 7th festival day and offerings were made to her.[13]

c. *Vaiśākha-tiruṇāḷ*

This festival was celebrated in the month of *Vaiśākha.* A record from Ponnūru, dated in Ś. 1041, mentions the celebration of a festival during this month for god Bhāvanārāyaṇa of the place.[14] Another from Danakapūḍi, dated in Ś. 1197, states that provision was made for the conduct of this festival according to the *śāstras* for god Bhāvanārāyaṇa of the village by a Nārāyaṇadāsu and his brothers.[15]

2. *Annual Festivals Celebrated on Particular Tithis in Particular Months*

a. *Citrā-Paurṇima*

The *Citra-paurṇima* festival was celebrated on the full-moon day in the month of *Cittrai* or *Caitra,* when the asterism *Citra* or Virginis holds sway. This festival was celebrated in the temples of Śrī Venkaṭēśa of Tirumala and Gōvindarāja of Tirupati.

This was celebrated in Ś. 1515, for Śrī Venkaṭēśa. On this day, *tirumanjanam* was conducted with gingelly oil and *candanam* while the god and Nāccimār were seated in the Śrī *Ahōbila-maṭha,* constructed by Ādi-van-Saṭhakōpa jiyar at Tirumala. After the *tirumanjanam* offerings were made to them and an *āsthānam* or *koluvu* was conducted.[16]

This festival was celebrated for god Gōvindarāja in Ś. 1518.[17] A Rāmacandra Ayyan made provision in Ś. 1553, for the celebration of this festival. On this day, *tirumanjanam* was conducted for the god and his Nāccimār while seated in a garden *maṇṭapa Candanam,* musk and *gaṁbura-karpūram* were used for the decoration of the deities.[18]

b. *Tai-Amāvāsya*

The *Tai-Amāvāsya* was celebrated on the new moon day in the Tamil month of *Tai* for gods Gōvindarāja and Śrī Raghunātha of Tirupati. For Gōvindarāja it was conducted in Ś. 1414, while seated in a *maṇṭapa,* constructed on the bund of the

10. *Ibid.*, IV. 27. Tirumala.
11. *Ibid.*, V. 2. Tirumala.
12. *Ibid.*, VI. 21. Tirupati.
13. *Ibid.*, VI. 22. Tirupati.
14. *S.I.I.* VI. 121. Ponnūru.
15. *Ibid.*, X. 435, Ganikapūḍi.
16. *T.T.D.I.* VI. 10. Tirupati.
17. *Ibid.*, VI. 12. Tirupati.
18. *Ibid.*, VI. 21. Tirupati.

tank of Tiruvēnkaṭajiyar.[19] This festival was celebrated for god Raghunātha in S. 1410.[20]

c. *Panguṇi-Amāvāsya*

This festival was celebrated on the new moon day of the Tamil month of *Panguṇi* for god Aḷagiya-Singar in Ś. 1390, *tirumanjanam* was performed for him as part of the festival.[21]

3. *Annual Festivals Celebrated on the Days of Particular Stars in Particular Months*

a. *Tirukārttikai*

This festival was celebrated on the full moon day in the month of *Kārtika* when the moon was in conjunction with the asterism *Kṛttika*. It was celebrated for Śrī Venkatēśa of Tirumala and Śrī Gōvindarāja, Śrī Raghunātha and Śrī Varadarāja Perumāḷ of Tirupati.

This festival was celebrated at Tirumala in Ś. 1385.[22] On this day the god witnessed the *kūṭam* or bonfire and returned to the *Yāmunaitturaiyvān-maṇṭapa*.[23]

During this festival procession was taken through the streets in Ś. 1407 and offerings were made to god Gōvindarāja after the procession.[24]

This festival was celebrated for god Raghunātha also in Ś. 1402,[25] and for god Śrī Varadarāja Perumāḷ in Ś. 1518 both at Tirupati.[26]

In S. 1462, Dēvarasayyangāru of Guḍiya Chillūru granted money for providing eight offerings to god Ahōbalēśvara during this festival held on the 15th day in the bright half of *Kārttika*, when the image was taken out in procession in a palanquin.[28]

b. *Tai-Pūsam*

This festival was celebrated in the Tamil month of *Tai* on the occasion of the asterism *Pūsam* or *Puṣya*. It was celebrated for many gods at Tirupati for god Gōvindarāja in Ś. 1468,[29] for Raghunātha in Ś. 1434,[30] for Janārdana Perumāḷ in Ś. 1469,[31] and for god Varadarāja Perumāḷ in Ś. 1518.[32]

19. *T.T.D.I.* VI. 97, 118. Tirupati.
20. *Ibid.*, II. 88. Tirupati.
21. *Ibid.*, II. 38 Tirumala.
22. *Ibid.*, II. 18. Tirumala.
23. *Ibid.*, II. 123. Tirupati.
24. *Ibid.*, II. 83, 132. Tirupati.
25. *Ibid.*, II. 88. Tirupati.
26. *Ibid.*, VI. 12. Tirupati.
28. 58 of 1918. Lower Ahōbalam.
29. *T.T.D.I.* V. 67, Tirupati.
30. *Ibid.*, V. 101. Tirupati.
31. *T.T.D.I.* III. 28. Tirumala,
32. *Ibid.*, VI. 12. Tirupati,

c. *Māsi-Maghā*

This festival was celebrated in the month of *Māsi* on the day of the asterism of *Maghā*. It was celebrated in Ś. 1434, for god Gōvindarāja. On this day a holy bath was given to him in the tank at Tirucchukanūr and offerings were made while he was returning.[33] In Ś. 1458, arrangements were made for the propitiation of the god while seated in the *Rāmabhaṭṭar-maṇṭapam*.[34] A procession was also conducted on this day in Ś. 1515.[35] A Rāmāpuram accountant made provision in S. 1518, for the propitiation of this god while seated in the *Kanakkappiḷḷai maṇṭapa*, situated below the Kṛṣṇadupaṭṭu tank on the way to Tirumala Nāyakkar's garden.[36] In S. 1454, Rāmabhaṭṭarāyan made provision for offerings to god Kāḷahastīśvara when the god's image rested in the *maṇṭapa* built by him at Toṇḍamānnaṟṟūr, during this festival.[37]

d. *Arpasi-Purāḍham*

The day of the star *Purāḍham* or *Pūrvāṣāḍha* in the Tamil month of *Arpasi* was of importance at Tirumala. A festival was celebrated in S. 1458, on the day of this star occurring in the month of *Arpasi* for god Śrī Venkaṭēśa of Tirumala.[38] In Ś. 1465, *tirumanjanam* was conducted for the god, Nāccimār and Sēnai Mudaliyār on this day.[39]

e. *Panguṇi-Uttiram*

Panguṇi-Uttiram corresponds to the day of *Uttiram* in the Tamil month of *Panguṇi.*

This festival was celebrated in the temple of god Gōvindarāja of Tirupati in Ś. 1452.[40] Rāmabhaṭṭar, the able general and viceroy of the Vijayanagara emperor, Acyutarāya, arranged in Ś. 1454 for *tirumanjanam* to be given to the god on this day.[41] In Ś. 1504, a certain Appala-Cinnappan, made arrangements for making offerings, to the god on this day while seated in a *maṇṭapa*, constructed by him in his garden in Tirupati, after returning from the Rāmabhaṭṭar's garden *maṇṭapa*.[42]

For goddess Alarmēlmangai-Nācciyār, the consort of Śrī Venkaṭēśa, this festival was celebrated from Ś. 1468 and *tirumanjanam* was conducted for her on this occasion. After the *tirumanjanam* she was propitiated with offerings.[43]

For goddess Padmāvatīdēvī, abiding in Tiruchānūr also, this festival was celebrated while she was seated in the garden known as Alarmēlmangai-Nācciyar *toṭṭam* at Tiruchānūr.[44]

33. *T.T.D.I.* III. 31. Tirupati.
34. *Ibid.*, IV. 80. Tirumala.
35. *Ibid.*, VI. 11. Tirupati.
36. *Ibid.*, VI. 12. Tirupati.
37. 18 of 1922 Kāḷahasti.
38. *T.T.D.I.* IV. 83. Tirumala.
39. *Ibid.*, V. 8. Tirumala.
40. *Ibid.*, IV. 18. Tirupati.
41. *Ibid.*, IV. 18. Tirupati.
42. *Ibid.*, VI. 4. Tirupati.
43. *Ibid.*, V. 71. Tirumala.
44. *Ibid.*, V. 128. Tirupati.

This festival was celebrated in Ś. 1410 for god Raghunātha of Tirupati also.[45] In the temple of god Viṭṭhalēśvara Perumāḷ of the same place, this festival was celebrated from Ś. 1467 and gingelly oil, green gram and *candanam* were used for the *tirumanjanam* of the god.[46]

This festival is also important in Śaiva temples. In Ś. 1455, it was celebrated for god Kāḷahastīśvara of Kāḷahasti. Rāmabhaṭṭar made provision for making offerings to this god when he halted at the pavilion in the garden on this day, for the merit of Acyutaraya and his qneen, Varadājidēvīaṁma.[47]

d. *Vaikāsi-Viśākha*

This festival falls on the day of the asterism of *Viśākha* on the full moon day in the Tamil month of *Vaikāsi*. The festival is celebrated in honour of Dharmaputra or the god of death. The day is also said to be the one on which god Subrahmaṇya was born.

This festival was celebrated for god Śrī Viṭṭhalēśvara Perumāḷ of Tirupati in Ś. 1467. For god Janārdana Perumāḷ this festival was celebrated in S. 1469 and for god Varadarāja Perumāḷ in Ś. 1518 and provision was made for the conduct of *tirumanjanam* to all these deities on this day.[48]

4. *Annual Festivals Celebrated on the Days of Particular Tithis*

a. *New Moon Days* (*Amāvasya*)

This festival was celebrated in several temples. In Ś. 1458, offerings were made to god Śrī Venkaṭēśa of Tirumala on all the twelve new moon days occurring in every year.[49] A record from Sūḷūrpēṭ, dated in the 24th year of the reign of the Telugu-Cōḍa king, Vijayagaṇḍagōpāla, mentions the gift of a *sarvamānya* land to god Tirunāgīśvara of Singalantapuram *alias* Suralūr for carrying the god in procession on the new moon days.[50] Mamiḍiamma instituted this festival in Ś. 1168 for god Śrīkūrmanātha of Śrīkūrmam.[51] In Ś. 1183, a gift was made by Siddama and Vijayadēvalu, the sons of *mahāmaṇḍalēśvara* Bhīmadēva, to god Śrī Mārga Nārāyaṇa Perumāḷ of Penṭrāla, for the celebration of this festival.[52] Koṇḍapeddimanci, the palace official of Kākātīya Pratāparudra, made a gift in Ś. 1242, to the temple of Anantagōpīnātha of Roṁpicherla for the celebration of this festival.[53] In the 26th year of the reign of the Cōḷa king, Kulōttungacōḷa, a gift was made by the residents of Kannanallūr for the extra supply of food offerings to god Kāḷahastīśvara of Kāḷahasti on the new moon days.[54]

45. *Ibid.*, II. 88. Tirupati.
46. *Ibid.*, V. 66. Tirupati.
47. 18 of 1922. Kāḷahasti.
48. *T.T.D.I.* V. 66, 101. VI. 12. Tirupati
49. *Ibid.*, IV. 83. Tirumala.
50. *N.D.I.* III. Sūḷūrpēṭ. 3. Sūlūrpēṭa.
51. *S.I.I.* V. 1304. Śrīkūrmam.
52. *N.D.I.* II. Kandukūr. 63. Peṇṭrāla.
53. *S.I.I.* X. 529. Roṁpicherla.
54. 157 of 1922. Kālahasti.

b. *Daśamī-Festival*

This festival was celebrated on *Daśamī*, the 10th day of each half of every month. A record from Guṟṟaṁpāḍu, dated in Ś. 1453, mentions the gift of a *sunka* or toll-income of the place by *mahāmaṇḍalēśvara* Tirumalayya to god Kēśavaperumāḷ of the village, for conducting the *daśamī-mahōtsavas*, for the merit of his overlord, Salakarāju Tiṁmarāju.[55] Another, from Veludurti, dated in Ś. 1472, mentions the gift of taxes on *pēṇṭas* or markets or toll-income or *magama*, by Kunapuli Iṁmaḍi Basivi nāyuḍu. to god Cennarāya of the place for offering worship during the *daśāmi-mahōtsavas.*[56] A record dated in Ś. 1474, states that the 18 communities of the village of Koppara agreed to present to the Raghupati temple the grain consumed by each family on one day in the year, together with 2 *vis* of jaggery from each sugar cane mill, in order to conduct the *daśamī* festivals, in that temple.[57] In Ś. 1477, two devotees named Parvatayya and Anantayya, donated the *vipravinōdi-vartana* for the celebration of the *daśamī-mahōtsavas* of gods Cennakēśava and Hanumān of the village of Meḍiguḍidinne, in the *Gaṇḍikōta-sīma*, of *Chandragiri-rājyya*. The gift was made on the holy occasion of Śrī Rāma Navami.[58] An inscription from Īpūru, dated in Ś. 1496, mentions that the *Daśamī* services were conducted in the temple of god Allāḍanātha of the place.[59]

c. *Ekādaśī*

Ekādaśī, or the 11th day in each half of the every month, is an important tithi for all Vaiṣṇavas. It was therefore celebrated in many Viṣṇu temples. A record from the Tirumala temple, dated in Ś. 1458, mentions that offerings were made to god Śrī Vēnkaṭēśa of the place on each of the 25 *ēkādaśī* days, occurring in every year.[60] Another, from Jaladanki, dated in Ś. 1197, mentions the gift made to god Cennakēśavadēva of the place for the conduct of this festival.[61]

d. *Dvādaśī*

Dvādaśī or the 12th day of each half of the month was an equally important day. In Ś. 1412, offerings were made to god Śrī Venkaṭēśa of Tirumala on this day.[62]

e. *Kumāra-Punnami*

A record from Śrīkūrmam, dated in Ś. 1199, mentions the gift of land for conducting the *Kumāra-Punnami* festival for god Śrīkūrmanātha of the place by Siṣṭudēvuravutulu.[63]

55. 379 of 1938-39. Guṟṟampāḍu.
56. 295 of 1937-38. Veludurti.
57. 328 of 1915. Kopparam.
58. 346 of 1940-41. Mēḍidinne.
59. *S.I.I.* X. 747. Īpūru.
60. *T.T.D.I.* IV. 83. Tirumala.
61. *N.D.I.* II. Kāvali. 22. Jaladanki.
62. *T.T.D.I.* II. 91. Tirumala.
63. *S.I.I.* V. 1236. Śrīkūrmam.

f. *Suparṇōtsva-Paurṇami*

An inscription from Sekuru, dated in Ś. 1496, registers the gift of land for services on the day of the *Suparṇōtsava-paurṇami* festival celebrated for god Tiruvēnkaṭēśvara, at *Sangamasthāna*, by Krottipalli Venkaya.[64]

5. *Annual Festivals Celebrated on the Days of Particular Stars*

Like months, week days and *tithis* particular stars were also considered important and the days on which they were in the ascendence were considered festive days.

a. *Mūlam*

The day of the star *Mūla* was important at Tirumala and Tirupati. A festival was celebrated on this day in Ś. 1560, for god Gōvindarāja of Tirupati. Procession was conducted on the *Garuḍa-vāhanam* through the four inner streets in Tirupati on eleven days of the star Mulam in every year excluding the two days of the *Vaikāsi-Brahmōtsavam* and *Āṇi-Brahmōtsavam*. After the procession, *tirumanjanam* was given for the god and his Nāccimār.[65]

b. *Svāti*

The day of the *Svāti-nakṣatra* was significant in the Śrīkūrmam temple. An individual named Tīrthapādadāsa instituted a festival in Ś. 1161 to be conducted on the *Svātinakṣatram* day every month for god Śrīkūrmanātha of Śrīkūrmam.[66]

c. *Ārdra and Pūrvaphalguṇi*

The days of the stars *Ārdra* and *Pūrvaphalguṇi* were of particular importance at Drākshārāma. A record from the place dated in Ś. 1038, mentions the institution of the *Ārdra* festival for god Bhīmēśvara in the month of *Mārgaśira* and a festival for the goddess on the day of the *Pūrvaphalguṇi-nakṣatra*, in the month of *Āśvayuja*, by king Parāntaka.[67]

d. *Punarvasu*

The star *Punarvasu* was also considered important in the Tirumala and Tirupati temples. On the 13 days of the star, special offerings were made to god Śrī Venkaṭēśa, Śrī Rāma and other deities in Ś. 1458.[68] In Ś. 1468 it was celebrated for god Raghunātha enshrined in Tirupati in every month, *Punarvasu* being his birth-star.[69]

e. *Mṛgaśirṣa*

The day of the star *Mṛgaśira* was also of importance in the same temple. In Ś.

64. 162 of 1917. Śēkūru.
65. *T.T.D.I.* VI. 23. Tirupati.
66. *S.I.I.* V. 1303. Śrīkūrmam.
67. *S.I.I.* IV. 1214. Drākshārāma.
68. *T.T.D.I.* IV. 83. Tirumala.
69. *Ibid.*, IV. 82. Tirumala.

1458, on the 13 days of the star, in every year a festival was celebrated and special offerings were made to deities.[70]

f. *Śravaṇam*

The day of the star *Śravaṇam* was also a festival day in the temples of Tirumala and Tirupati. In Ś. 1459, *tirumanjanam* was conducted on every day of the star, in every month, being the birth-star of Śrī Venkaṭēśa.[71] A record from Tirupati, dated in Ś. 1469, mentions that arrangements were made for *Śravaṇa-tirumanjanam* to be conducted for god Śrī Janārdana Perumāḷ of Tirupati on the day of the *Śravaṇam* being his birth-star.[72]

g. *Uttiram*

The day of the star *Uttiram* or *Uttara* was also of special importance in the temple of Tirumala. A festival was celebrated in Ś. 1458, on the 13 days of the star occurring in every year for god Śrī Venkaṭēśa.[73]

h. *Viśākhā*

The day of the star *Viśākhā* was of special significance in the temple of Tirupati. A festival was celebrated on this day for god Gōvindarāja. In Ś. 1518 procession was conducted for the god while seated in *Pallayan-tulam* vehicle and his two consorts in palanquin, through the eight streets on seven days of the star *Viśākhā* yearly. After the procession, *tirumanjanam* was conducted for them while seated in a *maṇṭapam*.[74]

i. *Pūram*

This festival was celebrated on the day of the star *Pūram* which was the birth day of Āṇḍāl, enshrined in the precincts of the temple of god Gōvindarāja of Tirupati. On this occasion. provision was made in Ś. 1557, for offering to be made to the god and his consorts, while seated in a *maṇṭapam* in the temple of Lakṣmī-nārāyaṇa perumāḷ of Tirupati.[75]

6. *Annual Festivals Celebrated on Particular Week Days*

Like months, *tithis* and days of stars, particular days of the week were also celebrated in temples.

a. *Friday*

A record from Tirupati dated in Ś. 1519, states that an individual named Nārāyaṇa made provision for offerings to be made on all the 53 Fridays occurring in every year to god Śrī Venkaṭēśa and his consorts.[76]

70. *Ibid.*, IV. 83. Tirumala.
71. *Ibid.*, IV. 99. Tirumala.
72. *Ibid*, IV. 101. Tirupati.
73. *Ibid.*, IV. 83. Tirumala.
74. *Ibid.*, VI. 12. Tirupati.
75. *Ibid.*, VI. 22. Tirupati.
76. *Ibid.*, 20. Tirupati.

b. *Saturday*

A record from Pālakol, dated in Ś. 1238, states that a certain Rāyanārāyaṇa Cakravarti, the son of Upēndradēva Cakravarti, gifted three puttis of land for the celebration of the *Śanivāramahōtsava* or *Saturday*-festival in the *Śanivāra-maṇṭapa*, built by him for god Koppēśvaramahādēva of this place.[77]

c. *Sunday*

A certain Nārāyaṇa made provision, in order to propitiate the *utsava-mūrti* or procession image of Śrī Venkaṭēśa of Tirumala on all the 53 Sundays occurring in every year.[78] A gift of 25 *paṭṭi* of land was made to provide for extra offerings to god Kāḷahastīśvara of Kāḷahasti on Sundays by the residents of Kannanallūr in the *Poyagaināḍu*, a *dēvādāna* of Tirukkāḷatti-Uḍaiyar.[79]

7. *Festivals Celebrated on Ayanam Days* (*Sankrāntis*)

The day on which the sun entered each *rāsi* or division of the Zodiac was also considered auspicious and was celebrated.

a. *Ayana-Sankrānti*

A record from Tirumala, dated in the 14th year of the reign of Koppātra Mahēndra Panmār, states that provision was made by Samavai *alias* Kāḍavan Perundēvī, for the conduct of *tirumanjanam* on the two *Ayana-sankrāntis* and two *Viṣu-sankrānti* days for god Śrī Venkaṭēśa of Tirumala.[80]

b. *Sankramaṇam*

This *Sankramaṇam* festival was celebrated at Tirupati for god Śrī Gōvinda-perumāḷ in Ś. 1415. On this day the god was taken in procession through the streets. In Ś. 1414 provision was made for the conduct of *tirumanjanam* for the god.[81] The same festival was celebrated for Śrī Venkaṭēśa of Tirumala in Ś. 1395.[82]

c. *Uttarāyaṇa-Sankramaṇam*

In the 23rd year of the reign of the Cōḷa king, Rājarāja, arrangements were made for making offerings on each *Uttarāyaṇa-sankramaṇam* for god Nāyanār.[83]

d. *Ādi-Ayanam*

This festival had a double significance. Firstly, it denoted the commencement of the *Ḍakṣināyana* or the change of the sun from the northern to the southern half to the zodiac. Secondly, it denoted the commencement of the accounts year of the

77. *S.I.I.* V. 138. Pālakol.
78. *T.T.D.I.* VI. 20. Tirupati.
79. 157 of 1922. Kāḷahasti.
80. *T.T.D.I.* I. 8. Tirumala.
81. *Ibid.*, II. 91, 100. Tirupati.
82. *T.T.D.I.* II. 50. Tirumala.
83. *Ibid.*, I. 18. Yōgimallavaram.

temples. The *Āḍi-ayanam* festival was celebrated on the first day of the month of *Āḍi* and was also known as *Anivari-Āsthānam.* In Ś. 1414, this festival was celebrated in the temple of god Gōvindarāja of Tirupati.[84] In Ś. 1457, offerings were made to the god while he witnessed the opening of the new year accounts.[85] *Tirumanjanam* was conducted on this day in Ś. 1461, for the god, Nāccimār, Sēnai Mudaliyār and Śrī Sudarśana while seated in a *maṇṭapam.*[86]

This festival was also celebrated at Tirumala for god Śrī Venkaṭēśa in Ś. 1415 and the yearly accounts were started afresh on this day.[87] Provision was made in Ś. 1460, for making offerings to the god on this occasion.[88]

This festival was celebrated for god Viṭṭhala of Tirupati also in Ś. 1467 and *tirumanjanam* was conducted.[89] In the temple of god Raghunātha also this festival was celebrated in Ś. 1410 and *tirumanjanam* was conducted for him.[90]

e. *Makara-Samkranti*

This is same as the *Uttarāyaṇa.* This festival was celebrated on the day on which the sun enters the asterism *Makara* or Capricornus in the Tamil month of *Tai.* This festival was celebrated in the temples of Tirumala and Tirupati. The first mention of the celebration of this festival is recorded in an inscription from Tirupati dated in Ś. 1230.[91] Provision was made in Ś. 1389, for the celebration of this festival for god Śrī Gōvindarāja of Tirupati.[92] In Ś. 1416, *padiavēṭṭai* was conducted for this god, on this day.[93] The god, Nāccimār and Sēnai Mudaliyan were given *tirumanjanam* while seated in the *Tillaikkuvayattan-maṇṭapam* on this day in Ś 1452.[94] In S. 1467, the god proceeded to the *Āḷvār-tirtham* on this day.[95] In Ś. 1466, *tirumanjanam* was conducted and *āsthānam* was held in the *Lakṣmīdēvī-maṇṭapam.*[96]

This festival was celebrated in the temple of Śrī Venkaṭēśa of Tirumala, also in Ś. 1389. An *ardhōdaya* occurred on this day in S. 1470 and special offerings were made for the god on this day.[97]

This festival was celebrated for Gōvinda Kṛṣṇa in Ś. 1468 in the month of *Tai,*[98] and for god Vitthala in Ś. 1467, on this day, *tirumanjanam* was conducted.[99]

84. *Ibid.*, II. 95. Tirumala.
85. *Ibid.*, IV. 51. Tirumala.
86. *Ibid.*, IV. 135. Tirupati.
87. *Ibid.*, II. 115, 116. Tirumala, Tirupati.
88. *Ibid.*, IV. 130. Tirupati.
89. *Ibid.*, V. 66. Tirupati.
90. *Ibid.*, II. 88. Tirupati.
91. *Ibid.*, I. 98. Tirupati.
92. *Ibid.*, II. 30. Tirupati.
93. *Ibid.*, II. 127. Tirupati.
94. *Ibid.*, IV. 44. Tirupati.
95. *Ibid.*, IV. 66 Tirupati.
96. *Ibid.*, V. 29, 53. Tirupati.
97. *Ibid.*, II. 31, V. 121. Tirumala.
98. *Ibid.*, V. 82. Tirupati.
99. *Ibid.*, V. 66. Tirupati.

For god Acyuta Perumāḷ, *tirumanjanam* was conducted on this day in Ś. 1468.[100] For god Raghunātha also this festival was celebrated in Ś. 1410.[101]

f. *Cittirai-viṣu or Mēṣa-Samkrānti*

Cittirai-viṣu is celebrated on the first day of the Tamil month of *Cittrai.* This day is of particular importance because it denoted the entry of the sun into zodaical sign of *Mēṣa* or Aries.

This festival was celebrated in the temples of both Tirupati and Tirumala. *Tirumanjanam* was conducted for the deities and various kinds of offerings were made. The first mention of the celebration of this festival for Gōvindarāja is recorded in an inscription dated in Ś. 1230.[102] On this day *tirumanjanam* was conducted with sandal paste and oil. In Ś. 1415, the god was seated in the *Citrakūṭa-maṇṭapam* after the *tirumanjanam.*[103] In Ś. 1416, he was seated in the *Śrīkaraṇa-maṇṭapam.*[104] Articles required for *tirumanjanam* of the deities like oil and *candanam* were supplied in Ś. 1457. After the *tirumanjanam* they were seated in a *maṇṭapam* in a garden on this day.[105]

This festival was celebrated for god Raghunātha of Tirupati also in Ś. 1410.[106] A certain Īyūṇṇi Periya perumāḷ made arrangements in Ś. 1430 for the celebration of a festival for god on this day.[107] In Ś. 1439, offerings were made to god, his brother, Lakṣmaṇa and his consort, Sītā dēvī.[108]

This festival was celebrated for god Lakṣmīnārāyaṇa Perumāḷ in S. 1468. In the temple of god Viṭṭhala, this festival was conducted in Ś. 1467 and arrangements were made for *tirumanjanam.*[109]

In the temple of Śrī Venkaṭēśa of Tirumala, this festival was celebrated in S. 1466.[110]

g. *Arpasi-Viṣu*

This festival was celebrated on the day on which the Tamil month *Arpasi* began. It was celebrated in the temples of Raghunātha, Gōvindarāja and Viṭṭhala of Tirupati. It was celebrated for god Raghunātha in Ś. 1410,[111] for god Gōvindarāja in Ś. 1418, and for god Viṭṭhala in Ś. 1467.[112] *Tirumanjanam* was an important item in this festival.

100. *Ibid.*, V. 91. Tirupati.
101. *Ibid.*, II. 88. Tirupati.
102. *Ibid.*, I. 98. Tirupati.
103. *Ibid.*, II. 105. Tirupati.
104. *Ibid.*, II. 132. Tirupati.
105. *Ibid.*, IV. 39. Tirupati.
106. *Ibid.*, II. 88. Tirupati.
107. *Ibid.*, III. 12. Tirumala.
108. *Ibid.*, III. 118. Tirumala.
109. *T.T.D.I.* V. 66. Tirupati.
110. *Ibid.*, V. 38. Tirupati.
111. *Ibid.*, II. 88. Tirupati.
112. *Ibid.*, V. 66. Tirupati.

8. *Annual Festivals with Mythological Significance*

a. *Śri-Jayanti*

This festival, also known as *Śrī Jayanti, Janmāṣṭami* and *Gōkulāṣṭami* was celebrated popularly all over India. It is intended to commemorate the birth of Kṛṣṇa, the most popular of all the incarnations of Viṣṇu. There is an interesting mythology behind this incident. Kṛṣṇa was born on the 8th day of the dark half of the month of Srāvaṇa in a Jail in which his parents were confined. The children that preceded him were all killed by his uncle, Kamsa. Kṛṣṇa's father, Vāsudēva, smuggled the child to Gōkula, a cowherd colony and left him in the care of Nanda. This festival commemorates the birth of this great epic hero.

This festival was celebrated in many places like Tirumala, Tirupati, Śrīkūrmam and Siṁhāchalam. In the temple of god Gōvindarāja this festival has been in vogue since Ś. 1412.[113] For god Raghunātha also this festival was celebrated in Ś. 1410.[114]

In the temple of god Śrī Venkaṭēśa of Tirumala, this festival was celebrated from Ś. 1412.[115] In Ś. 1515 special *tirumanjanam* was conducted on this day.[116]

For god Varadarāja perumāḷ of Tirupati also this festival was celebrated in Ś. 1518, various kinds of offerings were made to the god and His consorts on this day.[117]

For god Śrī Kṛṣṇa of Tirupati this festival was celebrated in Ś. 1416. Offerings were made to him on this day at the time of his auspicious birth.[118]

In the temple of god Janārdana perumāḷ, this festival was celebrated in Ś. 1409. On this day, *tirumanjanam* was conducted for the god with gingelly oil, green gram and *candanam*.[119]

This festival was celebrated in the temple of Śrīkūrmanātha of Śrīkūrmam in S. 1168. One *gaṇḍa-māḍa* was gifted for the celebration of this festival.[120] In S. 1188, an ascetic, named Narahari tīrtha, granted a sum of three *māḍas* for the easy delivery of Dēvakīdēvī, the mother of Kṛṣṇa.[121]

For god Narasiṁhanātha of Siṁhāchalam also this festival was celebrated in Ś. 1209 and provision was made for its conduct.[122]

A record from Niṭṭūru, dated in S. 1472, mentions that gifts were made on the occasion of the *Kṛṣna-Jayanti* for god Cennakēśava of the place for *Bhāgavata-sēva* and *mantrapuṣpam* during worship.[123]

113. *Ibid.*, II. 91. Tirumala.
114. *Ibid.*, II. 96. Tirumala.
115. *Ibid.*, II. 88, 91. Tirupati.
116. *Ibid.*, VI. 10. Tirupati.
117. *Ibid.*, VI. 12. Tirupati.
118. *Ibid.*, II. 132. Tirupati.
119. *Ibid.*, V. 101. Tirupati.
120. *S.I.I.* V. 1310. Śrīkūrmam.
121. *Ibid.*, V. 1251, 1252. Śrīkūrmam.
122. *S.I.I.* VI. 896. Siṁhāchalam.
123. 23 of 1953-54. Niṭṭūru.

b. *Uri-Āḍi Festival*

Urai is a kind of rope bag and *āḍi* means playing with this. This festival was celebrated in commemoration of the childhood pranks of Śrī Kṛṣṇa. It was celebrated in the month of *Āvaṇi* on the day very next to the day of the *Śrī Kṛṣṇa Jayanti.* On this day pots decorated with colours and designs are hung in a rope bag, tied to one end of a rope, the other end being held by a man at a distance. A number of people gather there in order to catch the pots but the man holding the rope pulls the rope when the people try to catch the pots. This is an imitation of Kṛṣṇa's childhood pranks of jumping up and catching the pots filled with curds, milk and butter.

The first mention of this festival in the temple of god Gōvindarāja is recorded in an inscription dated in Ś. 1413. Arrangements were made in Ś. 1416, for making offerings to the god after his witnessing the *uri-āḍī.*[124] While Gōvindarāja was witnessing the *uri-āḍi* in Ś. 1455, offerings were made to Śrī Kṛṣṇa. A certain Kōyilkēḷvi-annan-Rāmānuja Jiyar made provision, in Ś. 1515 for the conduct of this festival for Gōvindarāja, his two consorts and Śrī Kṛṣṇa, in a *maṭham* situated in Tirupati.[125] This festival was instituted by Tāḷḷapākam Tirumallayyangār.[126]

For god Śrī Venkaṭēśa of Tirumala this festival was celebrated in Ś. 1452.[127] A certain Cina Tirumalayyangār made arrangements, in Ś. 1469, for the celebration of this festival at Tirumala. On this day bamboos were supplied by *Tiruppanipiḷḷai* for arranging the *uri-āḍi,* 100 silk cloths and 100 cloths for the decoration of the *uri*-tree. *Pañcāmṛtam*, fruits and cocoanuts were offered to the tree after the decoration.[128]

Tirumal Tātācārya made provision in Ś. 1505 for the celebration of this festival in front of his house.[129]

This festival was celebrated on a grand scale for god Śrī Kṛṣṇa at Tirumala. Its first mention is recorded in an inscription dated in Ś. 1413.[130] On this day, offerings were made to the god while he was seated on the outer pial of his shrine when he proceeded for an oil bath.[131] In Ś. 1457, oil-bath was arranged for the god while he was in the cradle arranged in the *Tirumāmaṇi-maṇṭapam* after the procession through the streets on this day.[132] A devotee, named Tiruvēngaḷappan, made provision in S. 1467 for the supply of butter to Śrī *Veṭṭaivadu* Kṛṣṇa in front of the *Rāmānujakūṭam* while going for *ennai-aḍal* or oil-bath on this day at Tirumala.[133] Turmeric powder was distributed among the devotees while Śrī Kṛṣṇa was going in procession through the streets.[134]

124. *T.T D.I.* II. 96, 127. Tirupati.
125. *Ibid.*, VI. 10. Tirupati, IV. 26. Tirumala.
126. *Ibid.*, VI. 122. Tirupati.
127. *Ibid.*, IV. Tirumala.
128. *Ibid.*, V. 99. Tirupati.
129. *Ibid.*, VI. 5. Tirumala.
130. *Ibid.*, II. 116. Tirupati.
131. *Ibid.*, II. 121. Tirupati.
132. *Ibid.*, IV. 46. Tirumala.
133. *Ibid.*, V. 47. Tirumala.
134. *Ibid.*, V. 60. Tirumala.

c. *Dīpāvaḷi*

The *Dīpāvaḷi*, festival is coupled with by another name *Naraka-Caturthi*, celebrated on the 14th and 15th days of the dark fortnight in the month of *Arpasi*. A demon, named Naraka, is said to have been destroyed by Śrī Kṛṣṇa on this day and the festival is intended to commemorate his victory. The word *dīpāvaḷi* means a row of lamps and it originated perhaps from the custom of illuminating villages on this festive occasion.

This festival was celebrated in the temples of both Viṣṇu and Śiva. This festival was in vogue in the temple of Śrī Venkaṭēśa of Tirumala, Śrī Gōvidarāja, Varadarāja, Viṭṭhala of Tirupati and Kṣirārāmēśvara of Pālakol. On this day, *tirumanjanam* was conducted for god Śrī Venkaṭēśa and his body was smeared with sandal and was decorated with one moon-shaped full round flower-garland and taken in procession.[135] In Ś. 1468, Appaḷḷāṇḍār made provision for this festival occurring in the month of *Arpasi*.[136]

In Ś. 1413, arrangements were made for the conduct of *tirumanjanam*, for god Gōvindarāja and his consorts and the deities were smeared with sandal and taken in procession and decorated with one moon-shaped full round flower garland.[137] In Ś. 1416, numerous lights were lit on this occasion in the month of *Kārtika*.[138]

For god Varadarāja of Tirupati, this festival was celebrated in Ś. 1518. Offerings were made to him and to his consorts on this day.[139] In Ś. 1467, this festival was celebrated also for Viṭṭhalēśvarasvāmi. On this day *tirumanjanam* was conducted and lights were lit.[140]

A record from Pālakol, dated in Ś. 1218, mentions that, land was given for the celebration of this festival for god Koppēśvaramahādēva of the place, by Udayamahādēvī, the queen of Kōna Gaṇapatidēva.[141] Another, from the same place, dated in Ś. 1238, states that provision was made for the celebration of this festival for the same god by Rāyanārāyaṇa Cakravarti, the son of Upēndradēva Cakravarti.[142]

d. *Śrīrāma Navami*

Śrīrāmanavami is the anniversary of the birth of the Śrī Rāma, the seventh incarnation of Viṣṇu. It is celebrated in the month of *Caitra* on the ninth day of the bright fortnight when the asterism *Punarvasu* is in the ascendence. This festival was celebrated in temples of Śrī Rāma, Gōvindarāja and Gōpālakṛṣṇa of Tirupati and Śrī Venkaṭēśa and Narasiṁha of Tirumala.

The first instance of the celebration of this festival in the temple of Śrī Rāma is recorded in an inscription dated in Ś. 1416. On this day, offerings were made to the god at the shrine of Hanumān immediately after his arrival there after a procession

135. *Ibid.*, II. 94. Tirumala.
136. *T.T.D.I.* V. 82. Tirupati.
137. *Ibid.*, II. 94. Tirumala.
138. *Ibid.*, II. 127. Tirupati.
139. *Ibid.*, VI. 12. Tirupatti.
140. *Ibid.*, V. 66. Tirupati.
141. *S.I.I.* V. 125. Pālakol.
142. *Ibid.*, V. 138. Pālakol.

was arranged through the streets.[143] Offerings were made in Ś. 1439, to god Raghunātha at the *maṇṭapam* after the *Yāmajāgara-vṛata* (keeping the vigil during the night) along with his brother, Lakṣmaṇa and consort, Sītā on this day.[144] In Ś. 1462 Śrī Rāma, Sītā and Lakṣmaṇa were seated on a swing on this day. After the swing they were taken to the *maṇṭapam* and seated in it.[145]

This festival was also celebrated for god Gōvindarāja of Tirupati in S. 1468.[146] A certain individual made provision in Ś. 1557 for offerings during this festival. On this day, offerings were prepared in the temple kitchen of Śrī Gōvindarāja and offered to Śrī Cakravarti Tirunaṁganār or Śrī Rāma.[147]

It was also celebrated for god Śrī Venkaṭēśa of Tirumala in Ś. 1426.[148] Offerings were made in Ś. 1470 to god Śrī Periya Perumāḷ.[149] For Aḷagiya-Singar or Narasiṁha, enshrined within the temple of Śrī Venkaṭēśa of Tirumala also this festival was celebrated in Ś. 1415.[150]

In Ś. 1476, the *vipravinōdins* presented the *vartana* paid to them year after year by the *mahājanas* of Kōvilkunṭḷa for the Śrīrāma-Jayanti festival of god Pāṇḍaranga of the place.[151]

e. *Rāmāyaṇa-Pattābhiṣēkam Festival*

This festival was obviously celebrated in order to commemorate the return of Śri Rāma, to his capital, Ayōdhyā, accompanied by his monkey allies and his coronation at the capital. Venkaṭaṁman, the resident of Cinnahōttūr, near Vijayanagaram, arranged in S. 1536, for the celebration of the *Rāmāyaṇa-Paṭṭābhiṣēkam* festival at Tirumala. This festival was celebrated on the day next to that of the *Śrī Rāma Navami* festival, combined with the star *Pūsam*, being the 10th day of the bright fortnight of the month of the *Phālguna*. On this day, *tirumanjanam* was conducted for the processional image and his consorts, to Śrī Rāma, Sītā, Lakṣmaṇa, Sēnai Mudaliyār, Hanumān, Sugrīva and Angada, while seated in the *Veṇṛumalaiyiṭṭanmaṇṭapam*. It is interesting to note that during the course of this festival, the *Vāyupurāṇam* was recited and various kinds of offerings were made to the deities.[152]

f. *Gajēndra-Mōkṣam Festival*

This festival was obviously intended for the commemoration of an event which figures popularly in Viṣṇava mythology, embodied in the *Śrīmadbhagavata*. In the garden of *Ritumat*, on the mountain *Trikūṭa* to which Gajēndra, the lord of

143. *T.T.D.I.* II. 133. Tirumula.
144. *Ibid.*, III. 118. Tirumala.
145. *Ibid.*, IV. 157. Tirumala.
146. *Ibid.*, V. 82. Tirupati.
147. *Ibid.*, V. 22. Tirupati.
148. *Ibid.*, III. 3. Tirumala.
149. *Ibid.*, V. 121. Tirumala.
150. *Ibid.*, II. 101. Tirumala.
151. 694 of 1917. Kōvelakuṇṭla.
152. *T.T.D.I.* VI. 18. Tirumala.

elephants, repaired one day to quench its thirst. As soon as it got down into the water, a crocodile caught hold of one of the legs of the elephant. For a long time, the elephant struggled to liberate itself from the crocodile but was unsuccessful. At last, with a lotus flower in its trunk it began to praise Viṣṇu and so besought his help. Pleased with the prayers of the elephant, Viṣṇu appeared on the scene at once and killed the crocodile with his *cakra* and saved Gajēndra.

In Ś. 1461, one of the Tirumala temple accountants made provision for the celebration of *Gajēndra-mōkṣam* festival in Tirupati. *Ankurārpaṇam* was conducted for the commencement of the festival, the *hōmam* was made and a sacred thread was tied to the god's wrist. After this, *snapana-tirumanjanam* was conducted for Gōvindarāja, Nāccimār, Sēnai Mudaliyār and Śrī Sudarśana while seated in a *manṭapam* and flower garlands were supplied for the god, for his vehicle, Garudāḷvār and for his elephant devotee, Gajēndrāḷvar. The *manṭapam* in which they were seated was decorated. The *Gaēnjdra-mōkṣa-ślōkas* were recited. Procession was conducted through the eight streets on *Garuḍavāhanam.*[153]

g. *Tulaśī-Mahātmyam Festival*

This special festival was instituted by Bhūlōkan an accountant of the temple of Gōvindarāja at Tirupati, in Ś. 1514. The *Tulaśī* or ocimum sanctum plant is most sacred for Viṣṇu and it has a mythological significance contained in the *Tulaśī Mahātmyam.* The festival was celebrated on the day of the *dvādaśī* next to the day which followed the *Mukkōṭi-ēkādaśī* during the Tamil month of *Mārgaḷi.*

During this festival god Gōvindarāja was taken out in a procession and a special bath or *tirumanjanam* was given to him with oil, *candanam* and *kalabha candanam.* On this occasion the *Tulaśī-Mahātmyam* and *Prabhandham* were recited before the god.[154]

h. *Vaikuṇṭha-Ekādaśī*

The *Vaikuṇṭha Ekādaśī* otherwise known as *Mukkōṭi Ekādaśī* festival is celebrated on the eleventh day of the bright fortnight in the month of *Mārgaśira* or *Mārgaḷi.*

This festival has an interesting mythological significance. It is stated that on one occasion a demon, named Mura, harassed the gods. Unable to bear this, the gods went to *Vaikuṇṭha* and sought the protection of Viṣṇu. There upon Viṣṇu came down to the earth on an *ēkādaśī* day and killed the demon. Hence this day came to be known as *Vaikuṇṭha ēkādaśī.* The word *mukkōṭi* means three crores. The god is said to have been accompanied by three crores of deities when he came down to the earth on this day. Hence the day came to be known as *Mukkṭōi-ēkādaśī.*

i. *Mārgaḷi-Tirudvādaśī* (*Mukkōṭi-festival*)

This festival, so named because it occurs in the Tamil month of *Mārgaḷi,* immediately after the *Mukkōti-ēkādaśi.* It is known as the *Mukkōṭi-dvādaśī* festival.

153. *Ibid.,* IV. 135. Tirupati.
154. *Ibid.,* VI. 9. Tirupati.

It was celebrated in the temples of Gōvindarāja of Tirupati and Śrī Venkaṭēśa and Śrī Varāhasvāmi of Tirumala. The first mention of this festival in the temples of Tirumala and Tirupati occurs in a record dated in the 14th year of Koppātra Mahēndra Panmār.[155] Samavai arranged for the celebration of the *Mārgaḷi-tirudvādaśī* for the image of Maṇavāṭa Perumāḷ *alias* Śrī Venkaṭēśvara.[156] In Ś. 1413, the deity was seated in a *maṇṭapam* on this day[157] and 32 lights were lit on the bank of the *Svāmi-puṣkariṇi*.[158] In Ś. 1465, god Śrī Venkaṭēśa, Nāccimār and Tiruvaḷi-Āḷvan were taken out in a procession and seated in the front *maṇṭapam* at the shrine of Gnanappiran or Śrī Varahāsvāmi after Śrī Sudarśana's bath in the holy tank, named the *Svāmi·Puṣkariṇi*, in the early morning.[159] In the same year provision was made for the conduct of *tirumanjanam* with oil, *candanam*, milk, honey and curds. After the *tirumanjanam* the deities were decorated with *candanam* musk and refined camphor.[160]

This festival was also celebrated for god Śrī Varāhasvāmi at Tirumala. Offerings were made to this god in Ś. 1464, while Tiruvali-Āḷvan was bathing in the holy tank of the *Svāmi Puṣkaṛiṇi* on this day.[161]

For god Gōvindarāja this festival was celebrated from Ś. 1415. A record of S. 1466, mentions the details about this festival. On the morning of this day procession was conducted through streets with the god seated on *Garuḍavāhanam* along with his two consorts on palanquin accompanied by Sēnai Mudaliyār of Śrī Viśvakśēna seated on a palanquin. After the procession they were seated in the Lakṣmīdēvī *maṇṭapam* and *tirumanjanam* was conducted and offerings were made.[162]

j. *Utthāna-Ekādaśī*

This festival is celebrated on the 11th lunar day of the bright fortnight of the lunar month *Kārtika*. This festival was succcded by *Utthāna-Dvādaśī*.

In Ś. 1412 this festival was celebrated for god Gōvindarāja of Tirupati in Ś. 1412. Procession was arranged through the streets for this god.[163]

For god Venkatatturaivar or *Ugra* Śrīnivāsasvāmi of Tirumala also this festival was celebrated in Ś. 1452.[164]

k. *Utthāna-Dvādaśī*

On this day god Viṣṇu is believed to wake up to activity after his four months repose. This festival is also known as *Kaiśika-dvāadśi* and *Kāiśikapurāṇam* festival. It is celebrated on the 12th lunar day of the bright fortnight of the lunar month of *Kārtika*. It is celebrated only in the Vaiṣṇava temples. In Ś. 1351, this festival was

155. *Ibid.*, I. 9. Tirumala.
156. *Ibid.*, I. 9. Tirumala.
157. *Ibid.*, II. 96. Tirumala.
158. *Ibid.*, IV. 129. Tirumala.
159. *Ibid.*, V. 8. Tirumala.
160. *Ibid.*, V. 10. Tirumala.
161. *Ibid.*, V. 5, 64. Tirumala.
162. *Ibid.*, II. 116, V. 29. Tirupati,
163. *T.T.D.I.* II. 91. Tirumala,
164. *Ibid.*, IV. 6. Tirumala,

celebrated for god Śrī Venkaṭēśa of Tirumala. Incense and civet were smeared to the body of the god, during this festival.[165] Offerings were made to him on this day in Ś. 1415 immediately after hearing the reading of the *Kaiśikapurāṇam*.[166] A devotee, named Tirumala Kumāra Tātācāryar, made provision in S. 1505 for the celebration of this festival. The recitation of *Kaiśikapurānam* was arranged on this day.[167]

This festival was also celebrated in the temple of god Gōvindarāja of Tirupati in Ś. 1412. On this day, procession through the streets was conducted for the god.[168] Arrangements were made by Kṛṣṇamangai, for making offerings to god after hearing the recitation of the *Kaiśikapurāṇam* on this day in his temple.[169]

For god Gōpālakṛṣṇan also this festival was celebrated in Ś 1468. An Annaciyār made provision in Ś. 1468, for the celebration of this festival occurring in the month of *Kārtika*.[170]

In the temple of god Raghunātha also this festival was celebrated in Ś. 1467. On this day, the recitation of *Kaiśikapurāṇam* was arranged.[171]

This festival was celebrated for god Śrī Narasiṁha in Ś. 1452,[172] in the month of *Kārtika* and the recitation of *Kaiśikapurāṇam* was arranged.[173]

In Ś. 1483, land was given on the day of the *Utthāna-dvādaśi* to god Cennakēśavadēvā of Miḍutūru by *Daḷavāyi* Bhadri nāyaniṁgāru for the merit of his father, Ciddela Boṁminēḍu.[174]

k. *Mahānavāmi*

This festival was celebrated for god Raghunātha in Ś. 1410.[175] Provision was made in Ś. 1270, for the celebration of the navaratri festival in the month of Asvayuja for god Śrī Āndhra-rāmalingasvāmi of a temple in the *Podila-sima*, by the famous Vijayanagara king, Acyutarāya.[176]

l. *Vijaya-Daśamī Festival*

This festival was celebrated on the day next to that of Śrī Lakṣmīdēvī festival in the Tamil month of *Puraṭṭāsi*. It was conducted in commemoration of the successful termination of the *ajñātavāsa* of the Pāṇḍavas. On this day, the *śami* (prosppis-spicegera) tree was worshipped. This is the tree on which the Pāṇḍavas deposited their weapons while they were serving king Virāṭa *in cognito*. This festival was celebrated for god Gōvindarāja of Tirupati and Śrī Venkaṭēśa of Tirumala. This

165. *Ibid.*, I. 192. Tirumala.
166. *Ibid.*, II. 115. Tirumala.
167. *Ibid.*, VI. 5. Tirumala.
168. *Ibid.*, II. 91. Tirumala.
169. *Ibid.*, V. 40. Tirupati.
170. *Ibid.*, V. 82. Tirupati.
171. *Ibid.*, V. 60. Tirumala.
172. *Ibid.*, IV. 6. Tirumala.
173. *Ibid.*, IV. 46. Tirumala.
174. 413 of 1926. Miḍuṭūru.
175. *T.T.D.I.* II. 88. Tirupati.
176. *N.D.I.* I. C.P. 23. Kūchipūḍi.

festival is also known as the *Vannimaram* festival. In Ś. 1515, a certain Nārāyaṇar made arrangements for the celebration of this festival for god Gōvindarāja. During this festival *Āsthānam* was conductrd and various kinds of offerings were made to the god and his consorts while seated in a *maṇṭapam*, decorated with flowers.[177] The accountants of Rāmāpuram made provision in Ś. 1518, for offerings to god while seated in a *maṇṭapam* situated in the village on the way to the Rāmāpuram garden.[178]

This festival was celebrated for god Śrī Venkaṭēśa of Tirumala in Ś. 1457. Offerings were made to him while he was worshipping the *śami* tree.[179]

m. *Śivarātri*

Śivarātri is celebrated only in Śiva temples. It is celebrated on the night of the 14th day of the dark half of the month of *Māgha* in honour of Śiva, one of the Hindu Trinity.

The significance of the festival lies in the fact that god Śiva originated from the primeval linga on this day. So it came to be known as *Śivarātri.*

There is an interesting story connected with this *Śivarātri.* On one occasion, Viṣṇu asserted his greatness as the sustainer of the world and Brahmā also did so on the ground that he was its creator. While the two were engaged in this dispute there appeared a linga resembling the great cosmic fire, with hundreds of tongues of flames flazing out of it. Stopping their quarrels Brahmā and Viṣṇu decided to find out the origin and end of this huge pillar. The former assumed the form of a swan or *haṁsa* and flew up in the air in order to find out the top while the latter took the form of a boar or *varāha* and burrowed into the earth in order to find out the bottom. The attempt of these two proved futile. Thus humiliated they went to the pillar and began to praise it. Pleased with their prayers Śiva manifested himself in the body of this fiery linga on this *Śivarātri* day.

A record from Pālakol dated in Ś. 1218, mentions that, land was given for the celebration of the *Śivarātri* by Udayamahādēvī for the merit of her husband, Kōna Gaṇapatidēva and of herself, to god Kṣīrārāmēśvara of the place.[179] Another from Mōkṣaguṇḍam, dated in Ś. 1691, states that one *kuṁcam* of land was granted to god Sāṁbaśiva of the place by Tāḍicherla Venkaṭanarasu for the celebration of this festival.[180] In Ś. 1326, on the *Śivarātri* day, the Vijayanagara king, Harihara, presented a *maṇṭapa* to god Mallikārjuna of Śrīśailam.[181] In Ś. 1327, in the reign of the Vijayanagara king, Dēvarāya, the king confirmed the grant of the village of Tṁmaḍiyarahaḷḷi and of the *kānika* money realised on the days of *Śivarātri* to the temple of Mallikārjuna of Chandragiri, previously made by Kampana Oḍeya and Cikka Oḍeya.[182] A record dated in Ś. 1321, states that while Muktiśāntabikṣavṛtti was ruling as the pontiff of Śrīśailam, the *Dēvarakōṇḍapekkaṇḍru* and other guilds came

177. *Ibid.*, VI. 12. Tirupati.
178. *Ibid.*, IV. 69, 149, 157. Tirumala.
179. *S.I.I.* V. 125. Pālakol.
180. 256 of 1949-50. Mokshaguṇḍam.
181. 11 of 1915. Śrīśailam.
182. 313 of 1922. Kāḷahasti.

to Śrīśailam, for the *Śivarātri* festival and donated *mūlavisamu* on *perikalu* to god Mallikārjuna of the place.[183] Another from Srīśailam, dated in Ś. 1370, mentions the gift of fees by a merchant guild for the conduct of the *Śivarātri* festival in the temple of god Mallikārjuna of the place.[184] In Ś. 1483, a certain *Daḷavāyi* Bhadri nāyaka endowed land to god Cenna Mallikārjunadēva of Śrīgiri for the maintenance of a *satra* for the pilgrims visiting the place at the time of this festival.[185] In Ś. 1484, ten *māḍas* of gold levied on the members of the Vīra Śaiva community for a lamp in the temple of Vīrabhadra at Neṁmikallu on the occasion of the *Śivarātri.*[186] The Reddi king Kōmaṭivēma, gave the village of Pinapāḍu on the occasion of the *Śivarātri* before Śrīparvata to Śankara.[187]

n. *Dahanadēvara-utsava*

This festival was celebrated in honour of the burning of three cities by Śiva. There is an interesting mythology connected with this festival. On one occasion Śiva killed three *asuras* who dwelt in three forts constructed of metals and who caused great damage to the *Suras* and *Ṛṣis*. The *dēvas* approached Brahmā to consult him as to the means of destroying these *asuras* and the latter told them that they could only be killed with a single arrow and such a weapon could be wielded by Śiva and directed them to pray to him for help. They prayed accordingly and succeeded inducing Śiva to undertake the task of killing the *asuras*. The gods served Śiva in their own capacities. Viṣṇu became his arrow, Agni its barb and Yama its feather. Śiva made the *Vēdas* his bow and Sāvitri the bow-string. Brahmā became his charioteer. With the three barbed arrow consisting of Sōma, Agni and Viṣṇu the castles with their inhabitants were burnt by Śiva. So he came to be known as Tripurāntakamūrti. Hence this festival came to be known as *Tripuradahana-utsava* or the festival commemorating the burning of the three cities. A record from Tripurāntakam contains the gift of a forest for the celebration of *tripuradahana-dēvara-utsava* for god Tripurāntaka by Srī Viśvēśvaradēva.[188]

c. *Yugādi*

The *Yugādi* means the commencement of a *Yuga* or epoch. According to Hindu belief, there are four *yugas* i.e., *kṛta*, *trētā*, *dvāpara* and *kali*. Brahmā, the creator of this world, is supposed to have created this world on a particular day on which *Kali Yuga* commenced. This festival commemorates that day.

This festival is celebrated in temples with grandeur. It was celebrated in the temple of Śrī Venkaṭēśa of Tirumala and Śrī Gōvindarāja and Śrī Gōpāla Kṛṣṇa of Tirupati.

It has been in vogue since Ś. 1413 at Tirumala. During this festival the god was decorated with a full round flower garland of the shape of the full moon.[189] On

183. Mack. Colln. 15-3-2 P.25.
184. 40 of 1915. Śrīśailam.
185. 414 of 1926. Miḍaṭūru.
186. 686 of 1919. Nēmakallu.
187. *E.I.* XXI. pp. 267-277. Pinapāḍu.
188. *S.I.I.* X. 340. Tripurāntakam.

this day, *tirumanjanam* was conducted for him, Nāccimār and Sēnai Mudaliyār while seated in a *manṭapam*.[190] One of the temple councillors arranged in Ś. 1515, for holding an *āsthānam* or *durbar*.[191] The god was seated in the *Tirumāmaṇi-manṭapam* on this day and received offerings.[192]

For god Gōvindarāja of Tirupati, this festival was celebrated from Ś. 1413. On this day the god was decorated with a full round flower garland of the shape of the moon.[193] The god was taken in procession on *Tirucci* vehicle while Nāccimār accompanied him seated in palanquin in Ś. 1515.[194]

This festival was also celebrated for god Śrī Gōpālakṛṣṇa in Ś. 1468 in the month of *Panguṇi*.[195]

p. *Bhōgi*

The *Bhōgi* festival is observed on the last day of the *dakṣiṇāyana* or the period of the sun's progress from the northern solstice to the south. It is celebrated in honour of Indra, the god of Heavens and the controller of the clouds. There is an interesting myth attached to the festival also. In the *Dvāparayuga*, Lord Kṛṣṇa deserved to teach Indra a lesson since he was found to be rather arrogant. So he prevailed upon the *Yādavas*, his followers of *Bṛndāvan*, to offer sacrifices to the mountain Gōvardhana instead of the Indra on *Bhōgi-Paṇḍuga* day, stating that they were not agriculturists to care for the seasonal rains of Indra but were cowherds depending on the mountain Gōvardhana which afforded rich pasturage for their cattle. When Indra saw that he was balked of his legitimate offerings by the machinations of Śrī Kṛṣṇa, he grew angry and wanted to punish the *Yādavas* for listening to the evil advice of Kṛṣṇa. Induced by their master, the clouds began to rain heavily on the territory of the *Yādavas*, who, terrified at the severity of the rain, hastened to Śrī Kṛṣṇa and solicited his help. Kṛṣṇa thereupon lifted up the mountain Gōvardhana and held it aloft. The *Yādavas* with their cattle and other belongings took shelter under the mountain. Indra ordered the clouds to desist, recognised lord Viṣṇu in Śrī Kṛṣṇa and repented for his folly. Śrī Kṛṣṇa also relented and permitted the *Yādavas* to resume the old custom of celebrating the *Bhōgi* festival in honour of Indra.

This festival was celebrated in some temples. But very meagre information is available about this festival. In Ś. 1457, this festival was celebrated for Āṇḍāḷ Sūḍikkodutta-Nācciyār in the Gōvindarājasvāmi temple at Tirupati while seated in the *Śrīkaraṇa-manṭapam* after alighting from the temple car on this day, occurring previous to *Makara-Sankramaṇam* day during the *Mārgaḷi-nirāṭṭam* festival.[196]

q. *Ratha-Saptami*

Rath-Saptami is the seventh day after the *Yugādi* on which day the movement

189. *T.T.D.I.* II. 94. Tirumala.
190. *Ibid.*, V. 23. Tirumala.
191. *Ibid.*, VI. 10. Tirupati.
192. *Ibid.*, VI. 56. Tirumala.
193. *Ibid.*, II. 94. Tirumala.
194. *Ibid.*, VI. 10, Tirupati.
195. *Ibid.*, V. 82. Tirupati.
196. *Ibid.*, IV. 51. Tirumala.

of the sun in horizon is supposed to take tilt, if it is to the south it is *Dakṣiṇāyaṇa*, if it is to the north it is *Uttarāyaṇa.*

This festival was celebrated on the seventh day of the bright fortnight in the month of *Māgha*, known also as *Tai* when the sun is in the *Makara*. Some call it *Maghā-Saptami* deriving the name from the month in which it is considered auspicious. The word *Saptami* is derived from the Sanskrit word *Sapta* means seven and consequently the expression *Maghā-Saptamī* is taken to mean the seventh day of the car. Some people call it *Jayanti Saptami* which means the victorious seventh day after the full moon day and that going by the name *Mahāsaptami* which means the great seventh day in the fortnight. The name *Jaya-Saptami* originated perhaps from the belief that the observance of this festival brings success in all undertakings and the other.

This festival was celebrated in the temples of Tirupati, Tirumala and Moyiḷḷa-ceruvu. A record dated in Ś. 1459, states that arrangements were made for the celebration of the *Ratha Saptami* festival on the day of the *saptami* falling in the bright fortnight in the month of *Tai*. On this day *tirumanjanam* was conducted for god Gōvindarāja, Nāccimār and Sēnai Mudaliyār in the *Citrakūṭa-maṇṭapam*. After the *tirumanjanam* they were decorated with squeezed *candanam* and perfumed *candanam*. Procession was also conducted with *Sūryaprabhā* and other vehicles through the eight streets.[197]

For god Śrī Viṭṭhalēśvarasvāmi of Tirupati, this festival was celebrated in Ś. 1467 and *tirumanjanam* was conducted for this god with oil, green gram and *candanam*.[198]

It was celebrated for god Śrī Venkaṭēśa of Tirumala in Ś. 1466. Arrangements were made in Ś. 1485 for the celebration of this festival by Karaṇīkkan-Applayyan. On this day, *suddhi-ankurārpaṇam* was conducted and Brahmā sēnāpati was installed. In the early morning, a procession of Tiruvaḷi Āḷvan was arranged. After that, *hōmam* was made and *tirumanjanam* was conducted for the god and Nāccimār. *Candanam* was applied to the god's body, musk for the *tirunāmam* on his face. Various kinds of offerings were made to the god while seated on the *Sūryaprabhā* vehicle in the early morning, during the procession through the streets. *Cūrṇābhiṣēkam* or *abhiṣēka* with turmeric and sandal powder was conducted for the god, Nāccimār and Cakrattāḷvan while seated in the *Tirumāmaṇi-maṇṭapam*. After this, the god and Nāccimār were taken in *Bhavāni* or grand procession. After the *tīrthavāri* procession both of them were seated in the *Tirumāmaṇi-maṇṭapam*. They were taken on a procession in the right on the *Vaikuṇṭha vimānam*. After alighting from the *vāhanam*, they were propitiated with bed chamber offering.[199]

A record from Moyiḷḷacheruvu, dated in Ś. 1470, mentions the gift of taxes to god Cennakēśava of the place for services on this day in the temple.[200]

197. *Ibid.*, IV. 118. Tirupati.
198. *Ibid.*, V. 66. Tirupati.
199. *Ibid.*, V. 173. Tirumala.
200. 253 of 1937-38. Moyiḷḷacheṛuvu.

9. *Annual Festivals Without Mythological Significance*

a. *Adhyayanōtsvam*

The *Adhyayanōtsavam* is one of the important festivals, celebrated particularly in Vaiṣṇava temples, in the month of *Mārgaḷi*. *Adhyayana* means study and like human individuals the gods are also supposed to study the sacred texts. *Vēdapārāyaṇa* and the recitation of the Tamil *Prabhandham* during this festival, as evidenced by inscriptions, confirms this definition of the nature of this festival.

Numerous inscriptions indicate that this festival was celebrated in the temples of Śrī Venkaṭēśa of Tirumala and Gōvindarāja, Varadarāja and Lakṣmīnārāyaṇa perumāḷ of Tirupati.

The earliest mention of this festival, celebrated at Tirupati, is in a record dated in Ś. 1312 or 1390 A.D. and at Tirumala in an inscription dated in Ś. 1413 or 1491 A.D. The festival was divided into two equal halves, the earlier 10 days forming the first half or *pagalpattu* i.e., day time part and the latter 10 days forming the second half or *irā-pattu* i.e., night time part. The duration of the festival varied from a minimum of ten days to a maximum of 25 days. A record dated in Ś. 1312 mentions the provision made for the supply of the articles necessary for tbe festival. The *tiruppāvai* was sung on each of the ten days and the *Sāttumurai* was celebrated on the last day of this festival.[201] A devotee, named Nallār Angaṇḍai, made arrangements in Ś. 1407, for the celebration of this festival commencing on the day of *Iyalpa* and ending on the *Nuṟṟandāḍi* for god Gōvindarāja.[202] In Ś. 1430, during this festival, the god was seated in a *maṇṭapam* within the shrine of Kulaśēkharāḷvār.[203] The famous Vaiṣṇava teacher, Kandāḍai Rāmānujayyangār, made arrangements in Ś. 1452 for the celebration of this festival.[204] According to a record dated in Ś. 1457, offerings were made to god Gōvindarāja while seated in a *maṇṭapam* on the bank of the *puṣkarini* on the day of the commencement of the festival, on the 6th day, on the *Sāttumurai* day on the *Nuṟṟandāḍi* day.[205] In Ś. 1465, the god and Nāccimār went to the shrine of Nammāḷvār from the *Tillaikkuvattyan-maṇṭapam* after hearing the *Kanninunsiruttaṁbu-prabhandham* as *Kanninun-sirut-tambu-sirappu* on the 11th day of the latter ten days of the festival.[206] We learn from an inscription, dated in Ś. 1468, that the god and his consorts were decorated with 74 cloths and seated in the *Lakṣmīdēvī-maṇṭapam* on the day of the *Nuṟṟandāḍi*.[207]

The *Adhyayanōtsavam* was also celebrated at Tirumala for god Tiruvēnkaṭa-muḍaiyān or Śrī Venkaṭēśa during the Tamil month of *Mārgaḷi*. A record dated in Ś. 1413 mentions the practice of repairing the pathway to the sacred waterfall, Ākāśagangā, during this festival.[208] The practice of taking the god to the *Sokkara-*

201. *T.T.D.I.* I. 183. Tirumala.
202. *Ibidi.*, II. 83. Tirupati.
203. *Ibid.*, III. 15. Tirumala.
204. *Ibid.*, IV. 3. Tirumala.
205. *Ibid.*, IV. 71. Tirupati.
206. *Ibid.*, V. 7. Tirupati.
207. *Ibid.*, V. 67. Tirupati.
208. *Ibid.*, II. 95. Tirumala.

koḍi and seating him in a *manṭapam* near the corner of the *prākāra* on his return seems to have introduced in Ś. 1415.[209] An interesting item of this festival, whose duration was reduced to 20 days in Ś. 1415, was the *Aḍaiyavalam* celebration including the *tiruvāymoḷi-sāttumurai.*[210] In Ś. 1426, this festival was celebrated for 24 days, commencing on the day of *Iyalpatuvvākkam* and ending on the day of *tanniramudu-tiruttanal.*[211] One record states that the god was seated in the *Periya-tirumanṭapam* on the day of the *Iyalpa-sirappu* during this festival.[212] The practice of singing the *Kilaroli-ilamai-tiruvāyṁoḷi* on the 12th day of this festival was introduced in Ś. 1441.[213] The duration of this festival was increased to 24 days in Ś. 1452 and 25 days in Ś. 1458.[214] In Ś. 1465, the god and Nāccimār were seated in the *Tirumāmaṇi-manṭapam*, specially decorated for the occasion, and heard the recitation of *Kanninun-siruttaṁbu-Prabhandham* of Madhurakavi Āḷvār, on the 11th day of the festival.[215] In Ś. 1466, arrangements were made for making offerings by a religious teacher, named Ānandaṁpiḷḷai Ayyangār, on the day of *Kanninun-siruttaṁbu* festival.[216] A function, named *Kilaroli-ilamaisirappu*, involving the decoration of the deity with garlands and the offering of a rose water vessel on the 2nd day of the latter 10 days of the festival, was introduced in Ś. 1469.[217]

The *Adhyayanōtsavam* was also celebrated for god Raghunātha of Tirupati in Ś. 1429.[218] *Vēdaparāyaṇam* was gone through during the 12 days of the festival.[219] The god was taken out in procession on the 6th festival day and offerings were made on the 12th day which was the day of the *Sāttumuṛai.*[220]

This festival was also celebrated for god Śrī Varadarāja-perumāḷ for 12 days from Ś. 1469[221] and for Lakṣmīnārāyaṇaperumāḷ of Tirupati in Ś. 1557.[222]

b. *Tirupavitra-tirunāḷ or Pavitrōtsava*

The *Pavitrōtsavam* was celebrated for expiating for all the omissions and commissions made during the daily worship or during the festivals. It was celebrated in both Vaiṣṇava and Śaiva temples. We come to know of the celebration of this festival in the Tirumala temple first in Ś. 1385. The duration of the festival was five days, but it was reduced to four days in Ś. 1430 but was increased to five days in Ś. 1452.

The *Pavitrōtsavam* was celebrated in the month of *Āvaṇi* for god Śrī Venkaṭēśa

209. *Ibid.*, II. 109. Tirumala.
210. *Ibid.*, II. 123 Tirupati.
211. *Ibid.*, II. 138. Tirumala.
212. *Ibid*, III 2. Tirumala.
213. *Ibid.*, III. 132. Tirumala.
214. *Ibid.*, IV. 6. Tirumala.
215. *Ibid.*, V. 7. Tirupati.
216. *T.T.D.I.* V. 25. Tirupati.
217. *Ibid.*, V. 92. Tirupati.
218. *Ibid.*, III. 10. Tirumala.
219. *Ibid.*, III. 11. Tirumala.
220. *Ibid.*, III. 14. Tirumala.
221. *Ibid.*, V. 99. Tirupati.
222. *Ibid.*, VI. 22. Tirupati.

of Tirumala. It was instituted by Sāḷuva Mallayadēva *mahārāja* in Ś. 1385 and commenced with the *ankurārpaṇam* or sowing of nine kinds of seeds on the night of the *daśamī*. On the next or *ēkādaśi* day, the *Tirumāmaṇi-maṇṭapam* was decorated and on the *dvādaśī* day the god and his consorts were seated in it after putting on the *pavitram* or sanctified thread round the head, neck and wrist. Afterwards they were taken in procession through the streets. Provision was made for the supply of necessary articles like *sōmakuṁbham* or water pot, *pratimās* or images, *vajñōpavītams* or sacred thread, ornaments to the Ācarya, like *hastamātra* or the ornament for the hand and *karnamātra*, or the ornament for ears. During this function, various kinds of gifts of money, *paśu*, or cows, land and gold were made. Arrangements were also made for the preparation of five kinds of bed or *pancaśayanam* comprising the *ratnakaṁbaḷi* or carpet, *meṭṭai* or bed, *mayiliṛaku* or peacock's feathers, *kṛṣṇājinam* or deer skin and *paṭṭuccēlai* or silk cloth to the deity. Purāṇa-Bhaṭṭar and *brāhmanas* were appointed for chanting the *Vēdas* during this festival. Threads of various colours like red, black, green, blue and yellow were supplied for making *paṁcavarṇa-nūl* or thread of five colours. A donation was also made to the smith for the supply of *parvatam* or the plank with the image of the deity painted on it and *makaratōraṇam* or ornamental arch shaped wooden frame with two crocodiles.[223] A record dated in Ś. 1430 states that this festival was celebrated for four days.[224] In Ś. 1452, the duration of this festival was increased to five days.[225]

A record from the Śiva temple at Gangāpuram, dated in the 11th year of the Latter Cāḷukyan king, Jagadēkamalla, mentions a gift of one *hāga* of land for the *Pavitra* ceremony of god Sagarēśvara by Kēśava setti with the approval of the mercantile community.[226] Another, from Ḍākūr, dated in Ś. 1078, mentions that gift were made for the celebration of *Caitra-Pavitra* festival or the *Pavitrōtsavam* in the month of *Caitra* to god Mayilēśvara by the local officials.[227] In Ś. 1213, a Khadēvāṇḍu made a gift to god Tripurāntaka of Tripurāntakam on the occasion of the *Pavitrārōhaṇa*.[228] The residents of Melpadi granted land for the *Pavitrārōhaṇa* festival for god Mahādēva of the Cōḷēndrasimhēśvara temple, situated in Mērpaḍi, *alias* Rājāśrayapuram in the *Tuy-nāḍu*.[229] Provision was made by Anavalli Viraiyaviran for the celebration of this festival for god Mukkanna at Kalavāy.[230]

c. *Kalyāṇōtsavam*

This festival, also known as the marriage festival, or *tirukkaḷyāṇam* is common to both Vaiṣṇava or Śaivite temples. The duration of the festival was of five days.

The first instance of the celebration of this festival at Tirupati is recorded in an

223. *Ibid.*, II. 18. Tirumala.
224. *Ibid*, III. 15. Tirumala.
225. *Ibid.*, IV. 3. Tirumala.
226. *K.I.A.P.* Mn. 48. Gangāpuram.
227. *Ibid.*, Md. 4. Ḍākūr.
228. *S.I.I.* X. 466. Tripurāntakam.
229. 96 of 1921. Mēlpāḍi.
230. 362 of 1939-40. Kalvaguṇṭa.

inscription dated in Ś. 1469. This record mentions the *Vaivāhikōtsavam* of god Gōvindarāja, celebrated in the Tamil month of *Cittirai*, with *sāttumurai* on the day of the star *Rōhiṇi*. On the first day of the festival, nine kinds of seeds were sown and the soma image was installed. On this day, in the early morning the god and his consorts had *tirumanjanam* while seated in the *Telleikku-vayttan-maṇṭapam*. Provision was made for the supply of *candanam* for the *kalabham* decoration, musk for *tirunāmam* or *ūrdhvapuṇḍram* and refined camphor for the face. The worship of image *Jayādi-maṇḍalam* with rice while seated in the swing after the procession on *Garuḍavāhanam* and his consorts on palanquin is an interesting item of this festival. After the midday worship, the feet of the god were cleaned with milk and garlands were exchanged while the two consorts were seated on the *Haṁsavāhanam* and *Cātakapakṣivāhaṇam* and the god in swing. *Hōmam* was arranged for the marriage ceremony while the deities were seated in the *maṇṭapam* after returning from the swing *maṇṭapam*. Arrangements were made for the decoration of the marriage seat or *manai* and the marriage garments were supplied to the god and his consorts. A mirror was arranged before the god and his consorts. *Kanyādānam* was also arranged on the first day itself.

Tirumanjanam was conducted in the morning of the second day of the festival and the deities were taken in procession on the *Tiruci*-vehicle. They saw the *Dhruva* star. After the *vasantam* decoration, the god and his consorts were taken in the *vasantam* procession and *candanam* was distributed among the devotees and the temple officials. In the evening, *tirumanjanam* was conducted and after that the deities were taken out for the night procession on the *Śēṣavāhanam*.

Tirumanjanam was conducted in the morning of the third day of the festival once again. Arrangements were made for taking out the night procession on the *Vaikuṇṭha-vimānam* vehicle.

On the fourth day, there was *tirumanjanam* in the morning. Procession was arranged for the god in the night on the *Hanumanta-vāhanam* while his consorts were seated in a palanquin.

As usual, *tirumanjanam* was conducted for them in the morning of the 5th festival day and the god and his consorts were propitiated with offerings.[231]

The first mention of the celebration of this festival at Tirumala is in a record dated in S. 1468. A certain Tāḷḷapākam Tiruvēnkaṭanāthar made provision for the celebration of the *vaivāhikōtsavam* for Śrī Venkaṭēśa for five days commencing on the day of the star *Anurādha* and ending with the day of the star *uttirāḍham* occurring in the month of *Panguṇi*. This festival was commenced with *ankurārpaṇam* and the installation of Sōma and Brahmā images. *Tirumanjanam* was conducted for the god and his consorts while seated in the *Tirumāmaṇi-maṇṭapam*. After the *tirumanjanam* the god was decorated with musk and refined camphor. The function was commenced by the priests while the deities were seated in the swing after the procession through the streets. The feet of the god were washed with milk while seated in the swing along with consorts after the exchange of garlands while the two consorts seated on *Haṁsavāhanam* and *Cātaka-pakṣi-vāhanam*. The *nīrājana* or

231. *T.T.D.I.* V. 99. Tirupati.

karpūra-hārati was offered to them while seated on the *Pancavarna-pīṭham* or bridal chair decorated with patterns set with five kinds of coloured flour. At the *abhijin-muhūrtham* or auspicious hour, *hōmam* was performed after the procession through the streets at Tirumala. A curtain was held between the lord and his consorts. Various kinds of *dakṣiṇas* like *suvarṇapuṣpam, punyāha-vācana-dakṣiṇa* and *sūkta-dakṣiṇa* were made. After this, the *gandhōdaka-tirumanjanam* or *candana-abhiṣēkam* or ablution with sandal water was conducted and the deities were decorated with *candanam,* musk and camphor. After the night procession offerings were made in the *Tirumaṛai* or wedding chamber. Arrangements were made for the worship of the star *Dhruva* during the night.

During the 2nd day, the *candana-vasantōtsavam* was conducted while the deities were in the *vasantōtsava* procession and after that they were decorated with *candanam* or sandal. After the procession, gingelly oil and green gram were supplied for the conduct of *vasanta-tirumanjanam.* Immediately after the *vasanta-tirumanjanam* they used to have the ordinary ablution and were decorated with musk refined camphor and sandal. They were taken in the night procession on the *Śēṣa-vāhanam.*

On the third day, ablution was conducted and *hōmam* was made. *Āsthānam* was arranged on this day. After the night procession they were seated in the *Vaikuṇṭha-vimānam.*

On the fourth day of this festival, *tirumanjanam* was conducted and the deities were decorated. One *pāyasa-cāru prasādam* was supplied for *hōmam* and *candanam* was distributed among the *sumangaḷis* or married women. After the night procession, the god was seated on the *Haṁsa-vāhanam* and his consorts in the palanquin.

On the fifth day also *tirumanjanam* was conducted and they were taken out for the night procession. Offerings were made after the procession while the god was seated on *naṁbiran* or the elephant vehicle and his consorts in the palanquin.[232]

A certain Tiruvenadayyar instituted in S. 1475, the *peṇḍili-tiruṇāḷ* or the marriage festival for god Śrī Venkaṭēśa. On all the five days procession was arranged and the swing was arranged on four days commencing from the second festival day and ending with the fifth festival day. The Śrī Vaiṣṇavas chanted the *Iyal-prabhandham* of the Āḷvārs during the procession through the streets. Offerings were made while the god was seated the in bed-chamber.[233] Provision was made in Ś. 1479, for the supply of *candanam* for *kalabham* decoration of the god while seated in the temple car on the 5th festival day of *peṇḍili-tiruṇāḷ.*[234]

This festival was celebrated in other temples also. Provision was made in Ś. 1179, by *mahāmaṇḍalēśvara* Nārāyaṇa perumāḷ for its celebration for god Mārga-nārāyaṇa perumāḷ of Penṭrāla.[235] A *kaḷyāṇamaṇṭapa* was erected in Ś, 1476, by Bhōjanapalle Śrīnīvāsayyangar for the purpose of conducting the *kaḷyānamahōtsava* for god Kēśava perumāḷ of Saṁbaṭūru *alias* Śrī Bhāṣyapuram.[236] In Ś. 1564, a

232. *Ibid.*, V. 71. Tirumala.

234. *Ibid.*, V. 159. Tirupati.

235. *N.D.I.* II. Kandukūr. 60. Peṇṭrāla,

236. 279 of 1937-38. Saṁbaṭūrụ.

Barugugāru made arrangements for the performance of the *kaḷyāṇamahōtsava* for god Cennakēśava perumāḷ of Gārladinne.[237]

This festival was celebrated in the Śiva temples also. But the information is meagre. A record from Drākshārāma, dated in Ś. 1075, mention that gifts were made for feeding ascetics on all the days of the marriage festival of god Bhīmēśvara of the place.[238] Lakṣmīdēvī, the queen of Bayyaraja, gave a lamp on the occasion of this festival to the same god in Ś. 1079.[239] An undated record from the same place mentions the gift of two seats of gold to be used at the time of the *Vivāha-mahōtsava* of god Bhīmēśvara of the place.[240] This festival was celebrated in Ś. 1216 for the goddess Trailōkya-Sundari and Tripurāntaka-mahādēva of Tripurāntakam by the temple authorities.[241] The Eastern Cāḷukyan king, Visvēśvara, erected in Ś. 1329, a *maṇṭapa* for the *kaḷyānam* festivals of god Dharmēśa of Panchadhārla.[242] A Salakarāju Tirumala Dēvamahārāyalu made provision in Ś. 1456 for the celebration of the marriage festivities for god Nāgēśvaradēva of Muttukūru.[243]

d. *Vasantōtsavam*

The *Vasantōtsavam* is a grand festival celebrated in temples. On this occasion, the processional images are dressed in white cloths and water mixed with large quantities of saffron, known as vasantam was splashed on them. Hence the festival is called *Vasantōtsava.* This festival is also known as the *Damanārōhaṇa-Vasantōtsava* festival at Tirupati, and it is known as *Gaurakkuḷi-Vasantōtsavam* at Tirumala.

The duration of this festival varied from three days to nine days. A record dated in Ś. 1416, mentions that this festival was celebrated for three days, commencing from the day of the *Cittirai* star in the Tamil month of *Cittirai* for god Gōvindarāja of Tirupati.[244] Another record, dated in Ś. 1460, gives details stating that the *vasantōtsavam* was celebrated for five days, commencing on the day of the star *Uttarābhādrā*, in the month of *Panguṇi* and ending on the day of the star *Kṛttikā*.

This festival was started with *ankurārpaṇam* and the installation of the Sōma image. One *mārakkal* of paddy was spread beneath the above image and the sacrificial fire was lit. Then *tirumanjanam* was performed with five liquids i.e., milk, curds, ghee honey and coconut water. Then the images were taken to a specially decorated *Vasantōtsava-maṇṭapa* where coloured water was sprinkled over the images. After this the deities were taken out in procession in the *Vaikuṇtha-vimānam.*[245]

The *Damanārōhaṇa-vasantōtsava-tiruṇāḷ* was celebrated for god Gōvindarāja for five days in Ś. 1466, commencing with *ankurārpaṇam* on the day of the star *Svāti,* in the month of *Panguni* and ending with the day of *Sāttumuṛai* on the day of the star

237. *N.D.I.* III. Podili. 13. Gārladinne.
238. *S.I.I.* IV. 1098. Drākshārāma.
239. *Ibid* , IV. 1209. Drākshārāma.
240. *Ibid.*, X. 479. Tripurāntakam.
241. *E.I.* XIX. pp. 164-174. Panchadhārla.
242. *N.D.I.* I. Gudur. 82. Muttukūr.
243. *S.I.I.* IV. 1351. Drākshārāma.
244. *T.T.D.I.* II. 127. Tirupati.
245. *Ibid.*, III. 127. Tirupati.

Uttirāḍam. The seed sowing ceremony was conducted on the day of *ankurārpaṇam*. One roll of threads was tied to the main pots and the *Mahāmēru* pots. Ghee was supplied for arranging *hōmam* and milk and honey and curds for the god's *tirumanjanam*. During the course of the festival various kinds of *dānas* like *bhūdānam* or the gift of land, *ghaṭa-dānam* or gift of pots and *suvarṇadānam* or gift or gold were made. *Damana* leaves or twigs, *candanam* for the *kalabham* decoration, rose water vessel, musk and refined camphor for the forehead were supplied. On all the five days, the deity was seated in the *Lakṣmīdēvī-maṇṭapam* and various kinds of offerings were made, The recitation of *Vēdas* and the *Tiruvāymoḷi* of Naṁmāḷvār was also arranged during this festival.[246]

This vasanta festival was also celebrated in the Tirumala temple of Śrī Venkaṭēśa. We know from an inscription, that a certain Periya-Peṁma nāyaka of the Yādavarāya dynasty, visited the temple on the occasion of the *Vasanta* festival and this shows that this festival was celebrated in this temple even before the Yādavarāya rule.[247]. In Ś 1437, god Malaikiniyaninṟa-Perumāḷ, Nāccimār and Sēnai Mudaliyār witnessed the *Gaurakkuli-vasanta* festival conducted in a *maṇṭapam* constructed in a flower garden.[248] This festival was celebrated on the day next to that of the floating festival.[249] On the first day, *tirumanjanam* was conducted and the god was decorated with musk and refined camphor. *Āsthānam* or durbar was arranged during the festival.[250] In Ś. 1483, Tirumalarājayyan instituted this festival for five days. During this festival procession was conducted on the *Puṣpa-vāhanam* on the 5th day. On the first day, the god was seated on the *Śēṣa-vāhanam*, on the 2nd day on the *Haṁsa-vāhanam*, on the 3rd day on the *Garuḍa-vāhanam*, on the 4th day on the *Vaikuṇṭha-vimānam* and on the 5th day on the *Yānai-Naṁbiran* or elephant vehicle.[251]

In Ś. 1325, a merchant guild named the *Nānādēśi* and others made a gift to goddess Guṟṟala Paramēśvarı on the occasion of the *Vasantōtsava* of god Narasiṁha of Addanki.[252] A record from Udayagiri, dated in Ś. 1508 mentions gifts made for the celebration of *vasanta-mahōtsava* for god Raghunāyakulu of the place.[253] The *vasanta* festival was celebrated for god Śrīkūrmanātha of Śrīkūrmam in the *Caitra* month for 9 days in Ś. 1750.[254] An Anavalli Viraiviran made provision for the celebration of this festival for god Mukkannār at Kalavay.[255] An inscription from Uyyālavāḍa mentions that a certain Narasiṁha, the *uligam* of a *Mahārāja* made gifts for the celebration of *Vasantōtsava* for god Ahōbalēśvara of Ahōbalam.[256]

246. *Ibid.*, V. 25. Tirupati.
247. *Ibid.*, I. 113. Tirumala.
248. *Ibid.*, III. 105. Tirumala.
249. *Ibid.*, III. 127. Tirumala.
250. *Ibid.*, V. 93. Tirumala.
251. *Ibid.*, V. 168. Tirumala.
252. 205 of 1935-36. Boggaram.
253. *N.D.I.* III. Udayagiri. 23.
254. *S.I.I.* V. 1159. Śrīkūrmam.
255. 362 of 1939-40. Kalavaguṇṭa.
256. 244 of 1953-54. Uyyālavāda.

e. *Doḷamahōtsava or Swing Festival*

This festival, also known as *ūnjal-tirunāḷ*, was celebrated both in the Śiva and Viṣṇu temples. On this day, the god was placed in a swing. This duration of the festival was for five days in the Tirumala and Tirupati temples. The first instance of the celebration of this festival in Tirupati is recorded in Ś. 1430. But in the temple of Śrī Venkaṭēśa of Tirumala it was celebrated in Ś. 1395.

A certain Appa Piḷḷai made provision in Ś. 1430 for the celebration of the *Annā-ūnjal-tirunāḷ* for Śrī Gōvindarāja commencing with *ankurārpaṇam* on the day of the star *Cittirai*, during the month of *Āḍi* and ending with *sāttumuṛai*, on the day of the star *Uttirāḍham*. It was celebrated for the merit and welfare of Vira Narasingaraya Maharaya. *Ārādhanam* was gone through while the god was seated in the *anna-ūnjal* or swan shaped swing arranged in a *maṇṭapam*. After the procession through the streets along with his consorts he returned to the *Tiruppaḷḷiarai* or the bed chamber.[257]

This festival has been in vogue at Tirumala since Ś. 1395, Sāḷuva Narasiṁharāya instituted it in this year. On the first day the *Sōma-pratimā* or image was put into the *sōmakuṁbham* or water pot and *ankurārpaṇam* was done, indicating the commencement of the festival on the 6th lunar day. Oil was supplied for the conduct of *snapana-tirumanjanam* for Śrī Venkaṭēśa and his consorts. Offerings were made after the ablution. Rice was spread underneath the sleeping bedstead, while the deities rested on it. Water squeezed sandal paste was supplied for fixing on the chest of the god. After the rest, the deities were seated on the *Annā-ūnjal* and assembly or darbar was conducted. On the last day of the festival the *antya-hōma* i.e., final *hōma* was arranged and a variety of offerings were made to the deity.[258]

In the Bhīmēśvara temple of Drākshārāma, this festival was celebrated in Ś. 1197, on the day of *Davana-paurṇima*. A village was granted for the celebration of this *ḍolōtsava* in the same year by the Oḍḍādi chief, Arjunadēva. In Ś. 1209, another village was given for the celebration of this festival in the Telugu month *Caitra* on the day of the *Davana-paurṇima* by Akkamadēvī.[259]

g. *Pallavōtsavam*

The *Pallavōtsavam* was celebrated in the temples of both Śrī Venkaṭēśa of Tirumala and Śrī Gōvindarāja of Tirupati. The duration of this festival was for five days in both the temples. But in the Tirumala temple, the festival was celebrated in the month of *Māsi* and in the Tirupati temple it was celebrated in the month of *Cittira* or *Cittirai*.

In Ś. 1469, a Śrīnivāsa Ayyangār made provision for the celebration of this festival in the temple of Śrī Venkaṭēśa of Tirumala. It was conducted for five days every year in the month of *Māsi*. Abhiseka was done for three days during this festival. Arrangements were made for the decoration of the deity. After the decoration, god Śrī Venkaṭēśa, Nāccimār, Sēnai Mudaliyār and Śrī Bhāṣyakārar were

257. *T.T.D.I.* III. 13. Tirupati.
258. *Ibid.*, II. 50. Tirumala,
259. *S.I.I.* IV. 1140. Drākshārāma.

seated in a *maṇṭapam*, situated in the Ulagamundan flower garden at Tirumala. During the three days of the festival, a *tirumanjana-āsthānam* was conducted. After the *āsthānam* the deities were taken to the *Tirumāmaṇi-maṇṭapam* and thence to the bed-chamber.

On the last or *Sāttumuṟai* day of the festival, various kinds of offerings were made to the deity. During the course of this festival, the recitation of *Sahasranāma, Tiruvēnkaṭamahātmyam* and *Vēdapārāyaṇam* were gone through. The *Tirucci* vehicle and the *Vaikuṇṭha-vimānam* were carried by the *Sabhaiyār* on the last day.[260]

In the Gōvindarāja temple at Tirupati, this festival was celebrated for five days commencing from the day of the star *Uttiraṭṭāḍi* and ending on the day of the star *Kṛttikai*, in the month of *Cittirai* in every year. On the first day, the *suddhi-ankurārpaṇam* ceremony was performed and *tirumanjanam* was done with gingelly oil for the god and Nāccimār on all the five days. *Tirumanjanam* was conducted with *candanam*. After the *tirumanjaman, madhuparkam* was offered and the deities were seated in *Tillaikkuvayṭṭan-maṇṭapam*. After the procession through the streets, they were seated in the *Lakṣmīdēvi-maṇṭapam*. During this function, various images like *Jayādi-pratimā, Brahma-pratimā, Garuḍa-pratimā, Sēṣa-pratimā, Adhidevatā-pratimā, Nārāyaṇa-pratimā* and *Varuṇa-pratimā* were installed for *anugraham* or blessing from the god for the commencement of the festival. On the first day of the festival, the deities were taken in procession on the *Śēṣa-vāhanam* and on the *tirucci* vehicle on the 2nd, 3rd and 4th days and on the *Vaikuṇṭha-vimānam* on the last day of this festival. During this processions fire works named *pedil-bāṇam* and *candra-bāṇam* were fired. On the 5th festival day, offering named *kunukku-paḍi* was offered to the *mūlabēram* of Śrī Gōvindarāja. Provision for this was made in Ś. 1485 by Savandappayyar.[261]

g. *Plavōtsavam ; or Floating Festival*

This festival was celebrated annually, separate from the floating festival celebrated during the *Brahmōtsavam* and Summer festivals. The floating festival was instituted by Sāḷuva Gōvindarāja in Ś. 1461 for Gōvindarāja of Tirupati. The duration of the festival was of nine days.[262]

This festival was also celebrated at Tirumala for Śrī Venkaṭēśa for nine days in Ś. 1455.[263]

For god Śrī Rāma, also it was celebrated in Ś. 1454.[264] A record from Madanapalle, dated in Ś. 1535, mentions that provision was made for the supply of flower garlands during the floating festivals of the goddess Nāccāru of Tirupati conducted in the *Mukkōṭi-tirtha* by Venkaṭapatidēva at the request of *mahāmaṇḍalēśvara* Gōbūri Śēṣādrirāja.[265]

260. *T.T.D.I.* V. 72. Tirupati.
261. *Ibid.*, V. 173. Tirupati.
262. *Ibid.*, IV. 133. Tirupati.
263. *Ibid.*, IV. 23. Tirumala.
264. *Ibid.*, III. 18. Tirupati.
265. *E.I.* XIX pp. 89-96. Kandukūr.

h. *Mahālakṣmīdēvī Festival*

This festival was celebrated for Gōvindarāja of Tirupati in Ś. 1452 for 16 days.[266] Elaborate arrangements were made in Ś 1458 this connection.

During the first day *ankurārpaṇam* was gone through. Offerings were made, *Vēdapārāyaṇam* was done and ghee and *dharbha* grass were supplied for *hōmam*. After lighting the fire, *pañcāmṛta-tirumanjanam* was conducted and the *śami* tree was worshipped with garlands and cocoanuts. Procession was conducted while Śrī Gōvindarāja was seated on the horse vehicle, his consorts in the palanquin and Śrī Visvaksēna on the horse vehicle. Offerings were made to the god while striking the *śami* tree with an arrow.[267]

This festival was also celebrated for god Śrī Vēnkaṭēśa of Tirumala, for five days. In Ś. 1457, the famous Vijayanagara king, Acyutarāya, visited the Tirumala temple and made arrangements for the celebration of this new festival for the god and his consort, Alarmēlmangai-Nācciyār. During this festival the Sōma image was installed and paddy was spread under it. The images of Śēṣa and others and the *Brhmāṇḍamaṇḍalam* were also set up. *Ankurārpaṇam* was then performed. After this ceremony, *hōmam* was made. The *Kalpamantra Śrī-Sūkta*, *Lakṣmīsahasranāmam* and *Lakṣmī-gāyatri* were recited. The recitation of the *Vēdas* and *Purāṇas* was also done on all the five days. Five kinds of *paḍi* offerings were made to the deities while seated in the seven *maṇṭapas*, constructed by the king in the name of his queen, his son, his father and mother and himself. Provision was also made for the conduct of *tirumanjanam* during the five days.[268]

i. *Pāḍiya-*Vēṭṭi *or Hunting Festival*

The hunting festival or *Pārivēṭa mahōtsava* or *Pāḍiya-vēṭṭai* was commonly celebrated in both Vaiṣṇava and Śaivaite temples. Apart from being a part of the *Brahmōtsavam*, this festival was also separately celebrated. The duration of the festival was one day and it was celebrated for god Śrī Vēnkaṭēśa of Tirumala and Gōvindarāja, Śrī Raghunātha, Varadarāja, Viṭṭhalarāja, Acyutaperumāḷ and Śrī Kṛṣṇa of Tirupati and god Cennakēśava of Mōraguḍi. It was also celebrated for god Bhīmēśvara of Drākshārāma.

This festival was celebrated in Tirupati for god Gōvindarāja in Ś. 1468.[269] Procession was arranged on the horse vehicle and in the palanquin. In Ś. 1469, Sevvu Nāyakkar made provision for the celebration of this festival for the god while seated in a *maṇṭapam* constructed by him.[270] During this festival, *pillankulam* of the flutes and *tirumanivadam* or garlands were distributed in Ś. 1479.[271] A donation was made in Ś. 1504, for the celebration of this festival on this day, the god was seated in a

266. *T.T.D.I.* IV. 3. Tirumala.
267. *Ibid.*, IV. 95. Tirupati.
268. *Ibid.*, IV. 54. Tirumala.
269. *Ibid.*, V. 88. Tirupati.
270. *Ibid.*, V. 102. Tirupati.
271. *T.T.D.I.* V. 102. Tiruputi.

maṇṭapam, decorated with flowers and an *āsthānam* or durbar was arranged.[272] Procession was also arranged in Ś. 1515.[273]

It was celebrated in the temple of Acyutaperumāḷ of Tirupati in Ś. 1466, and Varadarāja perumāḷ in Ś. 1469. In the temple of Viṭṭhalēśvara this festival was celebrated in Ś. 1468. *Tirumanjanam* was conducted for god Gōvindarāja and his consorts on this day being celebrated on the very next day of the *Makara-sankrāmaṇam.* Offerings were made at the *Pāḍiyavēṭṭai-maṇṭapam*, a deer was brought for the hunting function during this festival.[274]

This festival was celebrated for god Śrī Rāma in Ś. 1468. A certain Sevvu Nāyakkar made provision in Ś. 1469 for making offerings to the god while seated in a *maṇṭapam.* God Hanumān was brought to the site of the *Pongalveli* on this day.[275] In Ś. 1468, a cash gift was made for conducting this festival. Procession was arranged on the horse vehicle and after the procession, *tirumanjanam* was conducted for Raghunātha, Lakṣmaṇa and Sītā while seated in a *maṇṭapam.* Arrangements were made for the supply of *candanam* for the *kalabham* decoration, musk and refined camphor.[276]

For god Gōvinda Kṛṣṇa abiding in the temple of Śrī Gōvindarāja, this festival was celebrated in Ś. 1468.[277]

A certain Kucaya nāyaka, constructed a *maṇṭapa* for seating on the occasion of the hunting festival celebrated for god Bhīmēśvara of Drākshārāma in Ś. 1349.[278] A record from Moraguḍi mentions the gift of the *vipravinodi* community for the *pārivēṭa-mahōtsava* of god Cennakēśava perumāḷ on the *Sankrānti* days.[279]

j. *Sahasra-nāmārcana-Festival*

Worship with 1008 appelations of the god is known as *Sahasra-nāmārcana.* This festival was celebrated for god Śrī Venkaṭēśa of Tirumala for five days commencing with the *ankurārpaṇam* on the day of the star *Makhā* and including the *Adhivāsam* ceremony on the day of the star *Uttiram* and ending with the day of the star *Cittirai,* in the month of *Māsi* every year. In Ś. 1473, a certain Sūrappa nāyakkar, granted a village for the conduct of this festival. On the first day, *ankurārpaṇam* was done and images like those of Jayaḍi, Sōma, Aṣṭamangaḷa images, Nāyaka images, Pārvatī, Śrī and Bhū were worshipped. The *dhvaja* or the flag was hoisted. After this, *pañcāmṛta-snapana* was conducted with milk, curds, honey ghee and sugar for three days and *Madhuparkam* was also offered. During this festival the recitation of the *Iyal-Prabhandham* of the Āḻvārs was also arranged. On three days, the god was seated on the *Garuḍa-vāhanam, Śēṣavāhanam* and *Pallayamtulam* or palanquin and taken in procession. After the procession, he and his Nāccimār were seated in

272. *Ibid.*, VI. 3. Tirupati.
273. *Ibid.*, VI. 11. Tirupati.
274. *Ibid.*, V. 88. Tirupati.
275. *Ibid.*, V. 102. Tirupati.
276. *Ibid.*, V. 71. Tirumala.
277. *S.I.I.* IV. 1353. . Drakshārāma.
278. 369 of 1932-33. Moragudi.
279. *T.T.D.I.* V. 127. Tirumala.

a *maṇṭapam*, decorated with flowers. Various kinds of flowers like jasmine, night lotus, and red lotus were supplied for the *Sahastra-nāmārcana* and *Sahasranāmam* was recited by an *Ācārya* before the god. On the last day of the festival or the *sāttumuṛai* day, offerings were made to Śrī Gñānappiran and *tirumanjanam* was conducted for him.[280]

k. *Koḍai-tirunāḷ or Summer Festival*

This festival was celebrated for 20 days in the temple of god Gōvindarāja of Tirupati. A record dated in Ś. 1407, mentions that the *Koḍai-tirunāḷ* was celebrated for 20 days for god Gōvindarāja.[281] On the 8th festival day, the god was seated in the *Nirāḷi-maṇṭapam* and on the 7th day of the latter 10 days he was seated in the *Appā-piḷḷai-maṇṭapam.*[282] A record, dated in Ś. 1434, mentions that on the 6th festival day, *tirumanjanam* was conducted and the deity was seated in the *maṇṭapam* on the 9th day of the latter 10 days of the festival.[283] We know from an inscription dated in Ś. 1437, that the god and his consorts were seated in a *maṇṭapam* in a garden on the western side of the Singarkōil on the 6th festival day of the latter 10 days of the festival.[284] *Tirumanjanam* was conducted on the 2nd day of the festival in Ś. 1452.[285] It is known from a record dated in Ś. 1467, that damsels were engaged for the recitation of *Sankīrtanaś* during the festival.[286] In Ś. 1504, special provision was made for the propitiation of the god on the first day of the festival after he returned from Ellappa-piḷḷai garden.[287] On the 20th day of the festival, the god was seated in a *maṇṭapam* on the bank of the *Gōvinda-Puṣkariṇi* in order to see the floating festival celebrated in Ś. 1528.[288]

For god Śrī Vēnkaṭēśa of Tirumala this festival was celebrated for 20 days. For the first time, the *Koḍai-tirunāḷ* was celebrated at Tirumala in Ś. 1326. On the 7th day of this festival, provision was made for offerings.[289] The deity was seated in the *Vasanta-maṇṭapa* in Ś. 1389, on the occasion of the *tirupaḷḷi-odattirunāḷ* or floating festival on the day of the *tuvvākam* in the latter 10 days of the festival.[290] In Ś. 1402, during the 20 days of the summer festival, the god was taken out on a pleasant walk and refined camphor was presented to him.[291] A record, dated in Ś. 1467, mentions that the *Sankīrtanas* were honoured and worshipped during the 20 days of the festival.[292] On all the days of the festival the god was seated in the swing arranged in a stone car and on the 20th day he and his consorts were seated

280. *Ibid.*, II. 83. Tirupati.
281. *Ibid.*, III. 11, 21, Tirumala.
282. *T.T.D.I* III. 28. Tirumala.
283. *Ibid.*, III. 118. Tirumala.
284. *Ibid.*, IV. 3. Tirumala.
285. *Ibid.*, V. 53. Tirupati.
286. *Ibid.*, VI. 4. Tirupati.
287. *Ibid.*, VI. 13. Tirupati.
288. *Ibid.*, I. 191. Tirumala.
289. *Ibid.*, II. 31. Tirumala.
290. *Ibid.*, IV. 146. Tirumala.
291. *Ibid.*, V. 47. Tirumala.
292. *Ibid.*, V. 32. Tirumala.

on the swing in Ś. 1466.[293] In. Ś 1468, *tirumanjanam* was conducted for the god and his consorts while seated in the garden *maṇṭapam* on the 5th day of the festival.[294] Provision was made in Ś. 1480, for the conduct of *tirumanjanam* on the 3rd day of the festival. *Candanam* was supplied to cover his body and for the *kalabham* decoration and refined camphor for his face and musk for *tirunāmam* or *ūrdhvapuṇḍram*.[295]

10. *Miscellaneous Festivals*

a. *Vanabhōjanam Festival*

This festival was celebrated on the day of the star *Tiruvēṇam* or *Śravaṇam* occuring in the month of *Kārtikai*. In Ś. 1466, three silk cloths and three garlands were presented to god Śrī Gōvindarāja and Nāccimār after the *śirappu-naivēdyam* on this *Vanabhōjanam* festival day.[295]

This festival was also celebrated for Śrī Vēnkaṭēśa of Tirumala. It was instituted by Tirumala Ayyangār. On this day, *tirumanjanam* was conducted for the god and the *śirappu-āsthānam* function was conducted in a garden in the 12 *maṇṭapams* constructed in the name of 12 managements.[296]

For god Lakṣmīnārāyaṇa perumāḷ of Tirupati also this festival was celebrated in Ś. 1468.[297]

b. *Tōppu-tirunāḷ*

The *Tōppu-tirunāḷ* or garden festival was celebrated in Ś. 1415, for god Śrī Vēnkaṭēśa of Tirumala. The duration of the festival was for 20 days. Two *appāpaḍi* were given on the two days of the *tuvvākkam* during the earlier 10 days and latter 10 days of the festival.[298]

This festival was celebrated for god Gōvindarāja of Tirupati in Ś. 1434.[299] In Ś. 1486, it was celebrated for god Ahōbalēśvara of Ahōbalam. For this purpose Parānkuśa Vān Saṭhagōpa Jiyyamgāru, the trustee of the temple, assigned a piece of land for providing offerings on this day to god when he visited the tank constructed by him on the way to *Bhārgava-tīrtham*.[300]

c. *New Harvest Festival*

This festival was celebrated in the temples of Raghunātha and Gōvindarāja of Tirupati and Śrī Venkaṭēśa of Tirumala. It was celebrated like the May Day games. In Ś. 1402, this festival was celebrated for god Raghunātha of Tirupati.[301] It is

293. *Ibid.*, V. 84. Tirumala.
294. *Ibid.*, V. 161. Tirupati.
295. *Ibid.*, V. 25, 66. Tirupati.
296. *Ibid.*, V. 47A. Tirumala.
297. *Ibid.*, V. 68. Tirupati.
298. *T.T.D.I.* II. 113. Tirumala.
299. *Ibid.*, III. 28. Tirumala.
300. 73 of 1915. Ahōbalam.
301. *T.T.D.I.* II. 73. Tirupati.

also known as the *Tiruppuḍiyiḍu* festival.[302] In Ś. 1457, it was celebrated in Tirupati, but we don't know for whom it was celebrated.[303]

In S. 1426, the new harvest offerings were made to god Śrī Vēnkaṭēśa of Tirumala.[304] In Ś. 1465, on this day, *tirumanjanam* was performed for the god and Nāccimār and Sēnai Mudaliyār while seated in the *Tirumamaṇi-maṇṭapam* after the procession on this festival day on the day of the star *Rōhiṇī*, in the Tamil month of *Tai*. After *tirumanjanam,* the god was decorated with refined camphor, *candanam* and musk. *Āsthānam* was conducted during this festival.[305] Various kinds of offerings were made in the *Tirumāmaṇi-maṇṭapam* during the *Alaikadir* or new harvest festival for god Śrī Venkaṭēśa.[306]

d. *Vasanta-paurṇima*

This festival was celebrated for god Narasiṁha, enshrined in the temple of Śrī Vēnkaṭēśa of Tirumala. A record from Tirumala, dated in Ś. 1390, mentions that *tirumanjanam* was conducted for Aḷagiya-Singar on this day.[307]

Another, from Tirumala, dated in Ś. 1452, states that offerings were made to Aḷagiya-Śingar enshrined in Śrīnivāsapuram in Tirupati, immediately after receiving *tirumanjanam* on this day, being his annual birth-star.[308]

e. *Gaurīvrata*

This festival was celebrated in honour of Pārvatī, the consort of Śiva, one of whose names is Gaurī. A record from Drākshārāma, dated in S. 1174, mentions the gift of the village of Śankubhīmāpuram in Oḍḍādi to god Bhīmanātha of the place for the purpose of celebrating the *Gaurī-vrata* on the full-moon day of the month of *Jēṣṭa* by Sūramadēvī, the daughter of Vīrapa nāyaka for the merit of his parents.[309]

f. *Kottamāvāsya-yātra*

An inscription from Drākshārāma, dated in Ś. 1096, mentions that an individual instituted the *Kottamāvāsya-yātra* and the *Māghadarśanotsava* for god Bhīmēśvara of Drākshārāma.[310]

g. *Car Festival*

The car festival or *rathamahotsava* was commonly celebrated in both Viṣṇu and Śiva temples. It was celebrated both as part of the *Brahmotsavam* and as a separate festival. A record, dated in Ś. 1463, mentions the gift of a village for the

302. *Ibid.*, II. 88. Tirupati.
303. *Ibid.*, IV. 69. Tirumala.
304. *Ibid.*, III. 3. Tirumala.
305. *Ibid.*, V. 9. Tirumala.
306. *Ibid.*, VI. 51. Tirumala.
307. *Ibid.*, II. 38. Tirumala.
308. *Ibid.*, IV. 3. VI. 160. Tirumala and Tirupati.
309. *S.I.I* IV. 1043. Drākshārāma.
310. *Ibid.*, IV. 1162. Drākshārāma.

annual car festival celebrated for god Vīrabhadra of Lēpākṣi by king Acyutarāya,[311] at the request of Vīrapaṇṇa Mahīpati. Another, from Ellanūr, dated in Ś. 1592, states that, a decision was taken by the Reḍḍis and *Karaṇams* of the place, to subscribe at the rate of two *rūkas* for every hundred of the total land assessment or *sistu-bēriju* for conducting this festival for god Śrī Vēnkaṭēśvara of the place.[312]

h. *Garuḍōtsava*

Garuḍa or the king of birds is the favourite vehicle of Viṣṇu. The *Garuḍa-vāhana* or the Garuḍa-vehicle is the most significant of all the vehicles of this god. It was customary to place the god on this *vāhana* and take out a procession on important occasions. Devotees made special gifts for conducting this procession. In Ś. 1635, a Timmā Reḍḍi of Peddanapāḍu, made provision for the celebration of *Garuḍōtsava* for god Madanagōpāla-Kṛṣṇasvāmi of the place.[313] A record from Vallūru, dated in Ś. 1760, mentions that Lakṣmammā made provision for the celebration of *Garuḍōtsava* for god Cennakēśava of Vallūru.[314]

i. *Capparam Festival*

Inscriptions mention a festival known as the *capparam* festival. The word *capparam* means a small car. Obviously, this festival involved the taking out of a deity seated in this car in a procession. In Ś. 1569, a number of inhabitants of the Peda-*Nandyāla-sīma* made provision for the conduct of this festival which was kept in abeyance because of some troubles and it was now revived.[315]

j. *Kanu Festival*

A subsidiary festival, named *Kanu,* was also celebrated during the *Mārgaḷi-nirāṭṭotsava.* This festival was celebrated for god Gōvindarāja and his consort, Śrī Gōvādōvī or Āṇḍāl for god Raghunātha of Tirupati and for Śrī Vēnkaṭēśa of Tirumala. For the goddess Āṇḍāḷ, this festival was celebrated in Ś. 1451. On this day, an offering was made to the deity and it was distributed among the married women after receiving *kanninir* or a holy bath in the *Gōvinda-Puṣkariṇi.* During the procession through the streets, turmeric was distributed among the married women. On this day, lights were set up in the middle of the tank and Śrī Kṛṣṇa was brought to the temple of Āṇḍāḷ during the festival. Offerings were made to Śrī Gōvindarāja while seated in a garden.[316] In Ś. 1457, offerings were made to Āṇḍāḷ immediately after the bath in the *Puṣkariṇi.*[317]

In S. 1426, this festival celebrated for Śrī Venkaṭēśa of Tirumala and in S. 1410 for god Śrī Raghunātha of Tirupati.[318]

311. *C.P.* 19 of 1937-38. Lēpākshi.
312. 7 of 1953-54. Ellanūru,
313. 262 of 1937-38. Peddanapāḍu.
314. 426 of 1938-39. Vallūru.
315. C.P. 13 of 1937-38.
316. *T.T.D.I.* III. 181. Tirupati.
317. *Ibid.*, IV. 51. Tirumala.
318. *Ibid.*, III. 3, Tirupati, II. 88. Tirupati.

k. *Kēdāravigarata Festival*

A record from Kāḷahasti, dated in Ś. 1489, in the reign of king Sadāśiva Rāya, registers the gift of money for meeting the expenses of the *Kēdāravigarata* festival on the *bahuḷacaturthaśī* day in the month of *Puraṭṭāsi* by a *dēvakarmi* of the temple.[319]

11. *Instituted Festivals*

a. *Āśvayuja*

A record from the Tirumala temple, dated in Ś. 1351, mentions a festival instituted by Vijayanagara king, Dēvarāya, which was to be conducted during the month of *Āśvayuja*, commencing from the day of the star *Punarvasu* and ending on the day of the *Svāti* star for god Śrī Vēnkaṭēśa of Tirumala.[320]

b. *Tirumugakkaṭu Festival*

This festival was instituted for god Śrī Vēnkaṭēśa of Tirumala by Kumāra-Tātācāryār in Ś. 1505 to be celebrated every year for one day in the month of *Arpasi*. During the course of this festival, a special crown or *kiriṭa* made of flowers by the Śrī Vaiṣṇavas of the temple was placed on the head of the deity.[321]

c. *Avilāli Garden Festival*

A certain individual, named Kōnēri, a resident of Avilāli village, made arrangements in Ś. 1506, for the celebration of the Avilāli garden festival for god Gōvindarāja in the month of *Tai*. On this day, the god was taken in procession in a palanquin, accompanied by Sēnai Mudaliyār in the *Tirucci*-vehicle. After the procession they were seated in a *maṇṭapam* in this village and a special *tirumanjanam* was conducted for the god.[322]

d. *Tiruppūvōla-tirunāḷ*

This special festival of five days' duration, during which the god was decorated with flowers, was instituted for god Gōvindarāja of Tirupati, by Meykkōṭṭi Tiṁmappa nāyykar in Ś. 1514. On this day, procession was conducted through the eight streets of Tirupati with the god seated in a *pallayaṁtulam* vehicle with his consorts accompanied in a palanquin and Sēnai Mudaliyār in the *Tirucci*-vehicle. After this, there was *tirumanjanam* followed by decoration with *candanam* musk and camphor. An *āsthānam* or durbar was also conducted during this day.[323]

e. *Kāṭhaka-mahōtsava*

This special festival was instituted by the Later Pallava chief, Kopperunjiñga, for god Bhīmēśvara of Drākshārāma, in his name.[324]

319. 183 of 1924. Kāḷahasti.
320. *T.T.D.I.* I. 192. Tirumala.
321. *Ibid.*, VI. 5. Tirumala.
322. *Ibid.*, VI. 6. Tirupati.
323. *Ibid.*, VI. 9. Tirupati.
324. *S.I.I.* IV. 1342. Drākshārāma.

f. *Gaṇḍagopāla-tirunāḷḷu*

The Telugu-Cōḍa chief, Gaṇḍagōpāladēva Cōḍa, instituted a festival, named the *Gaṇḍagopāla-tirunāḷḷu*, for god Cennakēśava of Narasaraopēṭ in Ś. 1219 and granted land for its celebration.[325]

g. *Kamaṭhēndra-mahōtsava*

The Śrīvaiṣṇavas of the temple of god Śrīkūrmanātha of Śrīkūrmam instituted a festival named *Kamaṭhēndramahōtsava* for god Śrīkūrmanātha and Lakṣmī in order to please sage Parandhāma in Ś. 1510.[326]

12. *Other Festivals*

a. *Grāmapradakṣiṇa Festival*

The *grāmapradakṣiṇa* festival was celebrated in the temples of Śrīkūrmam and Siṁhāchalam. On this day, the god was taken in procession around the village. In Ś. 1155, a gift was made for taking god Śrīkūrmanātha of Śrīkūrmam with Śrī and Bhū on *grāmapradakṣiṇa* on the day of the *Bharaṇi-nakṣatra* every month.[327] A gift of ten *malla-māḍas* was made by Narasiṁhamahāmuni in Ś. 1168, for conducting the same festival on his birthday, the day of the *Uttarāṣāḍhā-nakṣatra*, every month.[328] Arrangements were made in Ś. 1167, for the celebration of this festival every month.[329] A gift of ten *māḍas* was made in Ś. 1167 for the conduct of this festival on the day of the *Sankrānti* in every month.[330] This festival was also celebrated in the temple of Śrī Narasiṁhanātha of Siṁhāchalam.[331] In Ś. 1459, Haṁmanatayyan made arrangements for providing offerings to god Kāḷahastīśvara of Kāḷahasti on the *giripradakṣiṇa* day celebrated at Kāḷahasti.[332]

b. *Pandi-utsava*

Another festival, whose significance is not known, is the *Pandi-utsava* celebrated for god Kumārasvāmi of Drākshārāma for which a piece of land was given in Ś. 1044.[333]

c. *Gāṇṭi-utsava*

An inscription dated in Ś. 1174, mentions the gift of land for the celebration of a festival named *gāṇṭi-utsava*, for god Tripurāntakēśvara of Tripurāntakam by Viśvēśvaraśivadēva.[334]

325. *S.I.I.* IV. 661. Narasarāopēṭ.
326. *Ibid.*, V. 1300. Śrīkūrmam.
327. *Ibid.*, V. 1275. Śrīkūrmam.
328. *Ibid.*, V. 1291. Śrīkūrmam.
329. *Ibid.*, V. 1305. Śrīkūrmam.
330. *Ibid.*, V. 1308. Śrīkūrmam.
331. *Ibid.*, VI. 1198. Siṁhāchalam.
332. 175 of 1924. Kāḷahasti.
333. *S.I.I.* IV. 1250. Drākshārāma.
334. *Ibid.*, X. 340. Tripurāntakam.

d. *Carapu Festival*

Another popular annual celebration was the *Cerapu* festival whose meaning is not clear. A record from Kosinēpalle, dated in Ś. 1476, mentions the gift of the *tyāga-vartana*, or a kind of income due from the *mahājanas* of the village of Kosinēpalle by the *Vipravinōdins* for the celebration of the annual *Cerapu* festival of god Kōna Tiruvēngaḷanātha of the place.[335]

e. *Pāśu-bandham Festival*

In Ś. 1467, arrangements were made for the celebration of the *Pāśubandham* festival, in the month of *Āvaṇi*. But we don't know for whom it was celebrated.[336]

f. *Mucakunda-Mōkṣam Festival*

An inscription, dated in Ś. 1528, mentions the provision made for the celebration of the *Mucukunda-mōkṣam* festival for god Gōvindarāja of Tirupati. This was obviously in commemoration of god Viṣṇu granting salvation to a great devotee of his, named Mucukunda.[337]

g. *Nūliparva-mahōtsava*

A gift was made to god Tripurāntaka of Tripurāntakam by Pōtireḍḍi Tallaya reḍḍi in Ś. 1257, on the occasion of *Nūliparva-mahōtsava.*[338]

13. *The Brahmōtsavam*

Festivals celebrated in temples may be classified into obligatory, optional and miscellaneous. The obligatory festivals are those enjoined by the *Śāstras* and *Āgamas* to be celebrated at specified times. Their non-celebration would be considered as a serious omission, while their restitution would call for special purificatory rites. To this class belongs the *Brahmōtsavam*. According to the *Venkaṭācalamahātmyam*, it was originally instituted and conducted by Brahma. Actually, however, it was instituted for the first time by a woman devotee, named Samavai, in the 10th century and later special *Brahmōtsavams* were instituted by other devotees.

(a) *The Brahmōtsavam at Tirumala*

Numbers of Festivals

The earliest epigraph from Tiruchānūr, dated in the 14th year of the reign of king Sattiviṭanka, states that an image of silver, made in imitation of Śrī Venkaṭēśa, was installed under the name of Manavālapperumāḷ by Samavai. This queen arranged for the conduct of a festival with a procession for this image for nine days in the month of *Puraṭṭāsi*. In the same year, she made a further provision for the celebration of another festival for the same image with two processions each day for

335. 393 of 1940-41. Kosinīpalle.
336. *T.T.D.I.* V. 60. Tirumala.
337. *Ibid.*, VI. 15. Tirupati.
338. *S.I.I.* X. 548. Tripurāntakam.

seven days, in the month of *Mārgaḷi.*[339] These are the first known references to the celebration of the *Brahmōtsavam* at Tirumala.

As against the two festivals, celebrated in the 10th century, seven festivals came to be celebrated in Ś. 1367. This increase in the number was due to several festivals being instituted during the intervening period. The Yādavarāya chief, Vīra Narasinga, instituted the *Panguṇi-Brahmōtsavam* and his queen, Yādavarāya-Nācci, arranged for the celebration of the *Brahmōtsavam* in the month of *Āḍi.* The famous Vijayanagara rulers, Bukka I, Harihara I and Dēvarāya II, instituted *Brahmōtsavams* in the months of *Kārtikai. Māsi* and *Arpasi* respectively. Again, the number increased to eight in Ś. 1435, by the addition of another *Brahmōtsavam* instituted by King, Kṛṣṇarāya, in the month of *Tai.* By Ś. 1452, the number increased to nine by one more addition instituted by the Vijayanagara King, Acyutarāya. Two *Brahmōtsavams* were celebrated in the months of *Cittirai* and *Āṇi* which were instituted by Muluḍaiyār and Tāḷḷapākam Tirumalayyangār respectively and the number increased to eleven by the year Ś. 1462.[340] By the end of the 15th century, the *Brahmōtsavam* was celebrated in all the months except in the month of *Vaigāsi* and *Mārgaḷi.*

Duration of the Festival

The duration of the festival varied from time to time. The first *Brahmōtsavam* instituted by Samavai in the 10th century in the month of *Puraṭṭāsi* was celebrated for 9 days. The second festival instituted by her in the month of *Mārgaḷi* was of 7 days duration. It was continued for sometime up to Ś. 1351. In that year, Dēvarāya instituted the *Brahmōtsavam* which lasted for 9 days and it was continued up to the year Ś. 1416. Again, the duration was increased to 11 days and 12 days in Ś. 1426. In Ś. 1458 it was celebrated for 13 days. But the duration was reduced to 12 in Ś. 1467 and 11 days in Ś. 1473.

The *Brahmōtsavam* celebrated in the Śrī Vēnkaṭēśvara temple of Tirumala now-a-days is of 2 days duration.

Monthly Brahmōtsavams

Abundant information is available about the celebration of the *Brahmōtsavam* at Tirumala in all the months. It is curious, however, that this festival was not celebrated in the months of *Vaigāsi* and *Mārgaḷi.* This might be probably due to the fact that a festival. named *Tiruppuḷḷi-eḷucci,* lasting for 30 days, was celebrated in the month of *Mārgaḷi* and another festival, named *Koḍai-tirunāḷ* or the summer festival, was celebrated, lasting for 20 days, in the month of *Vāikāsi.* In modern times, the *Brahmōtsavam* is being celebrated at Tirumala only in the month of *Puraṭṭāsi* and an additional festival, once in three years,when there is an additional month of *Puraṭṭāsi.*

339. *T.T.D.I.* I. 9. Tirumala.
340. *Ibid.*, V. 129. Tirumala.

Cittirai-Brahmōtsavam

The earliest mention of the celebration of this festival at Tirumala is recorded in an inscription dated in Ś. 1368. It is also stated that the festival lasted for 9 days. Records dated in Ś. 1473 and Ś. 1515 mention the festival as lasting for 11 days.[341] In Ś. 1442, provision was made for the conduct of *tirumanjanam* on the 8th day of this festival. Immediately after the *tirumanjanam* an *Āsthānam* or durbar was held.[342] A devotee, named Venkaṭayyan, made arrangements in Ś. 1536 for the conduct of *Vasanta-tirumanjanam* on the 10th day of the festival. On this day, the god was taken in procession with his processional image seated on silver *Śēṣavāhanam*, and those of Nāccimar in a palanquin, Sēnai-Mudaliyār and Śrī Rāmānuja in the *Tirucci* vehicles. After the procession, they used to be seated in the *Vasanta-maṇṭapa* and *Vasanta-tirumanjanam* was conducted with saffron, rose-water, *candanam*, benjoin, turmeric, *palāsam* flowers.[343] In Ś. 1452, the car festival was celebrated.[344] On the day of the *Viḍayāṛri* or the last day, the deity proceeded to a *maṇṭapa* in Ś. 1462.[345]

Āṇi-Brahmōtsavam

In Ś. 1460, this festival was instituted by Tāḷḷapākkam Periya Tirumalai Iyangār.[346] The duration varied from 9 days in Ś. 1368 to 12 days in Ś. 1461, 13 days in Ś. 1466 and 11 days in Ś. 1473.[347] *Tirumanjanam* was conducted to god and Nāccimār and Sēnai Mudaliyār while seated in a flower garden on the *Viḍayāṛri* day.[348] On the same day offerings were made in Ś. 1467 while the god seated in the bed chamber of *Seṛri* arranged in the shrine of Periya Perumāḷ.[349] *Āsthānam* or durbar was conducted in Ś. 1466 during this festival.[350] In the same year, on the day of the star *Tiruveṇam* in the month of *Āṇi*, *ankurārpaṇam* was performed and provision was made by Tāḷḷapākkam Tirumalai Ayyangār for the conduct of *tirumanjanam*.[351] *Puṣpayāgam* was celebrated in Ś. 1465 for the god during this festival.[352] On the 7th festival day, a procession was taken out to the flower *maṇṭapam* and offerings were made while he was being decorated with garlands in the shrine of Uḍaiyavār. In the same year, on the first festival day, *tirukkalyāṇam* or marriage was celebrated. On the 8th day, the car procession was arranged. Offerings were made to him while granting permission to the gods on the 10th

341. *Ibid.*, I. 221, VI. 10. Tirumala.
342. *Ibid.*, III. 139, Tirupati.
343. *Ibid.*, VI. 18. Tirumala.
344. *Ibid.*, IV. 3. Tirumala.
345. *Ibid.*, IV. 149. Tirumala.
346. *Ibid.*, V. 129. Tirumala.
347. *Ibid.*, IV. 129. Tirumala.
348. *Ibid.*, IV. 163. Tirumala.
349. *Ibid.*, V. 43. Tirumala.
350. *Ibid.*, V. 12. Tirumala.
351. *Ibid.*, V. 19. Tirumala.
352. *T.T.D.I.* V. 8. Tirumala.

festival days. The 11th or the *Viḍayaṛṛi* day was the last day of the festival.[353] In Ś 1462, on the 5th festival day offerings were made to Śrī Kṛṣṇa and on the 9th day offerings were made to the *utsava-mūrti* of Periya Perumāḷ in front of the *Sankīrtana-Bhaṇḍāram* of the Tāḷḷapākam poets, situated in the first *prākāra* of the temple.[354]

Āḍi-Brahmōtsavam

This *Brahmōtsavam* was instituted by Yādavarāya Nācci, the queen of the Yādavarāya King, Vīranarasinga. The duration of the festival is not clear, but in Ś. 1368, it was celebrated for 9 days and in Ś. 1458 it was celebrated for 13 days. Another member of this family, named Tiruvēnkaṭanātha Yādavarāyar, granted a village in the 8th year of his reign for the celebration of this *Brahmōtsavam.*[355] *Ankurārpaṇam* or sowing of seeds, *dhvajārōhaṇam* or flag-hoisting and the car festival were the component items of this festival.[356] Avasaram Cennappa made provision in Ś. 1508, for making certain offerings to the god and his consort, Alarmēlmangai-Nācciyār, on the day of the star, *Punarvasu*, being the day of the *Vidayāṛṛi* festival during this *Brahmōtsavam.*[357]

Āvaṇi-Brahmōtsavam

The duration of this festival was 13 days in Ś. 1458 but it was reduced to 11 days in Ś. 1473. It was instituted by Tiruninra-urudaiyār, the Tirumala temple accountant. The festival was commenced in Ś. 1367 with the *dhvajārōhaṇam* and with *ankurārpaṇam* in Ś. 1458 and ended with the *Viḍayāṛṛi* festival.[358] Procession was arranged for the god in a car in Ś. 1452.[359]

Puraṭṭāsi-Brahmōtsavam

The first *Brahmōtsuvam* celebrated at Tirumala was in the month of *Puraṭṭāsi.* The duration of the festival was for nine days when it was instituted by Samavai in the 10th century, and it increased to 13 days in Ś. 1460, but was reduced to 11 days in Ś. 1473. The festival commenced with the sowing of the seeds.[360]

A devotee, named Periyaperumaḷdāsar, made provision in Ś. 1415, for offerings to the god while the car halted in front of his house.[361] In the same year, one of the *Niyogis*, named Tiṁmana-Dannāyakkar, arranged for offerings.[362] In Ś. 1438, the

353. *Ibid.*, V. 47. Tirumala.
354. *Ibid.*, V. 99. Tirupati.
355. *Ibid.*, I. 99. Tirumala.
356. *Ibid.*, IV. 86, 110. Tirumala; I. 221. IV. 3. Tirumala.
357. *Ibid.*, VI. 7. Tirumala.
358. *Ibid.*, V. 129. Tirumala.
359. *Ibid.*, IV. 3. Tirumala.
360. *Ibid.*, IV. 86. 110. Tirumala.
361. *Ibid.*, II. 108, 110, 111. Tirupati.
362. *Ibid.*, II. 113, Tirumala. III. 2, 11.

car festival was celebrated on the 8th day of the festival,[363] but in Ś. 1442, it was celebrated on the 7th day. The god went to the Aḷagīyamanavālan grove after the procession.[364] On the 4th day of this festival, *Āsthānam* or durbar was arranged in Ś. 1553.[365] The *puṣpayāgam* was celebrated during this festival in Ś. 1429 and 1457.[366] In Ś. 1442 the 9th day was celebrated as the *Tīrthavāri* day.[367] But in Ś. 1460 the *Viḍayāṛṛi* was celebrated on the 13th day as the last day.[368] On the 9th day, the god was taken out in procession on the serpent vehicle.[369] The famous Vijayanagara King, Kṛṣṇarāya, donated a tax named *Pērāyam* in Ś. 1445, for the celebration of this festival.[370] A *satram* was maintained for 10 days during this festival and a gift was made for this purpose.[371] A gift was made in Ś. 1467, for the purchase of cloths intended for free distribution among the devotees visiting Tirumala during this festival occasion. Watersheds were also maintained in front of the temple, and in the same year a devotee, named Dēvarāya Bhaṭṭar, made provision for the extra supply of water during this festival for the pilgrims.[372]

Arpasi-Brahmōtsavam

The famous Vijayanagara King, Dēvarāya Mahārāya, instituted this festival in Ś. 1351, during the month of *Āśvayuja*, commencing from the day of the star *Punarvasu* and ending on the day of the star *Svāti*, being the *Tīrthavāri* day. This festival was commenced with *ankurārpaṇam* ceremony and ended with the *Viḍayāṛṛi* festival in Ś. 1458 and in Ś. 1460.[373] Various kinds of offerings were made to the god on this occasion and perfumes like incense, and civet were supplied for smearing the holy body of the god.[374] It is clear that, the duration of this festival varied from 9-13 days.[375] A devotee, named Eṭṭūr Tirumala Kumāra Tātācāryār, made arrangements in Ś. 1505, for the celebration of this festival. *Tirumanjanam* was conducted with the gingelly oil for the god and Nāccimār, on the 10 days of the festival. The seed-sowing ceremony was conducted and the deities were decorated. The *vasanta* function was celebrated with turmeric and *cūrnābhiṣēkam* was conducted. After this function, *snapana-tirumanjanam* was conducted. The vehicles, *Nanji-vāhanam* or *Haṁsa-vāhanam*, *Garuḍa-vāhanm* and *Ānai-vāhanam* or elephant vehicle, were also decorated. The *Iyal-prabhandham* was recited during this festival and the *adhivāsam* function was gone through. Offerings were made to Tirukkōḍi Āḷvān

363. *Ibid.*, III. 113, 142. Tirumala.
364. *Ibid.*, V. 2. Tirumala.
365. *Ibid.*, VI. 21. Tirupati
366. *Ibid.*, III. 11, 59. Tirumala.
367. *Ibid.*, IV. 107. Tirupati.
368. *Ibid.*, IV. 110. Tirumala.
369. *Ibid.*, IV. 114. Tirumala.
370. *Ibid.*, III. 159. Tirumala.
371. *Ibid.*, II. 51. Tirumala.
372. *Ibid.*, V. 51, 61. Tirumala.
373. *Ibid*, IV. 86, 110. Tirumala.
374. *Ibid.*, I. 192. Tirumala.
375. *Ibid.*, IV. 3. Tirumala.

while ascending and descending the flag-staff. It is interesting to note that on the 11th day of the festival, the god and his consorts were seated in a garden *maṇṭapam*. Procession was arranged through the streets at Tirumala. The *Puṣpayāgam* festival was also celebrated as a component item. Areca-nuts and betel were offered to the deities while the god seated in the bed-chamber and afterwards distributed among the devotees during the *āsthānam* and on the 6th festival day, the swing was arranged.[376]

Tai-Brahmōtsavam

The *Tai-Brahmōtsavam* was instituted by the Vijayanagara King, Śrī Kṛṣṇarāya. It was celebrated for 13 days in Ś. 1460 and reduced to 11 days in Ś. 1473. This festival was commenced with the hoisting of the flag in Ś. 1368.[377] On the 2nd day of the festival *pāḍiyavēṭṭai* or the hunting festival was celebrated in Ś. 1379.[378] On the 7th day the god was seated in a *maṇṭapam* situated in a flower garden in Ś. 1438,[379] and on the 8th day, the car festival was celebrated.[380] On the *Viḍayāṛṛi* day in Ś. 1457, the god and Sēnai Mudaliyār went to the flower garden of the *Sabhaiyār*[381] and in Ś. 1461, marriage was celebrated for the god.[382] King Kṛṣṇarāya Mahārāya arranged a swing festival in Ś. 1442, to be conducted on the 6th festival day.[383] In Ś. 1460, on the 9th festival day, *Śēṣavāhanam* procession was arranged by Malayannan.[384]

Kārtika-Brahmōtsavam

The *Kārtika-Brahmōtsavam* was instituted by the Vijayanagara King, Bukkarāya I. The duration of the festival is not known at the time of its institution. But in Ś. 1460, it was celebrated for 13 days and in Ś. 1473 for 11 days. This festival was commenced with the *ankurārpaṇam* and ended with the day of the *Viḍayāṛṛi*.[385] The car festival was celebrated in Ś. 1455, on the 8th day.[386] On the 7th festival day, the processional deity was seated in a garden *maṇṭapam* in Ś. 1462.[377] On the 9th day the god was taken in procession on the serpent vehicle in Ś. 1460,[388] and on the 6th day the god was taken to the *yāgaśālā* or sacrificial hall.[389] In Ś. 1466, the god

376. *Ibid.*, VI. 5. Tirumala.
377. *Ibid.*, I. 221. Tirumala.
378. *Ibid.*, II. 3. Tirupati.
379. *T.T.D.I.* III. 113. Tirumala.
380. *Ibid.*, IV. 87, 134, 156. Tirumala.
381. *Ibid.*, IV. 38. Tirumala.
382. *Ibid.*, IV. 134. Tirumala.
383. *Ibid.*, III. 142. Tirumala.
384. *Ibid.*, IV. 114. Tirumala.
385. *Ibid.*, IV. 86, 110. Tirumala.
386. *Ibid.*, IV. 27. Tirumala.
387. *Ibid.*, IV. 156. Tirumala.
388. *Ibid.*. IV. 114. Tirumala.
389. *Ibid.*, IV. 138. Tirumala.

was seated in a garden *maṇṭapa* situated near the hunting ground on the 7th festival day.[390]

Māsi-Brahmōtsavam

An individual, named Mullai Tiruvēnkaṭa-jiyar, instituted the *Māsi-Brahmōtsavam* in the name of the Vijayanagara King, Harihara II, in the year *Prabhava.* For this purpose, Harihara granted a village. In Ś. 1368, the festival was commenced with the raising of the flag.[391] The duration of the festival varied from 9 days to 11 and 13 days. The car festival was celebrated in Ś. 1452.[392] This festival was celebrated for 13 days in Ś. 1458 with the commencement of *Ankurārpaṇam* and ending with the day of *Viḍayāṟṟi.*[393] The *Tīrthavāri* festival was celebrated in Ś. 1460 as a component item.[394]

Panguṇi-Brahmōtsavam

The *Panguṇi-Brahmōtsavam* was instituted by Vīranarasinga Yādavarāyar.[395] In Ś. 1460, the duration of the festival was 13 days and reduced to 11 days in Ś. 1473. The car festival was conducted in Ś. 1415.[396] In Ś. 1438 the car festival was celebrated on the 8th day.[397] On the 7th festival day, the god was seated in a *maṇṭapam* in a flower garden. In Ś. 1418, the god was seated in the *Nāvalūṟṟu-maṇṭapam* on the day of the *Puṣpayāgam* festival.[398] Sugar water was offered to the god, when he halted at the *Tirumāmaṇi-maṇṭapam* after the car procession in Ś. 1429.[399] On the 9th day of the festival the god was taken out in procession on the *Śēṣavāhanam.*[400]

Component Items of the Brahmōtsavam

The festival was commenced with the sowing of nine kinds of seeds or *Ankurārpaṇam* and ended on the *Viḍayāṟṟi* day. In some cases it was started with the *Kāiyārcakram* and ended with the *Viḍayāṟṟi.*[401] The *Dhvajārōhaṇam* or the hoisting of the Garuḍa flag signified the commencement of the festival. Similarly, the *dhvajāvarōhaṇam* or the lowering of the flag indicates the conclusion of the festival.[402] In between these two, there were several other minor festivals like

390. *Ibid.*, V. 25. Tirupati.
391. *Ibid.*, I. 221. Tīrumala.
392. *Ibid.*, IV. 3. Tirumala.
393. *Ibid.*, IV. 86. Tirumala.
394. *Ibid.*, IV. 107. Tirupati.
395. *Ibid.*, I. 97. Tiruchanur.
396. *Ibid.*, II. 108. Tirupati.
397. *Ibid.*, III. 113. Tirumala.
398. *Ibid.*, II. 135. Tirumala.
399. *Ibid.*, III. 11. Tirumala.
400. *Ibid.*, IV. 114. Tirumala.
401. *Ibid.*, IV. 81, 82, 83, 84, 88. IV. 140.
402. *Ibid.*, V. 53. Tirupati.

Puṣpayāgam or presentation of sanctified flowers, *Pāḍiyavēṭṭai* or hunting festival, *Vasantōtsava* or sprinkling of coloured water, *Tirukkalyāṇam* or marriage festival, *Dōlōtsava* or the swing festival.[403] On certain occasions, the Vēdas and the *Prabandham* were recited in the presence of the deity. The durbar or *Āsthānam* was also arranged during the festival.[404] Processions were arranged during the day and night on various vehicles like *Śēṣavāhanam* or serpent vehicle, the *Garuḍavāhanam*, the *ratha* or the car vehicle and on the palanquin.[405]

General Items in the Festival

Very interesting information is available from the records about some general items of the *Brahmōtsavam.* During the festival the god used to be seated in a *maṇṭapa* situated in the *Saṁpangi-pradakṣiṇam* of the Tirumala temple.[406] Procession was arranged around the temple after the swing.[407] It is very interesting to note that the god went on a galloping ride on a horse to the *Svāmipuṣkariṇi* on the 8th festival day.[408] On the 9th day of each *Brahmōtsavam, tirumanjanam* was conducted for god Sudarśana in *tīrthavāri-maṇṭapam.*[409] The god was seated in front of the granary in order to hear the temple accounts on the 9th day of the festival.[410] The god was seated in the Varāha temple while the *Tirumōḷi* was sung.[411] During the *Brahmōtsavam,* the god went on a slow walk in the evenings for hearing the *Prabandham* of the Āḻvārs.[412] Devotees made special endowments for the construction of *maṇṭapam* in gardens and on the banks of the *Puṣkariṇi* and for offerings to god on this festival occasion.[413] On the *Tīrthavāri* day, the god was seated in front of the *Yāgaśālā* and in the Varāha shrine in the early morning.[414] The recitation of the *Sāttumuṛai* songs of the *Tiruvaymōḷi* was arranged on all the 7th days of all the 10 *Brahmōtsavams,*[415] and *kōyil-aḻvār-tirumanjanam* was conducted on all the preceding days of the *Brahmōtsavam.* The *Iyal Prabandham* of the Āḻvārs was recited on all the 5th festival days of the 10 *Brahmōtsavams.*[416] An interesting practice was to maintain a watershed in front of the temple during the 10 days of each *Brahmōtsavam* for the convenience of pilgrims.[417] Another noteworthy thing was to have the image halted before the *Sankīrtana-Bhaṇḍāram* or the room

403. *Ibid.*, II. 109, 129, 134, III. 167, IV. 46, 134, 159, V. 76. Tirumala.
404. Ibid., I. 213. Tirumala.
405. *T.T.D.I.* II. 134, IV. 6, 26, 157, V. 8.
406. *Ibid.*, II. 18. Tirumala.
407. *Ibid.*, II. 68. Tirumala.
408. *Ibid.*, II. 96. Tirumala.
409. *Ibid* , III. 15. Tirumala.
410. *Ibid.*, II. 115. Tirumala.
411. *Ibid.*, III. 132. Tirumala.
412. *Ibid.*, III 133. Tirumala.
413. *Ibid.*, IV. 23, 69; III. 173. Tirumala.
414. *Ibid.*, IV. 165. Tirumala.
415. *Ibid.*, V. 78. Tirupati.
416. *Ibid.*, V. 94. Tirumala.
417. *Ibid.*, V. 51. Tirumala.

in which the copper plates containing the songs of Tāḷḷapākam family were preserved.[418]

(b) *The Brahmōtsavam at Tirupati*

The celebration of the *Brahmōtsavam* was in vogue at Tirupati also from the 13th century. Inscriptional evidence mentions this festival as celebrated in four months for god Gōvindarāja. One record mentions the celebration of the festival in the month of *Vaikāsi.* Another, dated in Ś. 1466, mentions the celebration of the *Brahmōtsavam* in the month of *Āṇi.* A third inscription, dated in Ś. 1467, refers to the *Brahmōtsavam* celebrated in the month of *Māsi* and the fourth, dated in Ś. 1504, mentions the festival celebrated in the month of *Āvaṇi.* Today, only one *Brahmōtsavam* is being celebrated in the month of *Vaikāsi* and an additional festival once in three years when there is an additional month of *Vaikāsi.*

Details about the Brahmōtsavams

Inscriptions found at Tirupati supply interesting information about the *Brahmōtsavams* celebrated in the four months mentioned above.

Vaikāsi-Brahmōtsavam

The duration of the festival varied from 9 days to 13 days. According to one record, dated in the 4th year of the reign of the Telugu-Pallava King, Vijayagaṇḍa-gōpāla, land was granted to the *Śrī Bhaṇḍāram.* From the 2nd day of the festival, the *Tirumoḷi* was sung.[419] In Ś. 1368, offerings were made to Garuḍa, painted on the flag. The festival was commenced with the *Dhvajārōhaṇam.*[420] The god was taken in procession on the car during this festival in Ś. 1415.[421] In Ś. 1416 and in Ś. 1438, the car festival was celebrated on the 8th day.[422] On the 6th day of this festival, the god was seated in *Yānai-naṁbiran* or the elephant vehicle.[423] A certain Nāgappayyan made arrangements for a procession on the *Veḍupuṛai* or horse vehicle in Ś. 1528.[424] The god proceeded to the Raghunātha temple in Ś. 1415, in the *tiruvananıāḷ* or the serpent vehicle.[425] On the 9th day of the festival, in Ś. 1436, the god was seated in the *Śēṣa-vāhanam.*[426] The *Śēṣa-vāhanam* festival was conducted during the night procession in Ś. 1453.[427] In Ś. 1468 immediately after the car procession *pañcāṁṛta-abiṣēkam* was conducted for the god.[428] On the 9th day of the festival, offerings were made to the god at the time of hearing the accounts

418. *Ibid.*, IV. 6. Tirumala.
419. *Ibid.*, I. 61. Tirupati.
420. *Ibid.*, I. 215. Tirupati.
421. *Ibid.*, II. 105, 110, Tirupati, Tirumala.
422. *Ibid.*, II. 127, III. 110. Tirupati.
423. *Ibid.*, III. 119. Tirumala.
424. *Ibid.*, VI. 13. Tirupati.
425. *Ibid.*, II. 118. Tirupati.
426. *Ibid.*, III. 28. Tirumala.
427. *Ibid.*, V. 12 Tirumala.
428. *Ibid.*, V. 78. Tirupati.

in front of the granary.[429] It is interesting to note that the *pāḍiyavēṭṭai* or hunting festival was also celebrated in Ś. 1415,[430] as part of the *Brahmōtsavam.* In Ś. 1416, the *Puṣpayāgam* was celebrated during this festival.[431] On the *Puṣpayāgam* day, the god and his consorts and Sēnai-Mudaliyār used to visit the shrine of Tirumangaiāḷvār in Ś. 1442.[432] On the 6th day, various kinds of offerings were made to the god at the time of smearing turmeric paste while seated at the *Vasanta-maṇṭapam.*[433] It is interesting to notice that in Ś. 1455, the god used to witness *malaippu* or a kind of dance in the north-east corner of the north main street in Tirupati on the 12 days from the *Kaiyārsakkaram* day to the *Viḍayāṟṟi* festival of this *Brahmotsavam.*[434] In Ś. 1367, *Ankurārpaṇam* performed and a bracelet was put on the god's hand.[435] A devotee, named Tirumalaiyyar, made provision in Ś. 1458 for the offering of *candanam,* 100 areca-nuts and 200 betels to Tiruvaḷiāḷvan and a procession was arranged round the tank for procuring the holy earth for sowing the nine kinds of seeds on the day of the *Ankurārpaṇam.*[436] In Ś. 1469, the *Ankurār-paṇam* procession was arranged during three days.[437] The god was taken in procession on the 3rd, 4th and 6th festival days in a palanquin.[438] In Ś. 1407, marriage was celebrated for the god on the 5th festival day and on the 6th day, the god and his Nāccimār were seated in an *Ūnjal-maṇṭapam.* The *Vasanta* function was conducted. Procession was arranged on the 7th day to the *maṇṭapams.* On the 8th day of the festival, the god was taken on car procession and offerings were made to him after alighting from the car.[439] The *Tannīramudu* was also celebrated during this festival as a component part in Ś. 1456.[440] The Garuḍa flag was hoisted in Ś. 1444.[441] Offerings were made to Garuḍa while the flag was being mounted.[442] In Ś. 1453, a procession was taken out in the night with the god seated on the *Śēṣavāhanam.*[443] Several kinds of food offerings were made on various days of this festival e.g., the *tirukkoḍi-āḷvan paḍi* during the night procession, on the *kaiyārcakram* day, the *Haṁsavāhana-paḍi* in the night of the second day, the *Siṁhavāhana-paḍi* in the night of the 3rd day, the *Kṛṣṇāvataraṇam-paḍi* in the night of the 5th day, the *Madanagōpāla-vāhana-paḍi* in the night of the 7th day, the horse-vehicle *paḍi* on the 8th day and the *Śēṣavāhana-paḍi* on the 9th day.[444] In Ś. 1469, the god was seated

429. *Ibid.,* VI. 115. Tirumala.
430. *Ibid* , II. 112. 118. Tirupati.
431. *Ibid.,* II. 126. Tirupati.
432. *T.T.D.I.* III. 143. Tirupati.
433. *Ibid.,* II. 149. Tirupati.
434. *Ibid.* IV. 27 Tirumula.
435. *Ibid.,* II. 211. Tirumala.
436. *Ibid.,* IV. 96. Tirupati.
437. *Ibid.,* V. 99. Tirupati.
438. *Ibid.,* IV. 27. Tirumala.
439. *Ibid.,* II. 83, 127. Tirupati.
440. *Ibid..* V. 31. Tirumala.
441. *Ibid.,* III. 151. Tirupati.
442. *Ibid.,* IV. 117, 130. Tirupati.
443. *Ibid.,* IV. 12. Tirumala. V. 99.
444. *Ibid.,* V. 99. Tirumala.

in the *Rāyar-maṇṭapam* at the *Āḻvār-tirtham* on the *Tīrthavāri* day.[445] The floating festival was celebrated at the end of the *Brahmōtsavam* in Ś. 1468.[446] On the *Viḍayāṟṟi* or the last day of the festival in Ś. 1367, *tirumanjanam* was conducted and the god was seated in the Viṭṭhalasvāmi temple after the ablution.[447]

Āṇi-Brahmōtsavam

The *Āṇi-Brahmōtsavam* was instituted by the Yādavarāya-Nācci, the queen of Vīra Narasinga Yādavarāya, in the 30th year of his reign. For this purpose, she presented the taxes due from a village and a car for conducting the procession.[448] The duration of the festival was for 12 days in Ś. 1407, 9 days in Ś. 1426 and 13 days in Ś. 1445. The 12 days festival lasted from the *Kaiyār-cakram* to the *Viḍayāṟṟi* day. The festival was commenced with the hoisting of the Garuḍa flag.[449] On the 5th day, the marriage procession was taken out and after that the god and Nāccimār were seated on the swing in a *maṇṭapam*. On the 6th day, the god and his consorts were seated on the *ūnjal* for the *Casanta* function, and on the 8th day another car procession was taken out.[450] In Ś. 1368, this festival was commenced with the *Tirumūḷai-tirunāḷ* or *Ankurārpaṇam* and after the god putting the bracelet.[451] In Ś. 1458, the god went out on a procession to the tank bund in order to collect the earth for seed sowing.[452] On the 8th festival day, the god went on a galloping ride on the hourse vehicle in Ś. 1413.[453] On the 9th day, offerings were made to the god while hearing the accounts presented to him in front of the granary.[454] In Ś. 1439, *pongal* offerings were made in a *maṇṭapam* to the god and to cows on the hunting festival day.[455] In Ś. 1415, the god was taken out in procession on the *Śēṣavāhanam* to the Raghunātha temple.[456] In Ś. 1458, the god went in a procession on the *Śēṣavāhanam* to the temple of Śrī Narasiṁha, situated in Śrīnivāsapuram, a suburb of Tirupati.[457] The *Puṣpayāgam* festival was also celebrated during this *Brahmōtsavam* in Ś. 1460.[458] On the 6th festival day, the god was seated in the elephant vehicle.[459] The palanquin procession was arranged on the 3rd, 4th and 6th days of the festival,[460] and on 12 days, the god witnessed the malaippu, a dance in Ś. 1455. In Ś. 1457, on the 9th day of the festival, the god and Nāccimār went to the *Āḻvār-*

445. *Ibid.*, V. 92. Tirupati.
446. *Ibid.*, V. 68. Tirupati.
447. *Ibid.*, V. 92. Tirupati.
448. *Ibid*. I. 86. Tirupati.
449. *Ibid.*. III. 15, IV. 117. V. 47.
450. *Ibid.*, II. 83. Tirupati.
451. *Ibid.*, I. 221. Tirumala.
452. *Ibid.*, IV. 96. Tirupati.
453. *Ibid.*, II. 96. Tirupati.
454. *Ibid.*, II. 115. Tirumala.
455 *Ibid.*, III. 119. Tirumala.
456. *Ibid.*, II. 118. Tirupati.
457. *Ibid.*, IV. 76, 133. Tirumala.
458. *Ibid.*, IV. 114. Tirumala.
459. *T.T.D.I.* VI. 119. Tirumala.
460. *Ibid.*, IV. 27. Tirumala.

tīrtham to the north of Tirupati, in order to mix the holy *tīrtham*[461] The *Tannīramudu* and the *Tīrthavāri* functions were parts of this *Brahmōtsavam*.[462] On the *Viḍayāṟṟi* day which was the last day, floating festival was celebrated and *tirumanjanam* was conducted.[463]

Māsi-Brahmōtsavam

The first instance of this festival celebrated at Tirupati is recorded in an inscription dated in Ś. 1467. The festival was commenced with the *Ankurārpaṇam* on the day of the star *Ārdra* and ended with the *Tīrthavāri* on the day of the star *Viśākham*. Various kinds of offerings like *panca-havis-tiruppōnakam, nāli cāru, bali-prasādam* etc., were offered to the god and Nāccimār while in the bed-chamber arranged in the temple of Naṁmāḷvār at *Āḷvār-tīrtham* on the *Tīrthavāri* day in Ś. 1469. On the *Kaiyārcakram* day, offerings were made to god Śrī Venkaṭēśa and brought down to the Gōvindarāja temple. The *Iyalsaṭṭu* songs were recited while the god halted at the shrine of Śrī Rāmānuja in the temple of Śrī Gōvindarājan during the night procession. On the 4th and 5th festival days, the god was taken out in the flower palanquin. The *Vēnkaṭācalamahātmyam* was also recited during this festival.[464]

Āvaṇi-Brahmōtsavam

The first instance of the celebration of this festival for Gōvindarāja is recorded in an inscription dated in Ś. 1504. It was instituted in the name of Śrīnivāsa Ayyangār.[465]

Brahmōtsavam of other Gods at Tirupati

The *Brahmōtsavam* was also celebrated for god Raghunātha and Acyuta-Perumāḷ of Tirupati.[466]

(c) *Brahmōtsavam at other Places*

For god Varadarāja Perumāḷ of Tiruchānūr also this festival was celebrated.[467] An individual. named Tangeḍa Sēvappa, granted permission in Ś. 1634 to celebrate the *Brahmotsavam* for gods Gōpālasvāmin and Vīrēśvara at Tangeḍa.[468]

The Brahmōtsavam was celebrated for god Kāḷahastīśvara of Kāḷahasti in the months of *Puraṭṭāsi, Panguni, Māsi* and *Vaigāsi*. A gift of gold was made in Ś. 1461, by Ēkāṁbara Vinōdasēyyār for making offerings to the god at the *yāgaśālā-*

461. *Ibid.*, IV. 49. Tirupati.
462. *Ibid.*, IV. 31. 49. Tirumala.
463. *Ibid.*, V. 68. Tirupati, II. 110. V. 78. Tirupati.
464. *Ibid.*. V. 92. Tirupati.
465. *Ibid.*, VI. 9. Tirupati.
466. *Ibid.* V. 99. Tirupati.
467. *Ibid.*, VI. 1. Tirupati.
468. 378 of 1926. Tangeḍa.

manṭapa of the temple during the *Māsi-tirunāḷ*.[469] In Ś. 1323, a devotee, named Pūrṇagiri Padangal, granted lands for the celebration of festivals in the months of *Māsi* and *Panguṇi*.[470] In Ś. 1475, during the reign of the Vijayanagara King, Sadāśivārāya, 100 *paṇam* was given for offerings on the 7th day of the *Māsi* festival when the god Kāḷahastīśvara was taken out in procession and *Tirukkaḷyāṇam* was performed by the supervisors of the *Śrī Bhaṇḍāram* of the temple.[471] An individual, named Tērkumadam Iṁmaḍi Rudraśivācārya, made provision for the celebration of the festivals in the months of *Māsi*, *Vaigāsi* and *Puraṭṭāsi* in the temple of Kāḷahastīśvaram.[472]

The *Brahmōtsavam* was celebrated for god Paraśurāmēśvara at Guḍimallam in the month of *Cittrai*. The Cōḷā King, Rājarājadēva, made arrangements for the celebration of the *Cittirai-tirunāḷ* in the 2nd year of his reign.[473] In the 8th year of the reign of the Cōḷa king, Vikrama Cōḷa, provision was made for food offerings for god Paraśurāmēśvara during this festival.[474]

For god Kōdaṇḍarāmēśvara Toṇḍamānāḍ, this festival was celebrated in the month of *Puraṭṭāsi*. In the 34th year of the reign of the Cōḷa King, Maduraikoṇḍa Kōpparakēsari, the *Brahmōtsavam* was celebrated, lasting from the *Kēṭṭai* (yuta) *nakṣatra* to *Sthiya* (satabhigam) *nakṣatra*.[475]

469. 176 of 1924. Kāḷahasti.
470. *S.I.I.* VIII. 491. Kāḷahasti.
471. *Ibid.*, VIII. 485. Kāḷahasti.
472. 172 of 1924. Kāḷahasti.
473. *S.I.I.* VIII. 519. Guḍimallam.
474. *Ibid.*, VIII. 512. Guḍimallam.
475. *Ibid.*, VIII. 529. Toṇḍamanād.

BIBLIOGRAPHY

BOOKS

S.K. Ayyangar	A History of Tirupati.
T.A. Gopinatha Rao	Hindu Iconography
Rai Bahadur B.A. Gupte	Hindu Holidays and Ceremonials
P.V. Jagadisa Ayyar	South Indian Festivities
Kramrisch	The Hindu Temple
T.V. Mahalingam	South Indian Polity
Percy Brown	Indian Architecture
Dr. M. Rama Rao	Early Cāḷukyan Temples of Āndhradēśa
Dr. M. Rama Rao	Eastern Cāḷukyan Temples of Āndhradēśa
Dr. M. Rama Rao	Select Kākatīya Temples
Dr. M. Rama Rao	The Temples of Kaḷinga
Dr. M. Rama Rao	Temples of Tirumala, Tirupati and Tiruchānūr
K.A.N. Sastri	The Cōḷas
N. Venkataramanayya	Studies in the History of the Third Dynasty of Vijayanagara
T.K.T. Viraraghavacarya	History of Tirupati

JOURNALS, PERIODICALS ETC.

Bharati	Bhārati
Hyd. Arch. Ser.	Hyderabad Archaeological Series
J.A.H.R.S.	Journal of Āndhra Historical Research Society, Rājahmundry.
J.I.H.	Journal of Indian History, Trivēṇḍrum
K.I.A.P.	Kannada Inscriptions of Āndhra Pradēsh
K.S.	Kākatīya Saṁchika

L.R.	Local Records
M.E.R.	Annual Reports of Epigraphy, Madras
E.I.	Epigraphia Indica
I.A.	Indian Archaeology
I.A.	Indian Antiquary
M. Mss.	Mackenzii Manuscripts
N.D.I.	Nellore District Inscriptions by Butterworth and Vēṇugōpāl Chetty.
S.I.I.	South Indian Inscriptions
S.V.U.O.J.	Śrī Venkaṭēśvara University Oriental Journal, Tirupati
T.I.	Telangāna Inscriptions
T.D.E.R.	Epigraphy Report of the Tirupati, Tirumala Dēvasthānams, by Subrahmaṇyaśāstri
T.T.D.I.	Tirumala-Tirupati Dēvasthānam Inscriptions

GLOSSARY

GLOSSARY OF TECHNICAL TERMS

Architecture

Alpaprāsāda	Minor shrine
Āmalaka	Cogged stone
Antarāḷa	Ante-chamber
Āyatāsra	Oblong
Bahirdvāraśāla	A hall outside a gate
Balipīṭha	Sacrificial altar
Bhōga-maṇṭapa	The hall of enjoyment
Boḍigai	Bud
Cāmara-Vāhini	Cauri-bearer
Catustala	Four storeyed
Cuncu	Ornament on the edge of the roof
Dharma-maṇṭapa	A general hall
Dikpālakas	Guardians of the directions
Dīpasthaṁbha	Lamp-posts
Ḍōlā-maṇṭapa	Hall with a swing fitted in it
Ūnjal-maṇṭapa	
Dvāra	Doorway
Gāli-Gopuram	Main pagoda
Gāngēvarāya-maṇṭapa	A hall named after a Ganga king
Garbhagṛha	Sanctum
Garuḍasthaṁbha	Garuda pillar
Gopura	Pagoda
Jīrṇōddhāra	Renovation
Kaladaram	Stone foundation

Kalaśa — Finial, Vessel

Kalyāṇa-maṇṭapa — Hall in which the marriages of the deities are celebrated

Karavālabhairava-maṇṭapa — *Maṇṭapa* in which the image of Karavālabhairava was installed

Kōṣṭa — Niche

Kuḍyasthaṁbha / *Kūṭagāra* / *Sthaṁbhapañjara* — Architectural decorative ornament

Kuraḍu — Basement

Madhyarangam — Elevation between four pillars

Makara-mukha — Face of a *makara*

Makara-tōraṇa — Festoon issuing out of the month of the two crocodiles

Mēyakkal — Sloping terrace

Mṛgayārāma-maṇṭapa / *Pāḍiyavēṭṭai-maṇṭapa* — *Maṇṭapa* in a garden in which the hunting festival is celebrated

Mukhamaṇṭapa — Entrance hall

Nāśika — Gable

Nāṭya-maṇṭapa — Dance hall

Niluvu-maṇṭapa — Hall in the ground floor

Nirāḷi-maṇṭapa — Hall near a fountain

Pañjara — Cage

Paṭṭa — Band

Prabhā — Back piece

Pradakṣiṇa — Circum-ambulatory passage

Prākāra — Compound wall

Puṇyaśālā — Shrine

Pūrṇakalaśa — Water pot

Rathōtsava-maṇṭapa — Hall in which the images are prepared for the car festival

Śālā — Hall

Śanivāra-maṇṭapa — Hall used on Saturdays

Śikhara — Crown

Siṁhalalāṭa, kirtimukha — Lion's face

Sōpāna-mārga — Stepped pathway

Stūpi — Roof

Sukanāsa — Frontice piece

Tala — Storey

Taraṅga	Wave
Tirumuṭṭainadandal	Beautiful flooring
Tōraṇa	Festoon
Upapīṭha	Basement
Uttama-nīla-śila	Black granite
Vāhana-maṇṭapa	Vehicle hall
Vākiṭi-mogaśālā	Front hall
Vasanta-maṇṭapa	Hall in which the spring festival was celebrated
Vēdi	Platform
Vimāna	Tower
Vṛkṣacaitya	A temple of the Bōdhi tree
Yāga-maṇṭapa	Sacrificial hall
Yāḷi	Mythical animal

CLOTHS

Cini / *Mahā-cini*	Chinese silk
Ciralu	Cloths
Kaṁcuka	Short coat
Kaṭivastra	Loin cloth
Kuḷḷāvu	Cap
Kṣita-kṣauma	White silk
Pāgālu	Turban
Patina ciralu	Variety of cloths
Pītāṁbara	Yellow silk cloth
Rakta-kṣauma	Red silk
Venne-ciralu	White cloths

DEITIES

Mūlabēram	Stationary image
Dīpapratimā	Lampstand with an image
Mūrti	Image
Parivāradēvatas	Attendant deities
Utsava-mūrti	Processional image

FESTIVALS

Akṣatṛtīya	3rd day of the bright fortnight of the month of *Vaiśākha* celebrated at Siṁhāchalam
Amāvāsya	New moon day

Cūrṇābhisēkam	Pouring turmeric and sandal powder
Jātara	Annual festival
Makara-sankrānti } *Dakṣiṇāyaṇa-sankrānti*	Winter solstice
Mēsa-sankrānti	Zupiter's entry into the sign of aries
Pāḍiyavēṭṭai	Hunting festival
Siṁhayuktapuṇyakāla	The time of the entry of the Zupiter into the sign of Leo
Tiruṇāḷ	Festival
Tiruppuḷḷi-eḷucci	Psalm singing festival
Uttarāyaṇa-sankrānti	Summer solstice
Viṣu-sankrānti	The day on which the sun enters a particular *rāsi*
Utsava	Festival
Yāmajāgaravrata	Keeping the vigil during one eighth of a day

FLOWERS

Aśōka	Saraca indica
Campaka	Michelia chempaka
Cangalya	Crinum asiatica
Cēmanti	Crysanthemum cinerarifolium
Davana	Arfemesia indica
Doṇḍavanamāla	Garland reaching up to the feet
Guriminda	Abrus precatorius
Ippalu	Bassia lalifolia
Jāji	Jasmina flexile
Mādiphala	Citrus medica
Mālā	Flower garland
Malle	Jasmina officianala
Mārēḍu	Aegle marmelos
Mogalirēkulu	Pandanus Odoratissimus
Nandanavanam	Flower garden
Nērēḍu	Syzygium jambolana
Nimmalu	Citrus acida
Palāsam	Butea trondosa
Panasa	Jack fruit
Pāṭala	Sterospermum tetragonum
Ponna	Calophylum inophyllum
Tulaśī	Basil plant
Virajāji	Jasminium sp.

JEWELS

Addiga	Small ornament
Bāhuvalaya	Bangle
Bhujakīrti	Ornament for the shoulder
Biḷḷasaramulu	Short garlands
Graivēyaka	Neck ornament
Hāra	Garland
Kadiyam	Wrist ornament
Kaṇṭhamāla	Garland for the neck
Kaṇṭhi	A kind of neck ornament
Kaṭisūtra	Waist thread
Kavaca / *Mēlukaṭṭu*	Encasement
Kirīṭa	Crown
Māmiḍikāyapēru	Necklace of mangoes
Manjīra	Ornament worn below the ankle
Medanūlu-veṇḍi-cippapūlu	Flowers of gold made in imitation of the flowers
Navaratna-Prabhāvaḷi	An arch set with nine kinds of precious stones
Padakam	Pendant
Pahiṇḍi-pogada-pūvula-mālā	A garland of Mimusops elengi flowers
Pancavaktra-kōhaḷi	Lamp with five sections waved before the god
Paṭṭālu	Ankle ornament
Paṭṭam	An ornament for the brow
Śaṁkha-cakrāla-pathakam	Garland with *Śaṁkhas* and *cakras* alternatively
Puṣpamālā	Garland of flowers
Reṇḍu-māṇikyālu-kaṭṭina-pahiṇḍi-pāṇi	Hand set with precious stones
Śaṁkulu-navaratnālu-kaṭṭina-pahiṇḍi-pēṇulu-reṇḍu	Two hands set with *Śaṁkhas* and 9 previous stones
Sannaṁpūsapēru	Garland of small beads
Śikha-nāga-bhūṣaṇam	Serpant ornament stuck in the tuft of the hair
Śrīhastālu	Hand cover made of gold
Tāttarikōhala	Variety of lamp
Trisarimuktyālacēru	A garland of gold with three strings of pearls
Vaḷaya	Bangle

Vajramāṇikyāla-kaḍiyōlajoḍu	Ornaments for the ankles set with precious stones
Valitalaikkay beads	Ornaments
Vaijayantimālā	A garland hanging below the knees
Vanki	Ornament for the upper arm
Voṁmeccu	Basement work for setting the stones
Vuḍudhāra	Vessel with a hole in the centre with which water drips

GENERAL

Abhisēka	Ablution
Ācārya / *Guru*	Preceptor
Āgamas	Sacred texts related to the conduct of worship
Agrahāra	Village gifted to a single individual
Akhiladēśala-teliki-vēguru	Merchant guild of oil millers
Anga-range-bhōga	Bodily and external enjoyment
Ankurārpaṇam	Sowing of the seed
Arcaka	Priest
Arcana	Worship
Arca-avatāra	Worshippable form
Artha	Accumulation of material goods
Āsthānam	Durbar
Avatāra	Incarnation
Āyudha	Weapon
Bhāgavatasēva	Service by a devotee
Bhakti	Devotion
Bhujangatrāsa	Dance pose
Bṛndāvanam	A garden of *tulaśi* plants
Calivēndiri	Water-shed
Cāmara / *Vinjāmara*	Cauri
Candanalagi	Application of sandal paste
Darśana	Seeing the god
Dāsaris	Garland makers
Dharmam	Charity
Dēvabhōga	Gift made to god

Dēvakarmulu	Workers of the deity
Dēvasthānam	Temple
Dharma	Righteousness
Dhūpa-dīpa-naivēdya	Waving incense, lamp and offering
Dīpārādhana	Lighting lamps
Doṁmari	Acrobat
Dvibhanga	Body posture
Ghadiyārōpacāra	Kitchen service
Ghaṭikayantra	A clock like devise denoting time
Gōtra	Endymemic group
Iyalpa-ṭuvākkam	Commencement of the Tamil work of the Āḷvārs
Jñāna	Right knowledge attained through contemplation
Kāma	Satisfaction of physical desires
Kāṁśyapātra	Bronze vessels
Kāppu	Paste applied to the body of the deity
Kāse	Mason
Kāvaḍi	Scales carrying on one's shoulder
Kōlam	Coloured design
Kśīrābhiṣēka	Ablution with milk
Madhyāhnavēḷa	Midday
Mahājanas	Learnedmen
Mānadīpa	Stone pillar on which a lampstand is placed
Mānya	Land
Māpaṭi } *Rātri* }	Night
Maṭha	Monastery
Maṭhappura	Village gifted to a matha
Meyigāpu-arcana	Worship after the application of perfumes
Mithuna	Couples
Mōkṣa	Salvation
Muhūrtham	Auspicious moment
Nāga	Cobra
Naṁbi	A non-brahmin Vaisnava priest
Nandāviḷakku	Perpetual lamp
Niṣārdhāyamasamaya	One eighth part of the night
Paḷika	Vessel
Pañcāhavaṁvāru	Traders in five metals

Pañcāmṛta-abhiśēkha	Ablution with five liquids, viz. milk, honey curds, ghee, coconut water
Paṇyāram	Confectionary
Prasādam	Food offered to the deity
Pūjāri	Priest
Purāntaka	Śiva, the destroyer of three cities
Puruṣārthas	Principal objectives
Sādhana	Practice
Sahasradhāra	Plate with one thousand holes
Śākta	Texts relating to the Śakti cult
Śaivagāma	Āgama texts relating to Saivite texts
Sandhya	Conjunction between the day and night
Saptasantānas	Seven kinds of children, viz., tank, well, garden, temple, literacy work, treasure and son
Suvarnadhēnu	Golden calf
Sarvamānya	Exclusive gift of land
Saṭhagōpam	A replica of the feet of the deity
Satra	Choultry
Sejja-avasaram	Food offering made at the time of sending the god to bed
Sēvaka	Servant
Sṛti	Tune
Srōtriyam	Land granted to an orthodox brāhmin
Suradāmavṛtti	Duty of garland making
Tapsvins	Ascetics
Tirukkōnēri	Tank
Tīrtham	Holy water
Tiruman-kānikkay	Cash gifting
Tiruvaḷikakōla / *Divyakōla*	Torch
Tiruvardhajāmam	One eighth part of a day
Tiruvāymoli-sāttumuṛai	Last day on which the *Tiruvāymoḷi* is recited
Tiruvidayāṭṭam	Temple villages
Tōppu	Garden
Tuvvākam	Commencement
Ubhaiyam	Service
Udayakāla	Morning
Upakaraṇālu	Utensils

Upanayana	Investiture with sacred thread
Uyyāla-mancam	Swing cot
Valayacuṭṭina	Round compound
Vaiśya	3rd caste
Veda-khanduka	Land gifted for Vēdic learning
Vidyam	Betel leaves along with areca nut
Vinnapam	Submission
Virāsana	Sitting posture
Vipravinōdin	A brāhman community of entertainers
Viśvakarmakula	Goldsmith community
Vyatyastapāda	Knees crossed

MEASURES

Aḷākku, *Uḷākku*	Quantitative measures
Ankaṇa	Land measure
Garśe	Quantitative measure
Kalañju, *Marakkal*	(Molucca bean used as a weight) Weights
Kha, *Khaṇḍriga*	Land measure
Kunceḍu	Quantitative measure
Kuṇṭa	Land measure
Mattar	Land measure
Muṁmaḍi-bhīma-mānika	Quantitative measure
Nāli	Quantitative measure
Nandi-mānika	Quantitative measure
Puṭṭi	Land measure
Rājamāna-mānika	Quantitative measure
Sāniyamāna	Quantitative measure
Sāniyambāṭi-mānika	Quantitative measure
Tūm	Quantitative measure
Vittu-paṭṭu	Land measure

MUSICIANS

Āvaja	A kind of musical instrument

Bhāgavata	Minstrel
Bhērī	Skinned instrument
Bōyuviddhavillabhi	A kind of bamboo instrument
Brahmā-Viṇāsvastyyana	Auspicious saying played in a variety of lute
Dōlā	Drum
Ekaśaṁkulayāru *Dhavaḷaśaṁkulayāru*	Blowers of conches
Gīta	Song or music
Jagaḍavāṇḍru	Players on cymbal which consists of a number of rows of bells
Kāḷakāḍu	Player on the *kāhaḷam*
Karada	Skinned instrument
Kinnara	A variety of lute
Mangaḷagītālu	Auspicious songs
Mardala	Drum
Mukhurī	Blower of the bellows
Nāgasvara	Pipe
Naṭṭuvār	Dancers
Nṛtta	Dance
Nṛttāngana	Woman dancer
Pāḍuvār	Songsters
Paurāṇika	Reciter of *Purāṇa*
Śaṁkulayāru	Conch bearers
Vādya	Sound
Vaṁśakāra	Flutist
Vīṇā	Indian lute
Vīṇa-koluvu	Lute service
Vīraṇatiṇḍlayāru *Sannagāḷavāḍu* *Peddsgavurravāru* *Kahaḍlavaṇḍu*	Players of skinned instruments

OFFICIALS

Daṇḍanāyaka	Commander
Dēsāntari	Visitor
Dvārapālaka	Door-keeper

Karaṇam	Village accountant
Kāryābharaṇa	Agent
Lenka	Servant
Mahant	Ordained priest
Mahāpradhāna	Prime minister
Mahāpātra	Feudatory
Mantri	Minister
Mahāsāmanta	Great feudatory
Mathādhipati	Head of a *maṭha*
Muduseli	A kind of servant
Paḍālu	Servant
Paṭṭaṇasvāmin	Mayor
Paṭṭaṇasāhaṇādhipati	Cavalry commander
Samuddār	Tax contractor
Sēnāpati	Commander-in-chief
Tantrapāla	Gurard
Suṁka-māniyagāṁḍu	Tax-officer

PERFUMES

Agaru	Perfume
Dhūpa	Incense smoke
Guggilam	Incense
Karpūra	Camphor
Kastūri	Musk
Kuṁkuma	Red powder
Mēḍittacandanam	Sandal paste
Pacca-karpūra	Refined camphor
Pannīr	Rose water
Pulugu	Civet oil paste
Śrīgandha	Sandal
Tastakaṭṭai	Sandal paste
Tirucūrṇam	White powder used for the Vaiṣṇava mark

SERVANTS

Īyunni-Appayan	Person in-charge of fixing *muhūrtham*
Kaikkolar	Person in-charge of the decoration of the *maṇṭapas*

Kummara-svarūpam	Potters
Kangāṇippan	Supervisor
Mēkarai-svarūpam	Suppliers of brass vessels
Muttukkārar	Time-keeper
Nivandakkārar	Bearers of vehicles
Paccadikkarar	Distributors of *prasādam*
Śālai-vāsal	Manager of the water-sheds
Singa-muṟai	Fuel-suppliers
Sippiyār	*Śilpi*-engravers
Talaiyāri	Night watchman
Tevaiyāḷ	Cooks
Tiruveṭṭuvāḍai	Proclaimer
Tiruvīdhimunaiyār	Street-sweepers

TERRITORIAL DIVISIONS

Kōṭṭam *Maṇḍala* *Nāḍu* *Rājyya* *Sīma* *Sthala* *Viṣaya*	These were tagged on to the names of the places, in order to indicate particular territorial division of *Kamma-nāḍu, Vēngī viṣaya, Addanki-sthala, Penugoṇḍarājya, Tiruvēngāḍa-Koṭṭam, Nellore-sīma, Jayangoṇḍa-maṇḍala*

VEHICLES

Ānai-vāhanam	Elephant-vehicle
Gaja	Elephant
Kanaka-mayūra	Golden peacock
Mōhana-vāhana	Syren or demon vehicle
Nanja-vāhana	Hamsa or swan vehicle
Nīlai-tēr	Stone car
Padma-pīṭha	Lotus shaped seat
Pallaiyan-tulam	Palanquin
Samarabhūpāla-vāhana	War-chariot
Sindhūra	Elephant
Suvarṇāśva	Golden horse
Turanga	Horse

VESSELS

Arghya-pātra	Vessel with which water for washing the hands is offered
Kuḍuka	Ladle
Taṁbagariyalu	A variety of vessel

WEAPONS

Cakra	Disc
Ḍhakka	Hand drum
Dhanus	Bow
Kaṭhāri	Sword
Khēta	Shield
Śaṁkha	Conch
Triśūla	Three pronged weapon with a long han

1. Bhīmēśvara Temple, Drākshārāma

2. *Gōpura*—Bhīmēśvara Temple, Drākshārāma.

Plate IV.

1. Minor shrine—Madhukēśvara Temple, Mukhalingam.

2. Corner shrine—Madhukēśvara Temple, Mukhalingam.

1. Front view—Thousand Pillared Temple, Hanumakoṇḍa.

2. Side view—Thousand Pillared Temple, Hanumakoṇḍa.

Plate VI

1. Miniature shrine in the wall—Thousand Pillared Temple, Hanumakoṇḍa.

2. Back view—Rudrēśvara Temple, Pāḷaṁpēṭ.

Miniature shrines in the wall—Rudrēśvara temple, Pālaṁpēṭ.

2. Figure Brackets—Rudrēśvara Temple, Pālaṁpēṭ.

Plate VIII.

1. Vīrabhadra Temple, Lēpākshi.

2. *Kaḷyāṇamaṇṭapa*—Vīrabhadra Temple, Lēpākshi.

Plate IX.

1. Sculptures in a *maṇṭapa*—Vīrabhadra Temple, Lēpākshi.

2. Kṛṣṇarāya and his queens—Śrī Vēnkaṭēśvara Temple, Tirumala.

Plate X.

1. Vēnkaṭapatirāya and his queen—Śrī Vēnkaṭēśvara Temple, Tirumala.

2. *Vimāna*—Śrī Venkaṭēśvara Temple, Tirumala.